Praise for *Data Science on AWS*

"Wow—this book will help you to bring your data science projects from idea all the way
to production. Chris and Antje have covered all of the important concepts and the
key AWS services, with plenty of real-world examples to get you started
on your data science journey."

—*Jeff Barr, Vice President & Chief Evangelist,*
Amazon Web Services

"It's very rare to find a book that comprehensively covers the full end-to-end process of
model development and deployment! If you're an ML practitioner, this book is a must!"

—*Ramine Tinati, Managing Director/Chief Data Scientist*
Applied Intelligence, Accenture

"This book is a great resource for building scalable machine learning solutions on AWS
cloud. It includes best practices for all aspects of model building, including training,
deployment, security, interpretability, and MLOps."

—*Geeta Chauhan, AI/PyTorch Partner Engineering Head,*
Facebook AI

"The landscape of tools on AWS for data scientists and engineers can be absolutely
overwhelming. Chris and Antje have done the community a service by providing
a map that practitioners can use to orient themselves, find the tools they need to
get the job done and build new systems that bring their ideas to life."

—*Josh Wills, Author,* Advanced Analytics with Spark *(O'Reilly)*

"Successful data science teams know that data science isn't just modeling but needs a disciplined approach to data and production deployment. We have an army of tools for all of these at our disposal in major clouds like AWS. Practitioners will appreciate this comprehensive, practical field guide that demonstrates not just how to apply the tools but which ones to use and when."

—*Sean Owen, Principal Solutions Architect, Databricks*

"This is the most extensive resource I know about ML on AWS, unequaled in breadth and depth. While ML literature often focuses on science, Antje and Chris dive deep into the practical architectural concepts needed to serve science in production, such as security, data engineering, monitoring, CI/CD, and costs management. The book is state-of-the-art on the science as well: it presents advanced concepts like Transformer architectures, AutoML, online learning, distillation, compilation, Bayesian model tuning, and bandits. It stands out by providing both a business-friendly description of services and concepts as well as low-level implementation tips and instructions. A must-read for individuals and organizations building ML systems on AWS or improving their knowledge of the AWS AI and machine learning stack."

—*Olivier Cruchant, Principal ML Specialist Solutions Architect, Amazon Web Services*

"This book is a great resource to understand both the end-to-end machine learning workflow in detail and how to build operationally efficient machine learning workloads at scale on AWS. Highly recommend *Data Science on AWS* for anyone building machine learning workloads on AWS!"

—*Shelbee Eigenbrode, AI/ML Specialist Solutions Architect, Amazon Web Services*

"This book is a comprehensive resource for diving into data science on AWS. The authors provide a good balance of theory, discussion, and hands-on examples to guide the reader through implementing all phases of machine learning applications using AWS services. A great resource to not just get started but to scale and secure end-to-end ML applications."

—*Sireesha Muppala, PhD, Principal Solutions Architect, AI/ML, Amazon Web Services*

"Implementing a robust end-to-end machine learning workflow is a daunting challenge, complicated by the wide range of tools and technologies available; the authors do an impressive job of guiding both novice and expert practitioners through this task leveraging the power of AWS services."

—*Brent Rabowsky, Data Scientist, Amazon Web Services*

Data Science on AWS

*Implementing End-to-End, Continuous AI
and Machine Learning Pipelines*

Chris Fregly and Antje Barth

Beijing · Boston · Farnham · Sebastopol · Tokyo

Data Science on AWS

by Chris Fregly and Antje Barth

Copyright © 2021 Antje Barth and Flux Capacitor, LLC. All rights reserved.

Published by O'Reilly Media, Inc., 1005 Gravenstein Highway North, Sebastopol, CA 95472.

O'Reilly books may be purchased for educational, business, or sales promotional use. Online editions are also available for most titles (*http://oreilly.com*). For more information, contact our corporate/institutional sales department: 800-998-9938 or *corporate@oreilly.com*.

Acquisitions Editor: Jessica Haberman
Development Editor: Gary O'Brien
Production Editor: Katherine Tozer
Copyeditor: Charles Roumeliotis
Proofreader: Piper Editorial Consulting, LLC

Indexer: Judith McConville
Interior Designer: David Futato
Cover Designer: Karen Montgomery
Illustrator: O'Reilly Media, Inc.

April 2021:   First Edition

Revision History for the First Edition
2021-04-07:   First Release

See *http://oreilly.com/catalog/errata.csp?isbn=9781492079392* for release details.

978-1-492-07939-2

[LSI]

Table of Contents

Preface

With this practical book, AI and machine learning (ML) practitioners will learn how to successfully build and deploy data science projects on Amazon Web Services (AWS). The Amazon AI and ML stack unifies data science, data engineering, and application development to help level up your skills. This guide shows you how to build and run pipelines in the cloud, then integrate the results into applications in minutes instead of days. Throughout the book, authors Chris Fregly and Antje Barth demonstrate how to reduce cost and improve performance.

- Apply the Amazon AI and ML stack to real-world use cases for natural language processing, computer vision, fraud detection, conversational devices, and more.

- Use automated ML (AutoML) to implement a specific subset of use cases with Amazon SageMaker Autopilot.

- Dive deep into the complete model development life cycle for a BERT-based natural language processing (NLP) use case including data ingestion and analysis, and more.

- Tie everything together into a repeatable ML operations (MLOps) pipeline.

- Explore real-time ML, anomaly detection, and streaming analytics on real-time data streams with Amazon Kinesis and Amazon Managed Streaming for Apache Kafka (Amazon MSK).

- Learn security best practices for data science projects and workflows, including AWS Identity and Access Management (IAM), authentication, authorization, including data ingestion and analysis, model training, and deployment.

Overview of the Chapters

Chapter 1 provides an overview of the broad and deep Amazon AI and ML stack, an enormously powerful and diverse set of services, open source libraries, and infrastructure to use for data science projects of any complexity and scale.

Chapter 2 describes how to apply the Amazon AI and ML stack to real-world use cases for recommendations, computer vision, fraud detection, natural language understanding (NLU), conversational devices, cognitive search, customer support, industrial predictive maintenance, home automation, Internet of Things (IoT), healthcare, and quantum computing.

Chapter 3 demonstrates how to use AutoML to implement a specific subset of these use cases with SageMaker Autopilot.

Chapters 4–9 dive deep into the complete model development life cycle (MDLC) for a BERT-based NLP use case, including data ingestion and analysis, feature selection and engineering, model training and tuning, and model deployment with Amazon SageMaker, Amazon Athena, Amazon Redshift, Amazon EMR, TensorFlow, PyTorch, and serverless Apache Spark.

Chapter 10 ties everything together into repeatable pipelines using MLOps with Sage-Maker Pipelines, Kubeflow Pipelines, Apache Airflow, MLflow, and TFX.

Chapter 11 demonstrates real-time ML, anomaly detection, and streaming analytics on real-time data streams with Amazon Kinesis and Apache Kafka.

Chapter 12 presents a comprehensive set of security best practices for data science projects and workflows, including IAM, authentication, authorization, network isolation, data encryption at rest, post-quantum network encryption in transit, governance, and auditability.

Throughout the book, we provide tips to reduce cost and improve performance for data science projects on AWS.

Who Should Read This Book

This book is for anyone who uses data to make critical business decisions. The guidance here will help data analysts, data scientists, data engineers, ML engineers, research scientists, application developers, and DevOps engineers broaden their understanding of the modern data science stack and level up their skills in the cloud.

The Amazon AI and ML stack unifies data science, data engineering, and application development to help users level up their skills beyond their current roles. We show how to build and run pipelines in the cloud, then integrate the results into applications in minutes instead of days.

Ideally, and to get most out of this book, we suggest readers have the following knowledge:

- Basic understanding of cloud computing
- Basic programming skills with Python, R, Java/Scala, or SQL
- Basic familiarity with data science tools such as Jupyter Notebook, pandas, NumPy, or scikit-learn

Other Resources

There are many great authors and resources from which this book drew inspiration:

- Aurélien Géron's *Hands-on Machine Learning with Scikit-Learn, Keras, and TensorFlow* (O'Reilly) is a great hands-on guide to building intelligent ML systems with popular tools such as Python, scikit-learn, and TensorFlow.
- Jeremy Howard and Sylvain Gugger's *Deep Learning for Coders with fastai and PyTorch* (O'Reilly) is an excellent reference for building deep learning applications with PyTorch "without a PhD."
- Hannes Hapke and Catherine Nelson's *Building Machine Learning Pipelines* (O'Reilly) is a fantastic and easy-to-read reference for building AutoML pipelines with TensorFlow and TFX.
- Eric R. Johnston, Nic Harrigan, and Mercedes Gimeno-Segovia's *Programming Quantum Computers* (O'Reilly) is a great introduction to quantum computers with easy-to-understand examples that demonstrate the quantum advantage.
- Micha Gorelick and Ian Ozsvald's *High Performance Python* (O'Reilly) is an advanced reference that reveals many valuable tips and tricks to profile and optimize Python code for high-performance data processing, feature engineering, and model training.
- *Data Science on AWS* (*https://datascienceonaws.com*) has a site dedicated to this book that provides advanced workshops, monthly webinars, meetups, videos, and slides related to the content in this book.

Conventions Used in This Book

The following typographical conventions are used in this book:

Italic
: Indicates new terms, URLs, email addresses, filenames, and file extensions.

`Constant width`

> Used for program listings, as well as within paragraphs to refer to program elements such as variable or function names, databases, data types, environment variables, statements, and keywords.

`Constant width bold`

> Shows commands or other text that should be typed literally by the user.

 This element signifies a tip or suggestion.

 This element signifies a general note.

Using Code Examples

Supplemental material (code examples, exercises, etc.) is available for download at *https://github.com/data-science-on-aws*. Some of the code examples shown in this book are shortened to highlight a specific implementation. The repo includes additional notebooks not covered in this book but useful for readers to review. The notebooks are organized by book chapter and should be easy to follow along.

This book is here to help you get your job done. In general, if example code is offered with this book, you may use it in your programs and documentation. You do not need to contact us for permission unless you're reproducing a significant portion of the code. For example, writing a program that uses several chunks of code from this book does not require permission. Selling or distributing examples from O'Reilly books does require permission. Answering a question by citing this book and quoting example code does not require permission. Incorporating a significant amount of example code from this book into your product's documentation does require permission.

We appreciate, but do not require, attribution. An attribution usually includes the title, author, publisher, and ISBN. For example: "*Data Science on AWS* by Chris Fregly and Antje Barth (O'Reilly). Copyright 2021 Antje Barth and Flux Capacitor, LLC, 978-1-492-07939-2."

If you feel your use of code examples falls outside fair use or the permission given above, feel free to contact us at *permissions@oreilly.com*.

O'Reilly Online Learning

 For more than 40 years, *O'Reilly Media* has provided technology and business training, knowledge, and insight to help companies succeed.

Our unique network of experts and innovators share their knowledge and expertise through books, articles, and our online learning platform. O'Reilly's online learning platform gives you on-demand access to live training courses, in-depth learning paths, interactive coding environments, and a vast collection of text and video from O'Reilly and 200+ other publishers. For more information, visit *http://oreilly.com*.

How to Contact Us

Please address comments and questions concerning this book to the publisher:

O'Reilly Media, Inc.
1005 Gravenstein Highway North
Sebastopol, CA 95472
800-998-9938 (in the United States or Canada)
707-829-0515 (international or local)
707-829-0104 (fax)

We have a web page for this book, where we list errata, examples, and any additional information. You can access this page at *https://oreil.ly/data-science-aws*.

Email *bookquestions@oreilly.com* to comment or ask technical questions about this book.

For news and information about our books and courses, visit *http://oreilly.com*.

Find us on Facebook: *http://facebook.com/oreilly*

Follow us on Twitter: *http://twitter.com/oreillymedia*

Watch us on YouTube: *http://www.youtube.com/oreillymedia*

The authors regularly share relevant blog posts, conference talks, slides, meetup invites and workshop dates on Twitter or LinkedIn.

Follow the authors on Twitter: *https://twitter.com/cfregly* and *https://twitter.com/anbarth*

Find the authors on LinkedIn: *https://www.linkedin.com/in/cfregly* and *https://www.linkedin.com/in/antje-barth*

Acknowledgments

We would like to thank our O'Reilly development editor, Gary O'Brien, who helped us navigate the book-authoring process and, more importantly, made us laugh every time we chatted. Thanks, Gary, for letting us include source code and low-level hardware specifications in Chapter 1! We'd also like to thank Jessica Haberman, senior acquisitions editor, who offered key advice on everything from the initial book proposal to the final page count. After seven years of submitting book proposals, you helped us raise the bar to the point where the proposal was accepted! Special thanks to Mike Loukides and Nicole Taché from O'Reilly for your thoughtful advice early in the book-writing process, including the chapter outline, introductions, and summaries.

We would like to send a warm thank you to book reviewers who tirelessly reviewed—and re-reviewed—every page in this book. The reviewers are listed here in alphabetical order by first name: Ali Arsanjani, Andy Petrella, Brent Rabowsky, Dean Wampler, Francesco Mosconi, Hannah Marlowe, Hannes Hapke, Josh Patterson, Josh Wills, Liam Morrison, Noah Gift, Ramine Tinati, Robert Monarch, Roy Ben-Alta, Rustem Feyzkhanov, Sean Owen, Shelbee Eigenbrode, Sireesha Muppala, Stefan Natu, Ted Dunning, and Tim O'Brien. Your deep technical expertise and thorough feedback has been invaluable not just to this book but to the way we will present technical material in the future. You helped elevate this book from good to great, and we really enjoyed working with you all on this project.

Chris

I would like to dedicate this book to my late father, Thomas Fregly. Dad: You brought home my first Apple computer when I was 8 years old and forever changed my life. You helped me absorb your university calculus book at age 10 and further solidified my strong interest in mathematics. You taught me how to read voraciously, write succinctly, speak effectively, type quickly, and ask questions early. Watching you repair a boat engine while stranded on Lake Michigan, I am continuously inspired to dive deep and understand the hardware that powers my software. While walking around your office at the *Chicago Sun-Times*, I learned that everybody has an interesting story to tell, including the front-desk person, the CEO, and the maintenance staff. You said "Hello" to everybody equally, asked about their children, listened to their stories, and made them laugh with a funny story of your own. Holding your hand as we walked around your university campus as a child, I learned that it's OK to leave the sidewalk and carve out my own path through the grass. You said, "Don't worry, Chris, they'll eventually pave this path as it's clearly the shortest path from the engineering building to the cafeteria." You were right, Dad. Many years later, we walked that newly paved path as we grabbed your favorite drink, Diet Pepsi, from the cafeteria. From you, I learned to carve out my own path through life and not always follow the crowd.

While you did not live to see Windows 95, you, quite frankly, didn't miss much. And yes, Mac OS finally switched to Linux. You were right on that one, as well.

I would also like to thank my coauthor, Antje Barth, for working many late nights and weekends to help make this a fantastic book-writing experience. Even though we have a 8–9 hour time difference between San Francisco and Düsseldorf, you always made yourself available for virtual whiteboarding sessions, last-minute source-code improvements, and Oxford comma discussions. We have become even better friends because of this experience, and I could not have created such a dense and high-quality book without you. I look forward to working with you on many future projects to come!

Antje

I would like to thank Ted Dunning and Ellen Friedman for being great mentors and always encouraging me to take on new challenges. Ted, you always have words of wisdom to share when we talk that help me see things from a different perspective, whether it's been in preparing for a demo competition or advising us on how to help our readers get the most out of this book. Ellen, I still remember how you guided me to create compelling conference talk proposals when I started submitting talks for O'Reilly Strata and AI conferences. And up to this day, I put extra thought into coming up with catchy titles. Unfortunately, O'Reilly rejected my proposal to title this book *Alexa, Please Train My Model*.

You both lead by example when you say, "Help build a girl's dream of what they can accomplish." For that same reason, I'd like to dedicate this book to all the women and girls who are dreaming of or currently pursuing a career in technology. As long as you believe in yourself, there is nothing stopping you from fulfilling your dreams in this profession.

There have been so many more individuals who supported and encouraged me throughout my professional journey. I thank you all.

I would also like to thank Chris for being a fun and insightful coauthor. From the beginning, you always insisted on the highest standards, drove me to dive deep, and encouraged me to be curious and ask a lot of questions. You helped simplify my code, present my thoughts clearly, and finally accept the controversial Oxford comma!

CHAPTER 1

Introduction to Data Science on AWS

In this chapter, we discuss the benefits of building data science projects in the cloud. We start by discussing the benefits of cloud computing. Next, we describe a typical machine learning workflow and the common challenges to move our models and applications from the prototyping phase to production. We touch on the overall benefits of developing data science projects on Amazon Web Services (AWS) and introduce the relevant AWS services for each step of the model development workflow. We also share architectural best practices, specifically around operational excellence, security, reliability, performance, and cost optimization.

Benefits of Cloud Computing

Cloud computing enables the on-demand delivery of IT resources via the internet with pay-as-you-go pricing. So instead of buying, owning, and maintaining our own data centers and servers, we can acquire technology such as compute power, storage, databases, and other services on an as-needed basis. Similar to a power company sending electricity instantly when we flip a light switch in our home, the cloud provisions IT resources on-demand with the click of a button or invocation of an API.

"There is no compression algorithm for experience" is a famous quote by Andy Jassy, CEO, Amazon Web Services. The quote expresses the company's long-standing experience in building reliable, secure, and performant services since 2006.

AWS has been continually expanding its service portfolio to support virtually any cloud workload, including many services and features in the area of artificial intelligence and machine learning. Many of these AI and machine learning services stem from Amazon's pioneering work in recommender systems, computer vision, speech/text, and neural networks over the past 20 years. A paper from 2003 titled "Amazon.com Recommendations: Item-to-Item Collaborative Filtering" (*https://oreil.ly/*

UlCDV) recently won the Institute of Electrical and Electronics Engineers award as a paper that withstood the "test of time." Let's review the benefits of cloud computing in the context of data science projects on AWS.

Agility

Cloud computing lets us spin up resources as we need them. This enables us to experiment quickly and frequently. Maybe we want to test a new library to run data-quality checks on our dataset, or speed up model training by leveraging the newest generation of GPU compute resources. We can spin up tens, hundreds, or even thousands of servers in minutes to perform those tasks. If an experiment fails, we can always deprovision those resources without any risk.

Cost Savings

Cloud computing allows us to trade capital expenses for variable expenses. We only pay for what we use with no need for upfront investments in hardware that may become obsolete in a few months. If we spin up compute resources to perform our data-quality checks, data transformations, or model training, we only pay for the time those compute resources are in use. We can achieve further cost savings by leveraging Amazon EC2 Spot Instances for our model training. Spot Instances let us take advantage of unused EC2 capacity in the AWS cloud and come with up to a 90% discount compared to on-demand instances. Reserved Instances and Savings Plans allow us to save money by prepaying for a given amount of time.

Elasticity

Cloud computing enables us to automatically scale our resources up or down to match our application needs. Let's say we have deployed our data science application to production and our model is serving real-time predictions. We can now automatically scale up the model hosting resources in case we observe a peak in model requests. Similarly, we can automatically scale down the resources when the number of model requests drops. There is no need to overprovision resources to handle peak loads.

Innovate Faster

Cloud computing allows us to innovate faster as we can focus on developing applications that differentiate our business, rather than spending time on the undifferentiated heavy lifting of managing infrastructure. The cloud helps us experiment with new algorithms, frameworks, and hardware in seconds versus months.

Deploy Globally in Minutes

Cloud computing lets us deploy our data science applications globally within minutes. In our global economy, it is important to be close to our customers. AWS has the concept of a Region, which is a physical location around the world where AWS clusters data centers. Each group of logical data centers is called an *Availability Zone* (AZ). Each AWS Region consists of multiple, isolated, and physically separate AZs within a geographic area. The number of AWS Regions and AZs is continuously growing (*https://oreil.ly/qegDk*).

We can leverage the global footprint of AWS Regions and AZs to deploy our data science applications close to our customers, improve application performance with ultra-fast response times, and comply with the data-privacy restrictions of each Region.

Smooth Transition from Prototype to Production

One of the benefits of developing data science projects in the cloud is the smooth transition from prototype to production. We can switch from running model prototyping code in our notebook to running data-quality checks or distributed model training across petabytes of data within minutes. And once we are done, we can deploy our trained models to serve real-time or batch predictions for millions of users across the globe.

Prototyping often happens in single-machine development environments using Jupyter Notebook, NumPy, and pandas. This approach works fine for small data sets. When scaling out to work with large datasets, we will quickly exceed the single machine's CPU and RAM resources. Also, we may want to use GPUs—or multiple machines—to accelerate our model training. This is usually not possible with a single machine.

The next challenge arises when we want to deploy our model (or application) to production. We also need to ensure our application can handle thousands or millions of concurrent users at global scale.

Production deployment often requires a strong collaboration between various teams including data science, data engineering, application development, and DevOps. And once our application is successfully deployed, we need to continuously monitor and react to model performance and data-quality issues that may arise after the model is pushed to production.

Developing data science projects in the cloud enables us to transition our models smoothly from prototyping to production while removing the need to build out our own physical infrastructure. Managed cloud services provide us with the tools to automate our workflows and deploy models into a scalable and highly performant production environment.

Data Science Pipelines and Workflows

Data science pipelines and workflows involve many complex, multidisciplinary, and iterative steps. Let's take a typical machine learning model development workflow as an example. We start with data preparation, then move to model training and tuning. Eventually, we deploy our model (or application) into a production environment. Each of those steps consists of several subtasks as shown in Figure 1-1.

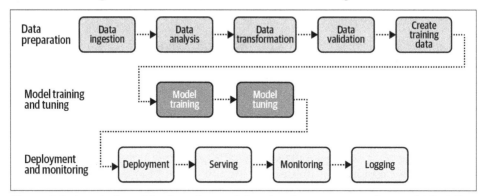

Figure 1-1. A typical machine learning workflow involves many complex, multidisciplinary, and iterative steps.

If we are using AWS, our raw data is likely already in Amazon Simple Storage Service (Amazon S3) and stored as CSV, Apache Parquet, or the equivalent. We can start training models quickly using the Amazon AI or automated machine learning (AutoML) services to establish baseline model performance by pointing directly to our dataset and clicking a single "train" button. We dive deep into the AI Services and AutoML in Chapters 2 and 3.

For more customized machine learning models—the primary focus of this book—we can start the manual data ingestion and exploration phases, including data analysis, data-quality checks, summary statistics, missing values, quantile calculations, data skew analysis, correlation analysis, etc. We dive deep into data ingestion and exploration in Chapters 4 and 5.

We should then define the machine learning problem type—regression, classification, clustering, etc. Once we have identified the problem type, we can select a machine learning algorithm best suited to solve the given problem. Depending on the algorithm we choose, we need to select a subset of our data to train, validate, and test our model. Our raw data usually needs to be transformed into mathematical vectors to enable numerical optimization and model training. For example, we might decide to transform categorical columns into one-hot encoded vectors or convert text-based columns into word-embedding vectors. After we have transformed a subset of the raw data into features, we should split the features into train, validation, and test feature sets to prepare for model training, tuning, and testing. We dive deep into feature selection and transformation in Chapters 5 and 6.

In the model training phase, we pick an algorithm and train our model with our training feature set to verify that our model code and algorithm is suited to solve the given problem. We dive deep into model training in Chapter 7.

In the model tuning phase, we tune the algorithm hyper-parameters and evaluate model performance against the validation feature set. We repeat these steps—adding more data or changing hyper-parameters as needed—until the model achieves the expected results on the test feature set. These results should be in line with our business objective before pushing the model to production. We dive deep into hyper-parameter tuning in Chapter 8.

The final stage—moving from prototyping into production—often presents the biggest challenge to data scientists and machine learning practitioners. We dive deep into model deployment in Chapter 9.

In Chapter 10, we tie everything together into an automated pipeline. In Chapter 11, we perform data analytics and machine learning on streaming data. Chapter 12 summarizes best practices for securing data science in the cloud.

Once we have built every individual step of our machine learning workflow, we can start automating the steps into a single, repeatable machine learning pipeline. When new data lands in S3, our pipeline reruns with the latest data and pushes the latest model into production to serve our applications. There are several workflow orchestration tools and AWS services available to help us build automated machine learning pipelines.

Amazon SageMaker Pipelines

Amazon SageMaker Pipelines are the standard, full-featured, and most complete way to implement AI and machine learning pipelines on Amazon SageMaker. SageMaker Pipelines have integration with SageMaker Feature Store, SageMaker Data Wrangler, SageMaker Processing Jobs, SageMaker Training Jobs, SageMaker Hyper-Parameter Tuning Jobs, SageMaker Model Registry, SageMaker Batch Transform, and SageMaker Model Endpoints, which we discuss throughout the book. We will dive deep into managed SageMaker Pipelines in Chapter 10 along with discussions on how to build pipelines with AWS Step Functions, Kubeflow Pipelines, Apache Airflow, MLflow, TFX, and human-in-the-loop workflows.

AWS Step Functions Data Science SDK

Step Functions, a managed AWS service, is a great option for building complex workflows without having to build and maintain our own infrastructure. We can use the Step Functions Data Science SDK to build machine learning pipelines from Python environments, such as Jupyter Notebook. We will dive deeper into the managed Step Functions for machine learning in Chapter 10.

Kubeflow Pipelines

Kubeflow is a relatively new ecosystem built on Kubernetes that includes an orchestration subsystem called *Kubeflow Pipelines*. With Kubeflow, we can restart failed pipelines, schedule pipeline runs, analyze training metrics, and track pipeline lineage. We will dive deeper into managing a Kubeflow cluster on Amazon Elastic Kubernetes Service (Amazon EKS) in Chapter 10.

Managed Workflows for Apache Airflow on AWS

Apache Airflow is a very mature and popular option primarily built to orchestrate data engineering and extract-transform-load (ETL) pipelines. We can use Airflow to author workflows as directed acyclic graphs of tasks. The Airflow scheduler executes our tasks on an array of workers while following the specified dependencies. We can visualize pipelines running in production, monitor progress, and troubleshoot issues when needed via the Airflow user interface. We will dive deeper into Amazon Managed Workflows for Apache Airflow (Amazon MWAA) in Chapter 10.

MLflow

MLflow is an open source project that initially focused on experiment tracking but now supports pipelines called *MLflow Workflows*. We can use MLflow to track experiments with Kubeflow and Apache Airflow workflows as well. MLflow requires us to build and maintain our own Amazon EC2 or Amazon EKS clusters, however. We will discuss MLflow in more detail in Chapter 10.

TensorFlow Extended

TensorFlow Extended (TFX) is an open source collection of Python libraries used within a pipeline orchestrator such as AWS Step Functions, Kubeflow Pipelines, Apache Airflow, or MLflow. TFX is specific to TensorFlow and depends on another open source project, Apache Beam, to scale beyond a single processing node. We will discuss TFX in more detail in Chapter 10.

Human-in-the-Loop Workflows

While AI and machine learning services make our lives easier, humans are far from being obsolete. In fact, the concept of "human-in-the-loop" has emerged as an important cornerstone in many AI/ML workflows. Humans provide important quality assurance for sensitive and regulated models in production.

Amazon Augmented AI (Amazon A2I) is a fully managed service to develop human-in-the-loop workflows that include a clean user interface, role-based access control with AWS Identity and Access Management (IAM), and scalable data storage with S3. Amazon A2I is integrated with many Amazon services including Amazon Rekognition for content moderation and Amazon Textract for form-data extraction. We can also use Amazon A2I with Amazon SageMaker and any of our custom ML models. We will dive deeper into human-in-the-loop workflows in Chapter 10.

MLOps Best Practices

The field of machine learning operations (MLOps) has emerged over the past decade to describe the unique challenges of operating "software plus data" systems like AI and machine learning. With MLOps, we are developing the end-to-end architecture for automated model training, model hosting, and pipeline monitoring. Using a complete MLOps strategy from the beginning, we are building up expertise, reducing human error, de-risking our project, and freeing up time to focus on the hard data science challenges.

We've seen MLOps evolve through three different stages of maturity:

MLOps v1.0
Manually build, train, tune, and deploy models

MLOps v2.0
Manually build and orchestrate model pipelines

MLOps v3.0
Automatically run pipelines when new data arrives or code changes from deterministic triggers such as GitOps or when models start to degrade in performance based on statistical triggers such as drift, bias, and explainability divergence

AWS and Amazon SageMaker Pipelines support the complete MLOps strategy, including automated pipeline retraining with both deterministic GitOps triggers as well as statistical triggers such as data drift, model bias, and explainability divergence. We will dive deep into statistical drift, bias, and explainability in Chapters 5, 6, 7, and 9. And we implement continuous and automated pipelines in Chapter 10 with various pipeline orchestration and automation options, including SageMaker Pipelines, AWS Step Functions, Apache Airflow, Kubeflow, and other options including human-in-the-loop workflows. For now, let's review some best practices for operational excellence, security, reliability, performance efficiency, and cost optimization of MLOps.

Operational Excellence

Here are a few machine-learning-specific best practices that help us build successful data science projects in the cloud:

Data-quality checks
> Since all our ML projects start with data, make sure to have access to high-quality datasets and implement repeatable data-quality checks. Poor data quality leads to many failed projects. Stay ahead of these issues early in the pipeline.

Start simple and reuse existing solutions
> Start with the simplest solution as there is no need to reinvent the wheel if we don't need to. There is likely an AI service available to solve our task. Leverage managed services such as Amazon SageMaker that come with a lot of built-in algorithms and pre-trained models.

Define model performance metrics
> Map the model performance metrics to business objectives, and continuously monitor these metrics. We should develop a strategy to trigger model invalidations and retrain models when performance degrades.

Track and version everything
> Track model development through experiments and lineage tracking. We should also version our datasets, feature-transformation code, hyper-parameters, and trained models.

Select appropriate hardware for both model training and model serving
> In many cases, model training has different infrastructure requirements than does model-prediction serving. Select the appropriate resources for each phase.

Continuously monitor deployed models
> Detect data drift and model drift—and take appropriate action such as model retraining.

Automate machine learning workflows
> Build consistent, automated pipelines to reduce human error and free up time to focus on the hard problems. Pipelines can include human-approval steps for approving models before pushing them to production.

Security

Security and compliance is a shared responsibility between AWS and the customer. AWS ensures the security "of" the cloud, while the customer is responsible for security "in" the cloud.

The most common security considerations for building secure data science projects in the cloud touch the areas of access management, compute and network isolation, encryption, governance, and auditability.

We need deep security and access control capabilities around our data. We should restrict access to data-labeling jobs, data-processing scripts, models, inference endpoints, and batch prediction jobs.

We should also implement a data governance strategy that ensures the integrity, security, and availability of our datasets. Implement and enforce data lineage, which monitors and tracks the data transformations applied to our training data. Ensure data is encrypted at rest and in motion. Also, we should enforce regulatory compliance where needed.

We will discuss best practices to build secure data science and machine learning applications on AWS in more detail in Chapter 12.

Reliability

Reliability refers to the ability of a system to recover from infrastructure or service disruptions, acquire computing resources dynamically to meet demand, and mitigate disruptions such as misconfigurations or transient network issues.

We should automate change tracking and versioning for our training data. This way, we can re-create the exact version of a model in the event of a failure. We will build once and use the model artifacts to deploy the model across multiple AWS accounts and environments.

Performance Efficiency

Performance efficiency refers to the efficient use of computing resources to meet requirements and how to maintain that efficiency as demand changes and technologies evolve.

We should choose the right compute for our machine learning workload. For example, we can leverage GPU-based instances to more efficiently train deep learning models using a larger queue depth, higher arithmetic logic units, and increased register counts.

Know the latency and network bandwidth performance requirements of models, and deploy each model closer to customers, if needed. There are situations where we might want to deploy our models "at the edge" to improve performance or comply with data-privacy regulations. "Deploying at the edge" refers to running the model on the device itself to run the predictions locally. We also want to continuously monitor key performance metrics of our model to spot performance deviations early.

Cost Optimization

We can optimize cost by leveraging different Amazon EC2 instance pricing options. For example, Savings Plans offer significant savings over on-demand instance prices, in exchange for a commitment to use a specific amount of compute power for a given amount of time. Savings Plans are a great choice for known/steady state workloads such as stable inference workloads.

With on-demand instances, we pay for compute capacity by the hour or the second depending on which instances we run. On-demand instances are best for new or stateful spiky workloads such as short-term model training jobs.

Finally, Amazon EC2 Spot Instances allow us to request spare Amazon EC2 compute capacity for up to 90% off the on-demand price. Spot Instances can cover flexible, fault-tolerant workloads such as model training jobs that are not time-sensitive. Figure 1-2 shows the resulting mix of Savings Plans, on-demand instances, and Spot Instances.

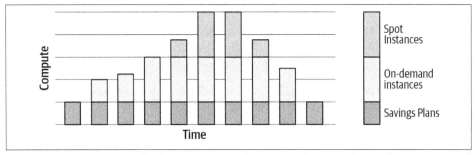

Figure 1-2. Optimize cost by choosing a mix of Savings Plans, on-demand instances, and Spot Instances.

With many of the managed services, we can benefit from the "only pay for what you use" model. For example, with Amazon SageMaker, we only pay for the time our model trains, or we run our automatic model tuning. Start developing models with smaller datasets to iterate more quickly and frugally. Once we have a well-performing model, we can scale up to train with the full dataset. Another important aspect is to right-size the model training and model hosting instances.

Many times, model training benefits from GPU acceleration, but model inference might not need the same acceleration. In fact, most machine learning workloads are actually predictions. While the model may take several hours or days to train, the deployed model likely runs 24 hours a day, 7 days a week across thousands of prediction servers supporting millions of customers. We should decide whether our use case requires a 24 × 7 real-time endpoint or a batch transformation on Spot Instances in the evenings.

Amazon AI Services and AutoML with Amazon SageMaker

We know that data science projects involve many complex, multidisciplinary, and iterative steps. We need access to a machine learning development environment that supports the model prototyping stage and equally provides a smooth transition to prepare our model for production. We will likely want to experiment with various machine learning frameworks and algorithms and develop custom model training and inference code.

Other times, we might want to just use a readily available, pre-trained model to solve a simple task. Or we might want to leverage AutoML techniques to create a first baseline for our project. AWS provides a broad set of services and features for each scenario. Figure 1-3 shows the entire Amazon AI and machine learning stack, including AI services and Amazon SageMaker Autopilot for AutoML.

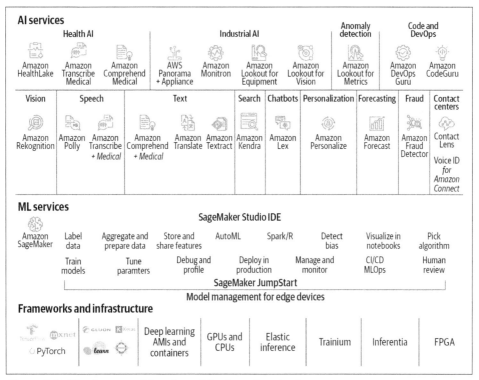

Figure 1-3. The Amazon AI and machine learning stack.

Amazon AI Services

For many common use cases, such as personalized product recommendations, content moderation, or demand forecasting, we can also use Amazon's managed AI services with the option to fine-tune on our custom datasets. We can integrate these "1-click" AI services into our applications via simple API calls without much (sometimes no) machine learning experience needed.

The fully managed AWS AI services are the fastest and easiest way to add intelligence to our applications using simple API calls. The AI services offer pre-trained or automatically trained machine learning models for image and video analysis, advanced text and document analysis, personalized recommendations, or demand forecasting.

AI services include Amazon Comprehend for natural language processing, Amazon Rekognition for computer vision, Amazon Personalize for generating product recommendations, Amazon Forecast for demand forecasting, and Amazon CodeGuru for automated source code reviews.

AutoML with SageMaker Autopilot

In another scenario, we might want to automate the repetitive steps of data analysis, data preparation, and model training for simple and well-known machine learning problems. This helps us focus our time on more complex use cases. AWS offers AutoML as part of the Amazon SageMaker service.

AutoML is not limited to SageMaker. Many of the Amazon AI services perform AutoML to find the best model and hyperparameters for the given dataset.

"AutoML" commonly refers to the effort of automating the typical steps of a model development workflow that we described earlier. Amazon SageMaker Autopilot is a fully managed service that applies AutoML techniques to our datasets.

SageMaker Autopilot first analyzes our tabular data, identifies the machine learning problem type (i.e., regression, classification) and chooses algorithms (i.e., XGBoost) to solve the problem. It also creates the required data transformation code to preprocess the data for model training. Autopilot then creates a number of diverse machine learning model candidate pipelines representing variations of data transformations and chosen algorithms. It applies the data transformations in a feature engineering step, then trains and tunes each of those model candidates. The result is a ranked list (leaderboard) of the model candidates based on a defined objective metric such as the validation accuracy.

SageMaker Autopilot is an example of transparent AutoML. Autopilot not only shares the data transformation code with us, but it also generates additional Jupyter notebooks that document the results of the data analysis step and the model candidate pipelines to reproduce the model training.

We can leverage SageMaker Autopilot in many scenarios. We can empower more people in our organization to build models, i.e., software developers who might have limited machine learning experience. We can automate model creation for simple-to-solve machine learning problems and focus our time on the new, complex use cases. We can automate the first steps of data analysis and data preparation and then use the result as a baseline to apply our domain knowledge and experience to tweak and further improve the models as needed. The Autopilot-generated model metrics also give us a good baseline for the model quality achievable with the provided dataset. We will dive deep into SageMaker Autopilot in Chapter 3.

Data Ingestion, Exploration, and Preparation in AWS

We will cover data ingestion, exploration, and preparation in Chapters 4, 5, and 6, respectively. But, for now, let's discuss this portion of the model-development workflow to learn which AWS services and open source tools we can leverage at each step.

Data Ingestion and Data Lakes with Amazon S3 and AWS Lake Formation

Everything starts with data. And if we have seen one consistent trend in recent decades, it's the continued explosion of data. Data is growing exponentially and is increasingly diverse. Today business success is often closely related to a company's ability to quickly extract value from their data. There are now more and more people, teams, and applications that need to access and analyze the data. This is why many companies are moving to a highly scalable, available, secure, and flexible data store, often called a *data lake*.

A data lake is a centralized and secure repository that enables us to store, govern, discover, and share data at any scale. With a data lake, we can run any kind of analytics efficiently and use multiple AWS services without having to transform or move our data.

Data lakes may contain structured relational data as well as semi-structured and unstructured data. We can even ingest real-time data. Data lakes give data science and machine learning teams access to large and diverse datasets to train and deploy more accurate models.

Amazon Simple Storage Service (Amazon S3) is object storage built to store and retrieve any amount of data from anywhere, in any format. We can organize our data with fine-tuned access controls to meet our business and compliance requirements. We will discuss security in depth in Chapter 12. Amazon S3 is designed for 99.999999999% (11 nines) of durability as well as for strong read-after-write consistency. S3 is a popular choice for data lakes in AWS.

We can leverage the AWS Lake Formation service to create our data lake. The service helps collect and catalog data from both databases and object storage. Lake Formation not only moves our data but also cleans, classifies, and secures access to our sensitive data using machine learning algorithms.

We can leverage AWS Glue to automatically discover and profile new data. AWS Glue is a scalable and serverless data catalog and data preparation service. The service consists of an ETL engine, an Apache Hive–compatible data catalog service, and a data transformation and analysis service. We can build data crawlers to periodically detect and catalog new data. AWS Glue DataBrew is a service with an easy-to-use UI that simplifies data ingestion, analysis, visualization, and transformation.

Data Analysis with Amazon Athena, Amazon Redshift, and Amazon QuickSight

Before we start developing any machine learning model, we need to understand the data. In the data analysis step, we explore our data, collect statistics, check for missing values, calculate quantiles, and identify data correlations.

Sometimes we just want to quickly analyze the available data from our development environment and prototype some first model code. Maybe we just quickly want to try out a new algorithm. We call this "ad hoc" exploration and prototyping, where we query parts of our data to get a first understanding of the data schema and data quality for our specific machine learning problem at hand. We then develop model code and ensure it is functionally correct. This ad hoc exploration and prototyping can be done from development environments such as SageMaker Studio, AWS Glue Data-Brew, and SageMaker Data Wrangler.

Amazon SageMaker offers us a hosted managed Jupyter environment and an integrated development environment with SageMaker Studio. We can start analyzing data sets directly in our notebook environment with tools such as pandas (*https:// pandas.pydata.org*), a popular Python open source data analysis and manipulation tool. Note that pandas uses in-memory data structures (DataFrames) to hold and manipulate data. As many development environments have constrained memory resources, we need to be careful how much data we pull into the pandas DataFrames.

For data visualizations in our notebook, we can leverage popular open source libraries such as Matplotlib (*https://matplotlib.org*) and Seaborn (*https:// seaborn.pydata.org*). Matplotlib lets us create static, animated, and interactive visualizations in Python. Seaborn builds on top of Matplotlib and adds support for additional statistical graphics—as well as an easier-to-use programming model. Both data visualization libraries integrate closely with pandas data structures.

The open source AWS Data Wrangler library (*https://oreil.ly/Q7gNs*) extends the power of pandas to AWS. AWS Data Wrangler connects pandas DataFrames with AWS services such as Amazon S3, AWS Glue, Amazon Athena, and Amazon Redshift.

AWS Data Wrangler provides optimized Python functions to perform common ETL tasks to load and unload data between data lakes, data warehouses, and databases.

After installing AWS Data Wrangler with `pip install awswrangler` and importing AWS Data Wrangler, we can read our dataset directly from S3 into a pandas DataFrame as shown here:

```
import awswrangler as wr


# Retrieve the data directly from Amazon S3
df = wr.s3.read_parquet("s3://<BUCKET>/<DATASET>/"))
```

AWS Data Wrangler also comes with additional memory optimizations, such as reading data in chunks. This is particularly helpful if we need to query large datasets. With chunking enabled, AWS Data Wrangler reads and returns every dataset file in the path as a separate pandas DataFrame. We can also set the chunk size to return the number of rows in a DataFrame equivalent to the numerical value we defined as chunk size. For a full list of capabilities, check the documentation (*https://oreil.ly/4sGjc*). We will dive deeper into AWS Data Wrangler in Chapter 5.

We can leverage managed services such as Amazon Athena to run interactive SQL queries on the data in S3 from within our notebook. Amazon Athena is a managed, serverless, dynamically scalable distributed SQL query engine designed for fast parallel queries on extremely large datasets. Athena is based on Presto, the popular open source query engine, and requires no maintenance. With Athena, we only pay for the queries we run. And we can query data in its raw form directly in our S3 data lake without additional transformations.

Amazon Athena also leverages the AWS Glue Data Catalog service to store and retrieve the schema metadata needed for our SQL queries. When we define our Athena database and tables, we point to the data location in S3. Athena then stores this table-to-S3 mapping in the AWS Glue Data Catalog. We can use PyAthena, a popular open source library, to query Athena from our Python-based notebooks and scripts. We will dive deeper into Athena, AWS Glue Data Catalog, and PyAthena in Chapters 4 and 5.

Amazon Redshift is a fully managed cloud data warehouse service that allows us to run complex analytic queries against petabytes of structured data. Our queries are distributed and parallelized across multiple nodes. In contrast to relational databases that are optimized to store data in rows and mostly serve transactional applications, Amazon Redshift implements columnar data storage, which is optimized for analytical applications where we are mostly interested in the summary statistics on those columns.

Amazon Redshift also includes Amazon Redshift Spectrum, which allows us to directly execute SQL queries from Amazon Redshift against exabytes of unstructured data in our Amazon S3 data lake without the need to physically move the data. Amazon Redshift Spectrum automatically scales the compute resources needed based on how much data is being received, so queries against Amazon S3 run fast, regardless of the size of our data.

If we need to create dashboard-style visualizations of our data, we can leverage Amazon QuickSight. QuickSight is an easy-to-use, serverless business analytics service to quickly build powerful visualizations. We can create interactive dashboards and reports and securely share them with our coworkers via browsers or mobile devices. QuickSight already comes with an extensive library of visualizations, charts, and tables.

QuickSight implements machine learning and natural language capabilities to help us gain deeper insights from our data. Using ML Insights, we can discover hidden trends and outliers in our data. The feature also enables anyone to run what-if analysis and forecasting, without any machine learning experience needed. We can also build predictive dashboards by connecting QuickSight to our machine learning models built in Amazon SageMaker.

Evaluate Data Quality with AWS Deequ and SageMaker Processing Jobs

We need high-quality data to build high-quality models. Before we create our training dataset, we want to ensure our data meets certain quality constraints. In software development, we run unit tests to ensure our code meets design and quality standards and behaves as expected. Similarly, we can run unit tests on our dataset to ensure the data meets our quality expectations.

AWS Deequ (*https://oreil.ly/a6cVE*) is an open source library built on top of Apache Spark that lets us define unit tests for data and measure data quality in large datasets. Using Deequ unit tests, we can find anomalies and errors early, before the data gets used in model training. Deequ is designed to work with very large datasets (billions of rows). The open source library supports tabular data, i.e., CSV files, database tables, logs, or flattened JSON files. Anything we can fit in a Spark data frame, we can validate with Deequ.

In a later example, we will leverage Deequ to implement data-quality checks on our sample dataset. We will leverage the SageMaker Processing Jobs support for Apache Spark to run our Deequ unit tests at scale. In this setup, we don't need to provision any Apache Spark cluster ourselves, as SageMaker Processing handles the heavy lifting for us. We can think of this as "serverless" Apache Spark. Once we are in possession of high-quality data, we can now create our training dataset.

Label Training Data with SageMaker Ground Truth

Many data science projects implement supervised learning. In supervised learning, our models learn by example. We first need to collect and evaluate, then provide accurate labels. If there are incorrect labels, our machine learning model will learn from bad examples. This will ultimately lead to inaccurate predictions. SageMaker Ground Truth helps us to efficiently and accurately label data stored in Amazon S3. SageMaker Ground Truth uses a combination of automated and human data labeling.

SageMaker Ground Truth provides pre-built workflows and interfaces for common data labeling tasks. We define the labeling task and assign the labeling job to either a public workforce via Amazon Mechanical Turk or a private workforce, such as our coworkers. We can also leverage third-party data labeling service providers listed on the AWS Marketplace, which are prescreened by Amazon.

SageMaker Ground Truth implements active learning techniques for pre-built workflows. It creates a model to automatically label a subset of the data, based on the labels assigned by the human workforce. As the model continuously learns from the human workforce, the accuracy improves, and less data needs to be sent to the human workforce. Over time and with enough data, the SageMaker Ground Truth active-learning model is able to provide high-quality and automatic annotations that result in lower labeling costs overall. We will dive deeper into SageMaker Ground Truth in Chapter 10.

Data Transformation with AWS Glue DataBrew, SageMaker Data Wrangler, and SageMaker Processing Jobs

Now let's move on to data transformation. We assume we have our data in an S3 data lake, or S3 bucket. We also gained a solid understanding of our dataset through the data analysis. The next step is now to prepare our data for model training.

Data transformations might include dropping or combining data in our dataset. We might need to convert text data into word embeddings for use with natural language models. Or perhaps we might need to convert data into another format, from numerical to text representation, or vice versa. There are numerous AWS services that could help us achieve this.

AWS Glue DataBrew is a visual data analysis and preparation tool. With 250 built-in transformations, DataBrew can detect anomalies, converting data between standard formats and fixing invalid or missing values. DataBrew can profile our data, calculate summary statistics, and visualize column correlations.

We can also develop custom data transformations at scale with Amazon SageMaker Data Wrangler. SageMaker Data Wrangler offers low-code, UI-driven data transformations. We can read data from various sources, including Amazon S3, Athena, Amazon Redshift, and AWS Lake Formation. SageMaker Data Wrangler comes with pre-configured data transformations similar to AWS DataBrew to convert column types, perform one-hot encoding, and process text fields. SageMaker Data Wrangler supports custom user-defined functions using Apache Spark and even generates code including Python scripts and SageMaker Processing Jobs.

SageMaker Processing Jobs let us run custom data processing code for data transformation, data validation, or model evaluation across data in S3. When we configure the SageMaker Processing Job, we define the resources needed, including instance types and number of instances. SageMaker takes our custom code, copies our data from Amazon S3, and then pulls a Docker container to execute the processing step.

SageMaker offers pre-built container images to run data processing with Apache Spark and scikit-learn. We can also provide a custom container image if needed. SageMaker then spins up the cluster resources we specified for the duration of the job and terminates them when the job has finished. The processing results are written back to an Amazon S3 bucket when the job finishes.

Model Training and Tuning with Amazon SageMaker

Let's discuss the model training and tuning steps of our model development workflow in more detail and learn which AWS services and open source tools we can leverage.

Train Models with SageMaker Training and Experiments

Amazon SageMaker Training Jobs provide a lot of functionality to support our model training. We can organize, track, and evaluate our individual model training runs with SageMaker Experiments. With SageMaker Debugger, we get transparency into our model training process. Debugger automatically captures real-time metrics during training and provides a visual interface to analyze the debug data. Debugger also profiles and monitors system resource utilization and identifies resource bottlenecks such as overutilized CPUs or GPUs.

With SageMaker training, we simply specify the Amazon S3 location of our data, the algorithm container to execute our model training code, and define the type and number of SageMaker ML instances we need. SageMaker will take care of initializing the resources and run our model training. If instructed, SageMaker spins up a distributed compute cluster. Once the model training completes, SageMaker writes the results to S3 and terminates the ML instances.

SageMaker also supports Managed Spot Training. Managed Spot Training leverages Amazon EC2 Spot Instances to perform model training. Using Spot Instances, we can reduce model training cost up to 90% compared to on-demand instances.

Besides SageMaker Autopilot, we can choose from any of the built-in algorithms that come with Amazon SageMaker or customize the model training by bringing our own model code (script mode) or our own algorithm/framework container.

Built-in Algorithms

SageMaker comes with many built-in algorithms to help machine learning practitioners get started on training and deploying machine learning models quickly. Built-in algorithms require no extra code. We only need to provide the data and any model settings (hyper-parameters) and specify the compute resources. Most of the built-in algorithms also support distributed training out of the box to support large datasets that cannot fit on a single machine.

For supervised learning tasks, we can choose from regression and classification algorithms such as Linear Learner and XGBoost. Factorization Machines are well suited to recommender systems.

For unsupervised learning tasks, such as clustering, dimension reduction, pattern recognition, and anomaly detection, there are additional built-in algorithms available. Such algorithms include Principal Component Analysis (PCA) and K-Means Clustering.

We can also leverage built-in algorithms for text analysis tasks such as text classification and topic modeling. Such algorithms include BlazingText and Neural Topic Model.

For image processing, we will find built-in algorithms for image classification and object detection, including Semantic Segmentation.

Bring Your Own Script (Script Mode)

If we need more flexibility, or there is no built-in solution that works for our use case, we can provide our own model training code. This is often referred to as "script mode." Script mode lets us focus on our training script, while SageMaker provides highly optimized Docker containers for each of the familiar open source frameworks, such as TensorFlow, PyTorch, Apache MXNet, XGBoost, and scikit-learn. We can add all our needed code dependencies via a requirements file, and SageMaker will take care of running our custom model training code with one of the built-in framework containers, depending on our framework of choice.

Bring Your Own Container

In case neither the built-in algorithms or script mode covers our use case, we can bring our own custom Docker image to host the model training. Docker is a software tool that provides build-time and runtime support for isolated environments called *Docker containers*.

SageMaker uses Docker images and containers to provide data processing, model training, and prediction serving capabilities.

We can use *bring your own container* (BYOC) if the package or software we need is not included in a supported framework. This approach gives us unlimited options and the most flexibility, as we can build our own Docker container and install anything we require. Typically, we see people use this option when they have custom security requirements, or want to preinstall libraries into the Docker container to avoid a third-party dependency (i.e., with PyPI, Maven, or Docker Registry).

When using the BYOC option to use our own Docker image, we first need to upload the Docker image to a Docker registry like DockerHub or Amazon Elastic Container Registry (Amazon ECR). We should only choose the BYOC option if we are familiar with developing, maintaining, and supporting custom Docker images with an efficient Docker-image pipeline. Otherwise, we should use the built-in SageMaker containers.

 We don't need to "burn" our code into a Docker image at build time. We can simply point to our code in Amazon S3 from within the Docker image and load the code dynamically when a Docker container is started. This helps avoid unnecessary Docker image builds every time our code changes.

Pre-Built Solutions and Pre-Trained Models with SageMaker JumpStart

SageMaker JumpStart gives us access to pre-built machine learning solutions and pre-trained models from AWS, TensorFlow Hub, and PyTorch Hub. The pre-built solutions cover many common use cases such as fraud detection, predictive maintenance, and demand forecasting. The pre-trained models span natural language processing, object detection, and image classification domains. We can fine-tune the models with our own datasets and deploy them to production in our AWS account with just a few clicks. We will dive deeper into SageMaker JumpStart in Chapter 7.

Tune and Validate Models with SageMaker Hyper-Parameter Tuning

Another important step in developing high-quality models is finding the right model configuration or model hyper-parameters. In contrast to the model parameters that are learned by the algorithm, hyper-parameters control how the algorithm learns the parameters.

Amazon SageMaker comes with automatic model tuning and validating capabilities to find the best performing model hyper-parameters for our model and dataset. We need to define an objective metric to optimize, such as validation accuracy, and the hyper-parameter ranges to explore. SageMaker will then run many model training jobs to explore the hyper-parameter ranges that we specify and evaluate the results against the objective metric to measure success.

There are different strategies to explore hyper-parameter ranges: grid search, random search, and Bayesian optimization are the most common ones. We will dive deeper into SageMaker Hyper-Parameter Tuning in Chapter 8.

Model Deployment with Amazon SageMaker and AWS Lambda Functions

Once we have trained, validated, and optimized our model, we are ready to deploy and monitor our model. There are generally three ways to deploy our models with Amazon SageMaker, depending on our application requirements: SageMaker Endpoints for REST-based predictions, AWS Lambda functions for serverless predictions, and SageMaker Batch Transform for batch predictions.

SageMaker Endpoints

If we need to optimize the model deployment for low-latency, real-time predictions, we can deploy our model using SageMaker hosting services. These services will spin up a SageMaker endpoint to host our model and provide a REST API to serve predictions. We can call the REST API from our applications to receive model predictions. SageMaker model endpoints support auto-scaling to match the current traffic pattern and are deployed across multiple AZs for high availability.

SageMaker Batch Transform

If we need to get predictions for an entire dataset, we can use SageMaker Batch Transform. Batch Transform is optimized for high throughput, without the need for real-time, low-latency predictions. SageMaker will spin up the specified number of resources to perform large-scale, batch predictions on our S3 data. Once the job completes, SageMaker will write the data to S3 and tear down the compute resources.

Serverless Model Deployment with AWS Lambda

Another option to serve our model predictions are AWS Lambda functions for serverless model servers. After training the model with SageMaker, we use an AWS Lambda function that retrieves the model from S3 and serves the predictions. AWS Lambda does have memory and latency limitations, so be sure to test this option at scale before finalizing on this deployment approach.

Streaming Analytics and Machine Learning on AWS

Until now, we assumed that we have all of our data available in a centralized static location, such as our S3-based data lake. In reality, data is continuously streaming from many different sources across the world simultaneously. In many cases, we want to perform real-time analytics and machine learning on this streaming data before it lands in a data lake. A short time to (business) insight is required to gain competitive advances and to react quickly to changing customer and market trends.

Streaming technologies provide us with the tools to collect, process, and analyze data streams in real time. AWS offers a wide range of streaming technology options, including Amazon Kinesis and Amazon Managed Streaming for Apache Kafka (Amazon MSK). We will dive deep into streaming analytics and machine learning in Chapter 11.

Amazon Kinesis Streaming

Amazon Kinesis is a streaming data service, which helps us collect, process, and analyze data in real time. With Kinesis Data Firehose, we can prepare and load real-time data continuously to various destinations including Amazon S3 and Amazon Redshift. With Kinesis Data Analytics, we can process and analyze the data as it arrives. And with Amazon Kinesis Data Streams, we can manage the ingest of data streams for custom applications.

Amazon Managed Streaming for Apache Kafka

Amazon MSK is a streaming data service that manages Apache Kafka infrastructure and operations. Apache Kafka is a popular open source, high-performance, fault-tolerant, and scalable platform for building real-time streaming data pipelines and applications. Using Amazon MSK, we can run our Apache Kafka applications on AWS without the need to manage Apache Kafka clusters ourselves.

Streaming Predictions and Anomaly Detection

In the streaming data chapter, we will focus on analyzing a continuous stream of product review messages that we collect from available online channels. We will run streaming predictions to detect the sentiment of our customers, so we can identify which customers might need high-priority attention.

Next, we run continuous streaming analytics over the incoming review messages to capture the average sentiment per product category. We visualize the continuous average sentiment in a metrics dashboard for the line of business (LOB) owners.

The LOB owners can now detect sentiment trends quickly and take action. We also calculate an anomaly score of the incoming messages to detect anomalies in the data schema or data values. In case of a rising anomaly score, we can alert the application developers in charge to investigate the root cause.

As a last metric, we also calculate a continuous approximate count of the received messages. This number of online messages could be used by the digital marketing team to measure effectiveness of social media campaigns.

AWS Infrastructure and Custom-Built Hardware

A key benefit of cloud computing is the ability to try infrastructure options that specifically match our workload. AWS provides many options for high-performance compute, networking, and storage infrastructure for our data science projects, as Figure 1-4 shows. Let's see each of these options, which we will reference throughout.

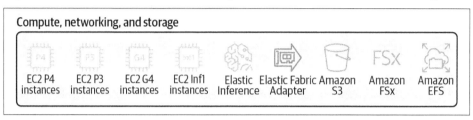

Figure 1-4. AWS infrastructure options for data science and machine learning projects.

SageMaker Compute Instance Types

AWS allows us to choose from a diverse set of instance types depending on our workload. Following is a list of instance types commonly used for data science use cases:

T instance type
> General-purpose, burstable-performance instances when we don't need consistently high levels of CPU but benefit from having fast CPUs when we need them

M instance type
> General-purpose instances with a good balance of compute, memory, and network bandwidth

C instance type
> Compute-optimized instances ideal for compute-bound workloads with high-CPU requirements

R instance type
> Memory-optimized instances optimized for workloads that benefit from storing large datasets in memory such as Apache Spark

P, G, Inferentia, and Trainium instance types
> High-performance compute instances with hardware accelerators or coprocessors such as GPUs or Amazon custom-built hardware such as AWS Inferentia for inference and AWS Trainium for training workloads

Amazon Elastic Inference Accelerator
> Network-attached coprocessors used by other instance types when additional compute power is needed for specific workloads, such as batch transformations and inference

GPUs and Amazon Custom-Built Compute Hardware

Similar to how Amazon S3 provides storage in the cloud, Amazon Elastic Compute Cloud (Amazon EC2) provides compute resources. We can choose from over 350 instances for our business needs and workload. AWS also offers a choice of Intel, AMD, and ARM-based processors. The hardware-accelerated P4, P3, and G4 instance types are a popular choice for high-performance, GPU-based model training. Amazon also provides custom-build hardware optimized for both model training and inference.

P4d instances consist of eight NVIDIA A100 Tensor Core GPUs with 400 Gbps instance networking and support for Elastic Fabric Adapter (EFA) with NVIDIA GPUDirect RDMA (remote direct memory access). P4d instances are deployed in hyperscale clusters called *Amazon EC2 UltraClusters* that provide supercomputer-class performance for everyday ML developers, researchers, and data scientists. Each EC2 UltraCluster of P4d instances gives us access to more than 4,000 NVIDIA A100 GPUs, petabit-scale nonblocking networking, and high-throughput/low-latency storage via Amazon FSx for Lustre.

P3 instances consist of up to eight NVIDIA V100 Tensor Core GPUs and deliver up to 100 Gbps of networking throughput. P3 instances deliver up to one petaflop of mixed-precision performance per instance. P3dn.24xlarge instances also support EFA.

The G4 instances are a great option for cost-sensitive, small-scale training or inference workloads. G4 instances consist of NVIDIA T4 GPUs with up to 100 Gbps of networking throughput and up to 1.8 TB of local NVMe storage.

AWS also offers custom-built silicon for machine learning training with the AWS Trainium chip and for inference workloads with the AWS Inferentia chip. Both AWS Trainium and AWS Inferentia aim at increasing machine learning performance and reducing infrastructure cost.

AWS Trainium has been optimized for deep learning training workloads, including image classification, semantic search, translation, voice recognition, natural language processing, and recommendation engines.

AWS Inferentia processors support many popular machine learning models, including single-shot detectors and ResNet for computer vision—as well as Transformers and BERT for natural language processing.

AWS Inferentia is available via the Amazon EC2 Inf1 instances. We can choose between 1 and 16 AWS Inferentia processors per Inf1 instance, which deliver up to 2,000 tera operations per second. We can use the AWS Neuron SDK to compile our TensorFlow, PyTorch, or Apache MXNet models to run on Inf1 instances.

Inf1 instances can help to reduce our inference cost, with up to 45% lower cost per inference and 30% higher throughput compared to Amazon EC2 G4 instances. Table 1-1 shows some instance-type options to use for model inference, including Amazon custom-built Inferentia chip, CPUs, and GPUs.

Table 1-1. EC2 instance options for model inference

Model characteristics	EC2 Inf1	EC2 C5	EC2 G4
Requires low latency and high throughput at low cost	X		
Low sensitivity to latency and throughput		X	
Requires NVIDIA's CUDA, CuDNN or TensorRT libraries			X

Amazon Elastic Inference is another option to leverage accelerated compute for model inference. Elastic Inference allows us to attach a fraction of GPU acceleration to any Amazon EC2 (CPU-based) instance type. Using Elastic Inference, we can decouple the instance choice for model inference from the amount of inference acceleration.

Choosing Elastic Inference over Inf1 might make sense if we need different instance characteristics than those offered with Inf1 instances or if our performance requirements are lower than what the smallest Inf1 instance provides.

Elastic Inference scales from single-precision TFLOPS (trillion floating point operations per second) up to 32 mixed-precision TFLOPS of inference acceleration.

Graviton processors are AWS custom-built ARM processors. The CPUs leverage 64-bit Arm Neoverse cores and custom silicon designed by AWS using advanced 7 nm manufacturing technology. ARM-based instances can offer an attractive price-performance ratio for many workloads running in Amazon EC2.

The first generation of Graviton processors are offered with Amazon EC2 A1 instances. Graviton2 processors deliver 7x more performance, 4x more compute cores, 5x faster memory, and 2x larger caches compared to the first generation. We can find the Graviton2 processor in Amazon EC2 T4g, M6g, C6g, and R6g instances.

The AWS Graviton2 processors provide enhanced performance for video encoding workloads, hardware acceleration for compression workloads, and support for machine learning predictions.

GPU-Optimized Networking and Custom-Built Hardware

AWS offers advanced networking solutions that can help us to efficiently run distributed model training and scale-out inference.

The Amazon EFA is a network interface for Amazon EC2 instances that optimizes internode communications at scale. EFA uses a custom-built OS bypass hardware interface that enhances the performance of internode communications. If we are using the NVIDIA Collective Communications Library for model training, we can scale to thousands of GPUs using EFA.

We can combine the setup with up to 400 Gbps network bandwidth per instance and the NVIDIA GPUDirect RDMA for low-latency, GPU-to-GPU communication between instances. This gives us the performance of on-premises GPU clusters with the on-demand elasticity and flexibility of the cloud.

Storage Options Optimized for Large-Scale Model Training

We already learned about the benefits of building our data lake on Amazon S3. If we need faster storage access for distributed model training, we can use Amazon FSx for Lustre.

Amazon FSx for Lustre offers the open source Lustre filesystem as a fully managed service. Lustre is a high-performance filesystem, offering submillisecond latencies, up to hundreds of gigabytes per second of throughput, and millions of IOPS.

We can link FSx for Lustre filesystems with Amazon S3 buckets. This allows us to access and process data through the FSx filesystem and from Amazon S3. Using FSx for Lustre, we can set up our model training compute instances to access the same set of data through high-performance shared storage.

Amazon Elastic File System (Amazon EFS) is another file storage service that provides a filesystem interface for up to thousands of Amazon EC2 instances. The filesystem interface offers standard operating system file I/O APIs and enables filesystem access semantics, such as strong consistency and file locking.

Reduce Cost with Tags, Budgets, and Alerts

Throughout the book, we provide tips on how to reduce cost for data science projects with the Amazon AI and machine learning stack. Overall, we should always tag our resources with the name of the business unit, application, environment, and user. We should use tags that provide visibility into where our money is spent. In addition to the AWS built-in cost-allocation tags, we can provide our own user-defined allocation tags specific to our domain. AWS Budgets help us create alerts when cost is approaching—or exceeding—a given threshold.

Summary

In this chapter, we discussed the benefits of developing data science projects in the cloud, with a specific focus on AWS. We showed how to quickly add intelligence to our applications leveraging the Amazon AI and machine learning stack. We introduced the concept of AutoML and explained how SageMaker Autopilot offers a transparent approach to AutoML. We then discussed a typical machine learning workflow in the cloud and introduced the relevant AWS services that assist in each step of the workflow. We provided an overview of available workflow orchestration tools to build and automate machine learning pipelines. We described how to run streaming analytics and machine learning over real-time data. We finished this chapter with an overview of AWS infrastructure options to leverage in our data science projects.

In Chapter 2, we will discuss prominent data science use cases across industries such as media, advertising, IoT, and manufacturing.

## CHAPTER 2

Data Science Use Cases

In this chapter, we show how AI and machine learning have disrupted nearly every industry—and will continue to do so in the future. We discuss prominent use cases across industries such as media, advertising, IoT, and manufacturing. As more and more building blocks become available, more and more use cases become tangible. Cloud-native developers have access to these building blocks through ready-to-use AI services such as Amazon Rekognition, fully customizable ML services including Amazon SageMaker, and easy-to-access quantum computers with Amazon Braket.

AI and machine learning have become truly ubiquitous thanks to recent innovations in cloud computing, leaps in computing power, and explosions in data collection. This democratization of AI and machine learning is fueled by an explosion of AI services that are easy to integrate with applications, require very little maintenance, and offer pay-as-you-go pricing.

With no required PhD in data science, we can implement product recommendations to delight our customers, implement highly accurate forecasting models to improve our supply chain, or build virtual assistants to simplify our customer support—all with just a single API call! These AI services free up valuable human resources to focus on domain-specific and product-differentiating features.

Innovation Across Every Industry

Many AI and machine learning use cases fall in one of two categories: improving business operations or creating new customer experiences. Prominent examples that improve business operations are AI-powered demand forecasting, resource optimization, and fraud detection. Examples for creating new customer experiences include personalized product recommendations and enriched video-streaming experiences.

Without a doubt, AI and machine learning are driving innovation in every industry. Here are a few examples across various industries:

Media and entertainment
Companies are delighting customers with highly engaging, personalized content. AI also enables highly efficient and effective metadata extraction to make media content more easily discoverable and searchable by customers and media production workers.

Life sciences
Companies benefit from AI and machine learning for drug discovery, clinical trial management, drug manufacturing, digital therapeutics development, and clinical decision support.

Financial services
AI and machine learning improve compliance, surveillance, and fraud detection. They help to speed up document processing, create personalized pricing and financial product recommendations, and assist in trading decisions.

Automotive
AI and machine learning power autonomous driving, navigation, and connected vehicles.

Manufacturing
AI and machine learning support engineering design, manage supply chain inventory, and optimize maintenance, repair, and operations. They enhance the assembly line and underpin smart products or factories.

Gaming
The gaming industry leverages AI and machine learning to implement intelligent auto-scaling for their game servers as demand changes throughout the day.

Let's discuss some prominent AI use cases in more detail and see how we can start to implement them with ready-to-use AI services from AWS.

Personalized Product Recommendations

Over recent decades, consumers have experienced more and more personalized online product and content recommendations. Recommendations are everywhere, including Amazon.com suggesting the next product to buy and Amazon Prime Video recommending the next show to watch.

A lot of recommendation systems find similarities based on how customers collaborate with items in the catalog. An early implementation of such "collaborative filtering" is described in a 2003 paper by Amazon.com, "Amazon.com Recommendations: Item-to-Item Collaborative Filtering" (*https://oreil.ly/LbrdC*).

Today, sophisticated deep learning techniques understand customers' needs at the right time and within the right context. Whether we are shopping on the Amazon.com marketplace, listening to music on Prime Music, watching shows on Prime Video, reading ebooks on the Amazon Kindle, or listening to audiobooks with Audible, we will be presented with new personalized recommendations.

Simple recommendation systems often start as rule-based systems. As the number of users and products increase in our system, it becomes difficult to define rules that are specific enough to each user to provide meaningful recommendations. Broad rules are not typically specialized enough to keep customers coming back.

Even ML-based recommendation systems may face challenges. We also have to handle new users and new items entering our system where we don't have any data on which to base our recommendations. This is the classic "cold start" problem and should be addressed by anyone implementing a recommendation engine in the modern era. Cold start is when we have little or no historical event activity to use as a signal to build our recommender model for a given user or product.

Recommendations should also avoid the "popularity trap," which only recommends popular items and potentially misses delightful recommendations for nonpopular items. This can be solved with recommender systems that explore new items using algorithms such as multiarmed bandits, which we will discuss in Chapter 9.

Also, we'd like to handle real-time changes in a user's intent as they are using our application. This requires a real-time, dynamic recommendation system instead of traditional offline, precomputed recommendations served from a database.

With such a dynamic system, customers will appreciate the relevant and timely content—and our business will realize the following benefits from a more personalized customer experience:

Increase in product engagement
By recommending relevant content to users, we increase the stickiness of our website, encourage users to come back often, and give them reason to stay longer.

Increase in product conversions
Users are more likely to purchase more relevant products.

Increase in click-through rates
We will likely see higher click-through rates with personalized product updates targeted at the individual user.

Increase in revenue
> When customers are served the right recommendations at the right time, companies see an increase in revenue.

Reduction in churn
> We can reduce overall churn and reduce opt-outs from interesting email campaigns.

Over the last two decades, Amazon has continuously advanced its machine learning research focused on personalization. The paper "Two Decades of Recommender Systems at Amazon.com" (*https://oreil.ly/iXEXk*) by Smith and Linden (2017) provides a great summary of this journey.

> More insights into Amazon's scientific research and academic publications are available on Amazon (*https://www.amazon.science*).

Recommend Products with Amazon Personalize

Like a lot of machine learning, there is no single algorithm that addresses all those challenges in personalization. Wouldn't it be great if anyone could just tap into Amazon.com's extensive experience in creating personalized product and content recommendations and add this capability to our applications? Amazon Personalize offers exactly this.

Amazon Personalize reflects Amazon.com's decades of experience in creating, scaling, and managing personalization technology. Amazon Personalize makes it easy for developers to create individualized product recommendations as well as targeted marketing promotions. This AI service enables developers to build custom personalization models without having to deal with the complexity of managing our own machine learning infrastructure.

To start generating recommendations, we just provide Amazon Personalize with the continuous activity stream from our application (i.e., clicks, page views, signups, purchases) along with the inventory of the products we want to recommend, as shown in Figure 2-1.

The activity data comprises event information about how the user interacts with the system. Some example event activity includes user clicks, shopping cart additions, item purchases, and movie watches. This event activity represents a strong signal to build an effective recommendation model.

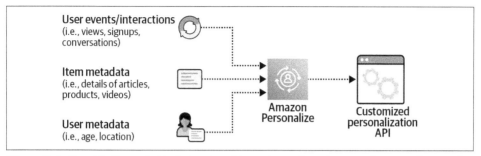

Figure 2-1. Provide the activity dataset and inventory of products to Amazon Personalize to start generating recommendations.

We can also provide additional metadata about the users and products involved in the event activity, such as the product category, product price, user age, user location, etc. While this additional metadata is optional, it is helpful when addressing the "cold start" scenario where we have little or no historical event activity to use as a signal to build our recommender model.

Additionally, Amazon Personalize has recently announced a new cold-start algorithm that combines neural networks and reinforcement learning to provide more relevant recommendations when little data is known about the user.

With this event activity and metadata in place, Amazon Personalize trains, tunes, and deploys a custom recommender model for our users and products. Amazon Personalize performs all steps of the machine learning pipeline, including feature engineering, algorithm selection, model tuning, and model deploying. Once Amazon Personalize selects, trains, and deploys the best model for our dataset, we simply call the Amazon Personalize `get_recommendations()` API to generate recommendations in real time for our users:

```
get_recommendations_response = personalize_runtime.get_recommendations(
        campaignArn = campaign_arn,
        userId = user_id
)

item_list = get_recommendations_response['itemList']
recommendation_list = []
for item in item_list:
    item_id = get_movie_by_id(item['itemId'])
recommendation_list.append(item_id)
```

Trained with the popular MovieLens dataset that contains millions of user-movie ratings, Amazon Personalize generates the following recommended movies for our sample user:

Shrek
Amelie
Lord of the Rings: The Two Towers
Toy Story 2
Good Will Hunting
Eternal Sunshine of the Spotless Mind
Spirited Away
Lord of the Rings: The Return of the King
Schindler's List
Leon: The Professional

Generate Recommendations with Amazon SageMaker and TensorFlow

Multitask recommenders create a model that optimizes two or more objectives at the same time. The model performs transfer learning by sharing variables between the tasks during model training.

In the following TensorFlow example that uses the TensorFlow Recommenders (TFRS) library (*https://oreil.ly/XdDII*), we will find a model that trains a recommender to predict ratings (ranking task) as well as predict the number of movie watches (retrieval task):

```
user_model = tf.keras.Sequential([
  tf.keras.layers.experimental.preprocessing.StringLookup(
      vocabulary=unique_user_ids),
  # We add 2 to account for unknown and mask tokens.
  tf.keras.layers.Embedding(len(unique_user_ids) + 2, embedding_dimension)
])

movie_model = tf.keras.Sequential([
  tf.keras.layers.experimental.preprocessing.StringLookup(
      vocabulary=unique_movie_titles),
  tf.keras.layers.Embedding(len(unique_movie_titles) + 2, embedding_dimension)
])

rating_task = tfrs.tasks.Ranking(
    loss=tf.keras.losses.MeanSquaredError(),
    metrics=[tf.keras.metrics.RootMeanSquaredError()],
)

retrieval_task = tfrs.tasks.Retrieval(
        metrics=tfrs.metrics.FactorizedTopK(
            candidates=movies.batch(128).map(self.movie_model)
        )
)
```

Generate Recommendations with Amazon SageMaker and Apache Spark

Amazon SageMaker supports serverless Apache Spark (both Python and Scala) through SageMaker Processing Jobs. We will use SageMaker Processing Jobs throughout the book to perform data-quality checks and feature transformations. However, in this section we will generate recommendations using SageMaker Processing Jobs with Apache Spark ML's collaborative filtering algorithm called *Alternating Least Squares* (ALS). We would use this algorithm if we already have a Spark-based data pipeline and want to generate recommendations using that pipeline.

Here is the *train_spark.py* file that generates recommendations with Apache Spark ML and ALS:

```python
import pyspark
from pyspark.sql import SparkSession
from pyspark.sql.functions import *
from pyspark.ml.evaluation import RegressionEvaluator
from pyspark.ml.recommendation import ALS
from pyspark.sql import Row

def main():
    ...
    lines = spark.read.text(s3_input_data).rdd
    parts = lines.map(lambda row: row.value.split("::"))
    ratingsRDD = parts.map(lambda p: Row(userId=int(p[0]),
                                         movieId=int(p[1]),
                                         rating=float(p[2]),
                                         timestamp=int(p[3])))
    ratings = spark.createDataFrame(ratingsRDD)
    (training, test) = ratings.randomSplit([0.8, 0.2])

    # Build the recommendation model using ALS on the training data
    als = ALS(maxIter=5,
              regParam=0.01,
              userCol="userId",
              itemCol="itemId",
              ratingCol="rating",
              coldStartStrategy="drop")
    model = als.fit(training)

    # Evaluate the model by computing the RMSE on the test data
    predictions = model.transform(test)
    evaluator = RegressionEvaluator(metricName="rmse",
                                    labelCol="rating",
                                    predictionCol="prediction")
    rmse = evaluator.evaluate(predictions)

    # Generate top 10 recommendations for each user
    userRecs = model.recommendForAllUsers(10)
    userRecs.show()
```

```
# Write top 10 recommendations for each user
userRecs.repartition(1).write.mode("overwrite")\
.option("header", True).option("delimiter", "\t")\
.csv(f"{s3_output_data}/recommendations")
```

Now let's launch the PySpark script within a serverless Apache Spark environment running as a SageMaker Processing Job:

```
from sagemaker.spark.processing import PySparkProcessor
from sagemaker.processing import ProcessingOutput

processor = PySparkProcessor(base_job_name='spark-als',
                             role=role,
                             instance_count=1,
                             instance_type='ml.r5.2xlarge',
                             max_runtime_in_seconds=1200)


processor.run(submit_app='train_spark_als.py',
              arguments=['s3_input_data', s3_input_data,
                         's3_output_data', s3_output_data,
              ],
              logs=True,
              wait=False
)
```

The output shows a user ID and list of recommendations (item ID, rank) sorted by rank from most recommended to least recommended:

```
|userId|      recommendations|
+------+--------------------+
|    12|[[46, 6.146928], ...|
|     1|[[46, 4.963598], ...|
|     6|[[25, 4.5243497],...|
+------+--------------------+
```

Detect Inappropriate Videos with Amazon Rekognition

Computer vision is useful for many different use cases, including content moderation of user-generated content, digital identity verification for secure login, and hazard identification for driverless cars.

Amazon Rekognition is a high-level AI service that identifies objects, including people, text, and activities found in both images and videos. Amazon Rekognition uses AutoML to train custom models to recognize objects specific to our use case and business domain.

Let's use Amazon Rekognition to detect violent content in videos uploaded by our application users. For example, we want to reject videos that contain weapons by using Amazon Rekognition's Content Moderation API as follows:

```
startModerationLabelDetection = rekognition.start_content_moderation(
    Video={
        'S3Object': {
            'Bucket': bucket,
            'Name': videoName,
        }
    },
)

moderationJobId = startModerationLabelDetection['JobId']

getContentModeration = rekognition.get_content_moderation(
    JobId=moderationJobId,
    SortBy='TIMESTAMP'
)

while(getContentModeration['JobStatus'] == 'IN_PROGRESS'):
    time.sleep(5)
    print('.', end='')

    getContentModeration = rekognition.get_content_moderation(
     JobId=moderationJobId,
     SortBy='TIMESTAMP')

display(getContentModeration['JobStatus'])
```

Here is the output that shows the detected labels. Note the Timestamp, which represents the offset from the start of the video, as well as the Confidence, which represents the confidence of Amazon Rekognition's prediction:

```
{'JobStatus': 'SUCCEEDED',
 'VideoMetadata': {'Codec': 'h264',
  'DurationMillis': 6033,
  'Format': 'QuickTime / MOV',
  'FrameRate': 30.0,
  'FrameHeight': 1080,
  'FrameWidth': 1920},
 'ModerationLabels': [{'Timestamp': 1999,
   'ModerationLabel': {'Confidence': 75.15272521972656,
    'Name': 'Violence',
    'ParentName': ''}},
  {'Timestamp': 1999,
   'ModerationLabel': {'Confidence': 75.15272521972656,
    'Name': 'Weapons',
    'ParentName': 'Violence'}},
  {'Timestamp': 2500,
   'ModerationLabel': {'Confidence': 87.55487060546875,
    'Name': 'Violence',
    'ParentName': ''}}]

Moderation labels in video
========================================
```

```
At 1999 ms: Violence (Confidence: 75.15)
At 1999 ms: Weapons (Confidence: 75.15)
At 2500 ms: Violence (Confidence: 87.55)
```

 We can further improve the confidence of Amazon Rekognition's predictions by training with our own dataset. This feature is called "custom labels"; it's supported by many of the Amazon AI services.

Demand Forecasting

Demand forecasting is used across many domains to predict demand in areas such as electricity usage, supply-chain inventory, call-center staffing, cash-flow planning, hospital-bed usage, and many other use cases. Forecasting is a time-series problem solved with popular algorithms such as Auto-Regressive Integrated Moving Average, Error Trend Seasonality, Non-Parametric Time Series, Prophet, and DeepAR++.

Businesses use everything from simple spreadsheets to complex time-series software to forecast future business outcomes such as product demand, resource needs, or financial performance. These approaches typically build forecast models using historical time-series data with the assumption that future demand is determined by past activity. These purely time-series approaches have a difficult time producing accurate forecasts with irregular trends and patterns. Also, these approaches often do not factor in important metadata that is relevant to the forecast, such as product price, product category, and store location.

Overforecasting can decrease efficiency and increase cost by overprovisioning resources that remain underutilized. Underforecasting can decrease customer satisfaction, lower revenue by starving the system of necessary resources, and require high-cost alternatives like paying overtime labor wages.

An effective demand forecast system demonstrates the following characteristics:

Analyze complex relationships rather than just time-series data
Combines time-series data with other metadata like product features and store locations.

Reduce forecast prediction time from months to hours
After automatically loading, inspecting, and identifying key dataset attributes, the system will quickly train, optimize, and deploy a custom model that fits our dataset.

Create forecasts for many different use cases

Build forecasts for virtually every use case, including supply chain, logistics, and finance, using a large library of algorithms to automatically determine the best fit for our specific use case.

Keep data secure

Every data point is protected with at-rest and in-flight encryption to keep sensitive information secure and confidential.

Automatically retrain and redeploy models when needed

When new data arrives—or when model evaluation metrics fall below a certain threshold—the model will be retrained and redeployed to improve the forecast predictions.

Predict Energy Consumption with Amazon Forecast

Amazon Forecast is a fully managed service based on the technology that powers Amazon.com's demand forecasting needs, such as efficient inventory management, immediate product fulfillment, and same-day delivery. Forecast uses machine learning to automatically train, tune, and optimize highly specialized demand forecast models from our dataset. We simply register our historical datasets—and related metadata—with Forecast to start generating demand predictions. Demand forecasts can be exported as CSVs, accessed via the AWS Console UI, or integrated into our application through the Forecast API.

Let's train a demand forecast model to predict individual household energy power consumption for the next 24 hours using Forecast's DeepAR++ algorithm and a public dataset from the UCI Machine Learning Repository (*https://oreil.ly/DYLJ7*).

Here is a snippet of the dataset, including the power consumption per customer:

timestamp	value	item
2014-01-01 01:00:00	38.34991708126038	client_12
2014-01-01 02:00:00	33.5820895522388	client_12
2014-01-01 03:00:00	34.41127694859037	client_12

Here is the schema that we define in Forecast to represent the public dataset:

```
forecast_schema ={
    "Attributes":[
        {
            "AttributeName":"timestamp",
            "AttributeType":"timestamp"
        },
        {
            "AttributeName":"target_value",
            "AttributeType":"float"
```

```
    },
    {
        "AttributeName":"item_id",
        "AttributeType":"string"
    }
  ]
}
```

Let's register the dataset with Forecast:

```
response=forecast.create_dataset(
                Domain="CUSTOM",
                DatasetType='TARGET_TIME_SERIES',
                DatasetName=forecast_dataset_name,
                DataFrequency=DATASET_FREQUENCY,
                Schema = forecast_schema
)
```

Now let's train the demand forecast model with Forecast:

```
forecast_horizon = 24 # hours

algorithm_arn = 'arn:aws:forecast:::algorithm/Deep_AR_Plus'

create_predictor_response = \
    forecast.create_predictor(PredictorName=predictor_name,
                        AlgorithmArn=algorithm_arn,
                        ForecastHorizon=forecast_horizon,
                        PerformAutoML= False,
                        PerformHPO=False,
                        EvaluationParameters= {
                            "NumberOfBacktestWindows": 1,
                            "BackTestWindowOffset": 24
                        },
                        InputDataConfig= {
                            "DatasetGroupArn": forecast_dataset_group_arn
                        },
                        FeaturizationConfig= {
                            "ForecastFrequency": "H",
                            "Featurizations": [{
                                "AttributeName": "target_value",
                                "FeaturizationPipeline":
                                [{
                                    "FeaturizationMethodName": "filling",
                                    "FeaturizationMethodParameters": {
                                        "frontfill": "none",
                                        "middlefill": "zero",
                                        "backfill": "zero"
                                    }
                                }]
                            }]
                        })
```

Let's make a prediction:

```
forecastResponse = forecastquery.query_forecast(
    ForecastArn=forecast_arn,
    Filters={"item_id":"client_12"}
)
```

Predict Demand for Amazon EC2 Instances with Amazon Forecast

AWS uses Forecast to predict demand for Amazon EC2 instances within Amazon Redshift clusters. As new data is ingested into Forecast, the Amazon Redshift control plane queries Forecast to adjust the size of the Amazon EC2 warm pool for Amazon Redshift, as shown in Figure 2-2.

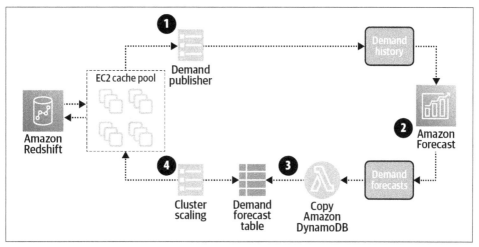

Figure 2-2. Amazon Redshift control plane adjusts the warm-pool cache of Amazon EC2 instances using Forecast.

The steps in Figure 2-2 can be described as follows:

1. Changes to Amazon EC2 warm-pool cache demand are published to S3.
2. Forecast ingests demand data from S3 and then creates new forecast predictions.
3. A Lambda function copies the new forecast predictions to Amazon DynamoDB.
4. The Amazon EC2 cluster scaler reads the forecast predictions from DynamoDB and adjusts the warm-pool cache size based on projected demand.

Identify Fake Accounts with Amazon Fraud Detector

Each year, tens of billions of dollars are lost to online fraud across the world. Online companies are especially prone to bad-actor attacks trying to defraud the system by creating fake user accounts and purchasing items with stolen credit cards. Typical fraud detection systems that detect bad actors often rely on business rules that are slow to adapt to the latest fraud techniques.

Effective fraud detection and privacy-leak prevention systems include the following characteristics:

Stop bad actors before they affect our business
Flag suspicious activity before bad actors can do real harm.

High-quality fraud-detection models without a lot of data
Pre-trained algorithms can analyze even the smallest amount of historical event data and still provide a high-quality fraud-detection model.

Let fraud teams move faster and with more control
Automatically handle the complex tasks required to build, train, tune, deploy, and update our fraud-detection models when new event data is available.

Amazon Fraud Detector is a fully managed service that identifies potentially fraudulent online activities such as online payments and fake accounts. Amazon Fraud Detector uses machine learning and 20 years of fraud-detection expertise from AWS and Amazon.com.

With Amazon Fraud Detector, we create a fraud-detection model with just a few clicks, a relatively small amount of historical data, and minimal code. We simply upload our historical online event data, such as online transactions and account registrations—and Amazon Fraud Detector does the rest, including training, tuning, and deploying a custom fraud-detection model for our business.

Here is the code that trains Amazon Fraud Detector on our transaction dataset:

```
response = client.create_model_version(
    modelId        = MODEL_NAME,
    modelType      = 'ONLINE_FRAUD_INSIGHTS',
    trainingDataSource = 'EXTERNAL_EVENTS',
    trainingDataSchema = trainingDataSchema,
    externalEventsDetail = {
        'dataLocation'     : S3_FILE_LOC,
        'dataAccessRoleArn': ARN_ROLE
    }
)
```

Here is the code to predict whether a given transaction is fraudulent:

```
pred = client.get_event_prediction(
    detectorId = DETECTOR_NAME,
    detectorVersionId = DETECTOR_VER,
    eventId = str(eventId),
    eventTypeName = EVENT_TYPE,
    eventTimestamp = timestampStr,
    entities = [{'entityType': ENTITY_TYPE,
    'entityId':str(eventId.int)}],
    eventVariables = record)

record["score"] = pred['modelScores'][0]['scores']\
                     ["{0}_insightscore".format(MODEL_NAME)]
```

Here is the output of the Amazon Fraud Detector prediction showing the relevant data, prediction outcome, and prediction confidence:

ip_address	email_address	state	postal	name	phone_number	score	outcomes
84.138.6.238	synth1@yahoo.com	LA	32733	Brandon Moran	(555)784 - 5238	5.0	[approve]
194.147.250.63	synth2@yahoo.com	MN	34319	Dominic Murray	(555)114 - 6133	4.0	[approve]
192.54.60.50	synth3@gmail.com	WA	32436	Anthony Abbott	(555)780 - 7652	5.0	[approve]
169.120.193.154	synth4@gmail.com	AL	34399.0	Kimberly Webb	(555)588 - 4426	938.0	[review]
192.175.55.43	synth5@hotmail.com	IL	33690.0	Renee James	(555)785 - 8274	16.0	[approve]

Enable Privacy-Leak Detection with Amazon Macie

A well-instrumented application produces many logs and metrics to increase insight and maintain high system uptime to avoid customer dissatisfaction. However, sometimes these logs contain sensitive account information such as home zip codes or credit card numbers. We need a system that monitors our data for sensitive information, detects access to this sensitive information, and sends notifications if unauthorized access is detected or data is leaked.

Effective systems to detect and monitor access to sensitive information have the following characteristics:

Continuously assess data sensitivity and evaluate access controls
Attacker ROI math dictates that an S3 bucket with sensitive customer data and loosely configured IAM roles is an easy target. We stay ahead of this by continuously monitoring our entire S3 environment and generating actionable steps to respond quickly when needed.

Support many data sources
Assess data sensitivity and evaluate access controls across many different data sources, such as S3, Amazon Relational Database Service (Amazon RDS), Amazon Aurora, emails, file shares, collaboration tools, etc.

Maintain regulatory compliance

In addition to monitoring and protecting sensitive data, compliance teams are required to provide evidence that they are enforcing data security and privacy to meet regulatory compliance requirements.

Identifying sensitive data during data migrations

When migrating large volumes of data into AWS, we want to know if the data includes sensitive data. If so, we likely need to update the security access controls, encryption settings, and resource tags when the data is migrated.

Amazon Macie is a fully managed security service that uses machine learning to identify sensitive data like personally identifiable information in our AWS-based data sources, such as S3. Macie provides visibility into where this data is stored—and who is accessing the data. By monitoring access to sensitive data, Macie can send an alert when it detects a leak—or risk of a leak.

Macie continuously identifies sensitive data and evaluates the security and access controls to this data. Macie helps maintain data privacy and security across all of our data and provides comprehensive options for scheduling our data-sensitivity and access-control analysis to maintain our data privacy and compliance requirements.

We can schedule daily, weekly, or monthly discovery jobs to generate our findings, including evaluation results, time stamps, and historical records of all buckets and objects scanned for sensitive data. These findings are summarized in a standard report compliant with data privacy and protection audits to ensure long-term data retention. For data migrations, Macie automates the configuration of data protection and role-based access policies as our data moves into AWS.

Conversational Devices and Voice Assistants

Whether it's Alexa or any of those other famous home voices, all of them use state-of-the-art deep learning technologies in the field of automatic speech recognition (ASR) and natural language understanding (NLU) to recognize the intent of our spoken text.

Speech Recognition with Amazon Lex

Using Amazon Lex to build conversational interfaces for voice and text, we have access to the same deep learning technologies that power Amazon Alexa. Amazon Lex is a fully managed service that uses ASR to convert speech to text. Amazon Lex also uses NLU to recognize the intent of the text. We can build custom responses to a wide set of voice and text queries, such as, "Where is the IT help desk in this office?" and "Reserve this room for the next 30 minutes."

Text-to-Speech Conversion with Amazon Polly

Amazon Polly is an automated text-to-speech service with dozens of human voices across a broad set of languages, dialects, and genders. We can use Amazon Polly to build speech-enabled applications that turn text into human-like speech for accessibility purposes, for example.

Speech-to-Text Conversion with Amazon Transcribe

Amazon Transcribe is an ASR service that makes it easy for developers to add speech-to-text capability to their real-time and batch applications. Amazon Transcribe converts speech to text by processing audio either in batch or real time. Popular use cases for Amazon Transcribe include creating image captions and video subtitles.

Text Analysis and Natural Language Processing

Natural language processing (NLP) is a field of artificial intelligence that focuses on machines' ability to read, understand, and derive meaning from human languages. It is a field that has been studied for a very long time, with research publications dating back to the early 1900s.

Fast-forwarding to 2021, we still experience ground-breaking NLP research with new language models emerging nearly on a monthly basis. In later chapters, we will discuss the evolution of NLP algorithms, discuss the novel Transformer neural-network architecture, and dive deeper into the BERT family of NLP algorithms.

Effective text analysis and cognitive search systems have the following characteristics:

Fast time to discover
New documents should become searchable quickly and without errors that require human correction.

Efficient processing workflows
Document-processing workflows should be automated to increase speed and quality while reducing human effort, custom code, and cost.

Translate Languages with Amazon Translate

In today's global economy, we need to appeal to international users by translating our content into many localized, region-specific, multilingual versions. Popular use cases include on-demand translation of user-generated content, real-time translations for communication apps, and multilingual sentiment analysis of social media content.

Amazon Translate is a neural machine translation service that creates more accurate and fluent translations than traditional statistical and rule-based translation models.

Classify Customer-Support Messages with Amazon Comprehend

Customer Obsession is one of Amazon's key leadership principles—customer focus is important for every business and industry. And in many cases, a customer's experience is largely influenced by the quality of customer support. In this section, we will use Amazon Comprehend to classify the sentiment of sample customer-support messages.

Text classification is a popular task in the field of NLP. As described earlier, we can use Amazon Comprehend as a fully managed NLP service to implement text classification without much machine learning experience.

More broadly, Amazon Comprehend can recognize important entities, key phrases, sentiment, language, and topics from our text documents. Important entities include names, places, items, and dates. Key phrases include "good morning," "thank you," and "not happy." Sentiment includes "positive," "neutral," and "negative." Amazon Comprehend currently supports many languages, and new languages are added frequently.

 Amazon Comprehend also supports a set of healthcare APIs called *Amazon Comprehend Medical*. Amazon Comprehend Medical has been pre-trained on extensive healthcare datasets and can identify medical conditions, medications, tests, treatments, procedures, anatomy, and protected health information.

Let's take a look at how we can use Amazon Comprehend's out-of-the-box Sentiment Analysis API to classify sample product reviews with just a few lines of code.

First, let's use Amazon Comprehend's `create_document_classifier()` API to create the classifier:

```
training_job = comprehend.create_document_classifier(
    DocumentClassifierName=comprehend_training_job_name,
    DataAccessRoleArn=iam_role_comprehend_arn,
    InputDataConfig={
        'S3Uri': comprehend_train_s3_uri
    },
    OutputDataConfig={
        'S3Uri': s3_output_job
    },
    LanguageCode='en'
)
```

Next, let's use the classifier to predict the sentiment of a sample *positive* review with Amazon Comprehend's `detect_sentiment()` API:

```
txt = """I loved it!  I will recommend this to everyone."""
```

```
response = comprehend.detect_sentiment(
    Text=txt
)
```

Here is the output:

```
{
    "SentimentScore": {
        "Mixed": 0.030585512690246105,
        "Positive": 0.94992071056365967,
        "Neutral": 0.0141543131828308,
        "Negative": 0.00893945890665054
    },
    "Sentiment": "POSITIVE",
    "LanguageCode": "en"
}
```

Next, let's use the classifier to predict the sentiment of a sample *negative* review with Amazon Comprehend's detect_sentiment() API:

```
txt = """Really bad.  I hope they don't make this anymore."""

response = comprehend.detect_sentiment(
    Text=txt
)
```

Here is the output for the *negative* review:

```
{
    "SentimentScore": {
        "Mixed": 0.030585512690246105,
        "Positive": 0.00893945890665054,
        "Neutral": 0.0141543131828308,
        "Negative": 0.94992071056365967
    },
    "Sentiment": "NEGATIVE",
    "LanguageCode": "en"
}
```

With Amazon Comprehend Custom Labels, we can train Amazon Comprehend to predict custom labels specific to our dataset.

> In Chapter 3, we will train a custom Amazon Comprehend model that classifies support messages into a star rating (1–5) as a finer-grained form of sentiment analysis. We will use the Amazon Customer Reviews Dataset.

Extract Resume Details with Amazon Textract and Comprehend

Organizations have long struggled to process semistructured documents efficiently to make them easy to index and search. Document processing usually requires significant customization and configuration. Amazon Textract, a fully managed service to accurately extract text from a document, uses optical character recognition (OCR) and machine learning to automatically extract information from our scanned documents.

More than just OCR, Amazon Textract also uses NLP to parse and save the specific words, phrases, dates, and numbers found in the document. Combined with Amazon Comprehend, Amazon Textract can build and maintain a smart index of our document contents. We can also use Amazon Textract to build automated document processing workflows and maintain compliance for our document archives.

After scanning and parsing a PDF resume, Amazon Textract generates this text-based version:

```
NAME
...
LOCATION
...
WORK EXPERIENCE
...
EDUCATION
...
SKILLS
C (Less than 1 year), Database (Less than 1 year),
Database Management (Less than 1 year),
Database Management System (Less than 1 year),
Java (Less than 1 year)
...
TECHNICAL SKILLS
Programming language: C, C++, Java
Oracle PeopleSoft
Internet of Things
Machine Learning
Database Management System
Computer Networks
Operating System worked on: Linux, Windows, Mac
...
NON-TECHNICAL SKILLS
Honest and Hard-Working
Tolerant and Flexible to Different Situations
Polite and Calm
Team-Player
```

Let's train Amazon Comprehend to understand a new concept called "SKILLS" that is specific to our resume domain:

```
comprehend_client = boto3.client('comprehend')

custom_recognizer_name = 'resume-entity-recognizer-'+ str(int(time.time()))

comprehend_custom_recognizer_response = \
    comprehend_client.create_entity_recognizer(
        RecognizerName = custom_recognizer_name,
        DataAccessRoleArn = iam_role_textract_comprehend_arn,
        InputDataConfig = {
            'EntityTypes': [
                {'Type': 'SKILLS'},
            ],
            'Documents': {
                'S3Uri': comprehend_input_doucuments
            },
            'EntityList': {
                'S3Uri': comprehend_input_entity_list
            }
        },
        LanguageCode='en'
    )
```

Using this new Skills entity recognizer that we built with Amazon Comprehend, we can perform entity recognition on the text-based resume that was extracted from the PDF with Amazon Textract earlier:

```
# Start a recognizer Job:
custom_recognizer_job_name = 'recognizer-job-'+ str(int(time.time()))

recognizer_response = comprehend_client.start_entities_detection_job(
    InputDataConfig = {
        'S3Uri': s3_test_document,
        'InputFormat': 'ONE_DOC_PER_LINE'
    },
    OutputDataConfig = {
        'S3Uri': s3_test_document_output
    },
    DataAccessRoleArn = iam_role_textract_comprehend_arn,
    JobName = custom_recognizer_job_name,
    EntityRecognizerArn = comprehend_model_response['EntityRecognizerProperties']\
                        ['EntityRecognizerArn'],
    LanguageCode = 'en'
)
```

Here is the output of our custom Amazon Comprehend entity recognizer that includes the text, offsets within the document, entity type (SKILLS), and prediction confidence:

Start offset	End offset	Confidence	Text	Type
9	39	0.9574943836014351	analytical and problem solving	SKILLS
8	11	0.7915781756343004	AWS	SKILLS
33	41	0.9749685544856893	Solution	SKILLS
20	23	0.9997213663311131	SQL	SKILLS
2	13	0.9996676358048374	Programming	SKILLS
25	27	0.9963501364429431	C,	SKILLS
28	32	0.9637213743240001	C++,	SKILLS
33	37	0.9984518452247634	Java	SKILLS
39	42	0.9986466628533158	PHP	SKILLS
44	54	0.9993487072806023	JavaScript	SKILLS

Cognitive Search and Natural Language Understanding

At one point or another, we have all struggled with finding a relevant piece of information buried deep in a website, enterprise content management system, corporate wiki, or corporate file share. We also know the pain of reanswering the same frequently asked questions over and over.

Surfacing relevant and timely search results is an age-old problem that has spawned many open source solutions, including Apache Lucene, Apache SOLR, and Elasticsearch. These solutions are rooted in older NLP techniques created many years ago. When interacting with these solutions, we typically issue keyword searches that, if entered incorrectly or out of order, could result in poor search results.

Cognitive search is a modern solution to the age-old problem of discovering information. Rooted in modern NLU, cognitive search allows end users to issue natural language questions that a human would naturally ask.

Amazon Kendra uses machine learning, NLU, and cognitive search to tackle the enterprise search problem in a modern way. Instead of issuing traditional keyword searches that require extra effort to distill, we can ask Amazon Kendra full natural language questions such as, "On which floor is the IT department located in this office?" and get a specific answer such as "19th floor."

Amazon Kendra integrates with many different data sources, including Amazon S3, SharePoint, Salesforce, ServiceNow, Amazon RDS Databases, OneDrive, and many more. It supports all types of data schemas, including structured, unstructured, and semistructured. It also supports many different formats, including PDF, HTML, rich text, Microsoft Word, and PowerPoint.

While Amazon Kendra comes out of the box with various pre-trained models optimized across multiple domains, we can train Amazon Kendra with our datasets to improve the accuracy of the results. In addition, Amazon Kendra actively learns and retrains itself based on end-user usage patterns, including explicit feedback such as thumbs up and thumbs down on specific search results.

Combining Amazon Kendra and Lex, we can build a support chatbot across a broad range of devices to help answer frequently asked questions. In this example, we also include the popular workforce-collaboration tool Slack, as shown in Figure 2-3.

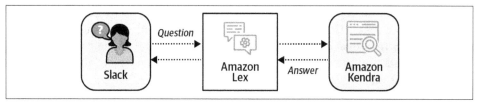

Figure 2-3. Using Slack, Amazon Lex, and Amazon Kendra to automatically answer questions.

The following is a sample conversation where Antje is using a Slackbot to ask questions during a live workshop. The chatbot answers commonly asked questions from attendees. This allows hosts of the workshop to focus on more-complicated questions that require human intervention:

> *Antje*: "Hi there."
>
> *Slackbot*: "Hello! How can I help?"
>
> *Antje*: "Do you record this workshop?"
>
> *Slackbot*: "Yes, this workshop is being recorded."
>
> *Antje*: "Where do I find the recording?"
>
> *Slackbot*: "The recording will be shared at *https://youtube.datascienceonaws.com* within 24 hours."
>
> *Antje*: "Do you know how to get started with SageMaker?"
>
> *Slackbot*: "I think the answer to your question is: On the Amazon SageMaker Studio page, under Get Started, choose Quick Start, then select Create Studio Domain."

Intelligent Customer Support Centers

Quality customer support is important for every industry and business (as noted earlier, Customer Obsession is a key leadership principle at Amazon). In many cases, customer support directly affects the customer's perception of the business. Amazon Connect is a cloud contact center solution that implements machine learning to provide intelligent contact center features. With Connect Wisdom, customer support agents can simply enter a question, such as "What is the exchange policy for books?"

and Wisdom returns the most relevant information and best answer. Wisdom also runs machine learning on live-call transcripts to automatically identify customer issues and recommend responses to the agents.

Contact Lens for Amazon Connect adds machine learning capabilities to Amazon Connect, a cloud contact center service based on the same technology that powers Amazon's customer service. Contact Lens uses speech-to-text transcription, NLP, and cognitive search capabilities to analyze customer–agent interactions.

By automatically indexing call transcripts, Contact Lens lets us search for specific words, phrases, and sentiment—as well as redact sensitive information from transcripts to avoid leaks. Contact Lens helps supervisors spot recurring themes with interactions in real time, automatically trains agents to improve their customer support skills, and continuously categorizes contacts based on keywords and phrases used by the customer.

With Contact Lens for Amazon Connect, contact center supervisors have a single view into customer–agent interactions, product feedback trends, and potential compliance risks. Amazon Connect replicates successful interactions, highlights product feedback anomalies, and escalates poor customer–agent interactions to a supervisor.

Industrial AI Services and Predictive Maintenance

As part of the AWS for Industrial service portfolio, AWS offers a range of AI services and hardware, including Amazon Lookout for Metrics, Lookout for Vision, Lookout for Equipment, Amazon Monitron, and AWS Panorama.

We can create accurate anomaly detection models using Amazon Lookout for Metrics. After uploading our data, Lookout for Metrics will automatically inspect the data and build the anomaly detection model. If the model detects anomalies, the service will group related anomalies together and assign a severity score. Lookout for Metrics comes with built-in connectors to popular data sources, including Amazon S3, Amazon Redshift, Amazon CloudWatch, Amazon RDS, and a variety of SaaS applications. The anomaly detection model leverages human-in-the-loop feedback to continuously improve over time.

We can spot product defects using Amazon Lookout for Vision. Lookout for Vision implements computer vision to identify visual defects in objects. It can help automate the detection of damages to parts, identify missing components, or uncover process issues in our manufacturing lines. Lookout for Vision already comes with a pre-trained anomaly detection model. We simply fine-tune it to our specific images.

We can monitor the health and efficiency of our equipment using Amazon Lookout for Equipment. We upload our historical equipment sensor data to Lookout for Equipment, and the service will build a custom machine learning model to detect any abnormal equipment behavior. Additionally, the service will automatically send an alert so we can take action. Lookout for Equipment works with any time series analog data, including sensor data such as temperature, flow rates, etc.

We can implement an end-to-end predictive maintenance use case with Amazon Monitron, which includes equipment sensors, a gateway device to securely connect to AWS, and a managed service to analyze the data for abnormal machine patterns. Amazon Monitron captures the sensor data from our equipment, identifies healthy sensor patterns, and trains a machine learning model specific to that equipment. We can provide feedback to improve the model via an Amazon Monitron mobile app, for example.

We can enable our on-premises cameras for computer vision via AWS Panorama, which comes with a hardware appliance that we can connect to our network and existing cameras. We can then deploy computer vision applications to the appliance to process the video streams from the connected cameras. Camera device manufacturers can use the AWS Panorama SDK to build new cameras that run computer vision models at the edge.

Home Automation with AWS IoT and Amazon SageMaker

We live in a world where we estimate five billion people own some sort of mobile device, and more than half of our internet traffic happens through mobile devices. In addition, the industrial Internet of Things (IoT) revolution boasts many more billions of connected sensors and devices across our homes, office buildings, factories, cars, ships, planes, oil drills, agricultural fields, and many more.

This trend toward mobile and IoT devices also pushed computing to the edge, whether we need to analyze and preprocess data before it is sent and ingested into central data lakes (for data-privacy compliance reasons, for example) or improve user experience by serving application responses faster, eliminating the latency of a round trip to the cloud. We also see more and more machine learning happening at the edge. And while the training of machine learning models often requires powerful compute resources, making inferences against these models typically requires far less computational power.

Performing inference at the edge helps to reduce latency and cost as we are saving the round-trip time to the cloud. We can also capture and analyze the prediction results faster, trigger some action locally, or send the analyzed data back to the cloud to retrain and improve our machine learning models.

AWS IoT Greengrass deploys the model from S3 to the edge to make predictions with edge-local data. AWS IoT Greengrass also syncs the model inference results back to an S3 bucket. This prediction data can then be used to retrain and improve the

SageMaker model. AWS IoT Greengrass supports over-the-air deployments, runs locally on each device, and extends AWS to those devices.

Figure 2-4 shows a home automation use case running AWS IoT Greengrass on a local home automation server called the "edge device." AWS IoT Greengrass deploys a SageMaker model to the edge device and processes data received from camera, light switches, and light bulbs using an edge version of Lambda running on the edge device.

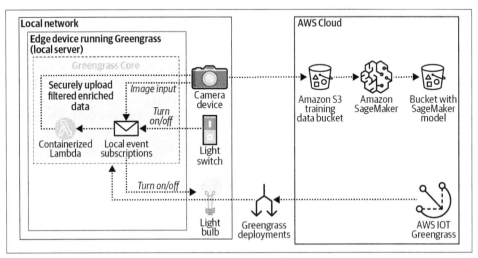

Figure 2-4. Home automation use case with AWS IoT Greengrass.

AWS provides a wide range of services to implement machine learning at the edge, including AWS IoT Greengrass for model deployment to the edge, SageMaker Neo for model optimization, and SageMaker Edge Manager for managing models at the edge. We will dive deeper into SageMaker Neo and Edge Manager in Chapter 9.

Extract Medical Information from Healthcare Documents

In the healthcare space, AWS offers many dedicated services. The services have been developed specifically for the characteristics and needs of healthcare data and comply with healthcare regulations. As part of the Amazon AI HIPAA-eligible healthcare portfolio of services, AWS offers Amazon Comprehend Medical, Amazon Transcribe Medical, and Amazon HealthLake.

Comprehend Medical is an NLP service that has been pre-trained specifically on medical language. Comprehend Medical automates the extraction of health data from medical texts, such as doctors' notes, clinical trial reports, or patient health records.

Transcribe Medical is an ASR service that has been similarly pre-trained on medical language. We can use Transcribe Medical to transcribe medical speech into text. With a simple API call, we can automate clinical documentation workflows or even subtitle telemedicine.

HealthLake is a secure data lake that complies with the Fast Healthcare Interoperability Resources industry standard. In addition to storing, indexing, and transforming healthcare data, Amazon HealthLake leverages machine learning to identify, understand, and extract medical information from the raw data, such as medical reports and patient notes. We can use Amazon QuickSight, Athena, and SageMaker to run advanced analytics and machine learning on our healthcare data.

Self-Optimizing and Intelligent Cloud Infrastructure

The Amazon AI/ML services that we have introduced so far are not the only services that provide sophisticated machine learning. In fact, more and more existing AWS services are being enriched with machine learning capabilities, and new machine-learning-powered services are being introduced across a variety of use cases. Let's take a quick look at some of these hidden gems.

Predictive Auto Scaling for Amazon EC2

Amazon EC2, short for Elastic Compute Cloud, provides virtual server instances in the AWS cloud. One of the challenges in running our applications on those Amazon EC2 instances is how we make sure to scale the number of instances to serve the current workload, basically matching supply with demand. Luckily, there's Amazon EC2 Auto Scaling, which helps us with exactly that. Based on changes in demand, we can configure Amazon EC2 Auto Scaling to automatically add or remove compute capacity. This dynamic scaling approach is still reactive, though, as it acts on monitored traffic and Amazon EC2 instance utilization metrics.

We can take this a level further to a proactive approach in combination with a service called *AWS Auto Scaling*. AWS Auto Scaling provides a single interface to set up automatic scaling of multiple AWS services, including Amazon EC2. It combines dynamic and predictive scaling. With predictive scaling, AWS uses machine learning algorithms to predict our future traffic based on daily and weekly trends and provisions the right number of Amazon EC2 instances in advance of anticipated changes, as shown in Figure 2-5.

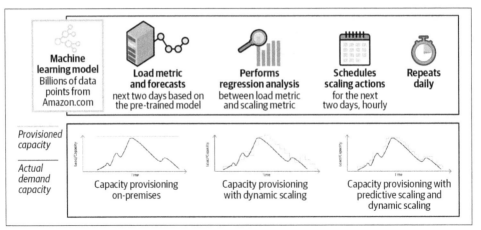

Figure 2-5. Predictive scaling with AWS Auto Scaling anticipates traffic changes to provision the right number of Amazon EC2 instances.

Anomaly Detection on Streams of Data

Streaming technologies provide us with the tools to collect, process, and analyze data streams in real time. AWS offers a wide range of streaming technology options, including Amazon MSK and Amazon Kinesis. While we dive deeper into streaming analytics and machine learning with Amazon Kinesis and Apache Kafka in Chapter 10, we want to highlight Kinesis Data Analytics as a simple and powerful way to create streaming applications with just a few lines of code.

Kinesis Data Analytics provides built-in capabilities for anomaly detection using the Random Cut Forest (RCF) function in Kinesis Data Analytics to build a machine learning model in real time and calculate anomaly scores for numeric values in each message. The score indicates how different the value is compared to the observed trend. The RCF function also calculates an attribution score for each column, which reflects the anomaly of the data in that particular column. The sum of all attribution scores of all columns is the overall anomaly score.

Cognitive and Predictive Business Intelligence

Many machine learning applications and models assume data being readily available in a data lake (discussed in Chapter 4). In reality, though, much of the world's data is stored and processed in structured, relational databases. In order for us to apply machine learning to this structured data, we have to either export the data or develop a custom application to read the data before applying any machine learning. Wouldn't it be great if we could use machine learning straight from our business intelligence service, our data warehouse, or our databases? Let's see how to do this on AWS.

Ask Natural-Language Questions with Amazon QuickSight

Amazon QuickSight is a business intelligence service that performs interactive queries and builds visualizations on data sources such as Amazon Redshift, Amazon RDS, Amazon Athena, and Amazon S3. QuickSight can also detect anomalies, create forecasts, and answer natural-language questions from our data through QuickSight ML Insights and QuickSight Q.

QuickSight ML Insights runs the RCF algorithm to identify change in millions of metrics, across billions of data points. ML Insights also enables forecasting based on the observed metrics. The RCF algorithm automatically detects seasonality patterns in our data, excludes any outliers, and imputes missing values.

With QuickSight Q, we can ask natural-language questions such as, "What are the best-selling product categories in the US state of California?" QuickSight uses machine learning to understand the question, apply the question to our data, and create a chart to answer our question, as shown in Figure 2-6. We will dive deep into QuickSight in Chapter 5.

Figure 2-6. QuickSight Q understands natural-language questions and automatically creates charts to answer the questions.

Train and Invoke SageMaker Models with Amazon Redshift

Amazon Redshift is a fully managed data warehouse that allows us to run complex analytic queries against petabytes of structured data. Using Amazon Redshift ML, we can use our data in Amazon Redshift to train models with SageMaker Autopilot as new data arrives. SageMaker Autopilot automatically trains, tunes, and deploys a model. We then register and invoke the model in our Amazon Redshift queries as a user-defined function (UDF). Figure 2-7 shows how we make predictions with the

`USING FUNCTION` SQL clause. We will show a more detailed example of Amazon Redshift ML and SageMaker Autopilot in Chapter 3.

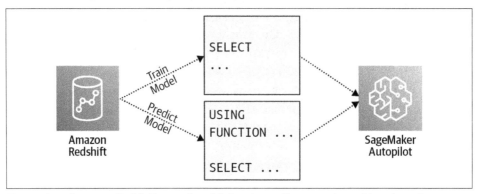

Figure 2-7. Amazon Redshift uses SageMaker Autopilot to train and invoke a Sage‐Maker model as a UDF.

 We can create a UDF to invoke any AWS service using Lambda Functions. This sample UDF invokes a Lambda Function:

```
USING FUNCTION invoke_lambda(input VARCHAR)
RETURNS VARCHAR TYPE LAMBDA_INVOKE WITH
(lambda_name='<LAMBDA_NAME>') SELECT invoke('<INPUT>');
```

Invoke Amazon Comprehend and SageMaker Models from Amazon Aurora SQL Database

Aurora, a MySQL- and PostgreSQL-compatible relational database, is natively inte‐grated with Amazon Comprehend and Amazon SageMaker, as shown in Figure 2-8.

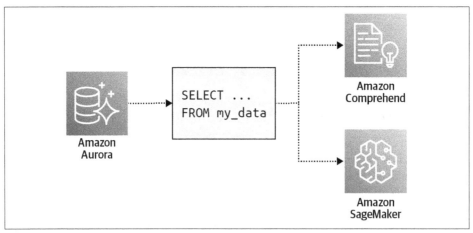

Figure 2-8. Aurora ML can invoke models in Amazon Comprehend and SageMaker.

We can use either built-in SQL functions (with Amazon Comprehend) or custom-written SQL functions (with Amazon SageMaker) in our queries to apply machine learning to the data. As shown in previous sections, we could leverage Amazon Comprehend for customer sentiment analysis (built-in SQL function) on maybe a product review or use Amazon SageMaker for any custom-developed machine learning model integration.

Let's say we have some sample product reviews in a relational table:

```
CREATE TABLE IF NOT EXISTS product_reviews (
        review_id INT AUTO_INCREMENT PRIMARY KEY,
        review_body VARCHAR(255) NOT NULL
);

INSERT INTO product_reviews (review_body)
VALUES ("Great product!");
INSERT INTO product_reviews (review_body)
VALUES ("It's ok.");
INSERT INTO product_reviews (review_body)
VALUES ("The worst product.");
```

Then, we can use the following built-in SQL functions to let Amazon Comprehend return us the sentiment and confidence score:

```
SELECT review_body,
        aws_comprehend_detect_sentiment(review_body, 'en') AS sentiment,
        aws_comprehend_detect_sentiment_confidence(review_body, 'en') AS confidence
   FROM product_reviews;
```

This would show a result similar to this:

```
review_body            sentiment       confidence
-------------------------------------------------------
Great product!         POSITIVE        0.9969872489
It's ok.               POSITIVE        0.5987234553
The worst product.     NEGATIVE        0.9876742876
```

Invoke SageMaker Model from Amazon Athena

Similarly, we can use Amazon Athena, a service that lets us use SQL queries to query data stored in Amazon S3, and invoke SageMaker machine learning models for inference directly from those queries, as shown in Figure 2-9.

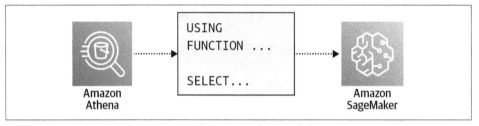

Figure 2-9. Amazon Athena can invoke SageMaker models.

We define a UDF with the USING FUNCTION SQL statement that invokes a custom-built Amazon SageMaker Endpoint that serves the sentiment predictions. Any subsequent SELECT statement in the query can then reference the function to pass values to the model.

Here's a simple example:

```
USING FUNCTION predict_sentiment(review_body VARCHAR(65535))
    RETURNS VARCHAR(10) TYPE
    SAGEMAKER_INVOKE_ENDPOINT WITH (sagemaker_endpoint = '<ENDPOINT_NAME>')

SELECT predict_sentiment(review_body) AS sentiment
    FROM "dsoaws"."amazon_reviews_tsv"
    WHERE predict_sentiment(review_body)="POSITIVE";
```

Run Predictions on Graph Data Using Amazon Neptune

Amazon Neptune is a fully managed graph database that allows us to build and run applications across highly connected datasets. Neptune ML implements graph neural networks (GNNs) to make predictions using graph data. While algorithms such as XGBoost are designed for traditional tabular datasets, GNNs have been specifically designed to deal with the complexity of graphs and potentially billions of relationships. Neptune ML uses the open source Deep Graph Library and Amazon Sage-Maker to automatically choose, train, and deploy the best model for our graph data.

Educating the Next Generation of AI and ML Developers

Amazon and AWS offer many programs and services to help educate the next generation of AI/ML developers. Amazon's Machine Learning University program (*https:// oreil.ly/CnXwM*)—used to train Amazon employees—was released to the public in 2020. AWS Training and Certification (T&C) offers a broad range of on-demand and classroom training courses that help to prepare for the AWS Machine Learning specialty certification. In addition, AWS has partnered with Udacity, Coursera, and DeepLearning.AI to create several Massive Open Online Courses to give hands-on experience with the Amazon AI and machine learning stack.

In this section, we discuss the deep-learning-powered AWS devices that provide a fun and educational way to get hands-on experience with computer vision, reinforcement learning, and generative adversarial networks (GANs).

The developer-focused device family consists of the following: AWS DeepLens, Deep-Racer, and DeepComposer. AWS DeepLens is a wireless, deep-learning-enabled video camera. AWS DeepRacer is a fully autonomous 1/18th-scale race car driven by reinforcement learning. And AWS DeepComposer is a musical keyboard powered by GANs to transform our melodies into original songs.

Build Computer Vision Models with AWS DeepLens

AWS DeepLens is a deep-learning-enabled video camera that comes with a rich set of computer vision tutorials and pre-built models. If we want to learn how to build computer vision apps and see our first results in a matter of minutes, we can just use one of the many sample projects that come with pre-trained models and a simple inference function. The camera will perform local inference on the device against the deployed model.

If we are a more experienced developer, we can build and train our custom convolutional neural network (CNN) model in any of the supported deep-learning frameworks, such as TensorFlow, Apache MXNet, or Caffe, and then deploy the project to the AWS DeepLens device. Figure 2-10 shows a typical AWS DeepLens workflow.

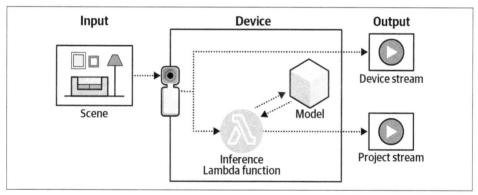

Figure 2-10. AWS DeepLens captures input video streams, processes the stream using a deployed model, and generates two output video streams.

AWS DeepLens is both an edge device and a camera. Therefore, AWS DeepLens runs AWS IoT Greengrass Core and can execute its own Lambda functions. New models are pushed to AWS DeepLens using AWS IoT Greengrass. The camera captures the input video stream and produces two output streams: a device stream that's passed through as is, and a project stream that is the result of the deployed model's processed video frames.

Any project we deploy needs to contain a Lambda function to process the input video frames, also called the *Inference Lambda function*. We first bundle that function together with a Lambda runtime and a trained model. Then we deploy the project using AWS IoT Greengrass to an AWS DeepLens device.

Learn Reinforcement Learning with AWS DeepRacer

AWS DeepRacer is a fully autonomous 1/18th-scale race car driven by reinforcement learning. The car is equipped with two cameras, a LIDAR sensor, and an on-board compute module. The compute module performs the inference in order to drive the car along a track.

Reinforcement learning is applied to a variety of autonomous decision-making problems. It gained broader popularity when the team of scientists, engineers, and machine learning experts at DeepMind (*https://deepmind.com*) released AlphaGo, the first computer program that defeated a professional human Go player back in 2015.

Go is an ancient, strategic board game known for its complexity. It was invented in China about three thousand years ago and is still being played by amateurs and in various professional leagues around the globe.

While AlphaGo learned the game by playing thousands of matches against human players, the subsequent release AlphaGo Zero learned Go by just playing against itself. This has revolutionized the field of reinforcement learning once more as it performed even better than the previous release and showed that the model was able to discover new knowledge and apply unconventional strategies to win.

At a high level, reinforcement learning is a machine learning method that aims at autonomous decision making by an agent to achieve a specific goal through interactions with an environment, as shown in Figure 2-11. Learning is achieved through trial and error.

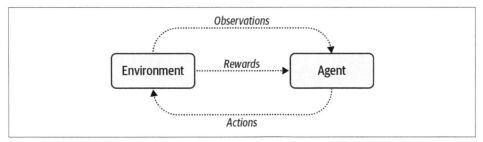

Figure 2-11. Reinforcement learning is a machine learning method that aims at autonomous decision making by an agent to achieve a specific goal through interactions with an environment.

We will dive deeper into reinforcement learning to compare models in production with multiarmed bandits in Chapter 9, but let's get back to our autonomous-car racing scenario. In our example, the agent is the AWS DeepRacer car, and the environment consists of track layouts, traveling routes, and traffic conditions. The actions include steer left, steer right, brake, and accelerate. Actions are chosen to maximize a reward function, which represents the goal of reaching the destination quickly without accidents. Actions lead to states. Figure 2-12 shows the AWS DeepRacer's flow of actions, rewards, and states.

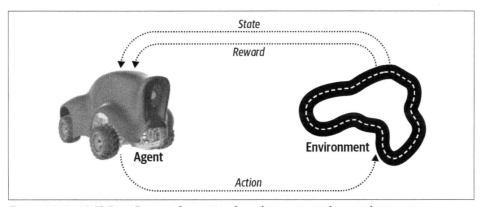

Figure 2-12. AWS DeepRacer takes action based on state and reward.

We don't even need a physical track or car to get started. We can start training our custom reinforcement learning model in the AWS DeepRacer console and use the AWS DeepRacer simulator to evaluate our model on a virtual track, as shown in Figure 2-13.

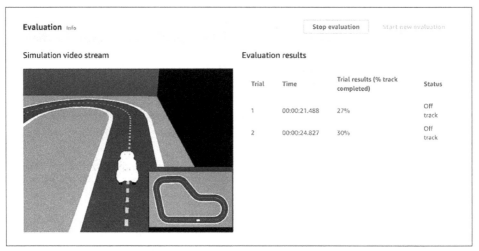

Trial	Time	Trial results (% track completed)	Status
1	00:00:21.488	27%	Off track
2	00:00:24.827	30%	Off track

Figure 2-13. Model evaluation using the AWS DeepRacer simulator. Source: AWS Deep-Racer Developer Guide (https://oreil.ly/rN3dR).

AWS also maintains a global AWS DeepRacer League and leaderboard that ranks vehicle performances from official AWS DeepRacer League racing events happening throughout the year, including both physical and virtual events.

Understand GANs with AWS DeepComposer

Yes, everyone looked a bit puzzled when AWS introduced the AWS DeepComposer device at the annual AWS re:Invent conference back in December 2019. Soon, however, we started hearing those distinctive sounds coming from hotel hallways throughout Las Vegas. AWS DeepComposer is a musical USB keyboard to help us learn generative AI. It is designed to work with the AWS DeepComposer service to turn a simple melody into an original song. An AWS DeepComposer device is shown in Figure 2-14.

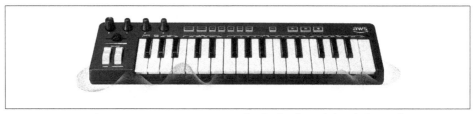

Figure 2-14. AWS DeepComposer is a musical USB keyboard that helps us learn generative AI. Source: AWS (https://oreil.ly/qk6zr).

Generative AI, specifically in the form of GANs, is used to generate new content from inputs we provide. This input can be images, text, or—yes—music. Generative AI models automatically discover and learn patterns in data and use this knowledge to generate new data based on the data they were trained on. GANs use two competing algorithms, a generator and a discriminator, to generate new content, as shown in Figure 2-15.

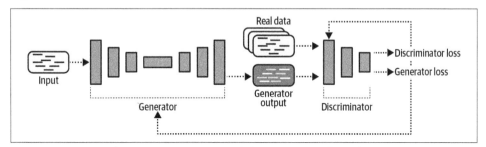

Figure 2-15. GANs leverage a generator and discriminator algorithm.

A generator is a CNN that learns to create new content based on the patterns of the input data. The discriminator is another CNN that is trained to actually differentiate between real and generated content. Both the generator and the discriminator are trained in alternating runs to force the generator to create more and more realistic content, while the discriminator improves at identifying synthetic content as opposed to real content.

Applied to our music example, when we play a melody on the keyboard, AWS Deep-Composer can add up to three additional accompaniment tracks to create a new composition. The generator network is adapted from the popular U-Net architecture used in Computer Vision and has been trained on a publicly available dataset of Bach's compositions.

Program Nature's Operating System with Quantum Computing

Building useful quantum applications requires new skills and a radically different approach to problem solving. Acquiring this expertise takes time and requires access to quantum technologies and programming tools.

Amazon Braket helps us explore the potential of quantum hardware, understand quantum algorithms, and retool for a quantum future. Figure 2-16 shows the flywheel of quantum computing growing the ecosystem through better hardware, more developers, and more use cases.

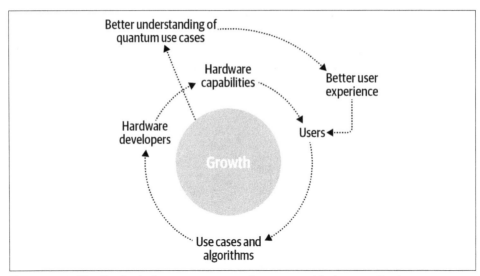

Figure 2-16. The flywheel of quantum computing grows with Amazon Braket.

There are many similarities between today's graphics processing units (GPUs) and tomorrow's quantum processing units (QPUs). GPUs revolutionized AI and machine learning though highly parallel, digital computations. GPUs also required a different set of skills, libraries (i.e., NVIDIA's CUDA), and hardware to take advantage of this massive parallelism. Additionally, GPU devices are "off-chip" relative to the CPU devices that traditionally manage the larger computation workflow. Synchronizing data between CPUs and GPUs requires special hardware and software to accommodate the physical separation.

Similarly, QPUs perform computations through massively parallel, quantum computations—many orders of magnitude more parallel than their digital counterparts. Additionally, QPUs require a different set of skills, libraries, and hardware. They are off-chip relative to CPUs and therefore require special hardware and software to perform the synchronization operations similar to GPUs, as shown in Figure 2-17.

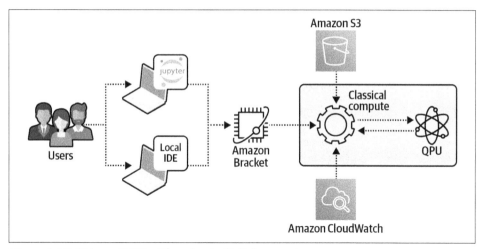

Figure 2-17. Using a QPU with a classic digital computer.

Quantum Bits Versus Digital Bits

Quantum bits (qubits) are the quantum computing equivalent of classical digital bits. However, their state (0 or 1) is probabilistic and therefore requires a READ operation before the value is known. This probabilistic state is referred to as "superposition" and is a key principle behind quantum computing.

Today's accessible quantum computers are around 70 to 100 qubits. However, a significant portion of these qubits are required for error correction given the relative "noisy" environment of the quantum hardware. Cryptography, for example, requires nearly 6,000 clean qubits to break 2048-bit RSA. Six thousand clean qubits requires approximately 1,000,000 error-correcting, redundant qubits to adjust for the noisy environment offered by current quantum hardware.

Quantum Supremacy and the Quantum Computing Eras

Until recently, we were in the "classically simulatable" phase where we could simulate the performance improvements of quantum computers. However, in 2019, we reached a point of "quantum supremacy" where we are no longer able to simulate and measure additional performance improvements from quantum computers due to limitations with today's digital computers.

The current era is called *Noisy Intermediate-Scale Quantum*. During this era, we are trying to correct for the noise introduced by the quantum computing environment, which requires very specific temperature and vacuum characteristics. Similar to error-correcting registers and RAM chips, we need error-correcting qubits and QRAM to enter the next era, called the *Error-Corrected Quantum Computer* era, as shown in Figure 2-18.

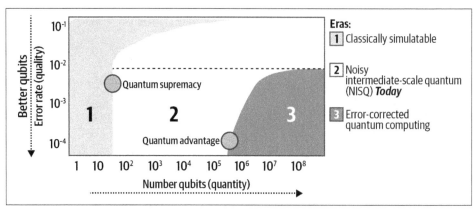

Figure 2-18. Quantum computing eras.

Cracking Cryptography

It is estimated that quantum computers are only 10 or so years away from cracking modern-day RSA cryptography. Today, cryptography is effective because we don't have enough computing power to perform the numeric factorization required to crack the code.

However, with an estimated 6,000 "perfect" qubits (no error correcting needed), we can crack the RSA code within just a few minutes. This is scary and has given rise to "quantum-aware" or "post-quantum" cryptography such as Amazon's s2n open source implementation of the TLS protocol (*https://oreil.ly/o3U7G*), which uses post-quantum cryptography as opposed to classical cryptography. We dive deeper into post-quantum cryptography in Chapter 12.

Molecular Simulations and Drug Discovery

Quantum computers have unique parallelization capabilities and can natively manipulate quantum mechanical states. Therefore, they have the potential to solve very important problems, such as mapping the electronic structure of molecules. Quantum simulations will likely lead to discovering new materials, catalysts, drugs, and high-temperature superconductors.

Logistics and Financial Optimizations

Optimization problems are ubiquitous across many domains, including supply chain logistics and financial services. Finding the optimal approach from an exponential set of possible options can saturate the resources of a classical digital computer. Quantum computers can break through this barrier and accelerate many optimization techniques, including linear programming algorithms and Monte Carlo methods.

Quantum Machine Learning and AI

Unfortunately, today's use of quantum computers in machine learning and AI is pretty limited. We have seen some early improvements in linear algorithms, such as support vector machines and Principal Component Analysis. We have also seen examples where quantum research has inspired improvements in classical recommendation algorithms (*https://oreil.ly/H99mZ*). In the future, error-correcting quantum computers will likely lead to a rich class of scalable and high-performance quantum machine learning and AI models.

Programming a Quantum Computer with Amazon Braket

Amazon Braket supports Jupyter Notebook and offers a Python SDK to allow developers to interact with a quantum computer. Using the Python SDK, we asynchronously submit tasks to a remote QPU. This is similar to how we submitted jobs and "rented" a shared computer back in the early days of computing to complete those jobs. This is also similar to offloading compute from a CPU to a GPU. The key difference, however, is that the CPU and GPU share classical digital fundamentals—the QPU does not.

The following code demonstrates how to build a quantum circuit involving multiple qubits. This example demonstrates how to perform "quantum teleportation" where information (*not* matter) is transported from one qubit to another without using classical digital circuits or network cables:

```python
from braket.aws import AwsDevice
from braket.circuits import Circuit, Gate, Moments
from braket.circuits.instruction import Instruction

device = AwsDevice("arn:aws:braket:::device/qpu/ionq/ionQdevice")

# Alice and Bob initially share a Bell pair.
circ = Circuit();
circ.h([0]);
circ.cnot(0,1);

# Define Alice's encoding scheme.
# Define four possible messages and their gates.
message = {
        "00": Circuit().i(0),
        "01": Circuit().x(0),
        "10": Circuit().z(0),
        "11": Circuit().x(0).z(0)
        }

# Alice selects a message to send.  Let's choose '01'.
m = "01"

# Alice encodes her message by applying the gates defined above.
```

```
circ.add_circuit(message[m]);

# Alice then sends her qubit to Bob so that Bob has both qubits.
# Bob decodes Alice's message by disentangling the two qubits.
circ.cnot(0,1);
circ.h([0]);

print(circ)

### OUTPUT ###

T  : |0|1|2|3|4|
q0 : -H-C-X-C-H-
         |   |
q1 : ---X---X---
T  : |0|1|2|3|4|
```

AWS Center for Quantum Computing

AWS has partnered with Caltech to build the AWS Center for Quantum Computing, scheduled to open in 2021. This center will focus on developing useful quantum applications, error-correcting qubits, quantum programming models, and new quantum hardware.

Increase Performance and Reduce Cost

What if we were able to double our code speed and reduce our server-pool size by half? We could potentially save significant money. What if we could automatically detect operational issues in our applications and see the recommended fixes to improve availability? Reducing application downtime is another huge cost-saving opportunity.

In this section, we introduce the fully managed services Amazon CodeGuru Reviewer, Amazon CodeGuru Profiler, and Amazon DevOps Guru. CodeGuru Reviewer and Profiler help us improve code performance and reduce our resource requirements, while Amazon DevOps Guru helps to detect operational issues and improve application availability.

Automatic Code Reviews with CodeGuru Reviewer

Code reviews are a well-known best practice for software development. The idea is that our code is reviewed by a more experienced set of team members to provide feedback on code performance, quality, and security. In addition to domain expertise, these experienced team members possess tacit knowledge of the team's coding idioms as well as an acute sense of code smell.

Sometimes, however, even the most experienced team member will miss subtle performance bottlenecks or mishandled exceptions. These reviewers are often focused on domain-specific issues such as poor implementation of the domain model or misconfigured service integrations. Additionally, reviewers are often limited to a static view of the code versus live metrics into the code's runtime. CodeGuru consists of CodeGuru Reviewer for automated code reviews and CodeGuru Profiler to monitor code performance.

CodeGuru Reviewer automates the code-review process and makes suggestions using machine learning models trained on millions of lines of code from hundreds of thousands of Amazon's internal code bases as well as 10,000+ open source projects on GitHub.

We simply point CodeGuru to our source code repository in a secure and private manner—CodeGuru will start making suggestions. CodeGuru analyzes all pull requests on our source code repositories and automatically flags critical defects such as credential leaks, resource leaks, concurrency race conditions, and inefficient use of AWS resources. It suggests changes to specific lines of code to remediate the defects, as shown in Figure 2-19.

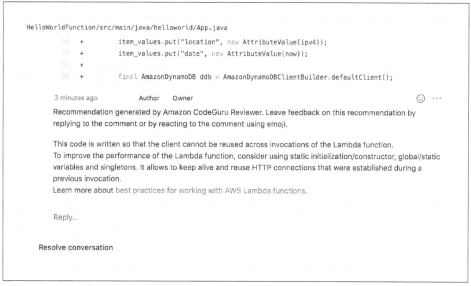

Figure 2-19. CodeGuru Reviewer analyzes our source code and adds suggestions to improve performance and reduce cost.

In this case, the original code from a Lambda function was creating a new DynamoDB client on every invocation instead of creating the client once and caching it. Without this change, we will waste unnecessary compute cycles and memory registers as we continuously re-create the same DynamoDB client object on every invocation. With this change, our Lambda functions can handle more requests per second, which results in fewer resources and lower cost.

CodeGuru Reviewer checks for Python and Java best practices, including connection pooling and exception handling. Reviewer includes Security Detector to detect security issues such as unsanitized arguments passed to OS-level Python subprocess calls. CodeGuru Reviewer also identifies code smells, reduces technical debt, and improves codebase maintainability.

Improve Application Performance with CodeGuru Profiler

CodeGuru Profiler can detect bottlenecks in our code at runtime by analyzing the application runtime profile, flagging the most expensive line of code, and providing intelligent recommendations. Profiler creates visualizations such as the flame graph in Figure 2-20 to identify where we should spend our time to optimize performance and save the most money.

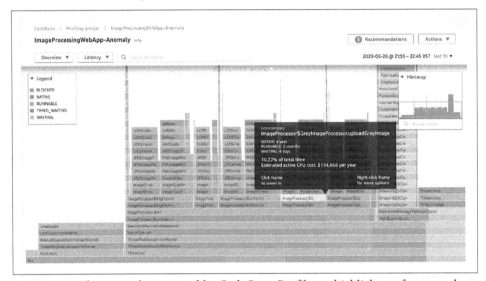

Figure 2-20. Flame graph generated by CodeGuru Profiler to highlight performance bottlenecks in our code.

The flame graph shows the call stack in human-readable form with the exact function names. When analyzing flame graphs, we should dive deep into any plateaus that we find. Plateaus often indicate that a resource is stalled waiting for network or disk I/O. Ideally, our flame graph will show a lot of narrow peaks and not a lot of plateaus.

Improve Application Availability with DevOps Guru

Amazon DevOps Guru is an ML-powered operations service that automatically detects operational issues in applications and recommends fixes. DevOps Guru looks at application metrics, logs, and events to identify any behavior that deviates from normal operating patterns, such as increased response latencies, elevated error rates, and excessive resource utilization. When such a pattern is recognized, DevOps Guru sends an alert together with a summary of related anomalies, the potential root cause, and a possible resolution.

Summary

In this chapter, we have shown many different use cases that can be solved with various AWS AI and machine learning services out of the box with little or no code. Whether we are application developers and don't know much about machine learning or experienced data scientists who want to focus on the difficult machine learning problems, the managed AI and machine learning services by Amazon are worth exploring.

We can easily enrich our applications with ready-to-use AI services, whether our business use case requires us to bring machine learning to the edge or we are just at the beginning of our AI/ML journey and want to find some fun educational ways to get started with computer vision, reinforcement learning, or GANs.

We've also shown some examples of how to put the high-level AI services to work, including Amazon Personalize for recommendations and Forecast for forecast demand.

We showed how machine learning powers a lot of existing AWS services, including predictive Amazon EC2 auto-scaling and warm-pooling. We also explored how to detect and prevent sensitive data leaks using Macie and prevent fraud using Amazon Fraud Detector. We covered how to improve the customer support experience with Amazon Contact Lens for Amazon Connect, Comprehend, Kendra, and Lex. We also described how we can automate source code reviews and identify performance and cost benefits using CodeGuru Reviewer, CodeGuru Profiler, and DevOps Guru.

In Chapter 3, we will discuss the concept of automated machine learning. We will show how to build predictive models in just a few clicks with Amazon SageMaker Autopilot and Amazon Comprehend.

## CHAPTER 3

Automated Machine Learning

In this chapter, we will show how to use the fully managed Amazon AI and machine learning services to avoid the need to manage our own infrastructure for our AI and machine learning pipelines. We dive deep into two Amazon services for automated machine learning, Amazon SageMaker Autopilot and Amazon Comprehend, both designed for users who want to build powerful predictive models from their datasets with just a few clicks. We can use both SageMaker Autopilot and Comprehend to establish baseline model performance with very low effort and cost.

Machine learning practitioners typically spend weeks or months building, training, and tuning their models. They prepare the data and decide on the framework and algorithm to use. In an iterative process, ML practitioners try to find the best performing algorithm for their dataset and problem type. Unfortunately, there is no cheat sheet for this process. We still need experience, intuition, and patience to run many experiments and find the best hyper-parameters for our algorithm and dataset. Seasoned data scientists benefit from years of experience and intuition to choose the best algorithm for a given dataset and problem type, but they still need to validate their intuition with actual training runs and repeated model validations.

What if we could just use a service that, with just a single click, finds the best algorithm for our dataset, trains and tunes the model, and deploys a model to production? Amazon SageMaker Autopilot simplifies the model training and tuning process and speeds up the overall model development life cycle. By spending less time on boiler-plate life-cycle phases such as feature selection and hyper-parameter tuning (HPT), we can spend more time on domain-specific problems.

By analyzing our data from S3, SageMaker Autopilot explores different algorithms and configurations based on many years of AI and machine learning experience at Amazon. SageMaker Autopilot compares various regression, classification, and deep learning algorithms to find the best one for our dataset and problem type.

The model candidates are summarized by SageMaker Autopilot through a set of automatically generated Jupyter notebooks and Python scripts. We have full control over these generated notebooks and scripts. We can modify them, automate them, and share them with colleagues. We can select the top model candidate based on our desired balance of model accuracy, model size, and prediction latency.

Automated Machine Learning with SageMaker Autopilot

We configure the SageMaker Autopilot job by providing our raw data in an S3 bucket in the form of a tabular CSV file. We also need to tell SageMaker Autopilot which column is the target. Then SageMaker Autopilot applies automated machine learning techniques to analyze the data, identify the best algorithm for our dataset, and generate the best model candidates.

SageMaker Autopilot analyzes and balances the dataset and splits the dataset into train/validation sets. Based on the target attribute we are trying to predict, SageMaker Autopilot automatically identifies the machine learning problem type, such as regression, binary classification, or multiclass classification. SageMaker Autopilot then compares a set of algorithms depending on the problem type. The algorithm choices include logistic regression, linear regression, XGBoost, neural networks, and others.

SageMaker Autopilot generates code to execute a set of model pipelines specific to each algorithm. The generated code includes data transformations, model training, and model tuning. Since SageMaker Autopilot is transparent, we have full access to this generated code to reproduce on our own. We can even modify the code and rerun the pipeline anytime.

After training and tuning the generated pipelines in parallel, SageMaker Autopilot ranks the trained models by an objective metric such as accuracy, AUC, and F1-score, among others.

SageMaker Autopilot uses a transparent approach to AutoML. In nontransparent approaches, as shown in Figure 3-1, we don't have control or visibility into the chosen algorithms, applied data transformations, or hyper-parameter choices. We point the automated machine learning (AutoML) service to our data and receive a trained model.

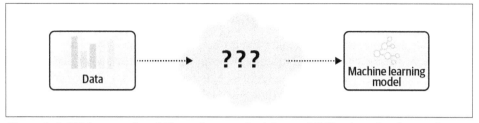

Figure 3-1. With many AutoML services, we don't have visibility into the chosen algorithms, applied data transformations, or hyper-parameter choices.

This makes it hard to understand, explain, and reproduce the model. Many AutoML solutions implement this kind of nontransparent approach. In contrast, SageMaker Autopilot documents and shares its findings throughout the data analysis, feature engineering, and model tuning steps.

SageMaker Autopilot doesn't just share the models; it also logs all observed metrics and generates Jupyter notebooks, which contain the code to reproduce the model pipelines, as visualized in Figure 3-2.

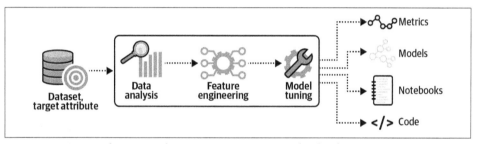

Figure 3-2. SageMaker Autopilot generates Jupyter notebooks, feature engineering scripts, and model code.

The data-analysis step identifies potential data-quality issues, such as missing values that might impact model performance if not addressed. The Data Exploration notebook contains the results from the data-analysis step. SageMaker Autopilot also generates another Jupyter notebook that contains all pipeline definitions to provide transparency and reproducibility. The Candidate Definition notebook highlights the best algorithms to learn our given dataset, as well as the code and configuration needed to use our dataset with each algorithm.

> Both Jupyter notebooks are available after the first data-analysis step. We can configure Autopilot to just do a "dry run" and stop after this step.

Track Experiments with SageMaker Autopilot

SageMaker Autopilot uses SageMaker Experiments to keep track of all data analysis, feature engineering, and model training/tuning jobs. This feature of the broader Amazon SageMaker family of ML services helps us organize, track, compare and evaluate machine learning experiments. SageMaker Experiments enables model versioning and lineage tracking across all phases of the ML life cycle.

A SageMaker Experiment consists of trials. A trial is a collection of steps that includes data preprocessing, model training, and model tuning. SageMaker Experiments also offers lineage tracking across S3 locations, algorithms, hyper-parameters, trained models, and model-performance metrics.

We can explore and manage SageMaker Autopilot experiments and trials either through the UI or using SDKs, such as the Amazon SageMaker Python SDK (*https://oreil.ly/nUN9I*) or the AWS SDK for Python (Boto3) (*https://oreil.ly/eiN8j*).

The SageMaker SDK is a high-level, SageMaker-specific abstraction on top of Boto3 and is the preferred choice for SageMaker model development and management.

Train and Deploy a Text Classifier with SageMaker Autopilot

Let's create a SageMaker Autopilot experiment to build a custom text classifier to classify social feedback on products that we are selling. The product feedback comes from various online channels, such as our website, partner websites, social media, customer support emails, etc. We capture the product feedback and want our model to classify the feedback into star rating classes, with 5 being the best feedback and 1 being the worst.

As input data, we leverage samples from the Amazon Customer Reviews Dataset (*https://oreil.ly/LjXva*). This dataset is a collection of over 150 million product reviews on Amazon.com from 1995 to 2015. Those product reviews and star ratings are a popular customer feature of Amazon.com. We will describe and explore this dataset in much more detail in Chapters 4 and 5. For now, we focus on the review_body (feature) and star_rating (predicted label).

Train and Deploy with SageMaker Autopilot UI

The SageMaker Autopilot UI is integrated into SageMaker Studio, an IDE that provides a single, web-based visual interface where we can perform our machine learning development. Simply navigate to Amazon SageMaker in our AWS Console and click SageMaker Studio. Then follow the instructions to set up SageMaker Studio and click Open Studio.

This will take us to the SageMaker Studio UI, where we can access the SageMaker Autopilot UI through the Experiments and trials menu. There, we can click Create Experiment to create and configure our first SageMaker Autopilot experiment.

In preparation for our SageMaker Autopilot experiment, we use a subset of the Amazon Customer Reviews Dataset to train our model. We want to train a classifier model to predict the `star_rating` for a given `review_body`. We created our input CSV file to contain the `star_rating` as our label/target column and the `review_body` column, which contains the product feedback:

```
star_rating,review_body
5,"GOOD, GREAT, WONDERFUL"
2,"It isn't as user friendly as TurboTax."
4,"Pretty easy to use. No issues."
…
```

In other scenarios, we will likely want to use more columns from our dataset and let SageMaker Autopilot choose the most important ones through automated feature selection. In our example, however, we keep things simple and use the `star_rating` and `review_body` columns to focus on the steps to create the Autopilot experiment.

Next, we configure the SageMaker Autopilot experiment with a few input parameters that define the dataset, the target column to predict, and, optionally, the problem type, such as binary classification, multiclass classification, or regression. If we don't specify the problem type, SageMaker Autopilot can automatically determine the problem type based on the values it finds in the target column:

Experiment name
  A name to identify the experiment, e.g., *amazon-customer-reviews*.

Input data location
  The S3 path to our training data, e.g., *s3://<MY-S3-BUCKET>/data/amazon_reviews_us_Digital_Software_v1_00_header.csv*.

Target
  The target column we want to predict, e.g., `star_rating`.

Output data location
  The S3 path for storing the generated output, such as models and other artifacts, e.g., *s3://<MY-S3-BUCKET>/autopilot/output*.

Problem type

The machine learning problem type, such as binary classification, multiclass classification, and regression. The default, "Auto," allows SageMaker Autopilot to choose for itself based on the given input data, including categorical data.

Run complete experiment

We can choose to run a complete experiment or just generate the Data Exploration and Candidate Definition notebooks as part of the data analysis phase. In this case, SageMaker Autopilot stops after the data analysis phase and would not run the feature engineering, model training, and tuning steps.

Let's click Create Experiment and start our first SageMaker Autopilot job. We can observe the progress of the job in SageMaker Studio's Autopilot UI through preprocessing, candidate generation, feature engineering, and model tuning. Once SageMaker Autopilot completes the candidate generation phase, we can see the links to the two generated notebooks appearing in the UI: Candidate Generation and Data Exploration.

We can either download these files directly from the UI or automate the download from S3 directly. We can find the generated notebooks, code, and transformed data in the following structure:

```
amazon-customer-reviews/
    sagemaker-automl-candidates/
    ...
        generated_module/
        candidate_data_processors/
                    dpp0.py
                    dpp1.py
                    ...
            notebooks/
                SageMakerAutopilotCandidateDefinitionNotebook.ipynb
                SageMakerAutopilotDataExplorationNotebook.ipynb
        ...
    data-processor-models/
        amazon-cus-dpp0-1-xxx/
            output/model.tar.gz
        amazon-cus-dpp1-1-xxx/
            output/model.tar.gz
        ...
    preprocessed-data/
        header/
headers.csv
tuning_data/
        train/
            chunk_20.csv
            chunk_21.csv
            ...
        validation/
            chunk_0.csv
```

```
chunk_1.csv
    ...
```

When the feature engineering stage starts, we will see SageMaker Training Jobs appearing in the AWS Console or within SageMaker Studio directly. Each training job is a combination of a model candidate and the data preprocessor (dpp) code, named dpp0 through dpp9. We can think of those training jobs as the 10 machine learning pipelines SageMaker Autopilot builds to find the best-performing model. We can select any of those training jobs to view the job status, configuration, parameters, and log files. We will dive deep into feature engineering in Chapter 6 and SageMaker Training Jobs in Chapter 7.

Once the feature-engineering stage has completed, we can view the transformed data directly in S3 grouped by pipeline. The data has been divided into smaller chunks and split into separate train and validation datasets, as shown in the following:

```
transformed-data/
    dpp0/
        rpb/
            train/
                chunk_20.csv_out
                chunk_21.csv_out
                ...
            validation/
                chunk_0.csv_out
                chunk_1.csv_out
                ...
    dpp1/
        csv/
            train/
                chunk_20.csv_out
                chunk_21.csv_out
                ...
            validation/
                chunk_0.csv_out
                chunk_1.csv_out
                ...
    ..
    dpp9/
```

Finally, SageMaker Autopilot runs the model-tuning stage, and we start seeing the trials appear in SageMaker Studio's Autopilot UI. The model-tuning stage creates a SageMaker Hyper-Parameter Tuning Job. HPT, or hyper-parameter optimization (HPO), as it is commonly called, is natively supported by Amazon SageMaker and is usable outside of SageMaker Autopilot for standalone HPT jobs on custom models, as we will see in Chapter 8.

SageMaker Hyper-Parameter Tuning Jobs find the best version of a model by running many training jobs on our dataset using the algorithm and ranges of hyper-parameters that we specify. SageMaker supports multiple algorithms for HPT, including random search and Bayesian search. With random search, SageMaker chooses random combinations of hyper-parameters from the ranges we specify. With Bayesian search, SageMaker treats tuning as a regression problem. We will explore SageMaker's automatic model tuning functionality in Chapter 8.

We can find the corresponding training jobs listed in the SageMaker Training Jobs UI or within SageMaker Studio directly. Again, we can click and inspect any of these jobs to view the job status, configuration, parameters, and log files. Back in the SageMaker Autopilot UI, we can inspect the trials.

The four SageMaker Autopilot trial components make up a pipeline of the following jobs:

Processing Job
Splits the data into train and validation data and separates the header data

Training Job
Trains a batch transform model using the previously split training and validation data with the data preprocessor code (*dpp[0-9].py*) for each model candidate

Batch Transform Job
Transforms the raw data into features

Tuning Job
Finds the best-performing model candidates using the previously transformed algorithm-specific features by optimizing the algorithm configuration and parameters

Those four components preserve the model's lineage by tracking all hyper-parameters, input datasets, and output artifacts. After the model-tuning step is completed, we can find the final outputs and model candidates in the S3 bucket organized per model-candidate pipeline:

```
tuning/
    amazon-cus-dpp0-xgb/
        tuning-job-1-8fc3bb8155c645f282-001-da2b6b8b/
            output/model.tar.gz
        tuning-job-1-8fc3bb8155c645f282-004-911d2130/
            output/model.tar.gz
        tuning-job-1-8fc3bb8155c645f282-012-1ea8b599/
            output/model.tar.gz
    ...
    amazon-cus-dpp3-ll/
    ...
amazon-cus-dpp-9-xgb/
```

Note that the pipeline name (i.e., amazon-cus-dpp0-xgb) conveniently contains information on the settings used (dpp0 = data preprocessor pipeline dpp0, xgb = chosen algorithm XGBoost). In addition to programmatically retrieving the best-performing model, we can use SageMaker Studio's Autopilot UI to visually highlight the best model.

Deploying this model into production is now as easy as right-clicking on the name and selecting the Deploy model action. We just need to give our endpoint a name, select the AWS instance type we want to deploy the model on, e.g., ml.m5.xlarge, and define the number of instances to serve our model.

 There is an overview of all AWS instance types supported by Amazon SageMaker and their performance characteristics (*https:// oreil.ly/2AJ4c*).

Note that those instances start with ml. in their name.

Optionally, we can enable data capture of all prediction requests and responses for our deployed model. We can now click Deploy model and watch our model endpoint being created. Once the endpoint shows up as *In Service*, we can invoke the endpoint to serve predictions.

Here is a simple Python code snippet that shows how to invoke the model deployed to the SageMaker endpoint. We pass a sample review ("I loved it!") and see which star rating our model chooses. Remember, star rating 1 is the worst, and star rating 5 is the best:

```
import boto3
sagemaker_runtime = boto3.client('sagemaker-runtime')
csv_line_predict = """I loved it!"""
ep_name = 'reviews-endpoint'

response = sagemaker_runtime.invoke_endpoint(
        EndpointName=ep_name,
        ContentType='text/csv',
        Accept='text/csv',
        Body=csv_line_predict)

response_body = response['Body'].read().decode('utf-8').strip()
print(response_body)
```

Here is the star rating that our model predicts:

```
"5"
```

Our model successfully classified the review as a 5-star rating.

Train and Deploy a Model with the SageMaker Autopilot Python SDK

In addition to using the preceding SageMaker Autopilot UI, we can also launch a SageMaker Autopilot job using the Python SDK to train and deploy a text classifier in just a few lines of code, as follows:

```
import boto3
import sagemaker

session = sagemaker.Session(default_bucket="dsoaws-amazon-reviews")
bucket = session.default_bucket()
role = sagemaker.get_execution_role()
region = boto3.Session().region_name

sm = boto3.Session().client(service_name='sagemaker',
                            region_name=region)
```

We can specify the number of model candidates to explore and set a maximum run-time in seconds for each training job and the overall SageMaker Autopilot job:

```
max_candidates = 3

job_config = {
    'CompletionCriteria': {
      'MaxRuntimePerTrainingJobInSeconds': 600,
      'MaxCandidates': max_candidates,
      'MaxAutoMLJobRuntimeInSeconds': 3600
    },
}
```

Similar to the SageMaker Autopilot UI configuration, we provide an S3 input and output location and define the target attribute for predictions:

```
input_data_config = [
    {
    'DataSource': {
        'S3DataSource': {
            'S3DataType': 'S3Prefix',
            'S3Uri': 's3://<BUCKET>/amazon_reviews.csv'
        }
    },
    'TargetAttributeName': 'star_rating'
    }
]

output_data_config = {
    'S3OutputPath': 's3://<BUCKET>/autopilot/output/'
}
```

Next, we create our SageMaker Autopilot job. Note that we add a timestamp to the SageMaker Autopilot job name, which helps to keep the jobs unique and easy to track. We pass the job name, input/output configuration, job configuration, and execution role. The execution role is part of the AWS Identity and Access Management (IAM) service and manages service access permissions:

```
from time import gmtime, strftime, sleep
timestamp_suffix = strftime('%d-%H-%M-%S', gmtime())

auto_ml_job_name = 'automl-dm-' + timestamp_suffix
```

```
sm.create_auto_ml_job(AutoMLJobName=auto_ml_job_name,
                       InputDataConfig=input_data_config,
                       OutputDataConfig=output_data_config,
                       AutoMLJobConfig=job_config,
                       RoleArn=role)
```

The SageMaker Autopilot job has been created with a unique identifier, described as `AutoMLJobArn` previously. ARN (Amazon Resource Name) is often encoded in the form of `arn:partition:service:region:account-id:resource-id`. ARNs are used across all AWS services to specify resources unambiguously.

We can poll the SageMaker Autopilot job status and check if the data analysis step has completed:

```
job = sm.describe_auto_ml_job(AutoMLJobName=auto_ml_job_name)
job_status = job['AutoMLJobStatus']
job_sec_status = job['AutoMLJobSecondaryStatus']

if job_status not in ('Stopped', 'Failed'):
    while job_status in ('InProgress') and job_sec_status in ('AnalyzingData'):
        job = sm.describe_auto_ml_job(AutoMLJobName=auto_ml_job_name)
        job_status = job['AutoMLJobStatus']
        job_sec_status = job['AutoMLJobSecondaryStatus']
        print(job_status, job_sec_status)
        sleep(30)
    print("Data analysis complete")

print(job)
```

The code will return the following output (shortened):

```
InProgress AnalyzingData
InProgress AnalyzingData
...
Data analysis complete
```

Similarly, we can query for `job_sec_status in ('FeatureEngineering')` and `job_sec_status in ('ModelTuning')` for the two following SageMaker Autopilot steps.

Once the SageMaker Autopilot job has finished, we can list all model candidates:

```
candidates = sm.list_candidates_for_auto_ml_job(AutoMLJobName=auto_ml_job_name,
        SortBy='FinalObjectiveMetricValue')['Candidates']

for index, candidate in enumerate(candidates):
    print(str(index) + "  "
        + candidate['CandidateName'] + "  "
        + str(candidate['FinalAutoMLJobObjectiveMetric']['Value']))
```

This will generate output similar to this:

```
0    tuning-job-1-655f4ef810d441d4a8-003-b80f5233    0.4437510073184967
1    tuning-job-1-655f4ef810d441d4a8-001-7c10cb15    0.29365700483322144
2    tuning-job-1-655f4ef810d441d4a8-002-31088991    0.2874149978160858
```

We can also retrieve the best candidate:

```
best_candidate = \
    sm.describe_auto_ml_job(AutoMLJobName=auto_ml_job_name)['BestCandidate']

best_candidate_identifier = best_candidate['CandidateName']

print("Candidate name: " + best_candidate_identifier)

print("Metric name: " + \
    best_candidate['FinalAutoMLJobObjectiveMetric']['MetricName'])

print("Metric value: " + \
    str(best_candidate['FinalAutoMLJobObjectiveMetric']['Value']))
```

This will generate output similar to this:

```
Candidate name: tuning-job-1-655f4ef810d441d4a8-003-b80f5233
Metric name: validation:accuracy
Metric value: 0.4437510073184967
```

Now, let's deploy the best model as a REST endpoint. First, we need to create a model object:

```
model_name = 'automl-dm-model-' + timestamp_suffix

model_arn = sm.create_model(Containers=best_candidate['InferenceContainers'],
                            ModelName=model_name,
                            ExecutionRoleArn=role)

print('Best candidate model ARN: ', model_arn['ModelArn'])
```

The output should look similar to this:

```
Best candidate model ARN:
arn:aws:sagemaker:<region>:<account_id>:model/automl-dm-model-01-16-34-00
```

The preceding code reveals another detail that has been hidden in the UI. When we deploy our model as a REST endpoint, we actually deploy a whole inference pipeline. The inference pipeline consists of three containers.

Data transformation container
> This is essentially the "request handler" that converts the application inputs (e.g., review_body) into a format recognized by the model (i.e., NumPy arrays or tensors). The container hosts the model that SageMaker Autopilot trained for the feature engineering step.

Algorithm container
> This container hosts the actual model that serves the predictions.

Inverse label transformer container

This is the "response handler" that converts the algorithm-specific output (i.e., NumPy arrays or tensors) back into a format recognized by the invoker (e.g., `star_rating`).

Figure 3-3 shows an example of the inference pipeline.

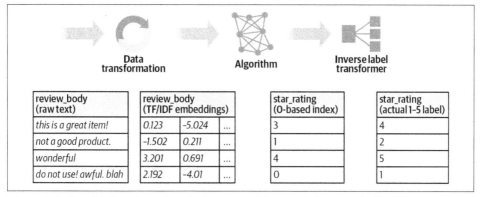

review_body (raw text)	review_body (TF/IDF embeddings)			star_rating (0-based index)	star_rating (actual 1–5 label)
this is a great item!	0.123	-5.024	...	3	4
not a good product.	-1.502	0.211	...	1	2
wonderful	3.201	0.691	...	4	5
do not use! awful. blah	2.192	-4.01	...	0	1

Figure 3-3. SageMaker Autopilot deploys a model as an inference pipeline.

We pass our reviews as raw text, and the data transformation container converts the text into TF/IDF vectors. TF/IDF stands for *term frequency–inverse document frequency* and causes more common terms to be downweighted and more unique terms to be upweighted. TF/IDF encodes the relevance of a word to a document in a collection of documents.

The algorithm container processes the input and predicts the star rating. Note that the algorithm in our example returns the prediction results as a 0-based index value. The task of the inverse label transformer container is to map the index (0,1,2,3,4) to the correct star rating label (1,2,3,4,5).

To deploy the inference pipeline, we need to create an endpoint configuration:

```
# EndpointConfig name
timestamp_suffix = strftime('%d-%H-%M-%S', gmtime())
epc_name = 'automl-dm-epc-' + timestamp_suffix

# Endpoint name
ep_name = 'automl-dm-ep-' + timestamp_suffix
variant_name = 'automl-dm-variant-' + timestamp_suffix

ep_config = sm.create_endpoint_config(
    EndpointConfigName = epc_name,
    ProductionVariants=[{
        'InstanceType': 'ml.c5.2xlarge',
        'InitialInstanceCount': 1,
        'ModelName': model_name,
```

```
        'VariantName': variant_name}])

create_endpoint_response = sm.create_endpoint(
        EndpointName=ep_name,
        EndpointConfigName=epc_name)
```

SageMaker Autopilot is now deploying the inference pipeline. Let's query for the endpoint status to see when the pipeline is successfully in service:

```
response = sm.describe_endpoint(EndpointName=autopilot_endpoint_name)
status = response['EndpointStatus']

print("Arn: " + response['EndpointArn'])
print("Status: " + status)
```

After a couple of minutes, the output should look similar to this:

```
Arn: arn:aws:sagemaker:<region>:<account_id>:endpoint/automl-dm-ep-19-13-29-52
Status: InService
```

We can now invoke the endpoint and run a sample prediction. We pass the review "It's OK." to see which star-rating class the model predicts:

```
sagemaker_runtime = boto3.client('sagemaker-runtime')
csv_line_predict = """It's OK."""

response = sagemaker_runtime.invoke_endpoint(
        EndpointName=ep_name,
        ContentType='text/csv',
        Accept='text/csv',
        Body=csv_line_predict)

response_body = response['Body'].read().decode('utf-8').strip()
```

Let's print the response:

```
response_body
'3'
```

Our endpoint has successfully classified this sample review as a 3-star rating.

 We can check the S3 output location again for all generated models, code, and other artifacts, including the Data Exploration notebook and Candidate Definition notebook.

Invoking our models using the SageMaker SDK is just one option. There are many more service integrations available in AWS. In the next section, we describe how we can run real-time predictions from within a SQL query using Amazon Athena.

Predict with Amazon Athena and SageMaker Autopilot

Amazon Athena is an interactive query service that lets us analyze data stored in S3 using standard SQL. Since Athena is serverless, we don't need to manage any infrastructure, and we only pay for the queries we run. With Athena, we can query large amounts of data (TB+) without needing to move the data to a relational database. We can now enrich our SQL queries with calls to a SageMaker model endpoint and receive model predictions.

To call SageMaker from Athena, we need to define a function with the USING FUNCTION clause, as shown in Figure 3-4. Any subsequent SELECT statement can then reference the function to invoke a model prediction.

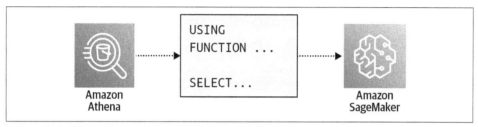

Figure 3-4. We can invoke a SageMaker model from Amazon Athena ML using a user-defined function.

Here's a simple SQL query that selects product reviews stored in an Athena table called `dsaws.product_reviews`. The function `predict_star_rating` then calls a SageMaker endpoint with the name `reviews` to serve the prediction:

```
USING FUNCTION predict_star_rating(review_body VARCHAR)
    RETURNS VARCHAR TYPE
    SAGEMAKER_INVOKE_ENDPOINT WITH (sagemaker_endpoint = 'reviews')

SELECT review_id, review_body,
        predict_star_rating(REPLACE(review_body, ',', ' '))
        AS predicted_star_rating
FROM dsoaws.product_reviews
```

The result should look similar to this (shortened):

review_id	review_body	predicted_star_rating
R23CFDQ6SLMET	The photographs of this book is a let down. I ...	1
R1301KYAYKX8FU	This is my go-to commentary for all of my semi...	5
R1CKM3AKI920D7	I can't believe I get to be the first to tell ...	5
RA6CYWHAHSR9H	There's Something About Christmas / Debbie Mac...	5
R1T1CCMH2N9LBJ	This revised edition by Murray Straus is an ex...	1
...	...	...

This example shows how easy it is to enrich our S3 data with machine learning prediction results using a simple SQL query.

Train and Predict with Amazon Redshift ML and SageMaker Autopilot

Amazon Redshift is a fully managed data warehouse that allows us to run complex analytic queries against petabytes of structured data. With Amazon Redshift ML, we can use our data in Amazon Redshift to create and train models with SageMaker Autopilot as new data arrives. Following is the code to train a text classifier model with training data retrieved from an Amazon Redshift query. The SELECT statement points to the data in Amazon Redshift we want to use as training data for our model. The TARGET keyword defines the column to predict. The FUNCTION keyword defines the function name used to invoke the model in a prediction Amazon Redshift query:

```
CREATE MODEL dsoaws.predict_star_rating
FROM (SELECT review_body,
             star_rating
      FROM dsoaws.amazon_reviews_tsv_2015)
TARGET star_rating
FUNCTION predict_star_rating
IAM_ROLE '<ROLE_ARN>'
SETTINGS (
  S3_BUCKET '<BUCKET_NAME>'
);
```

The preceding statement executes an Amazon Redshift query, exports the selected data to S3, and triggers a SageMaker Autopilot job to generate and deploy the model. Amazon Redshift ML then deploys the trained model and function in our Amazon Redshift cluster called predict_star_rating.

To make predictions with our trained Amazon Customer Reviews text classifier model, we query the review_body column in Amazon Redshift and predict the star_rating as follows:

```
SELECT review_body,
       predict_star_rating(review_body) AS "predicted_star_rating"
FROM dsoaws.amazon_reviews_tsv_2015
```

Here are sample query results that demonstrate Amazon Redshift ML:

review_body	predicted_star_rating
I love this product!	5
It's ok.	3
This product is terrible.	1

Automated Machine Learning with Amazon Comprehend

Amazon Comprehend is a fully managed AI service for natural language processing (NLP) tasks using AutoML to find the best model for our dataset. Amazon Comprehend takes text documents as input and recognizes entities, key phrases, language, and sentiment. Amazon Comprehend continues to improve as new language models are discovered and incorporated into the managed service.

Predict with Amazon Comprehend's Built-in Model

Sentiment analysis is a text classification task that predicts positive, negative, or neutral sentiment of a given input text. This is extremely helpful if we want to analyze product reviews and identify product-quality issues from social streams, for example.

Let's implement this text classifier with Amazon Comprehend. As input data, we leverage a subset of the Amazon Customer Reviews Dataset. We want Amazon Comprehend to classify the sentiment of a provided review. The Comprehend UI is the easiest way to get started. We can paste in any text and Amazon Comprehend will analyze the input in real time using the built-in model. Let's test this with a sample product review such as "I loved it! I will recommend this to everyone." After clicking Analyze, we see the positive-sentiment prediction and prediction confidence score under the Insights tab. The score tells us that Amazon Comprehend is 99% confident that our sample review has a positive sentiment. Now let's implement a custom model that classifies our product reviews into star ratings again.

Train and Deploy a Custom Model with the Amazon Comprehend UI

Comprehend Custom is an example of automated machine learning that enables the practitioner to fine-tune Amazon Comprehend's built-in model to a specific dataset. Let's reuse the Amazon Customer Reviews Dataset file from the previous SageMaker Autopilot example as our training data:

```
star_rating,review_body
5,"GOOD, GREAT, WONDERFUL"
2,"It isn't as user friendly as TurboTax"
4,"Pretty easy to use. No issues."
…
```

We can use the Comprehend UI to train a custom multiclass text classifier by providing a name for the custom classifier, selecting multiclass mode, and putting in the path to the training data. Next, we define the S3 location to store the trained model outputs and select an IAM role with permissions to access that S3 location. Then, we click Train classifier to start the training process. We now see the custom classifier show up in the UI with the status `Submitted` and shortly after with the status `Training`.

Once the classifier shows up as `Trained`, we can deploy it as a Comprehend Endpoint to serve predictions. Simply select the trained model and click Actions. Give the endpoint a name and click Create Endpoint.In the Comprehend UI, navigate to Real-time analysis and select the analysis type Custom. Select the custom endpoint from the endpoint drop-down list. Amazon Comprehend can now analyze input text using the custom text classifier model. Let's paste in the review "Really bad. I hope they don't make this anymore." and click Analyze.

We can see in the results that our custom model now classifies input text into the star ratings from 1 to 5 (with 5 being the best rating). In this example, the model is 76% confident that the review classifies as star-rating 2.

In just a few clicks, we trained a Comprehend Custom model on the Amazon Customer Reviews Dataset to predict a star rating from review text. That is the power of Amazon AI services.

Train and Deploy a Custom Model with the Amazon Comprehend Python SDK

We can also interact programmatically with Amazon Comprehend. Let's use the Amazon Comprehend Python SDK to train and deploy the custom classifier:

```
import boto3
comprehend = boto3.client('comprehend')

# Create a unique timestamp ID to attach to our training job name
import datetime
id = str(datetime.datetime.now().strftime("%s"))

# Start training job
training_job = comprehend.create_document_classifier(
    DocumentClassifierName='Amazon-Customer-Reviews-Classifier-'+ id,
    DataAccessRoleArn=iam_role_comprehend_arn,
    InputDataConfig={
        'S3Uri': 's3://<bucket>/<path>/amazon_reviews.csv'
    },
    OutputDataConfig={
        'S3Uri': 's3://<bucket>/<path>/model/outputs'
    },
```

```
    LanguageCode='en'
)
```

The input parameters are as follows:

DocumentClassifierName
 The name of the custom model

DataAccessRoleArn
 The ARN of the IAM role that grants Amazon Comprehend read access to our
 input data

InputDataConfig
 Specifies the format and location of the training data (S3Uri: S3 path to the training data)

OutputDataConfig
 Specifies the location of the model outputs (S3Uri: S3 path for model outputs)

LanguageCode
 The language of the training data

The training job will now run for some time depending on the amount of training
data to process. Once it is finished, we can deploy an endpoint with our custom classifier to serve predictions.

To deploy the custom model, let's first find out the ARN of the model that we need to
reference:

```
model_arn = training_job['DocumentClassifierArn']
```

With the model_arn, we can now create a model endpoint:

```
inference_endpoint_response = comprehend.create_endpoint(
    EndpointName='comprehend-inference-endpoint',
    ModelArn = model_arn,
    DesiredInferenceUnits = 1
)
```

The input parameters are as follows:

EndpointName
 A name for our endpoint.

ModelArn
 The ARN of the model to which the endpoint will be attached.

`DesiredInferenceUnits`

The desired number of inference units to be used by the model attached to this endpoint. Each inference unit represents a throughput of one hundred characters per second.

Once the model endpoint is successfully created and In Service, we can invoke it for a sample prediction. To invoke the custom model, let's find out the ARN of our endpoint:

```
endpoint_arn = inference_endpoint_response["EndpointArn"]
```

We can now run a prediction using comprehend.classify_document() along with text we want to classify and the ARN of our endpoint:

```
# Sample text to classify
txt = """It's OK."""

response = comprehend.classify_document(
    Text= txt,
    EndpointArn = endpoint_arn
)
```

The JSON-formatted response will look similar to this:

```
{
  "Classes": [
    {
      "Name": "3",
      "Score": 0.977475643157959
    },
    {
      "Name": "4",
      "Score": 0.021228035911917686
    },
    {
      "Name": "2",
      "Score": 0.001270478474907577
    }
  ],
  ...
}
```

Our custom classifier is 97% confident that our sample review deserves a 3-star rating. And with just a few lines of Python code, we trained an Amazon Comprehend Custom model on the Amazon Customer Reviews Dataset to predict a star rating from review text.

Summary

In this chapter, we discussed the concept of AutoML. We introduced SageMaker Autopilot's transparent approach to AutoML. SageMaker Autopilot offloads the heavy lifting of building ML pipelines while providing full visibility into the automated process. We demonstrated how to invoke machine learning models from SQL queries using Amazon Athena. We also showed how Amazon Comprehend uses AutoML to train and deploy a custom text classification model based on the public Amazon Customer Reviews Dataset in just a few clicks or lines of Python code.

In the following chapters, we will dive deep into building a custom BERT-based text classifier with Amazon SageMaker and TensorFlow to classify product reviews from different sources, including social channels and partner websites.

## CHAPTER 4

Ingest Data into the Cloud

In this chapter, we will show how to ingest data into the cloud. For that purpose, we will look at a typical scenario in which an application writes files into an Amazon S3 data lake, which in turn needs to be accessed by the ML engineering/data science team as well as the business intelligence/data analyst team, as shown in Figure 4-1.

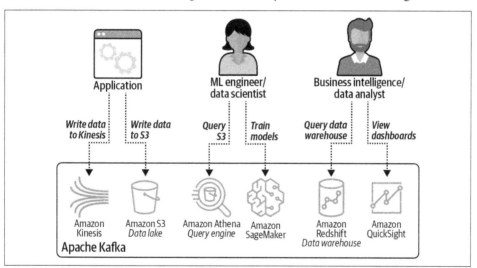

Figure 4-1. An application writes data into our S3 data lake for the data science, machine learning engineering, and business intelligence teams.

Amazon Simple Storage Service (Amazon S3) is fully managed object storage that offers extreme durability, high availability, and infinite data scalability at a very low cost. Hence, it is the perfect foundation for data lakes, training datasets, and models.

We will learn more about the advantages of building data lakes on Amazon S3 in the next section.

Let's assume our application continually captures data (i.e., customer interactions on our website, product review messages) and writes the data to S3 in the tab-separated values (TSV) file format.

As a data scientist or machine learning engineer, we want to quickly explore raw datasets. We will introduce Amazon Athena and show how to leverage Athena as an interactive query service to analyze data in S3 using standard SQL, without moving the data. In the first step, we will register the TSV data in our S3 bucket with Athena and then run some ad hoc queries on the dataset. We will also show how to easily convert the TSV data into the more query-optimized, columnar file format Apache Parquet.

Our business intelligence team might also want to have a subset of the data in a data warehouse, which they can then transform and query with standard SQL clients to create reports and visualize trends. We will introduce Amazon Redshift, a fully managed data warehouse service, and show how to insert TSV data into Amazon Redshift, as well as combine the data warehouse queries with the less frequently accessed data that's still in our S3 data lake via Amazon Redshift Spectrum. Our business intelligence team can also use Amazon Redshift's data lake export functionality to unload (transformed, enriched) data back into our S3 data lake in Parquet file format.

We will conclude this chapter with some tips and tricks for increasing performance using compression algorithms and reducing cost by leveraging S3 Intelligent-Tiering. In Chapter 12, we will dive deep into securing datasets, tracking data access, encrypting data at rest, and encrypting data in transit.

Data Lakes

In Chapter 3, we discussed the democratization of artificial intelligence and data science over the last few years, the explosion of data, and how cloud services provide the infrastructure agility to store and process data of any amount.

Yet, in order to use all this data efficiently, companies are tasked to break down existing data silos and find ways to analyze very diverse datasets, dealing with both structured and unstructured data while ensuring the highest standards of data governance, data security, and compliance with privacy regulations. These (big) data challenges set the stage for data lakes.

One of the biggest advantages of data lakes is that we don't need to predefine any schemas. We can store our raw data at scale and then decide later in which ways we need to process and analyze it. Data lakes may contain structured, semistructured, and unstructured data. Figure 4-2 shows the centralized and secure data lake repository that enables us to store, govern, discover, and share data at any scale—even in real time.

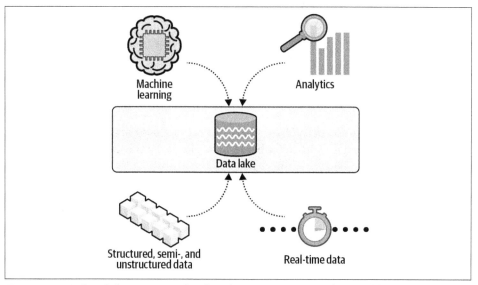

Figure 4-2. A data lake is a centralized and secure repository that enables us to store, govern, discover, and share data at any scale.

Data lakes provide a perfect base for data science and machine learning, as they give us access to large and diverse datasets to train and deploy more accurate models. Building a data lake typically consists of the following (high-level) steps, as shown in Figure 4-3:

1. Set up storage.
2. Move data.
3. Cleanse, prepare, and catalog data.
4. Configure and enforce security and compliance policies.
5. Make data available for analytics.

Each of those steps involves a range of tools and technologies. While we can build a data lake manually from the ground up, there are cloud services available to help us streamline this process, i.e., AWS Lake Formation.

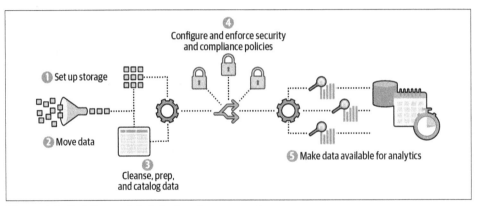

Figure 4-3. Building a data lake involves many steps.

Lake Formation (*https://oreil.ly/5HBtg*) collects and catalogs data from databases and object storage, moves data into an S3-based data lake, secures access to sensitive data, and deduplicates data using machine learning.

Additional capabilities of Lake Formation include row-level security, column-level security, and "governed" tables that support atomic, consistent, isolated, and durable transactions. With row-level and column-level permissions, users only see the data to which they have access. With Lake Formation transactions, users can concurrently and reliably insert, delete, and modify rows across the governed tables. Lake Formation also improves query performance by automatically compacting data storage and optimizing the data layout of governed tables.

S3 has become a popular choice for data lakes, as it offers many ways to ingest our data while enabling cost optimization with intelligent tiering of data, including cold storage and archiving capabilities. S3 also exposes many object-level controls for security and compliance.

On top of the S3 data lake, AWS implements the Lake House Architecture. The Lake House Architecture integrates our S3 data lake with our Amazon Redshift data warehouse for a unified governance model. We will see an example of this architecture in this chapter when we run a query joining data across our Amazon Redshift data warehouse with our S3 data lake.

From a data analysis perspective, another key benefit of storing our data in Amazon S3 is that it shortens the "time to insight" dramatically as we can run ad hoc queries directly on the data in S3. We don't have to go through complex transformation processes and data pipelines to get our data into traditional enterprise data warehouses, as we will see in the upcoming sections of this chapter.

Import Data into the S3 Data Lake

We are now ready to import our data into S3. We have chosen the Amazon Customer Reviews Dataset (*https://oreil.ly/jvgLz*) as the primary dataset for this book.

The Amazon Customer Reviews Dataset consists of more than 150+ million customer reviews of products across 43 different product categories on the Amazon.com website from 1995 until 2015. It is a great resource for demonstrating machine learning concepts such as natural language processing (NLP), as we demonstrate throughout this book.

Many of us have seen these customer reviews on Amazon.com when contemplating whether to purchase products via the Amazon.com marketplace. Figure 4-4 shows the product reviews section on Amazon.com for an Amazon Echo Dot device.

Figure 4-4. Reviews for an Amazon Echo Dot device. Source: Amazon.com.

Describe the Dataset

Customer reviews are one of Amazon's most valuable tools for customers looking to make informed purchase decisions. In Amazon's annual shareholder letters, Jeff Bezos (founder of Amazon) regularly elaborates on the importance of "word of mouth" as a customer acquisition tool. Jeff loves "customers' constant discontent," as he calls it:

> "We now offer customers…vastly more reviews, content, browsing options, and recommendation features…Word of mouth remains the most powerful customer acquisition tool we have, and we are grateful for the trust our customers have placed in us. Repeat purchases and word of mouth have combined to make Amazon.com the market leader in online bookselling."
>
> –Jeff Bezos, 1997 Shareholder ("Share Owner") Letter (*https://oreil.ly/mj8M0*)

Here is the schema for the dataset:

marketplace

Two-letter country code (in this case all "US").

customer_id

Random identifier that can be used to aggregate reviews written by a single author.

review_id

A unique ID for the review.

product_id

The Amazon Standard Identification Number (ASIN).

product_parent

The parent of that ASIN. Multiple ASINs (color or format variations of the same product) can roll up into a single product parent.

product_title

Title description of the product.

product_category

Broad product category that can be used to group reviews.

star_rating

The review's rating of 1 to 5 stars, where 1 is the worst and 5 is the best.

helpful_votes

Number of helpful votes for the review.

total_votes

Number of total votes the review received.

vine

Was the review written as part of the Vine program?

verified_purchase

Was the review from a verified purchase?

review_headline

The title of the review itself.

review_body

The text of the review.

review_date

The date the review was written.

The dataset is shared in a public Amazon S3 bucket and is available in two file formats:

- TSV, a text format: *s3://amazon-reviews-pds/tsv*
- Parquet, an optimized columnar binary format: *s3://amazon-reviews-pds/parquet*

The Parquet dataset is partitioned (divided into subfolders) by the column `product_category` to further improve query performance. With this, we can use a `WHERE` clause on `product_category` in our SQL queries to only read data specific to that category.

We can use the AWS Command Line Interface (AWS CLI) to list the S3 bucket content using the following CLI commands:

- `aws s3 ls s3://amazon-reviews-pds/tsv`
- `aws s3 ls s3://amazon-reviews-pds/parquet`

The AWS CLI tool provides a unified command line interface to Amazon Web Services. We can find more information on how to install and configure the tool (*https://aws.amazon.com/cli*).

The following listings show us the available dataset files in TSV format and the Parquet partitioning folder structure.

Dataset files in TSV format:

```
2017-11-24 13:49:53   648641286 amazon_reviews_us_Apparel_v1_00.tsv.gz
2017-11-24 13:56:36   582145299 amazon_reviews_us_Automotive_v1_00.tsv.gz
2017-11-24 14:04:02   357392893 amazon_reviews_us_Baby_v1_00.tsv.gz
2017-11-24 14:08:11   914070021 amazon_reviews_us_Beauty_v1_00.tsv.gz
2017-11-24 14:17:41  2740337188 amazon_reviews_us_Books_v1_00.tsv.gz
2017-11-24 14:45:50  2692708591 amazon_reviews_us_Books_v1_01.tsv.gz
2017-11-24 15:10:21  1329539135 amazon_reviews_us_Books_v1_02.tsv.gz
...
2017-11-25 08:39:15    94010685 amazon_reviews_us_Software_v1_00.tsv.gz
2017-11-27 10:36:58   872478735 amazon_reviews_us_Sports_v1_00.tsv.gz
2017-11-25 08:52:11   333782939 amazon_reviews_us_Tools_v1_00.tsv.gz
2017-11-25 09:06:08   838451398 amazon_reviews_us_Toys_v1_00.tsv.gz
2017-11-25 09:42:13  1512355451 amazon_reviews_us_Video_DVD_v1_00.tsv.gz
2017-11-25 10:50:22   475199894 amazon_reviews_us_Video_Games_v1_00.tsv.gz
2017-11-25 11:07:59   138929896 amazon_reviews_us_Video_v1_00.tsv.gz
2017-11-25 11:14:07   162973819 amazon_reviews_us_Watches_v1_00.tsv.gz
2017-11-26 15:24:07  1704713674 amazon_reviews_us_Wireless_v1_00.tsv.gz
```

Dataset files in Parquet format:

```
PRE product_category=Apparel/
                     PRE product_category=Automotive/
                     PRE product_category=Baby/
```

```
PRE product_category=Beauty/
PRE product_category=Books/
...
PRE product_category=Watches/
PRE product_category=Wireless/
```

Note that PRE stands for "prefix." For now, we can think of prefixes as folders in S3.

It is sometimes useful to use EXPLAIN in our queries to make sure the S3 partitions are being utilized. Spark, for example, will highlight which partitions are being used in Spark SQL. If our query patterns change over time, we may want to revisit updating the existing partitions—or even adding new partitions to match our business needs.

So which data format should we choose? The Parquet columnar file format is definitely preferred when running analytics queries since many analytics queries perform summary statistics (AVG, SUM, STDDEV, etc.) on columns of data. On the other hand, many applications write out data in simple CSV or TSV files, e.g., application log files. So let's actually assume we don't have the Parquet files ready to use as this allows us to show us how we can easily get there from CSV or TSV files.

In a first step, let's copy the TSV data from Amazon's public S3 bucket into a privately hosted S3 bucket to simulate that process, as shown in Figure 4-5.

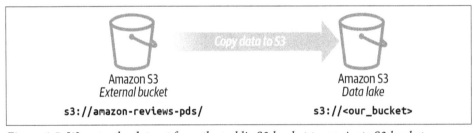

Figure 4-5. We copy the dataset from the public S3 bucket to a private S3 bucket.

We can use the AWS CLI tool again to perform the following steps.

1. Create a new private S3 bucket:

```
aws s3 mb s3://data-science-on-aws
```

2. Copy the content of the public S3 bucket to our newly created private S3 bucket as follows (only include the files starting with amazon_reviews_us_, i.e., skipping any index, multilingual, and sample data files in that directory):

```
aws s3 cp --recursive s3://amazon-reviews-pds/tsv/ \
        s3://data-science-on-aws/amazon-reviews-pds/tsv/ \
        --exclude "*" --include "amazon_reviews_us_*"
```

We are now ready to use Amazon Athena to register and query the data and transform the TSV files into Parquet.

Query the Amazon S3 Data Lake with Amazon Athena

Amazon Athena is an interactive query service that makes it easy to analyze data in Amazon S3 using standard SQL. With Athena, we can query raw data—including encrypted data—directly from our S3-based data lake. Athena separates compute from storage and lowers the overall time to insight for our business. When we register an Athena table with our S3 data, Athena stores the table-to-S3 mapping. Athena uses the AWS Glue Data Catalog, a Hive Metastore–compatible service, to store the table-to-S3 mapping. We can think of the AWS Glue Data Catalog as a persistent metadata store in our AWS account. Other AWS services, such as Athena and Amazon Redshift Spectrum, can use the data catalog to locate and query data. Apache Spark reads from the AWS Glue Data Catalog, as well.

Besides the data catalog, AWS Glue also provides tools to build ETL (extract-transform-load) workflows. ETL workflows could include the automatic discovery and extraction of data from different sources. We can leverage Glue Studio to visually compose and run ETL workflows without writing code. Glue Studio also provides the single pane of glass to monitor all ETL jobs. AWS Glue executes the workflows on an Apache Spark–based serverless ETL engine.

Athena queries run in parallel inside a dynamically scaled, serverless query engine. Athena will automatically scale the cluster depending on the query and dataset involved. This makes Athena extremely fast on large datasets and frees the user from worrying about infrastructure details.

In addition, Athena supports the Parquet columnar file format with tens of millions of partitions (i.e., by `product_category`, `year`, or `marketplace`) to improve the performance of our queries. For example, if we plan to run frequent queries that group the results by `product_category`, then we should create a partition in Athena for `product_category`. Upon creation, Athena will update the AWS Glue Data Catalog accordingly so that future queries will inherit the performance benefits of this new partition.

Athena is based on Presto, an open source, distributed SQL query engine designed for fast, ad hoc data analytics on large datasets. Similar to Apache Spark, Presto (*https://oreil.ly/WKcDS*) uses high-RAM clusters to perform its queries. However, Presto does not require a large amount of disk as it is designed for ad hoc queries (versus automated, repeatable queries) and therefore does not perform the checkpointing required for fault tolerance.

For longer-running Athena jobs, we can listen for query-completion events using Amazon CloudWatch Events. When the query completes, all listeners are notified with the event details, including query success status, total execution time, and total bytes scanned.

With a functionality called *Athena Federated Query*, we can also run SQL queries across data stored in relational databases, such as Amazon RDS and Aurora, nonrelational databases such as DynamoDB, object storage such as Amazon S3, and custom data sources. This gives us a unified analytics view across data stored in our data warehouse, data lake, and operational databases without the need to actually move the data.

We can access Athena via the AWS Management Console, an API, or an Open Database Connectivity (ODBC) or Java Database Connectivity (JDBC) driver for programmatic access. Let's take a look at how to use Amazon Athena via the AWS Management Console.

Access Athena from the AWS Console

To use Amazon Athena, we first need to quickly set up the service. First, click on Amazon Athena in the AWS Management Console. If we are asked to set up a "query result" location for Athena in S3, specify an S3 location for the query results (e.g., *s3://<BUCKET>/data-science-on-aws/athena/query-results.*)

In the next step, we create a database. In the Athena Query Editor, we see a query pane with an example query. We can start typing our query anywhere in the query pane. To create our database, enter the following CREATE DATABASE statement, run the query, and confirm that dsoaws appears in the DATABASE list in the Catalog dashboard:

```
CREATE DATABASE dsoaws;
```

When we run CREATE DATABASE and CREATE TABLE queries in Athena with the AWS Glue Data Catalog as our source, we automatically see the database and table metadata entries being created in the AWS Glue Data Catalog.

Register S3 Data as an Athena Table

Now that we have a database, we are ready to create a table based on the Amazon Customer Reviews Dataset. We define the columns that map to the data, specify how the data is delimited, and provide the Amazon S3 path to the data.

Let's define a "schema-on-read" to avoid the need to predefine a rigid schema when data is written and ingested. In the Athena Console, make sure that dsoaws is selected for DATABASE and then choose New Query. Run the following SQL statement to read the compressed (compression=gzip) files and skip the CSV header (skip.header.line.count=1) at the top of each file. After running the SQL statement, verify that the newly created table, amazon_reviews_tsv, appears on the left under Tables:

```
CREATE EXTERNAL TABLE IF NOT EXISTS dsoaws.amazon_reviews_tsv(
        marketplace string,
        customer_id string,
        review_id string,
        product_id string,
        product_parent string,
        product_title string,
        product_category string,
        star_rating int,
        helpful_votes int,
        total_votes int,
        vine string,
        verified_purchase string,
        review_headline string,
        review_body string,
        review_date string
) ROW FORMAT DELIMITED FIELDS TERMINATED BY '\t'
LINES TERMINATED BY '\n'
LOCATION 's3://data-science-on-aws/amazon-reviews-pds/tsv'
TBLPROPERTIES ('compressionType'='gzip', 'skip.header.line.count'='1')
```

Let's run a sample query like this to check if everything works correctly. This query will produce the results shown in the following table:

```
SELECT *
FROM dsoaws.amazon_reviews_tsv
WHERE product_category = 'Digital_Video_Download' LIMIT 10
```

marketplace	customer_id	review_id	product_id	product_title	product_category
US	12190288	R3FBDHSJD	B00AYB23D	Enlightened	Digital_Video_Download
...	...	...	...	...	...

Update Athena Tables as New Data Arrives with AWS Glue Crawler

The following code crawls S3 every night at 23:59 UTC and updates the Athena table as new data arrives. If we add another *.tar.gz* file to S3, for example, we will see the new data in our Athena queries after the crawler completes its scheduled run:

```
glue = boto3.Session().client(service_name='glue', region_name=region)

create_response = glue.create_crawler(
    Name='amazon_reviews_crawler',
    Role=role,
    DatabaseName='dsoaws',
    Description='Amazon Customer Reviews Dataset Crawler',
    Targets={
        'CatalogTargets': [
            {
                'DatabaseName': 'dsoaws',
                'Tables': [
                    'amazon_reviews_tsv',
```

```
            ]
        }
    ]
},
Schedule='cron(59 23 * * ? *)', # run every night at 23:59 UTC
SchemaChangePolicy={
    'DeleteBehavior': 'LOG'
},
RecrawlPolicy={
    'RecrawlBehavior': 'CRAWL_EVERYTHING'
}
)
```

Create a Parquet-Based Table in Athena

In a next step, we will show how we can easily convert that data into the Apache Parquet columnar file format to improve query performance. Parquet is optimized for
columnar-based queries such as counts, sums, averages, and other aggregation-based
summary statistics that focus on the column values versus row information.

By storing our data in columnar format, Parquet performs sequential reads for columnar summary statistics. This results in much more efficient data access and
"mechanical sympathy" versus having the disk controller jump from row to row and
having to reseek to retrieve the column data. If we are doing any type of large-scale
data analytics, we should be using a columnar file format like Parquet. We discuss the
benefits of Parquet in the performance section.

 While we already have the data in Parquet format from the public
dataset, we feel that creating a Parquet table is an important-
enough topic to demonstrate in this book.

Again, make sure that dsoaws is selected for DATABASE and then choose New Query
and run the following CREATE TABLE AS (CTAS) SQL statement:

```
CREATE TABLE IF NOT EXISTS dsoaws.amazon_reviews_parquet
WITH (format = 'PARQUET', \
      external_location = 's3://<BUCKET>/amazon-reviews-pds/parquet', \
      partitioned_by = ARRAY['product_category']) AS

SELECT marketplace,
       customer_id,
       review_id,
       product_id,
       product_parent,
       product_title,
       star_rating,
       helpful_votes,
```

```
            total_votes,
            vine,
            verified_purchase,
            review_headline,
            review_body,
            CAST(YEAR(DATE(review_date)) AS INTEGER) AS year,
            DATE(review_date) AS review_date,
            product_category

    FROM dsoaws.amazon_reviews_tsv
```

As we can see from the query, we're also adding a new year column to our dataset by converting the review_date string to a date format and then casting the year out of the date. Let's store the year value as an integer. After running the CTAS query, we should now see the newly created table amazon_reviews_parquet appear as well on the left under Tables. As a last step, we need to load the Parquet partitions. To do so, just issue the following SQL command:

```
MSCK REPAIR TABLE amazon_reviews_parquet;
```

We can automate the MSCK REPAIR TABLE command to load the partitions after data ingest from any workflow manager (or use an Lambda function that runs when new data is uploaded to S3).

We can run our sample query again to check if everything works correctly:

```
SELECT *
FROM dsoaws.amazon_reviews_parquet
WHERE product_category = 'Digital_Video_Download' LIMIT 10
```

Both tables also have metadata entries in the Hive Metastore–compatible AWS Glue Data Catalog. This metadata defines the schema used by many query and data-processing engines, such as Amazon EMR, Athena, Redshift, Kinesis, SageMaker, and Apache Spark.

In just a few steps, we have set up Amazon Athena to transform the TSV dataset files into the Apache Parquet file format. The query on the Parquet files finished in a fraction of the time compared to the query on the TSV files. We accelerated our query response time by leveraging the columnar Parquet file format and product_category partition scheme.

Continuously Ingest New Data with AWS Glue Crawler

New data is always arriving from applications, and we need a way to register this new data into our system for analytics and model-training purposes. AWS Glue provides sophisticated data-cleansing and machine-learning transformations, including "fuzzy" record deduplication. One way to register the new data from S3 into our AWS Glue Data Catalog is with a Glue Crawler, as shown in Figure 4-6.

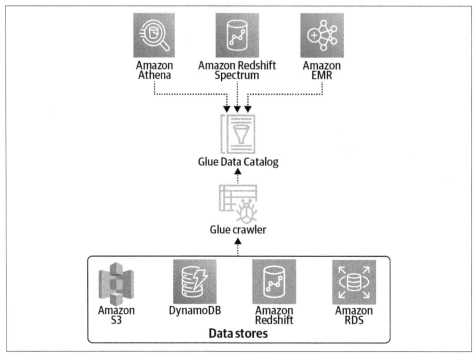

Figure 4-6. Ingest and register data from various data sources with AWS Glue Crawler.

We can trigger the crawler either periodically on a schedule or with, for example, an S3 trigger. The following code creates the crawler and schedules new S3 folders (prefixes) to be ingested every night at 23:59 UTC:

```
create_response = glue.create_crawler(
    Name='amazon_reviews_crawler',
    Role=role,
    DatabaseName='dsoaws',
    Description='Amazon Customer Reviews Dataset Crawler',
    Targets={
        'CatalogTargets': [
            {
                'DatabaseName': 'dsoaws',
                'Tables': [
                    'amazon_reviews_tsv',
                ]
            }
        ]
    },
    Schedule='cron(59 23 * * ? *)',
     SchemaChangePolicy={
```

```
        'DeleteBehavior': 'LOG'
    },
    RecrawlPolicy={
        'RecrawlBehavior': 'CRAWL_NEW_FOLDERS_ONLY'
    }
)
```

This assumes that we are storing new data in new folders. Typically, we use an S3 prefix that includes the year, month, day, hour, quarter hour, etc. For example, we can store application logs in hourly S3 folders with the following naming convention for the S3 prefix: *s3://<S3_BUCKET>/<YEAR>/<MONTH>/<DAY>/<HOUR>/*. If we want to crawl all of the data, we can use CRAWL_EVERYTHING for our RecrawlBehavior. We can change the schedule using a different cron() trigger. We can also add a second trigger to start an ETL job to transform and load new data when the scheduled Glue Crawler reaches the SUCCEEDED state.

Build a Lake House with Amazon Redshift Spectrum

One of the fundamental differences between data lakes and data warehouses is that while we ingest and store huge amounts of raw, unprocessed data in our data lake, we normally only load some fraction of our recent data into the data warehouse. Depending on our business and analytics use case, this might be data from the past couple of months, a year, or maybe the past two years. Let's assume we want to have the past two years of our Amazon Customer Reviews Dataset in a data warehouse to analyze year-over-year customer behavior and review trends. We will use Amazon Redshift as our data warehouse for this.

Amazon Redshift is a fully managed data warehouse that allows us to run complex analytic queries against petabytes of structured data, semistructured, and JSON data. Our queries are distributed and parallelized across multiple nodes. In contrast to relational databases, which are optimized to store data in rows and mostly serve transactional applications, Amazon Redshift implements columnar data storage, which is optimized for analytical applications where we are mostly interested in the data within the individual columns.

Amazon Redshift also includes Amazon Redshift Spectrum, which allows us to directly execute SQL queries from Amazon Redshift against exabytes of unstructured data in our Amazon S3 data lake without the need to physically move the data. Amazon Redshift Spectrum is part of the Lake House Architecture that unifies our S3 data lake and Amazon Redshift data warehouse—including shared security and row-and-column-based access control. Amazon Redshift Spectrum supports various open source storage frameworks, including Apache Hudi and Delta Lake.

Since Amazon Redshift Spectrum automatically scales the compute resources needed based on how much data is being retrieved, queries against Amazon S3 run fast, regardless of the size of our data. Amazon Redshift Spectrum will use pushdown filters, bloom filters, and materialized views to reduce seek time and increase query performance on external data stores like S3. We discuss more performance tips later in "Reduce Cost and Increase Performance" on page 119.

Amazon Redshift Spectrum converts traditional ETL into extract-load-transform (ELT) by transforming and cleaning data after it is loaded into Amazon Redshift. We will use Amazon Redshift Spectrum to access our data in S3 and then show how to combine data that is stored in Amazon Redshift with data that is still in S3.

This might sound similar to the approach we showed earlier with Amazon Athena, but note that in this case we show how our business intelligence team can enrich their queries with data that is not stored in the data warehouse itself. Once we have our Redshift cluster set up and configured, we can navigate to the AWS Console and Amazon Redshift and then click on Query Editor to execute commands.

We can leverage our previously created table in Amazon Athena with its metadata and schema information stored in the AWS Glue Data Catalog to access our data in S3 through Amazon Redshift Spectrum. All we need to do is create an external schema in Amazon Redshift, point it to our AWS Glue Data Catalog, and point Amazon Redshift to the database we've created.

In the Amazon Redshift Query Editor (or via any other ODBC/JDBC SQL client that we might prefer to use), execute the following command:

```
CREATE EXTERNAL SCHEMA IF NOT EXISTS athena FROM DATA CATALOG
    DATABASE 'dsoaws'
    IAM_ROLE '<IAM-ROLE>'
    CREATE EXTERNAL DATABASE IF NOT EXISTS
```

With this command, we are creating a new schema in Amazon Redshift called athena to highlight the data access we set up through our tables in Amazon Athena:

- FROM DATA CATALOG indicates that the external database is defined in the AWS Glue Data Catalog.

- DATABASE refers to our previously created database in the AWS Glue Data Catalog.

- IAM_ROLE needs to point to an Amazon Resource Name (ARN) for an IAM role that our cluster uses for authentication and authorization.

IAM is the AWS Identity and Access Management service, which enables us to manage and control access to AWS services and resources in our account. With an IAM role, we can specify the permissions a user or service is granted. In this example, the IAM role must have at a minimum permission to perform a LIST operation on the Amazon S3 bucket to be accessed and a GET operation on the Amazon S3 objects the bucket contains. If the external database is defined in an Amazon Athena data catalog, the IAM role must have permission to access Athena unless `CATALOG_ROLE` is specified. We will go into more details on IAM in a later section of this chapter when we discuss how we can secure our data.

If we now select `athena` in the Schema dropdown menu in the Amazon Redshift Query Editor, we can see that our two tables, `amazon_reviews_tsv` and `amazon_reviews_parquet`, appear, which we created with Amazon Athena. Let's run a sample query again to make sure everything works. In the Query Editor, run the following command:

```
SELECT
    product_category,
    COUNT(star_rating) AS count_star_rating
FROM
    athena.amazon_reviews_tsv
GROUP BY
    product_category
ORDER BY
    count_star_rating DESC
```

We should see results similar to the following table:

product_category	count_star_rating
Books	19531329
Digital_Ebook_Purchase	17622415
Wireless	9002021
...	...

So with just one command, we now have access and can query our S3 data lake from Amazon Redshift without moving any data into our data warehouse. This is the power of Amazon Redshift Spectrum.

But now, let's actually copy some data from S3 into Amazon Redshift. Let's pull in customer reviews data from the year 2015.

First, we create another Amazon Redshift schema called `redshift` with the following SQL command:

```
CREATE SCHEMA IF NOT EXISTS redshift
```

Next, we will create a new table that represents our customer reviews data. We will also add a new column and add `year` to our table:

```
CREATE TABLE IF NOT EXISTS redshift.amazon_reviews_tsv_2015(
    marketplace varchar(2) ENCODE zstd,
    customer_id varchar(8) ENCODE zstd,
    review_id varchar(14) ENCODE zstd,
    product_id varchar(10) ENCODE zstd DISTKEY,
    product_parent varchar(10) ENCODE zstd,
```

```
        product_title varchar(400) ENCODE zstd,
        product_category varchar(24) ENCODE raw,
        star_rating int ENCODE az64,
        helpful_votes int ENCODE zstd,
        total_votes int ENCODE zstd,
        vine varchar(1) ENCODE zstd,
        verified_purchase varchar(1) ENCODE zstd,
        review_headline varchar(128) ENCODE zstd,
        review_body varchar(65535) ENCODE zstd,
        review_date varchar(10) ENCODE bytedict,
        year int ENCODE az64)  SORTKEY (product_category)
```

In the performance section, we will dive deep into the SORTKEY, DISTKEY, and ENCODE attributes. For now, let's copy the data from S3 into our new Amazon Redshift table and run some sample queries.

For such bulk inserts, we can either use a COPY command or an INSERT INTO command. In general, the COPY command is preferred, as it loads data in parallel and more efficiently from Amazon S3, or other supported data sources.

If we are loading data or a subset of data from one table into another, we can use the INSERT INTO command with a SELECT clause for high-performance data insertion. As we're loading our data from the athena.amazon_reviews_tsv table, let's choose this option:

```
INSERT
INTO
    redshift.amazon_reviews_tsv_2015
    SELECT
        marketplace,
        customer_id,
        review_id,
        product_id,
        product_parent,
        product_title,
        product_category,
        star_rating,
        helpful_votes,
        total_votes,
        vine,
        verified_purchase,
        review_headline,
        review_body,
        review_date,
        CAST(DATE_PART_YEAR(TO_DATE(review_date,
        'YYYY-MM-DD')) AS INTEGER) AS year
    FROM
        athena.amazon_reviews_tsv
    WHERE
        year = 2015
```

We use a date conversion to parse the year out of our `review_date` column and store it in a separate `year` column, which we then use to filter records from 2015. This is an example of how we can simplify ETL tasks, as we put our data transformation logic directly in a `SELECT` query and ingest the result into Amazon Redshift.

Another way to optimize our tables would be to create them as a sequence of time-series tables, especially when our data has a fixed retention period. Let's say we want to store data of the last two years (24 months) in our data warehouse and update with new data once a month.

If we create one table per month, we can easily remove old data by running a `DROP TABLE` command on the corresponding table. This approach is much faster than running a large-scale `DELETE` process and also saves us from having to run a subsequent `VACUUM` process to reclaim space and resort the rows.

To combine query results across tables, we can use a `UNION ALL` view. Similarly, when we need to delete old data, we remove the dropped table from the `UNION ALL` view.

Here is an example of a `UNION ALL` view across two tables with customer reviews from years 2014 and 2015—assuming we have one table each for 2014 and 2015 data. The following table shows the results of the query:

```
SELECT
    product_category,
    COUNT(star_rating) AS count_star_rating,
    year
FROM
    redshift.amazon_reviews_tsv_2014
GROUP BY
    redshift.amazon_reviews_tsv_2014.product_category,
    year
UNION
ALL SELECT
    product_category,
    COUNT(star_rating) AS count_star_rating,
    year
FROM
    redshift.amazon_reviews_tsv_2015
GROUP BY
    redshift.amazon_reviews_tsv_2015.product_category,
    year
ORDER BY
    count_star_rating DESC,
    year ASC
```

product_category	count_star_rating	year
Digital_Ebook_Purchase	6615914	2014
Digital_Ebook_Purchase	4533519	2015

product_category	count_star_rating	year
Books	3472631	2014
Wireless	2998518	2015
Wireless	2830482	2014
Books	2808751	2015
Apparel	2369754	2015
Home	2172297	2015
Apparel	2122455	2014
Home	1999452	2014

Now, let's actually run a query and combine data from Amazon Redshift with data that is still in S3. Let's take the data from the previous query for the years 2015 and 2014 and query Athena/S3 for the years 2013–1995 by running this command:

```
SELECT
    year,
    product_category,
    COUNT(star_rating) AS count_star_rating
FROM
    redshift.amazon_reviews_tsv_2015
GROUP BY
    redshift.amazon_reviews_tsv_2015.product_category,
    year
UNION
ALL SELECT
    year,
    product_category,
    COUNT(star_rating) AS count_star_rating
FROM
    redshift.amazon_reviews_tsv_2014
GROUP BY
    redshift.amazon_reviews_tsv_2014.product_category,
    year
UNION
ALL SELECT
    CAST(DATE_PART_YEAR(TO_DATE(review_date,
    'YYYY-MM-DD')) AS INTEGER) AS year,
    product_category,
    COUNT(star_rating) AS count_star_rating
FROM
    athena.amazon_reviews_tsv
WHERE
    year <= 2013
GROUP BY
    athena.amazon_reviews_tsv.product_category,
    year
ORDER BY
    product_category ASC,
    year DESC
```

year	product_category	count_star_rating
2015	Apparel	4739508
2014	Apparel	4244910
2013	Apparel	854813
2012	Apparel	273694
2011	Apparel	109323
2010	Apparel	57332
2009	Apparel	42967
2008	Apparel	33761
2007	Apparel	25986
2006	Apparel	7293
2005	Apparel	3533
2004	Apparel	2357
2003	Apparel	2147
2002	Apparel	907
2001	Apparel	5
2000	Apparel	6
2015	Automotive	2609750
2014	Automotive	2350246

Export Amazon Redshift Data to S3 Data Lake as Parquet

Amazon Redshift Data Lake Export gives us the ability to unload the result of an Amazon Redshift query to our S3 data lake in the optimized Apache Parquet columnar file format. This enables us to share any data transformation and enrichment we have done in Amazon Redshift back into our S3 data lake in an open format. Unloaded data is automatically registered in the AWS Glue Data Catalog to be used by any Hive Metastore–compatible query engines, including Amazon Athena, EMR, Kinesis, SageMaker, and Apache Spark.

We can specify one or more partition columns so that unloaded data is automatically partitioned into folders in our Amazon S3 bucket. For example, we can choose to unload our customer reviews data and partition it by product_category.

We can simply run the following SQL command to unload our 2015 customer reviews data in Parquet file format into S3, partitioned by product_category:

```
UNLOAD (
    'SELECT marketplace, customer_id, review_id, product_id, product_parent,
        product_title, product_category, star_rating, helpful_votes, total_votes,
        vine, verified_purchase, review_headline, review_body, review_date, year
        FROM redshift.amazon_reviews_tsv_2015')
TO 's3://data-science-on-aws/amazon-reviews-pds/parquet-from-redshift/2015'
IAM_ROLE '<IAM_ROLE>'
```

```
PARQUET PARALLEL ON
PARTITION BY (product_category)
```

We can use the AWS CLI tool again to list the S3 folder and see our unloaded data from 2015 in Parquet format:

```
aws s3 ls s3://data-science-on-aws/amazon-reviews-pds/parquet-from-redshift/2015
```

Share Data Between Amazon Redshift Clusters

Amazon Redshift also implements a data sharing capability that allows us to securely share live data across Amazon Redshift clusters without the need to move data. Instead, we create a "data share" object that specifies the data to share and the list of Amazon Redshift clusters that are allowed to access the data. On the consuming Amazon Redshift cluster, we create a new database from the data share object and assign permissions to the relevant IAM users and groups to manage access to the database. The data sharing capability is useful if we need to share data among multiple business units, or if we want to share data from a central data warehouse cluster with additional BI and analytics clusters.

Choose Between Amazon Athena and Amazon Redshift

Amazon Athena is the preferred choice when running ad hoc SQL queries on data that is stored in Amazon S3. It doesn't require us to set up or manage any infrastructure resources—we don't need to move any data. It supports structured, unstructured, and semistructured data. With Athena, we are defining a "schema on read"—we basically just log in, create a table, and start running queries.

Amazon Redshift is targeted for modern data analytics on petabytes of structured data. Here, we need to have a predefined "schema on write." Unlike serverless Athena, Amazon Redshift requires us to create a cluster (compute and storage resources), ingest the data, and build tables before we can start to query but caters to performance and scale. So for highly relational data with a transactional nature (data gets updated), workloads that involve complex joins, or subsecond latency requirements, Amazon Redshift is the right choice.

Athena and Amazon Redshift are optimized for read-heavy analytics workloads; they are not replacements for write-heavy, relational databases such as Amazon Relational Database Service (RDS) and Aurora. At a high level, use Athena for exploratory analytics and operational debugging; use Amazon Redshift for business-critical reports and dashboards.

Reduce Cost and Increase Performance

In this section, we want to provide some tips and tricks to reduce cost and increase performance during data ingestion, including file formats, partitions, compression, and sort/distribution keys. We will also demonstrate how to use Amazon S3 Intelligent-Tiering to lower our storage bill.

S3 Intelligent-Tiering

We introduced Amazon S3 in this chapter as a scalable, durable storage service for building shared datasets, such as data lakes in the cloud. And while we keep the S3 usage fairly simple in this book, the service actually offers us a variety of options to optimize our storage cost as our data grows.

Depending on our data's access frequency patterns and service-level agreement (SLA) needs, we can choose from various Amazon S3 storage classes. Table 4-1 compares the Amazon S3 storage classes in terms of data access frequency and data retrieval time.

Table 4-1. Comparison of Amazon S3 storage classes

From frequent access				To infrequent access	
S3 Standard (default storage class)	S3 Intelligent-Tiering	S3 Standard-IA	S3 One Zone-IA	Amazon S3 Glacier	Amazon S3 Glacier Deep Archive
General-purpose storage Active, frequently accessed data Access in milliseconds	Data with unknown or changing access patterns Access in milliseconds Opt in for automatic archiving	Infrequently accessed (IA) data Access in milliseconds	Lower durability (one Zvailability zone) Re-creatable data Access in milliseconds	Archive data Access in minutes or hours	Long-term archive data Access in hours

But how do we know which objects to move? Imagine our S3 data lake has grown over time and we possibly have billions of objects across several S3 buckets in the S3 Standard storage class. Some of those objects are extremely important, while we haven't accessed others maybe in months or even years. This is where S3 Intelligent-Tiering comes into play.

Amazon S3 Intelligent-Tiering automatically optimizes our storage cost for data with changing access patterns by moving objects between the frequent-access tier optimized for frequent use of data and the lower-cost infrequent-access tier optimized for less-accessed data. Intelligent-Tiering monitors our access patterns and auto-tiers on a granular object level without performance impact or any operational overhead.

Parquet Partitions and Compression

Athena supports the Parquet columnar format for large-scale analytics workloads. Parquet enables the following performance optimizations for our queries:

Partitions and pushdowns

Partitions are physical groupings of data on disk to match our query patterns (i.e., `SELECT * FROM reviews WHERE product_category='Books'`). Modern query engines like Athena, Amazon Redshift, and Apache Spark will "pushdown" the `WHERE` into the physical storage system to allow the disk controller to seek once and read all relevant data in one scan without randomly skipping to different areas of the disk. This improves query performance even with solid state drives (SSDs), which have a lower seek time than traditional, media-based disks.

Dictionary encoding/compression

When a small number of categorical values are stored together on disk (i.e., `prod uct_category`, which has 43 total values in our dataset), the values can be compressed into a small number of bits to represent each value (i.e., `Books`, `Lawn_and_Garden`, `Software`, etc.) versus storing the entire string.

Type compression

When values of a similar type (i.e., String, Date, Integer) are stored together on disk, the values can be compressed together: (String, String), (Date, Date), (Integer, Integer). This compression is more efficient than if the values were stored separately on disk in a row-wise manner: (String, Date, Integer), (String, Date, Integer)

Vectorized aggregations

Because column values are stored together on disk, the disk controller needs to only perform one disk seek to find the beginning of the data. From that point, it will scan the data to perform the aggregation. Additionally, modern chips/processors offer high-performance vectorization instructions to perform calculations on large amounts of data versus flushing data in and out of the various data caches (L1, L2) or main memory.

See an example of row versus columnar data format in Figure 4-7.

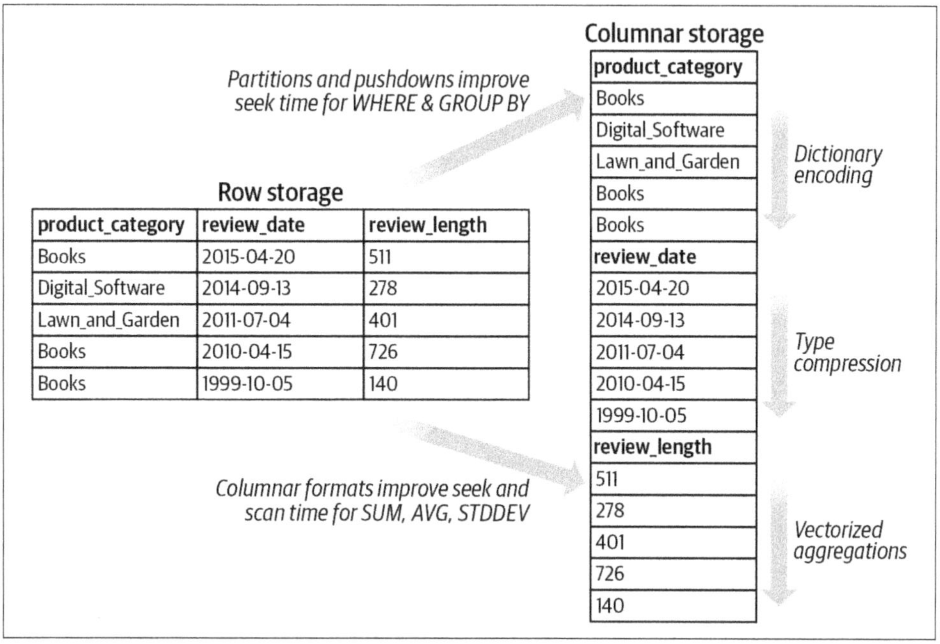

Figure 4-7. Using a columnar data format such as Parquet, we can apply various performance optimizations for query execution and data encoding.

Amazon Redshift Table Design and Compression

Here is the CREATE TABLE statement that we used to create the Amazon Redshift tables:

```
CREATE TABLE IF NOT EXISTS redshift.amazon_reviews_tsv_2015(
         marketplace varchar(2) ENCODE zstd,
         customer_id varchar(8) ENCODE zstd,
         review_id varchar(14) ENCODE zstd,
         product_id varchar(10) ENCODE zstd DISTKEY,
         product_parent varchar(9) ENCODE zstd,
         product_title varchar(400) ENCODE zstd,
         product_category varchar(24) ENCODE raw,
         star_rating int ENCODE az64,
         helpful_votes int ENCODE zstd,
         total_votes int ENCODE zstd,
         vine varchar(1) ENCODE zstd,
         verified_purchase varchar(1) ENCODE zstd,
         review_headline varchar(128) ENCODE zstd,
         review_body varchar(65535) ENCODE zstd,
         review_date varchar(10) ENCODE bytedict,
         year int ENCODE az64)  SORTKEY (product_category)
```

When we create a table, we can specify one or more columns as the SORTKEY. Amazon Redshift stores the data on disk in sorted order according to the SORTKEY. Hence, we can optimize our table by choosing a SORTKEY that reflects our most frequently used query types. If we query a lot of recent data, we can specify a timestamp column as the SORTKEY. If we frequently query based on range or equality filtering on one column, we should choose that column as the SORTKEY. As we are going to run a lot of queries in the next chapter filtering on product_category, let's choose that one as our SORTKEY.

 Amazon Redshift Advisor continuously recommends SORTKEYs for frequently queried tables. Advisor will generate an ALTER TABLE command that we run without having to re-create the tables—without impacting concurrent read and write queries. Note that Advisor does not provide recommendations if it doesn't see enough data (queries) or if the benefits are relatively small.

We can also define a distribution style for every table. When we load data into a table, Amazon Redshift distributes the rows of the table among our cluster nodes according to the table's distribution style. When we perform a query, the query optimizer redistributes the rows to the cluster nodes as needed to perform any joins and aggregations. So our goal should be to optimize the rows distribution to minimize data movements. There are three distribution styles from which we can choose:

KEY *distribution*
Distribute the rows according to the values in one column.

ALL *distribution*
Distribute a copy of the entire table to every node.

EVEN *distribution*
The rows are distributed across all nodes in a round-robin fashion, which is the default distribution style.

For our table, we've chosen KEY distribution based on product_id, as this column has a high cardinality, shows an even distribution, and can be used to join with other tables.

At any time, we can use EXPLAIN on our Amazon Redshift queries to make sure the DISTKEY and SORTKEY are being utilized. If our query patterns change over time, we may want to revisit changing these keys.

In addition, we are using compression for most columns to reduce the overall storage footprint and reduce our cost. Table 4-2 analyzes the compression used for each Amazon Redshift column in our schema.

Table 4-2. Compression types used in our Amazon Redshift table

Column	Data type	Encoding	Explanation
marketplace	varchar(2)	zstd	Low cardinality, too small for higher compression overhead
customer_id	varchar(8)	zstd	High cardinality, relatively few repeat values
review_id	varchar(14)	zstd	Unique, unbounded cardinality, no repeat values
product_id	varchar(10)	zstd	Unbounded cardinality, relatively low number of repeat values
product_parent	varchar(10)	zstd	Unbounded cardinality, relatively low number of repeat words
product_title	varchar(400)	zstd	Unbounded cardinality, relatively low number of repeat words
product_category	varchar(24)	raw	Low cardinality, many repeat values, but first SORT key is raw
star_rating	int	az64	Low cardinality, many repeat values
helpful_votes	int	zstd	Relatively high cardinality
total_votes	int	zstd	Relatively high cardinality
vine	varchar(1)	zstd	Low cardinality, too small to incur higher compression overhead
verified_purchase	varchar(1)	zstd	Low cardinality, too small to incur higher compression overhead
review_headline	varchar(128)	zstd	Varying length text, high cardinality, low repeat words
review_body	varchar(65535)	zstd	Varying length text, high cardinality, low repeat words
review_date	varchar(10)	bytedict	Fixed length, relatively low cardinality, many repeat values
year	int	az64	Low cardinality, many repeat values

While AWS CEO Andy Jassy maintains "there is no compression algorithm for experience," there is a compression algorithm for data. Compression is a powerful tool for the ever-growing world of big data. All modern big data processing tools are compression-friendly, including Amazon Athena, Redshift, Parquet, pandas, and Apache Spark. Using compression on small values such as varchar(1) may not improve performance. However, due to native hardware support, there are almost no drawbacks to using compression.

zstd is a generic compression algorithm that works across many different data types and column sizes. The star_rating and year fields are set to the default az64 encoding applied to most numeric and date fields. For most columns, we gain a quick win by using the default az64 encoding for integers and overriding the default lzo encoding in favor of the flexible zstd encoding for everything else, including text.

We are using bytedict for review_date to perform dictionary encoding on the string-based dates (YYYY-MM-DD). While it seemingly has a large number of unique values, review_date actually contains a small number of unique values because there are only ~7,300 (365 days per year × 20 years) days in a 20-year span. This cardinality is low enough to capture all of the possible dates in just a few bits versus using a full varchar(10) for each date.

While `product_category` is a great candidate for `bytedict` dictionary encoding, it is our first (and only, in this case) SORTKEY. As a performance best practice, the first SORTKEY should not be compressed.

While `marketplace`, `product_category`, `vine`, and `verified_purchase` seem to be good candidates for `bytedict`, they are too small to benefit from the extra overhead. For now, we leave them as `zstd`.

If we have an existing Amazon Redshift table to optimize, we can run the ANALYZE COMPRESSION command in Amazon Redshift to generate a report of suggested compression encodings as follows:

```
ANALYZE COMPRESSION redshift.customer_reviews_tsv_2015
```

The result will be a table like the following showing the % improvement in compression if we switch to another encoding:

Column	Encoding	Estimated reduction (%)
marketplace	zstd	90.84
customer_id	zstd	38.88
review_id	zstd	36.56
product_id	zstd	44.15
product_parent	zstd	44.03
product_title	zstd	30.72
product_category	zstd	99.95
star_rating	az64	0
helpful_votes	zstd	47.58
total_votes	zstd	39.75
vine	zstd	85.03
verified_purchase	zstd	73.09
review_headline	zstd	30.55
review_body	zstd	32.19
review_date	bytedict	64.1
year	az64	0

We performed this analysis on a version of the CREATE TABLE that did not specify any ENCODE attributes. By default, Amazon Redshift will use `az64` for numerics/dates and `lzo` for everything else (hence the 0% gain for the `az64` suggestions). We can also use the ALTER TABLE statement to change the compression used for each column.

Keep in mind that these are just suggestions and not always appropriate for our specific environment. We should try different encodings for our dataset and query the STV_BLOCKLIST table to compare the % reduction in physical number of blocks. For example, the analyzer recommends using `zstd` for our `SORTKEY`, `product_category`, but our experience shows that query performance suffers when we compress the SORT KEY. We are using the extra disk space to improve our query performance.

Amazon Redshift supports automatic table optimization and other self-tuning capabilities that leverage machine learning to optimize peak performance and adapt to shifting workloads. The performance optimizations include automatic vacuum deletes, intelligent workload management, automatic table sorts, and automatic selection of distribution and sort keys.

Use Bloom Filters to Improve Query Performance

Amazon Redshift is a distributed query engine and S3 is a distributed object store. Distributed systems consist of many cluster instances. To improve performance of distributed queries, we need to minimize the number of instances that are scanned and the amount of data transferred between the instances.

Bloom filters, probabilistic and memory-efficient data structures, help answer the question, "Does this specific cluster instance contain data that might be included in the query results?" Bloom filters answer with either a definite NO or a MAYBE. If the bloom filter answered with a NO, the engine will completely skip that cluster instance and scan the remaining instances where the bloom filter answered with a MAYBE.

By filtering out rows of data that do not match the given query, bloom filters result in huge performance gains for join queries. And since bloom filtering happens close to the data source, data transfer is minimized between the nodes in the distributed cluster during join queries. This ultimately increases query performance for data stores such as S3.

Amazon Redshift Spectrum actually automatically creates and manages bloom filters on external data such as S3, but we should be aware of their importance in improving query performance on distributed data stores. Bloom filters are a pattern used throughout all of distributed computing, including distributed query engines.

Materialized Views in Amazon Redshift Spectrum

Materialized views provide repeatable and predictable query performance on external data sources such as S3. They pretransform and prejoin data before SQL queries are executed. Materialized views can be updated either manually or on a predefined schedule using Amazon Redshift Spectrum.

Summary

In this chapter, we provided an overview on how we can load our data into Amazon S3, discussed the value of an S3 data lake, and showed how we can leverage services like Amazon Athena to run ad hoc SQL queries across the data in S3 without the need to physically move the data. We showed how to continuously ingest new application data using AWS Glue Crawler. We also introduced our dataset, the Amazon Customer Reviews Dataset, which we will be using through the rest of this book.

As different use cases require data in different formats, we elaborated on how we can use Athena to convert tab-separated data into query-optimized, columnar Parquet data.

Data in our S3 data lake often needs to be accessed not only by the data science and machine learning teams but also by business intelligence teams. We introduced the Lake House Architecture based on Amazon Redshift, AWS's petabyte-scale cloud data warehouse. We showed how to use Amazon Redshift Spectrum to combine queries across data stores, including Amazon Redshift and S3.

To conclude this chapter, we discussed the various data compression formats and S3 tiering options, showing how they can reduce cost and improve query performance.

In Chapter 5 we will explore the dataset in more detail. We will run queries to understand and visualize our datasets. We will also show how to detect data anomalies with Apache Spark and Amazon SageMaker Processing Jobs.

Explore the Dataset

In the previous chapter, we demonstrated how to ingest data into the cloud with Amazon Athena and Redshift. Amazon Athena offers ad hoc, serverless SQL queries for data in S3 without needing to set up, scale, and manage any clusters. Amazon Redshift provides the fastest query performance for enterprise reporting and business intelligence workloads—particularly those involving complex SQL with multiple joins and subqueries across many data sources, including relational databases and flat files. We created a data-catalog mapping for our S3-based data lake in S3 using AWS Glue Catalog. We ran ad hoc queries on our data lake with Athena. And we ran queries on our data warehouse with Amazon Redshift.

We also had a first peek into our dataset. As we've learned, the Amazon Customer Reviews Dataset consists of more than 150+ million of those customer reviews of products across 43 different product categories on the Amazon.com website from 1995 until 2015. The dataset contains the actual customer reviews text together with additional metadata. It comes in two formats: row-based tab-separated values (TSV) and column-based Apache Parquet.

In this chapter, we will use the SageMaker Studio integrated development environment (IDE) as our main workspace for data analysis and the model development life cycle. SageMaker Studio provides fully managed Jupyter Notebook servers. With just a couple of clicks, we can provision the SageMaker Studio IDE and start using Jupyter notebooks to run ad hoc data analysis and launch Apache Spark–based data-quality jobs.

We will use SageMaker Studio throughout the rest of the book to launch data processing and feature engineering jobs in Chapter 6, train models in Chapter 7, optimize models in Chapter 8, deploy models in Chapter 9, build pipelines in Chapter 10, develop streaming applications in Chapter 11, and secure our data science projects in Chapter 12.

Let's explore our dataset in more depth and analyze our data for correlations, anomalies, bias, imbalances, and useful business insights. The knowledge from this data analysis and exploration will prepare us for data bias, feature selection, and feature engineering in Chapter 6 as well as model bias, fairness, and explainability analysis in Chapters 7 and 9.

Tools for Exploring Data in AWS

Let's introduce some tools and services that will assist us in our data exploration task. In order to choose the right tool for the right purpose, we will describe the breadth and depth of tools available within AWS and use these tools to answer questions about our Amazon Customer Reviews Dataset.

To interact with AWS resources from Jupyter notebooks running within SageMaker Studio IDE, we leverage the AWS Python SDK Boto3 (*https://oreil.ly/byebi*) and the Python DB client PyAthena (*https://oreil.ly/DTQS8*) to connect to Athena, the Python SQL toolkit SQLAlchemy (*https://oreil.ly/q0DC0*) to connect to Amazon Redshift, and the open source AWS Data Wrangler library (*https://oreil.ly/rUvry*) to facilitate data movement between pandas and Amazon S3, Athena, Redshift, Glue, and EMR.

 The open source AWS Data Wrangler library (*https://oreil.ly/5Eq4H*) is not related to SageMaker Data Wrangler. This is an unfortunate name clash. AWS Data Wrangler is focused on general data ingestion into—and between—AWS storage services like Amazon S3, Athena, Redshift, etc., while SageMaker Data Wrangler is focused on ML-based data ingestion, analysis, and transformation for reproducible pipelines. We will describe SageMaker Data Wrangler in more detail later in this chapter and describe when to use one over the other.

Amazon EMR supports flexible, highly distributed, data-processing and analytics frameworks such as Apache Spark and Hadoop. Amazon EMR is a managed service with automated cluster setup and autoscaling and supports Spot Instances. Amazon EMR lets us run custom jobs with specific compute, memory, and storage parameters to optimize our analytics queries. Amazon EMR Studio is a unified IDE for data processing on AWS. SageMaker Studio also supports Amazon EMR through EMR-specific Jupyter kernels, including PySpark.

QuickSight is a fast, easy-to-use business intelligence service to build visualizations, perform ad hoc analysis, and build dashboards from many data sources—across many devices.

Visualize Our Data Lake with SageMaker Studio

In this section, we will start working with the Amazon SageMaker Studio IDE, which provides us with managed Jupyter notebooks. We will use the Amazon Customer Reviews Dataset which we introduced in Chapter 4. Here's another quick overview of the dataset schema:

marketplace
Two-letter country code (in this case, just "US").

customer_id
Random identifier used to aggregate reviews written by a single author.

review_id
Unique ID for the review.

product_id
Amazon Standard Identification Number (ASIN).

product_parent
Multiple ASINs (variations of the same product) can roll up into a single parent.

product_title
Title description of the product.

product_category
Broad product category used to group reviews.

star_rating
The review's rating of 1 to 5 stars, where 1 is the worst and 5 is the best.

helpful_votes
Number of helpful votes for the review.

total_votes
Total number of votes for the review.

vine
Was the review written as part of the Vine program?

verified_purchase
Was the review from a verified purchase?

review_headline
Title of the review.

review_body
> Actual text of the review.

review_date
> Date the review was submitted.

Prepare SageMaker Studio to Visualize Our Dataset

For our exploratory data analysis in this Jupyter notebook, we will use pandas (*https://pandas.pydata.org*), NumPy (*https://numpy.org*), Matplotlib (*https://matplotlib.org*), and Seaborn (*https://oreil.ly/ysj3B*), which are probably the most commonly used libraries for data analysis and data visualization in Python. Seaborn is built on top of Matplotlib, adds support for pandas, and offers more advanced visualizations with a streamlined API. We will also use PyAthena (*https://oreil.ly/d5wwh*), the Python DB Client for Amazon Athena, to run Athena queries right from our notebook:

```
import pandas as pd

import numpy as np

import matplotlib.pyplot as plt
%matplotlib inline
%config InlineBackend.figure_format='retina'

import seaborn as sns
```

 When using a Mac with a Retina display, make sure to specify the retina setting for much higher-resolution images with Matplotlib on a Mac.

Let's define the database and table holding our Amazon Customer Reviews Dataset information in Amazon Athena:

```
database_name = 'dsoaws'
table_name = 'amazon_reviews_parquet'
```

With that, we are now ready to run our first SQL queries right from the notebook.

Run a Sample Athena Query in SageMaker Studio

In the first example shown in the following, we will query our dataset to give us a list of the distinct product categories. PyAthena sets up a connection to the data source. We will then execute SQL commands with pandas, passing the SQL statement to execute and the PyAthena connection object:

```
# PyAthena imports
from pyathena import connect

# Set the Athena query results S3 bucket
s3_staging_dir = 's3://{0}/athena/staging'.format(bucket)

# Set up the PyAthena connection
conn = connect(region_name=region, s3_staging_dir=s3_staging_dir)

# The SQL statement to execute
sql_statement="""
SELECT DISTINCT product_category from {0}.{1}
ORDER BY product_category
""".format(database_name, table_name)

# Execute the SQL statement with pandas
import pandas as pd
pd.read_sql(sql_statement, conn)
```

Here is the result of the read_sql() call that queries all product categories:

product_category	product_category (continued)
Apparel	Luggage
Automotive	Major Appliances
Baby	Mobile_Apps
Beauty	Mobile_Electronics
Books	Music
Camera	Musical Instruments
Digital_Ebook_Purchase	Office Products
Digital_Music_Purchase	Outdoors
Digital_Software	PC
Digital_Video_Download	Personal_Care_Appliances
Digital_Video_Games	Pet Products
Electronics	Shoes
Furniture	Software
Gift Card	Sports
Grocery	Tools
Health & Personal Care	Toys
Home	Video
Home Entertainment	Video DVD
Home Improvement	Video Games
Jewelry	Watches
Kitchen	Wireless
Lawn and Garden	

We may need to use pandas cursors if we are working with a large dataset that exceeds the memory available to the notebook server. Pay attention to the file size when reading data into the DataFrame. We can easily exceed available memory when working with large datasets.

Dive Deep into the Dataset with Athena and SageMaker

We need to understand our data in order to prepare for the next steps of feature selection and feature engineering. We will run queries across the data to learn about data correlations, identify data anomalies, and class imbalances.

Let's use Athena, SageMaker Studio, Matplotlib, and Seaborn to track down answers to the following questions over the entire dataset:

1. Which product categories are the highest rated by average rating?

2. Which product categories have the most reviews?

3. When did each product category become available in the Amazon catalog based on the date of the first review?

4. What is the breakdown of star ratings (1–5) per product category?

5. How have the star ratings changed over time? Is there a drop-off point for certain product categories throughout the year?

6. Which star ratings (1–5) are the most helpful?

7. What is the distribution of review lengths (number of words)?

From this point, we will only show the Athena query and the results. The full source code to execute and render the results is available in the accompanying GitHub repo.

1. Which product categories are the highest rated by average rating?

Here is the SQL query that will answer this question:

```
SELECT product_category, AVG(star_rating) AS avg_star_rating
FROM dsoaws.amazon_reviews_parquet
GROUP BY product_category
ORDER BY avg_star_rating DESC
```

Let's plot the results in a horizontal bar chart using Seaborn and Matplotlib to provide a high-level overview of which product categories are more popular than others, on average. We may want to consider this distribution when we select our training dataset in the next few chapters.

Figure 5-1 shows that Amazon Gift Cards are the highest-rated product category, with an average star rating of 4.73, followed by Music Purchase, with an average of 4.64 and Music, with an average of 4.44.

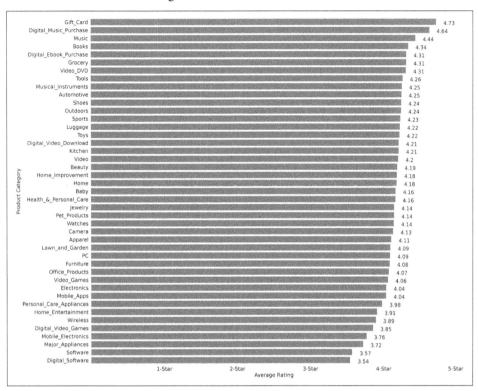

Figure 5-1. Gift Cards are the highest rated product category at the Amazon.com marketplace.

2. Which product categories have the most reviews?

Here is the SQL query that will answer this question:

```
SELECT product_category,
       COUNT(star_rating) AS count_star_rating
FROM dsoaws.amazon_reviews_parquet
GROUP BY product_category
ORDER BY count_star_rating DESC
```

Let's plot the result again in a horizontal bar chart using Seaborn and Matplotlib, shown in Figure 5-2.

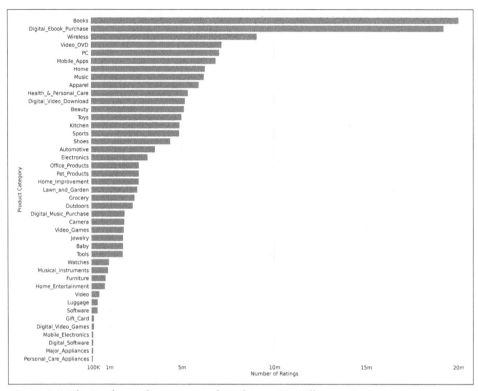

Figure 5-2. The Books product category has close to 20 million reviews.

We can see in Figure 5-2 that the "Books" product category has the most reviews, with close to 20 million. This makes sense as Amazon.com initially launched as the "Earth's Biggest Bookstore" (*https://oreil.ly/q11mI*) back in 1995.

The second most reviewed category is "Digital_Ebook_Purchase," representing Kindle book reviews. So we notice that book reviews—whether printed or as ebooks—still count the most reviews.

"Personal_Care_Appliances" has the least number of reviews. This could potentially be due to the fact that the product category was added more recently.

Let's check this out by querying for the first review in each category, which will give us a rough timeline of product category introductions.

3. When did each product category become available in the Amazon catalog?

The initial review date is a strong indicator of when each product category went live on Amazon.com. Here is the SQL query that will answer this question:

```
SELECT
        product_category,
        MIN(year) AS first_review_year
    FROM dsoaws.amazon_reviews_parquet
    GROUP BY product_category
    ORDER BY first_review_year
```

The result should look similar to this:

product_category	first_review_year
Books	1995
Video Games	1997
Office Products	1998
Pet Products	1998
Software	1998
Gift Card	2004
Digital_Video_Games	2006
Digital_Software	2008
Mobile_Apps	2010

We can see that personal care appliances were indeed added somewhat later to the Amazon.com catalog, but that doesn't seem to be the only reason for the low number of reviews. Mobile apps appear to have been added around 2010.

Let's visualize the number of first reviews per category per year, shown in Figure 5-3.

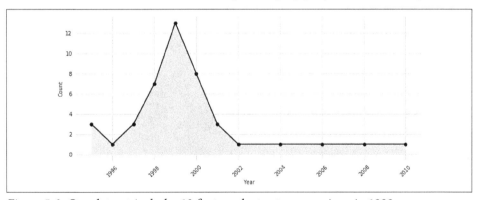

Figure 5-3. Our dataset includes 13 first product category reviews in 1999.

We notice that a lot of our first product category reviews (13) happened in 1999. Whether this is really related to the introduction of those product categories around this time or is just a coincidence created by the available data in our dataset, we can't tell for sure.

4. What is the breakdown of star ratings (1–5) per product category?

Here is the SQL query that will answer this question:

```
SELECT product_category,
       star_rating,
       COUNT(*) AS count_reviews
FROM dsoaws.amazon_reviews_parquet
GROUP BY  product_category, star_rating
ORDER BY  product_category ASC, star_rating DESC,
     count_reviews
```

The result should look similar to this (shortened):

product_category	star_rating	count_reviews
Apparel	5	3320566
Apparel	4	1147237
Apparel	3	623471
Apparel	2	369601
Apparel	1	445458
Automotive	5	2300757
Automotive	4	526665
Automotive	3	239886
Automotive	2	147767
Automotive	1	299867
...	...	...

With this information, we can also quickly group by star ratings and count the reviews for each rating (5, 4, 3, 2, 1):

```
SELECT star_rating,
       COUNT(*) AS count_reviews
FROM dsoaws.amazon_reviews_parquet
GROUP BY  star_rating
ORDER BY  star_rating DESC, count_reviews
```

The result should look similar to this:

star_rating	count_reviews
5	93200812
4	26223470
3	12133927
2	7304430
1	12099639

Approximately 62% of all reviews have a 5-star rating. We will come back to this relative imbalance of star ratings when we perform feature engineering to prepare for model training.

We can now visualize a stacked percentage horizontal bar plot, showing the proportion of each star rating per product category, as shown in Figure 5-4.

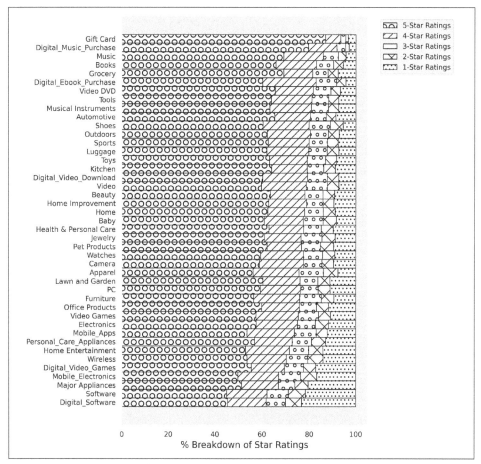

Figure 5-4. Distribution of reviews per star rating (5, 4, 3, 2, 1) per product category.

We see that 5- and 4-star ratings make up the largest proportion within each product category. But let's see if we can spot differences in product satisfaction over time.

5. How have the star ratings changed over time? Is there a drop-off point for certain product categories throughout the year?

Let's first have a look at the average star rating across all product categories over the years. Here is the SQL query that will answer this question:

```
SELECT year, ROUND(AVG(star_rating), 4) AS avg_rating
FROM dsoaws.amazon_reviews_parquet
GROUP BY year
ORDER BY year;
```

The result should look similar to this:

year	avg_rating
1995	4.6169
1996	4.6003
1997	4.4344
1998	4.3607
1999	4.2819
2000	4.2569
...	...
2010	4.069
2011	4.0516
2012	4.1193
2013	4.1977
2014	4.2286
2015	4.2495

If we plot this, as shown in Figure 5-5, we notice the general upward trend, with two lows in 2004 and 2011.

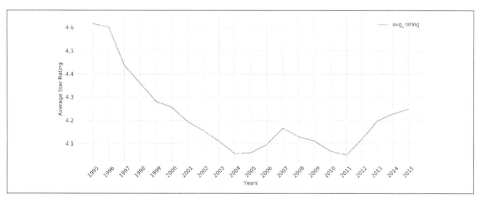

Figure 5-5. Average star rating across all product categories over time.

Let's take a look now at our top five product categories by number of ratings ('Books', 'Digital_Ebook_Purchase', 'Wireless', 'PC', and 'Home'). Here is the SQL query that will answer this question:

```
SELECT
    product_category,
    year,
    ROUND(AVG(star_rating), 4) AS avg_rating_category
FROM dsoaws.amazon_reviews_parquet
WHERE product_category IN
    ('Books', 'Digital_Ebook_Purchase', 'Wireless', 'PC', 'Home')
GROUP BY product_category, year
ORDER BY year
```

The result should look similar to this (shortened):

product_category	year	avg_rating_category
Books	1995	4.6111
Books	1996	4.6024
Books	1997	4.4339
Home	1998	4.4
Wireless	1998	4.5
Books	1998	4.3045
Home	1999	4.1429
Digital_Ebook_Purchase	1999	5.0
PC	1999	3.7917
Wireless	1999	4.1471

If we plot this now, as shown in Figure 5-6, we can see something interesting.

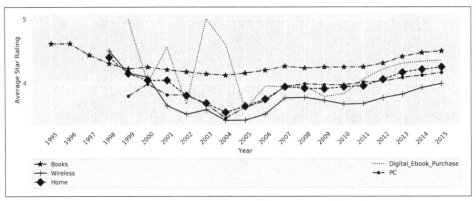

Figure 5-6. Average star rating over time per product category (top 5).

While books have been relatively consistent in `star_rating` with values between 4.1 and 4.6, the other categories are more affected by customer satisfaction. Digital ebook purchases (Kindle books) seem to spike a lot, dropping as low as 3.5 in 2005 and rising as high as 5.0 in 2003. This would definitely require a closer look into our dataset to decide whether this is due to limited reviews in that time or some sort of skewed data or if it really reflected the voice of our customers.

6. Which star ratings (1–5) are the most helpful?

Here is the SQL query that will answer this question:

```
SELECT star_rating,
       AVG(helpful_votes) AS avg_helpful_votes
FROM dsoaws.amazon_reviews_parquet
GROUP BY  star_rating
ORDER BY  star_rating DESC
```

The result should look similar to this:

star_rating	avg_helpful_votes
5	1.672697561905362
4	1.6786973653753678
3	2.048089542651773
2	2.5066350146417995
1	3.6846412525200134

We see that customers find negative reviews more helpful than positive reviews, which is visualized in Figure 5-7.

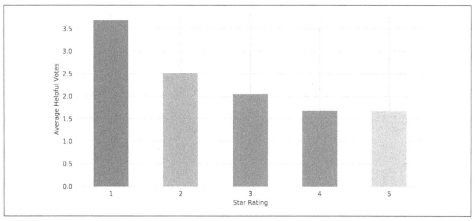

Figure 5-7. Customers find negative reviews (1-star ratings) the most helpful.

7. What is the distribution of review lengths (number of words)?

Here is the SQL query that will answer this question:

```
SELECT CARDINALITY(SPLIT(review_body, ' ')) as num_words
FROM dsoaws.amazon_reviews_parquet
```

We can describe the resulting distribution through percentiles:

```
summary = df['num_words']\
    .describe(percentiles=\
        [0.10, 0.20, 0.30, 0.40, 0.50, 0.60, 0.70, 0.80, 0.90, 1.00])
```

The summary result should look similar to this:

```
count    396601.000000
mean         51.683405
std         107.030844
min           1.000000
10%           2.000000
20%           7.000000
30%          19.000000
40%          22.000000
50%          26.000000
60%          32.000000
70%          43.000000
80%          63.000000
90%         110.000000
100%       5347.000000
max        5347.000000
```

If we plot this now, as shown in Figure 5-8, we can see that 80% of our reviews have 63 words or less.

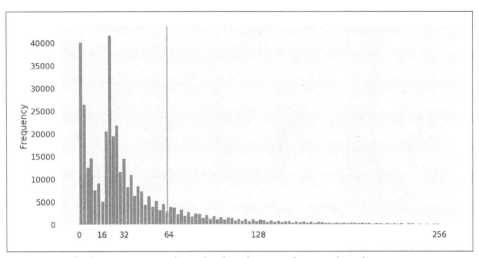

Figure 5-8. The histogram visualizes the distribution of review lengths.

Query Our Data Warehouse

At this point, we will use Amazon Redshift to query and visualize use cases. Similar to the Athena example, we first need to prepare our SageMaker Studio environment.

Run a Sample Amazon Redshift Query from SageMaker Studio

In the following example, we will query our dataset to give us the number of unique customers per product category. We can use the pandas `read_sql_query` function to run our SQLAlchemy query and store the query result in a pandas DataFrame:

```
df = pd.read_sql_query("""
        SELECT product_category, COUNT(DISTINCT customer_id) as num_customers
        FROM redshift.amazon_reviews_tsv_2015
        GROUP BY product_category
        ORDER BY num_customers DESC
""", engine)
```

```
df.head(10)
```

The output should look similar to this:

product_category	num_customers
Wireless	1979435
Digital_Ebook_Purchase	1857681
Books	1507711
Apparel	1424202
Home	1352314
PC	1283463
Health & Personal Care	1238075
Beauty	1110828
Shoes	1083406
Sports	1024591

We can see that the Wireless product category has the most unique customers providing reviews, followed by the Digital_Ebook_Purchase and Books categories. We are all set now to query Amazon Redshift for some deeper customer insights.

Dive Deep into the Dataset with Amazon Redshift and SageMaker

Now, let's query our data from 2015 in Amazon Redshift for deeper insight into our customers and find answers to the following questions:

1. Which product categories had the most reviews in 2015?

2. Which products had the most helpful reviews in 2015? How long were those reviews?

3. How did the star ratings change during 2015? Was there a drop-off point for certain product categories throughout the year?

4. Which customers wrote the most helpful reviews in 2015? How many reviews did they write? Across how many categories? What was their average star rating?

5. Which customers provided more than one review for the same product in 2015? What was their average star rating for each product?

As with the Athena examples, we will only show the Amazon Redshift SQL query and the results. The full source code to execute and render the results is available in the accompanying GitHub repo.

Let's run the queries and find out the answers!

1. Which product categories had the most reviews in 2015?

Here is the SQL query that will answer this question:

```
SELECT
    year,
    product_category,
    COUNT(star_rating) AS count_star_rating
FROM
    redshift.amazon_reviews_tsv_2015
GROUP BY
    product_category,
    year
ORDER BY
    count_star_rating DESC,
    year DESC
```

The result should look similar to this subset of data:

year	product_category	count_star_rating
2015	Digital_Ebook_Purchase	4533519
2015	Wireless	2998518
2015	Books	2808751
2015	Apparel	2369754
2015	Home	2172297
2015	Health & Personal Care	1877971
2015	PC	1877971
2015	Beauty	1816302
2015	Digital_Video_Download	1593521
2015	Sports	1571181
...	...	...

We notice that books are still the most reviewed product categories, but it's actually the ebooks (Kindle books) now. Let's visualize the result in a horizontal bar plot, as shown in Figure 5-9.

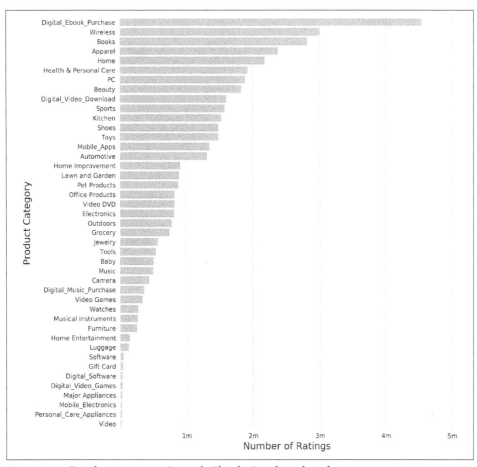

Figure 5-9. For the year 2015, Digital_Ebook_Purchase has the most reviews.

2. Which products had the most helpful reviews in 2015?

Also, how long were those reviews? Here is the SQL query that will answer this question:

```
SELECT
    product_title,
    helpful_votes,
    LENGTH(review_body) AS review_body_length,
    SUBSTRING(review_body, 1, 100) AS review_body_substring
FROM
    redshift.amazon_reviews_tsv_2015
ORDER BY
    helpful_votes DESC LIMIT 10
```

The result should look similar to this:

product_title	helpful_votes	review_body_length	review_body_substring
Fitbit Charge HR Wireless Activity Wristband	16401	2824	Full disclosure, I ordered the Fitbit Charge HR only after I gave up on Jawbone fulfilling my preord
Kindle Paperwhite	10801	16338	Review updated September 17, 2015 As a background, I am a retired Information Systems pro
Kindle Paperwhite	8542	9411	[[VIDEOID:755c0182976ece27e407ad23676f3ae8]]If you're reading reviews of the new 3rd generation Pape
Weslo Cadence G 5.9 Treadmill	6246	4295	I got the Weslo treadmill and absolutely dig it. I'm 6'2", 230 lbs. and like running outside (ab
Haribo Gummi Candy Gold-Bears	6201	4736	It was my last class of the semester, and the final exam was worth 30% of our grade. After a la
FlipBelt - World's Best Running Belt & Fitness Workout Belt	6195	211	The size chart is wrong on the selection. I've attached a photo so you can see what you really need.
Amazon.com eGift Cards	5987	3498	I think I am just wasting time writing this, but this must have happened to someone else. Something
Melanie's Marvelous Measles	5491	8028	If you enjoyed this book, check out these other fine titles from the same author: Abby's
Tuft & Needle Mattress	5404	4993	tl;dr: Great mattress, after some hurdles that were deftly cleared by stellar customer service. The
Ring Wi-Fi Enabled Video Doorbell	5399	3984	First off, the Ring is very cool. I really like it and many people that come to my front door (sale

We see that the "Fitbit Charge HR Wireless Activity Wristband" had the most helpful review in 2015, with a total of 16,401 votes and a decent-sized review length of 2,824 characters. It's followed by two reviews for the "Kindle Paperwhite," where people were writing longer reviews of 16,338 and 9,411 characters, respectively.

3. How did the star ratings change during 2015?

Also, was there a drop-off point for certain product categories throughout the year? Here is the SQL query that will answer this question:

```
SELECT
    CAST(DATE_PART('month', TO_DATE(review_date, 'YYYY-MM-DD')) AS integer)
    AS month,
    AVG(star_rating ::FLOAT) AS avg_rating
FROM redshift.amazon_reviews_tsv_2015
GROUP BY month
ORDER BY month
```

The result should look similar to this:

month	avg_rating
1	4.277998926134835
2	4.267851231035101
3	4.261042822856084
4	4.247727865199895
5	4.239633709986397
6	4.235766635971452
7	4.230284081689972
8	4.231862792031927

We notice that we only have data until August 2015. We can also spot that the average rating is slowly declining, as we can easily see in Figure 5-10. While we don't have a precise explanation, this decline was likely investigated in 2015.

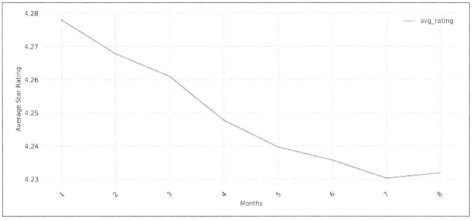

Figure 5-10. Average star rating throughout 2015 across all product categories.

Now let's explore whether this is due to a certain product category dropping drastically in customer satisfaction or is more of a trend across all categories. Here is the SQL query that will answer this question:

```
SELECT
    product_category,
    CAST(DATE_PART('month', TO_DATE(review_date, 'YYYY-MM-DD')) AS integer)
    AS month,
    AVG(star_rating ::FLOAT) AS avg_rating
FROM redshift.amazon_reviews_tsv_2015
GROUP BY product_category, month
ORDER BY product_category, month
```

The result should look similar to this (shortened):

product_category	month	avg_rating
Apparel	1	4.159321618698804
Apparel	2	4.123969612021801
Apparel	3	4.109944336469443
Apparel	4	4.094360325567125
Apparel	5	4.0894595692213125
Apparel	6	4.09617799917213
Apparel	7	4.097665115845663
Apparel	8	4.112790034578352
Automotive	1	4.325502388403887
Automotive	2	4.318120214368761
...	...	...

Let's visualize the result to make it easier to spot the trends, as shown in Figure 5-11.

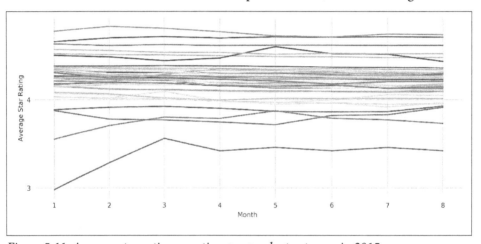

Figure 5-11. Average star rating over time per product category in 2015.

While the figure is a bit messy, we can see that most categories follow the same average star rating over the months, with three categories fluctuating more than others: "Digital Software," "Software," and "Mobile Electronics." They are, however, improving throughout the year, which is good.

4. Which customers wrote the most helpful reviews in 2015?

Also, how many reviews did they write? Across how many categories? What was their average star rating? Here is the SQL query that will answer the questions:

```
SELECT
    customer_id,
    AVG(helpful_votes) AS avg_helpful_votes,
    COUNT(*) AS review_count,
    COUNT(DISTINCT product_category) AS product_category_count,
    ROUND(AVG(star_rating::FLOAT), 1) AS avg_star_rating
FROM
    redshift.amazon_reviews_tsv_2015
GROUP BY
    customer_id
HAVING
    count(*) > 100
ORDER BY
    avg_helpful_votes DESC LIMIT 10;
```

The result should look similar to this:

customer_id	avg_helpful_votes	review_count	product_category_count	avg_star_rating
35360512	48	168	26	4.5
52403783	44	274	25	4.9
28259076	40	123	7	4.3
15365576	37	569	30	4.9
14177091	29	187	15	4.4
28021023	28	103	18	4.5
20956632	25	120	23	4.8
53017806	25	549	30	4.9
23942749	25	110	22	4.5
44834233	24	514	32	4.4

We can see the customers that wrote reviews that produced the most helpful votes on average (with more than one hundred reviews provided) across many different categories; the reviews generally reflected a positive sentiment.

5. Which customers provided more than one review for the same product in 2015?

Also, what was their average star rating for each product? Here is the SQL query that will answer this question:

```
SELECT
    customer_id,
    product_category,
    product_title,
    ROUND(AVG(star_rating::FLOAT), 4) AS avg_star_rating,
    COUNT(*) AS review_count
```

```
FROM
    redshift.amazon_reviews_tsv_2015
GROUP BY
    customer_id,
    product_category,
    product_title
HAVING
    COUNT(*) > 1
ORDER BY
    review_count DESC LIMIT 5
```

The result should look similar to this:

customer_id	product_category	product_title	avg_star_rating	review_count
2840168	Camera	(Create a generic Title per Amazon's guidelines)	5.0	45
9016330	Video Games	Disney INFINITY Disney Infinity: Marvel Super Heroes (2.0 Edition) Characters	5.0	23
10075230	Video Games	Skylanders Spyro's Adventure: Character Pack	5.0	23
50600878	Digital_Ebook_Purchase	The Art of War	2.35	20
10075230	Video Games	Activision Skylanders Giants Single Character Pack Core Series 2	4.85	20

Note that the `avg_star_rating` is not always a whole number. This means some customers rated the product differently over time.

It's good to know that customer 9016330 finds the Disney Infinity: Marvel Super Heroes Video Game to be 5 stars—even after playing it 23 times! Customer 50600878 has been fascinated enough to read *The Art of War* 20 times, but is still struggling to find a positive sentiment there.

Create Dashboards with Amazon QuickSight

QuickSight is a managed, serverless, and easy-to-use business analytics service that we can leverage to quickly build powerful visualizations. QuickSight automatically discovers the data sources in our AWS account, including MySQL, Salesforce, Amazon Redshift, Athena, S3, Aurora, RDS, and many more.

Let's use QuickSight to create a dashboard with our Amazon Customer Reviews Dataset. In just a few clicks, we can have a visualization of review counts per product category, accessible by any device, even our mobile phone. We can automatically refresh the dashboard after data ingestion using the QuickSight Python SDK. Using the QuickSight UI, we can see the imbalance in our dataset, as shown in Figure 5-12.

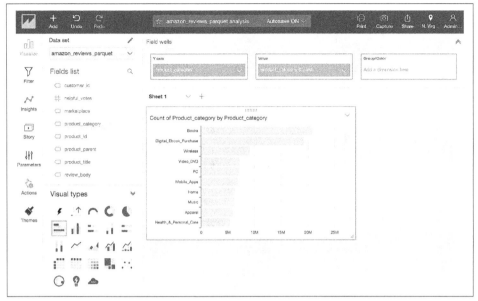

Figure 5-12. Visualizing review counts per product category in QuickSight.

The product categories Books and Digital_Ebook_Purchase have by far the most reviews. We will analyze and address this imbalance in more detail in the next chapter, when we prepare the dataset to train our models.

Detect Data-Quality Issues with Amazon SageMaker and Apache Spark

Data is never perfect—especially in a dataset with 150+ million rows spread across 20 years! Additionally, data quality may actually degrade over time as new application features are introduced and others are retired. Schemas evolve, code gets old, and queries get slow.

Since data quality is not always a priority for the upstream application teams, the downstream data engineering and data science teams need to handle bad or missing data. We want to make sure that our data is high quality for our downstream consumers, including the business intelligence, ML engineering, and data science teams.

Figure 5-13 shows how applications generate data for engineers, scientists, and analysts to consume—as well as which tools and services the various teams are likely to use when accessing that data.

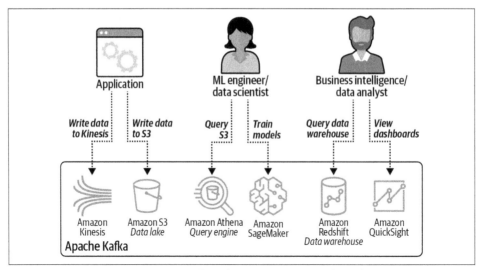

Figure 5-13. Engineers, scientists and analysts use various tools and services to access data.

Data quality can halt a data processing pipeline in its tracks. If these issues are not caught early, they can lead to misleading reports (i.e., double-counted revenue), biased AI/ML models (skewed toward/against a single gender or race), and other unintended data products.

To catch these data issues early, we use two open source libraries from AWS, Deequ (*https://oreil.ly/CVaTM*) and PyDeequ (*https://oreil.ly/K9Ydj*). These libraries use Apache Spark to analyze data quality, detect anomalies, and enable us to "notify the Data Scientist at 3 a.m." about a data issue. Deequ continuously analyzes data throughout the complete, end-to-end lifetime of the model, from feature engineering to model training to model serving in production. Figure 5-14 shows a high-level overview of the Deequ architecture and components.

Learning from run to run, Deequ will suggest new rules to apply during the next pass through the dataset. Deequ learns the baseline statistics of our dataset at model training time, for example, then detects anomalies as new data arrives for model prediction. This problem is classically called "training-serving skew." Essentially, a model is trained with one set of learned constraints, then the model sees new data that does not fit those existing constraints. This is a sign that the data has shifted—or skewed—from the original, expected distribution used during training.

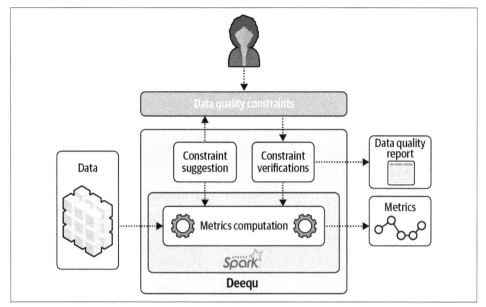

Figure 5-14. Deequ's components: constraints, metrics, and suggestions.

Since we have 150+ million reviews, we need to run Deequ on a cluster versus inside our notebook. This is the trade-off of working with data at scale. Notebooks work fine for exploratory analytics on small datasets but are not suitable to process large datasets or train large models. We will use a notebook to kick off a Deequ Spark job on a separate, ephemeral, and serverless Apache Spark cluster using SageMaker Processing Jobs.

SageMaker Processing Jobs

SageMaker Processing Jobs can run any Python script—or custom Docker image—on the fully managed, pay-as-you-go AWS infrastructure using familiar open source tools such as scikit-learn and Apache Spark. Figure 5-15 shows the SageMaker Processing Job container.

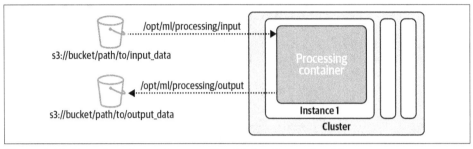

Figure 5-15. Container for an Amazon SageMaker Processing Job.

Fortunately, Deequ is a high-level API on top of Apache Spark, so we use SageMaker Processing Jobs to run our large-scale analysis job.

 Deequ is similar to TensorFlow Extended in concept—specifically, the TensorFlow Data Validation component. However, Deequ builds upon popular open source Apache Spark to increase usability, debug-ability, and scalability. Additionally, Apache Spark and Deequ natively support the Parquet format—our preferred file format for analytics.

Analyze Our Dataset with Deequ and Apache Spark

Table 5-1 shows just a few of the metrics that Deequ supports.

Table 5-1. Sample Deequ metrics

Metric	Description	Usage example
ApproxCountDistinct	Approximate number of distinct values using HLL+ +	ApproxCountDistinct("review_id")
ApproxQuantiles	Approximate quantiles of a distribution	ApproxQuantiles("star_rating", quantiles = Seq(0.1, 0.5, 0.9))
Completeness	Fraction of non-null values in a column	Completeness("review_id")
Compliance	Fraction of rows that comply with the given column constraint	Compliance("top star_rating", "star_rating >= 4.0")
Correlation	Pearson correlation coefficient	Correlation("total_votes", "star_rating")
Maximum	Maximum value	Maximum("star_rating")
Mean	Mean value; null valuesexcluded	Mean("star_rating")
Minimum	Minimum value	Minimum("star_rating")
MutualInformation	How much information about one column can be inferred from another column	MutualInformation(Seq("total_votes", "star_rating"))
Size	Number of rows in a DataFrame	Size()
Sum	Sum of all values of a column	Sum("total_votes")
Uniqueness	Fraction of unique values	Uniqueness("review_id")

Let's kick off the Apache Spark–based Deequ analyzer job by invoking the PySpark Processor and launching a 10-node Apache Spark Cluster right from our notebook. We chose the high-memory r5 instance type because Spark typically performs better with more memory:

```
s3_input_data='s3://{}/amazon-reviews-pds/tsv/'.format(bucket)
s3_output_analyze_data='s3://{}/{}/output/'.format(bucket, output_prefix)

from sagemaker.spark.processing import PySparkProcessor

processor = \
    PySparkProcessor(base_job_name='spark-amazon-reviews-analyzer',
                     role=role,
                     framework_version='2.4',
                     instance_count=10,
                     instance_type='ml.r5.8xlarge',
                     max_runtime_in_seconds=300)

processor.run(submit_app='preprocess-deequ-pyspark.py',
              submit_jars=['deequ-1.0.3-rc2.jar'],
              arguments=['s3_input_data', s3_input_data,
                         's3_output_analyze_data', s3_output_analyze_data,
              ],
              logs=True,
              wait=False
)
```

Following is our Deequ code specifying the various constraints we wish to apply to our TSV dataset. We are using TSV in this example to maintain consistency with the rest of the examples, but we could easily switch to Parquet with just a one-line code change:

```
dataset = spark.read.csv(s3_input_data,
                         header=True,
                         schema=schema,
                         sep="\t",
                         quote="")
```

Define the analyzers:

```
from pydeequ.analyzers import *

analysisResult = AnalysisRunner(spark) \
                    .onData(dataset) \
                    .addAnalyzer(Size()) \
                    .addAnalyzer(Completeness("review_id")) \
                    .addAnalyzer(ApproxCountDistinct("review_id")) \
                    .addAnalyzer(Mean("star_rating")) \
                    .addAnalyzer(Compliance("top star_rating", \
                                            "star_rating >= 4.0")) \
                    .addAnalyzer(Correlation("total_votes", \
                                             "star_rating")) \
```

```
                    .addAnalyzer(Correlation("total_votes",
                                             "helpful_votes")) \
            .run()
```

Define the checks, compute the metrics, and verify check conditions:

```
from pydeequ.checks import *
from pydeequ.verification import *

verificationResult = VerificationSuite(spark) \
        .onData(dataset) \
        .addCheck(
            Check(spark, CheckLevel.Error, "Review Check") \
                .hasSize(lambda x: x >= 150000000) \
                .hasMin("star_rating", lambda x: x == 1.0) \
                .hasMax("star_rating", lambda x: x == 5.0)  \
                .isComplete("review_id")  \
                .isUnique("review_id")  \
                .isComplete("marketplace")  \
                .isContainedIn("marketplace", ["US", "UK", "DE", "JP", "FR"])) \
        .run()
```

We have defined our set of constraints and assertions to apply to our dataset. Let's run the job and ensure that our data is what we expect. Table 5-2 shows the results from our Deequ job, summarizing the results of the constraints and checks that we specified.

Table 5-2. Deequ job results

check_name	columns	value
ApproxCountDistinct	review_id	149075190
Completeness	review_id	1.00
Compliance	Marketplace contained in US,UK, DE,JP,FR	1.00
Compliance	top star_rating	0.79
Correlation	helpful_votes,total_votes	0.99
Correlation	total_votes,star_rating	-0.03
Maximum	star_rating	5.00
Mean	star_rating	4.20
Minimum	star_rating	1.00
Size	*	150962278
Uniqueness	review_id	1.00

We learned the following:

- review_id has no missing values and approximately (within 2% accuracy) 149,075,190 unique values.

- 79% of reviews have a "top" star_rating of 4 or higher.

- `total_votes` and `star_rating` are weakly correlated.

- `helpful_votes` and `total_votes` are strongly correlated.

- The average `star_rating` is 4.20.

- The dataset contains exactly 150,962,278 reviews (1.27% different than `Approx CountDistinct`).

Deequ supports the concept of a `MetricsRepository` to track these metrics over time and potentially halt our pipeline if we detect degradation in data quality. Following is the code to create a `FileSystemMetricsRepository`, start tracking our metrics with a revised `AnalysisRunner`, and load our metrics for comparison:

```
from pydeequ.repository import *

metrics_file = FileSystemMetricsRepository.helper_metrics_file(spark,
    'metrics.json')
repository = FileSystemMetricsRepository(spark, metrics_file)
resultKey = ResultKey(spark, ResultKey.current_milli_time())

analysisResult = AnalysisRunner(spark) \
                    .onData(dataset) \
                    .addAnalyzer(Size()) \
                    .addAnalyzer(Completeness("review_id")) \
                    .addAnalyzer(ApproxCountDistinct("review_id")) \
                    .addAnalyzer(Mean("star_rating")) \
                    .addAnalyzer(Compliance("top star_rating", \
                                            "star_rating >= 4.0")) \
                    .addAnalyzer(Correlation("total_votes", \
                                            "star_rating")) \
                    .addAnalyzer(Correlation("total_votes", \
                                            "helpful_votes")) \
                    .useRepository(repository) \
                    .run()

df_result_metrics_repository = repository.load() \
    .before(ResultKey.current_milli_time()) \
    .forAnalyzers([ApproxCountDistinct("review_id")]) \
    .getSuccessMetricsAsDataFrame()
```

Deequ also suggests useful constraints based on the current characteristics of our dataset. This is useful when we have new data entering the system that may differ statistically from the original dataset. In the real world, this is very common because new data is coming in all the time.

In Table 5-3 are the checks—and the accompanying code—that Deequ suggests we add to detect anomalies as new data arrives into the system.

Table 5-3. Deequ suggestions for checks to be added

column	check	deequ_code
customer_id	`'customer_id'` has type Integral	`.hasDataType(\"customer_id\", Con strainableDataTypes.Integral)"`
helpful_votes	`'helpful_votes'` has no negative values	`.isNonNegative(\"helpful_votes\")"`
review_headline	`'review_headline'` has less than 1% missing values	`.hasCompleteness(\"review_headline \", lambda x: x >= 0.99, Some(\"It should be above 0.99!\"))"`
product_category	`'product_category'` has value range `'Books', 'Digital_Ebook_Purchase', 'Wireless', 'PC', 'Home', 'Apparel', 'Health & Personal Care', 'Beauty', 'Video DVD', 'Mobile_Apps', 'Kitchen', 'Toys', 'Sports', 'Music', 'Shoes', 'Digital_Video_Download', 'Automotive', 'Electronics', 'Pet Products', 'Office Products', 'Home Improvement', 'Lawn and Garden', 'Grocery', 'Outdoors', 'Camera', 'Video Games', 'Jewelry', 'Baby', 'Tools', 'Digital_Music_Purchase', 'Watches', 'Musical Instruments', 'Furniture', 'Home Entertainment', 'Video', 'Luggage', 'Software', 'Gift Card', 'Digital_Video_Games', 'Mobile_Electronics', 'Digital_Software', 'Major Appliances', 'Personal_Care_Appliances'`	`.isContainedIn(\"product_category \", Array(\"Books\", \"Digi tal_Ebook_Purchase\", \"Wireless\", \"PC\", \"Home\", \"Apparel\", \"Health & Personal Care\", \"Beauty \", \"Video DVD\", \"Mobile_Apps\", \"Kitchen\", \"Toys\", \"Sports\", \"Music\", \"Shoes\", \"Digi tal_Video_Download\", \"Automotive \", \"Electronics\", \"Pet Products \", \"Office Products\", \"Home Improvement\", \"Lawn and Garden\", \"Grocery\", \"Outdoors\", \"Camera \", \"Video Games\", \"Jewelry\", \"Baby\", \"Tools\", \"Digi tal_Music_Purchase\", \"Watches\", \"Musical Instruments\", \"Furniture \", \"Home Entertainment\", \"Video \", \"Luggage\", \"Software\", \"Gift Card\", \"Digital_Video_Games \", \"Mobile_Electronics\", \"Digi tal_Software\", \"Major Appliances \", \"Personal_Care_Appliances\"))"`
vine	`'vine'` has value range `'N'` for at least 99.0% of values	`.isContainedIn(\"vine\", Array(\"N \"), lambda x: x >= 0.99, Some(\"It should be above 0.99!\"))"`

In addition to the Integral type and not-negative checks, Deequ also suggests that we constrain `product_category` to the 43 currently known values, including Books, Soft ware, etc. Deequ also recognized that at least 99% of the `vine` values are N and < 1% of `review_headline` values are empty, so it recommends that we add checks for these conditions moving forward.

Detect Bias in Our Dataset

Using just a few lines of Python code with the Seaborn library, shown in the following, we can identify an imbalance in the number of reviews for three sample product categories across the five different `star_rating` classes in our pandas DataFrame. Figure 5-16 visualizes this imbalance for this sample of data.

```
import seaborn as sns

sns.countplot(data=df,
    x="star_rating",
    hue="product_category")
```

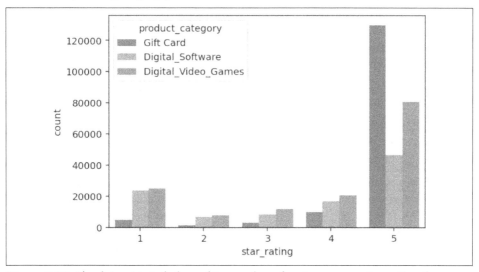

Figure 5-16. The dataset is imbalanced in number of reviews across star rating classes and product categories.

We will now use SageMaker Data Wrangler and Clarify to analyze imbalance and other potential bias in our dataset at scale.

Generate and Visualize Bias Reports with SageMaker Data Wrangler

SageMaker Data Wrangler is integrated with SageMaker Studio and is designed specifically for machine learning, data analysis, feature engineering, feature-importance analysis, and bias detection. With Data Wrangler, we can specify custom Apache Spark user-defined functions, pandas code, and SQL queries. Additionally, Data Wrangler provides over 300 built-in data transformations for feature engineering and bias mitigation. We will dive deeper into SageMaker Data Wrangler for feature engineering in Chapter 6. For now, let's analyze the dataset with Data Wrangler and SageMaker Clarify, a feature of Amazon SageMaker that we will use throughout the rest of this book to evaluate bias, statistical drift/shift, fairness, and explainability.

 The SageMaker Data Wrangler service is different from the open source AWS Data Wrangler project. AWS Data Wrangler is used primarily for data ingestion and moving data between AWS services. SageMaker Data Wrangler is the preferred tool for ML-focused data ingestion, analysis, and transformation as it maintains full data lineage throughout the machine learning pipeline.

Let's use SageMaker Data Wrangler to analyze class imbalance relative to the product_category column, or "facet," as it is commonly called in this context. Typically, we are analyzing sensitive facets like age and race. We have chosen to analyze the product_category facet since there may be differences in language used when writing gift card reviews versus software reviews, for example.

Class imbalance is one example of data bias and, if not mitigated, may lead to model bias where the model disproportionately favors an overrepresented class, such as Gift Card, at the expense of an underrepresented class, such as Digital_Software. This may result in higher training error for the underrepresented, disadvantaged class.

In other words, our model may more accurately predict the star_rating for gift cards versus software since our dataset has more gift cards reviews than software reviews. This is often called "selection bias" for the given facet, product_category in our case. We use SageMaker Data Wrangler and Clarify to generate a bias report with many metrics, including class imbalance (CI), difference in positive proportion labels (DPL), and Jensen–Shannon divergence (JS), among many others. Figure 5-17 shows a class imbalance for a subset of our dataset relative to the Gift Card product category and target star_rating of 5 and 4.

This bias report shows a class imbalance of 0.45 for the Gift Card product category facet. The class imbalance values range over the interval [-1, 1]. Values closer to 0 indicate a balanced distribution of samples relative to the facet being analyzed. Values closer to -1 and 1 indicate an imbalanced dataset and may require balancing before proceeding with feature selection, feature engineering, and model training.

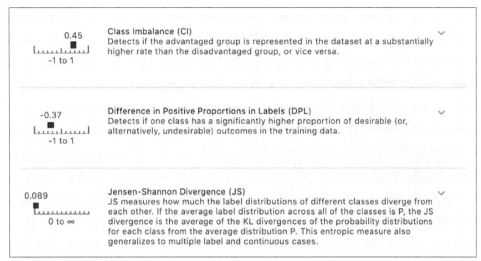

Figure 5-17. Detect class imbalance through a SageMaker Data Wrangler bias report.

In addition to detecting data bias with SageMaker Data Wrangler, SageMaker Clarify helps select the best columns (aka "features") for model training, detects bias in our models after training, explains model predictions, and detects statistical drift of model prediction inputs and outputs. Figure 5-18 shows where SageMaker Clarify is used throughout the remaining phases of the machine learning pipeline, including model training, tuning, and deployment.

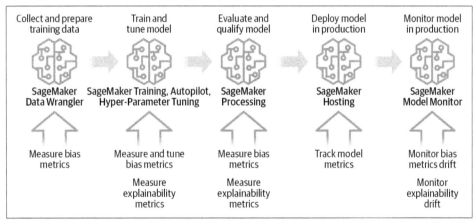

Figure 5-18. Measure data bias, model bias, feature importance, and model explainability with SageMaker Clarify.

In Chapter 7, we will calculate "post-training" metrics to detect bias in our model predictions in a similar fashion. In Chapter 9, we will calculate drift in data distributions and model explainability on our live models in production by setting thresholds for various distribution-distance metrics, comparing the live metrics to a baseline set of metrics created from our trained model before the model is deployed, and alerting us when the thresholds are exceeded after the model is deployed.

Detect Bias with a SageMaker Clarify Processing Job

We can also run Clarify as a SageMaker Processing Job to continually analyze our dataset at scale and calculate bias metrics as new data arrives. Following is the code to configure and run the SageMakerClarifyProcessor job using a DataConfig to specify our input dataset and BiasConfig to specify our product_category facet to analyze:

```
from sagemaker import clarify
import pandas as pd

df = pd.read_csv('./amazon_customer_reviews_dataset.csv')
bias_report_output_path = 's3://{}/clarify'.format(bucket)

clarify_processor = clarify.SageMakerClarifyProcessor(
        role=role,
        instance_count=1,
        instance_type='ml.c5.2xlarge',
        sagemaker_session=sess)

data_config = clarify.DataConfig(
        s3_data_input_path=data_s3_uri,
        s3_output_path=bias_report_output_path,
        label='star_rating',
        headers=df.columns.to_list(),
        dataset_type='text/csv')

data_bias_config = clarify.BiasConfig(
        label_values_or_threshold=[5, 4],
        facet_name='product_category',
        facet_values_or_threshold=['Gift Card'],
        group_name=product_category)

clarify_processor.run_pre_training_bias(
    data_config=data_config,
    data_bias_config=data_bias_config,
    methods='all',
    wait=True)
```

We are using methods='all' to calculate all data-bias metrics during this "pre-training" phase, but we can specify the list of metrics, including CI, DPL, JS, Kullback–Leibler divergence (KL), Lp-norm (LP), total variation distance (TVD), the Kolmogorov–Smirnov metric (KS), and conditional demographic disparity (CDD).

Once the SageMakerClarifyProcessor job finishes analyzing our dataset for bias, we view the generated bias reports in SageMaker Studio, as shown in Figure 5-19. In addition, SageMaker Clarify generates *analysis.json* with bias metrics and *report.ipynb* to visualize the bias metrics and share with our colleagues.

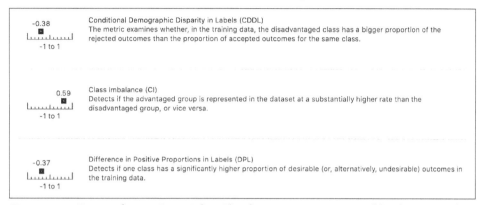

Figure 5-19. Extract from a SageMaker Clarify Bias Report generated by the SageMaker Processing Job.

Integrate Bias Detection into Custom Scripts with SageMaker Clarify Open Source

SageMaker also offers Clarify as a standalone, open source Python library (*https://oreil.ly/9qIUn*) to integrate bias and drift detection into our custom Python scripts. Following is an example using the smclarify Python library to detect bias and class imbalance from a Python script using a CSV file. To install this library, use pip install smclarify:

```
from smclarify.bias import report
import pandas as pd

df = pd.read_csv('./amazon_customer_reviews_dataset.csv')

facet_column = report.FacetColumn(name='product_category')

label_column = report.LabelColumn(
    name='star_rating',
    data=df['star_rating'],
    positive_label_values=[5, 4]
 )
group_variable = df['product_category']

report.bias_report(
    df,
    facet_column,
    label_column,
    stage_type=report.StageType.PRE_TRAINING,
    group_variable=group_variable
)
```

The result looks similar to this:

```
[{'value_or_threshold': 'Gift Card',
  'metrics': [{'name': 'CDDL',
    'description': 'Conditional Demographic Disparity in Labels (CDDL)',
    'value': -0.3754164610069102},
   {'name': 'CI',
    'description': 'Class Imbalance (CI)',
    'value': 0.4520671273445213},
   {'name': 'DPL',
    'description': 'Difference in Positive Proportions in Labels (DPL)',
    'value': -0.3679426717770344},
   {'name': 'JS',
    'description': 'Jensen-Shannon Divergence (JS)',
    'value': 0.11632161004661548},
   {'name': 'x',
    'description': 'Kullback-Leibler Divergence (KL)',
    'value': 0.3061581684888518},
   {'name': 'KS',
    'description': 'Kolmogorov-Smirnov Distance (KS)',
    'value': 0.36794267177703444},
   {'name': 'LP', 'description': 'L-p Norm (LP)', 'value': 0.5203495166028743},
   {'name': 'TVD',
    'description': 'Total Variation Distance (TVD)',
    'value': 0.36794267177703444}]},
}]
```

Mitigate Data Bias by Balancing the Data

We can mitigate the imbalances in our dataset by balancing the number of reviews across star rating classes and product categories, as shown in the following. Figure 5-20 visualizes the results for three sample product categories using Seaborn:

```
df_grouped_by = df.groupby(
  ["product_category", "star_rating"]
)[["product_category", "star_rating"]]

df_balanced = df_grouped_by.apply(
        lambda x: x.sample(df_grouped_by.size().min())\
        .reset_index(drop=True)
        )

import seaborn as sns

sns.countplot(data=df_balanced,
                        x="star_rating",
                        hue="product_category")
```

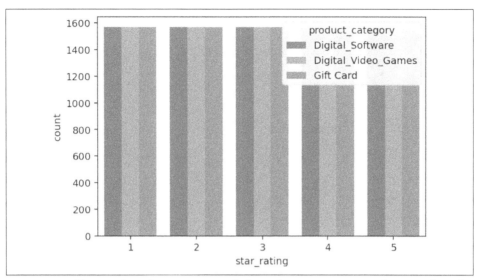

Figure 5-20. The number of reviews is now balanced across star rating classes and product categories.

We can rerun the bias analysis using SageMaker Clarify on the balanced dataset. The following is a sample result for the facet value "Gift Card":

```
[{'value_or_threshold': 'Gift Card',
  'metrics': [{'name': 'CDDL',
    'description': 'Conditional Demographic Disparity in Labels (CDDL)',
    'value': 0.0},
   {'name': 'CI',
    'description': 'Class Imbalance (CI)',
    'value': 0.3333333333333333},
   {'name': 'DPL',
    'description': 'Difference in Positive Proportions in Labels (DPL)',
    'value': 0.0},
   {'name': 'JS',
    'description': 'Jensen-Shannon Divergence (JS)',
    'value': 0.0},
   {'name': 'KL',
    'description': 'Kullback-Leibler Divergence (KL)',
    'value': 0.0},
   {'name': 'KS',
    'description': 'Kolmogorov-Smirnov Distance (KS)',
    'value': 0.0},
   {'name': 'LP', 'description': 'L-p Norm (LP)', 'value': 0.0},
   {'name': 'TVD',
    'description': 'Total Variation Distance (TVD)',
    'value': 0.0}]}]
```

We can see that all but one of the bias metrics values equal 0, which indicates an equal distribution across the three product categories. The class imbalance metric value of

0.33 is evenly balanced since we have three total product categories. The other two product categories, Digital_Software and Digital_Video_Games, also have a class imbalance metric value of 0.33, as shown in the following:

```
[{'value_or_threshold': 'Digital_Software',
  'metrics': [
   ...
   {'name': 'CI',
    'description': 'Class Imbalance (CI)',
    'value': 0.3333333333333333},
   ...
   ]}
]

[{'value_or_threshold': 'Digital_Video_Games',
  'metrics': [
   ...
   {'name': 'CI',
    'description': 'Class Imbalance (CI)',
    'value': 0.3333333333333333},
   ...
   ]}
]
```

A class imbalance metric value of 0.33 represents an evenly balanced dataset since we are analyzing three product categories. If we analyzed four product categories, the ideal class imbalance metric value would be 0.25 for all four product categories.

Detect Different Types of Drift with SageMaker Clarify

Statistical changes in data distributions are often called "shifts" in statistics terms or "drifts" in applied data science terms. There are multiple types of drifts, including "covariate," "label shift," and "concept shift." Covariate shifts occur in the data distribution of model inputs (independent variables). Label shifts occur in the data distribution of model outputs (dependent variables). Concept shifts occur when the actual definition of a label changes depending on a particular feature, such as geographical location or age group.

 Throughout the book, we use the terms *drift* and *shift* interchangeably to represent changes in statistical distributions. For more information on types of distribution drifts/shifts, see d2l.ai (*https://oreil.ly/HjtbC*).

Let's analyze concept drift by analyzing how different regions of the United States have different names for "soft drinks." The eastern region of the US calls soft drinks "soda," the northern-middle region calls them "pop," and the southern region calls them "coke." The change in labels relative to geographical location (the concept drift) is illustrated in Figure 5-21.

Figure 5-21. Concept shift on soft drink names in the US. Source: http://popvssoda.com.

Another example of concept drift involved one of our early book reviewers, who used the term "beef" to describe Chapter 9. While this term was initially interpreted as negative by the US- and Germany-based authors of this book, we realized that the term "beef" means something positive in the reviewer's geographical location and age group. If we were building a model to classify reviews of our book, we may want to adjust for this concept drift by factoring in the reviewers' location and age—or perhaps build separate models for different locations and age.

To detect covariate and label drift, we calculate baseline statistics during model training. We then can set thresholds using various statistical distribution-distance metrics discussed earlier, like KL, KS, LP, L-infinity norm, and more. These metrics answer various questions about the bias. For example, the divergence metric KL answers "How different are the distributions of star ratings for different product categories?" Whereas the KS metric answers "Which star ratings cause the greatest disparity per product category?"

If the calculated drift is greater than the given threshold, SageMaker can alert us and automatically trigger a retrain action, for example. To detect concept drift in the predicted labels relative to a particular feature, we capture live model inputs and outputs using SageMaker Model Monitor and send the model inputs to an offline human labeling workflow to create the ground truth labels. We compare the captured model outputs to the ground truth labels provided by humans using SageMaker Clarify. If the distribution of model outputs differs beyond a given threshold relative to the ground truth labels, SageMaker can notify us and automatically trigger a model retrain, for example. We demonstrate how to use SageMaker Model Monitor and Clarify to monitor live predictions in Chapter 9.

Also in Chapter 9, we demonstrate how SageMaker Model Monitor samples live model inputs and outputs, calculates model feature-importance and model-explainability statistics, and compares these statistics to a baseline created from our trained model. If SageMaker Model Monitor detects a shift in feature importance and model explainability relative to the baseline, it can automatically trigger a model retrain and notify the appropriate on-call scientist or engineer.

Analyze Our Data with AWS Glue DataBrew

We can use Glue DataBrew to analyze our data as well. While not natively integrated with SageMaker lineage and artifact tracking, DataBrew provides a slick, interactive visual interface to ingest and analyze data without writing any code. We can connect data sources from data lakes, data warehouses, and databases. Let's load the Amazon Customer Reviews Dataset (Parquet) into DataBrew and analyze some of the visualizations:

```
db.create_dataset(
    Name='amazon-reviews-parquet',
    Input={
        'S3InputDefinition': {
            'Bucket': 'amazon-reviews-pds',
            'Key': 'parquet/'
        }
    }
)
```

Once the dataset is created within DataBrew, we start seeing correlations and other summary statistics, as shown in Figure 5-22. Specifically, we can see a strong correlation between helpful_votes and total_votes, while star_rating is not correlated with either helpful_votes or total_votes.

In addition to correlations, DataBrew highlights missing cells, duplicate rows, and class imbalances, as shown in Figure 5-23.

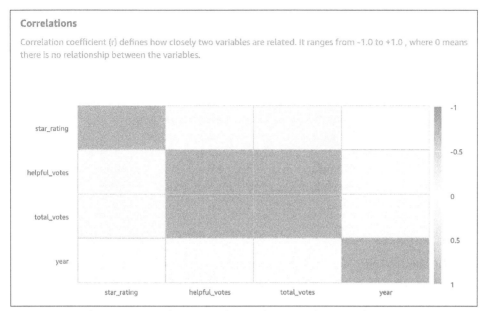

Figure 5-22. Glue DataBrew shows correlations between dataset columns.

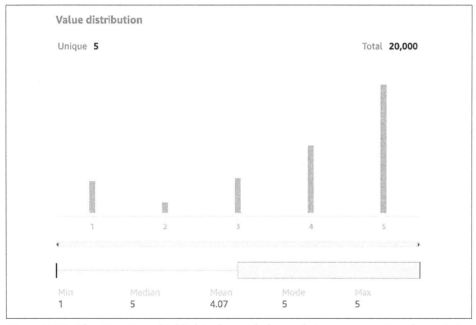

Figure 5-23. Glue DataBrew highlights class imbalances between star rating classes 1–5.

We can use Glue DataBrew for a lot of data analysis and transformation use cases, but we should use SageMaker Data Wrangler for machine-learning-based workloads to better track our data and model lineage throughout the pipeline.

Reduce Cost and Increase Performance

In this section, we want to provide some tips and tricks to reduce cost and increase performance during data exploration. We can optimize expensive SQL COUNT queries across large datasets by using approximate counts. Leveraging Redshift AQUA, we can reduce network I/O and increase query performance. And if we feel our Quick-Sight dashboards could benefit from a performance increase, we should consider enabling QuickSight SPICE.

Use a Shared S3 Bucket for Nonsensitive Athena Query Results

By choosing a shared S3 location for Athena query results across our team, we can reuse cached query results, improve query performance, and save on data-transfer costs. The following code sample highlights s3_staging_dir, which can be shared across different team members to improve the performance of commonly executed queries by reusing cached results:

```
from pyathena import connect
import pandas as pd

# Set the Athena query results S3 bucket
s3_staging_dir = 's3://{0}/athena/staging'.format(bucket)

conn = connect(region_name=region, s3_staging_dir=s3_staging_dir)

sql_statement="""
SELECT DISTINCT product_category from {0}.{1}
ORDER BY product_category
""".format(database_name, table_name)

pd.read_sql(sql_statement, conn)
```

Approximate Counts with HyperLogLog

Counting is a big deal in analytics. We always need to count users (daily active users), orders, returns, support calls, etc. Maintaining super-fast counts in an ever-growing dataset can be a critical advantage over competitors.

Both Amazon Redshift and Athena support HyperLogLog (HLL), a type of "cardinality-estimation" or COUNT DISTINCT algorithm designed to provide highly accurate counts (< 2% error) in a small amount of time (seconds) requiring a tiny fraction of the storage (1.2 KB) to store 150+ million separate counts. HLL is a probabilistic data structure that is common in counting use cases such as number of likes, number of page visits, number of click-throughs, etc.

 Other forms of HLL include HyperLogLog++, Streaming HyperLoglog, and HLL-TailCut+, among others. Count-Min Sketch and Bloom Filters are similar algorithms for approximating counts and set membership, respectively. Locality Sensitive Hashing (LSH) is another popular algorithm for calculating "fuzzy" similarity metrics on large datasets with a small footprint.

The way this works is that Amazon Redshift and Athena update a tiny HLL data structure when inserting new data into the database (think of a tiny hash table). The next time a count query arrives from a user, Amazon Redshift and Athena simply look up the value in the HLL data structure and quickly return the value—without having to physically scan all the disks in the cluster to perform the count.

Let's compare the execution times of both SELECT APPROXIMATE COUNT() and SELECT COUNT() in Amazon Redshift. Here is SELECT APPROXIMATE COUNT():

```
%%time
df = pd.read_sql_query("""
SELECT APPROXIMATE COUNT(DISTINCT customer_id)
FROM {}.{}
GROUP BY product_category
""".format(redshift_schema, redshift_table_2015), engine)
```

For this query, we should see output similar to this:

```
CPU times: user 3.66 ms, sys: 3.88 ms, total: 7.55 ms
Wall time: 18.3 s
```

Next up, SELECT COUNT():

```
%%time
df = pd.read_sql_query("""
SELECT COUNT(DISTINCT customer_id)
FROM {}.{}
GROUP BY product_category
""".format(redshift_schema, redshift_table_2015), engine)
```

For this query, we should see output similar to this:

```
CPU times: user 2.24 ms, sys: 973 µs, total: 3.21 ms
Wall time: 47.9 s
```

 Note that we run the APPROXIMATE COUNT first to factor out the performance boost of the query cache. The COUNT is much slower. If we rerun, both queries will be very fast due to the query cache.

We see that APPROXIMATE COUNT DISTINCT is 160% faster than regular COUNT DISTINCT in this case. The results were approximately 1.2% different—satisfying the < 2% error guaranteed by HLL.

Remember that HLL is an approximation and may not be suitable for use cases that require exact numbers (e.g., financial reporting).

Dynamically Scale a Data Warehouse with AQUA for Amazon Redshift

Existing data warehouses move data from storage nodes to compute nodes during query execution. This requires high network I/O between the nodes—and reduces overall query performance. AQUA (Advanced Query Accelerator) is a hardware-accelerated, distributed cache on top of our Amazon Redshift data warehouse. AQUA uses custom, AWS-designed chips to perform computations directly in the cache. This reduces the need to move data from storage nodes to compute nodes—therefore reducing network I/O and increasing query performance. These AWS-designed chips are implemented in field programmable gate arrays and help speed up data encryption and compression for maximum security of our data. AQUA dynamically scales out more capacity as well.

Improve Dashboard Performance with QuickSight SPICE

QuickSight is built with the "Super-fast, Parallel, In-memory Calculation Engine," or SPICE. SPICE uses a combination of columnar storage, in-memory storage, and machine code generation to run low-latency queries on large datasets. QuickSight updates its cache as data changes in the underlying data sources, including Amazon S3 and Redshift.

Summary

In this chapter, we answered various questions about our data using tools from the AWS analytics stack, including Athena and Amazon Redshift. We created a business intelligence dashboard using QuickSight and deployed a SageMaker Processing Job using open source AWS Deequ and Apache Spark to continuously monitor data quality and detect anomalies as new data arrives. This continuous data-quality monitoring creates confidence in our data pipelines and allows downstream teams, including data scientists and AI/ML engineers, to develop highly accurate and relevant models for our applications to consume. We also used Glue DataBrew and SageMaker Data Wrangler to analyze our data for correlations, anomalies, imbalances, and bias.

In Chapter 6, we will select and prepare features from our dataset to use in the model training and optimization phases in Chapters 7 and 8, respectively.

Prepare the Dataset for Model Training

In the previous chapter, we explored our dataset using SageMaker Studio and various Python-based visualization libraries. We gained some key business insights into our product catalog using the Amazon Customer Reviews Dataset. In addition, we analyzed summary statistics and performed quality checks on our dataset using SageMaker Processing Jobs, Apache Spark, and the AWS Deequ open source library.

In this chapter, we discuss how to transform human-readable text into machine-readable vectors in a process called "feature engineering." Specifically, we will convert the raw `review_body` column from the Amazon Customer Reviews Dataset into BERT vectors. We use these BERT vectors to train and optimize a review-classifier model in Chapters 7 and 8, respectively. We will also dive deep into the origins of natural language processing and BERT in Chapter 7.

We will use the review-classifier model to predict the `star_rating` of product reviews from social channels, partner websites, etc. By predicting the `star_rating` of reviews in the wild, the product management and customer service teams can use these predictions to address quality issues as they escalate publicly—not wait for a direct inbound email or phone call. This reduces the mean time to detect quality issues down to minutes/hours from days/months.

Perform Feature Selection and Engineering

AI and machine learning algorithms are numerical-optimization methods that operate on numbers and vectors instead of raw text and images. These vectors, often called "embeddings," are projected into a high-dimensional vector space. The algorithms perform optimizations in this high-dimensional vector space.

One-hot encoding is a form of embedding for categorical data in a tabular dataset. With one-hot encoding, we represent each categorical value with a unique vector of

0s and 1s. The number of dimensions—the size of each vector—is equal to the number of unique categorical values.

One of the most important aspects of AI and machine learning, feature engineering usually requires more time than any other phase in the typical machine learning pipeline. Feature engineering helps to reduce data dimensionality, prevent certain features from statistically dominating the algorithm, speed up model-training time, reduce numerical instabilities, and improve overall model-prediction accuracy.

With many feature-engineering iterations and visualizations, we will start to really understand our dataset, including outliers, correlations, and principal components. Analyzing the features in the context of our models, we will also gain intuition about which features are more important than others. Some features will improve model performance, while other features show no improvement or reduce model performance.

Careless feature engineering can lead to disastrous results. At worst, poor feature engineering can lead to socially destructive models that propagate racial, gender, and age bias. At best, poor feature engineering produces suboptimal models that make poor movie recommendations, overstate revenue forecasts, or create excess inventory.

While domain experts can certainly help evaluate which features to include and how they should be engineered, there are certain "latent" features hidden in our datasets not immediately recognizable by a human. Netflix's recommendation system is famous for discovering new movie genres beyond the usual drama, horror, and romantic comedy. For example, they discovered very specific genres such as "Gory Canadian Revenge Movies," "Sentimental Movies About Horses for Ages 11–12," "Romantic Crime Movies Based on Classic Literature," and "Raunchy Mad Scientist Comedies."

Many of these "secret" genres were discovered using Netflix's Viewing History Service, also called "VHS"—a throwback to the popular video-tape format from the 1980s and 1990s.

At a high level, feature engineering is divided into three logical types: selection, creation, and transformation. Not all may apply to our use case, but they should all be considered and explored.

Feature selection identifies the data attributes that best represent our dataset. In addition, feature selection filters out irrelevant and redundant attributes using statistical methods. For example, if two data points are highly correlated, such as total_votes and helpful_votes, then perhaps only one is needed to train our model. Selecting only one of these attributes helps to reduce feature dimensionality and train models faster while preserving model accuracy.

Feature creation combines existing data points into new features that help improve the predictive power of our model. For example, combining `review_headline` and `review_body` into a single feature may lead to more accurate predictions than does using them separately.

Feature transformation converts data from one representation to another to facilitate machine learning. Transforming continuous values such as a timestamp into categorical "bins" like hourly, daily, or monthly helps to reduce dimensionality. While we lose some information and granularity during the binning transformation, our models may actually benefit from the broader generalization. Two common statistical feature transformations are normalization and standardization. Normalization scales all values of a particular data point between 0 and 1, while standardization transforms the values to a mean of 0 and standard deviation of 1. Standardization is often preferred as it better handles outliers than normalization does and allows us to compare features of different units and scales. These techniques help reduce the impact of large-valued data points, such as number of reviews (represented in thousands), versus small-valued data points, such as `helpful_votes` (represented in tens). Without these techniques, the model could potentially favor the number of reviews over `help ful_votes` given the order of magnitude difference in values.

Let's walk through a typical feature engineering pipeline from feature selection to feature transformation, as shown in Figure 6-1.

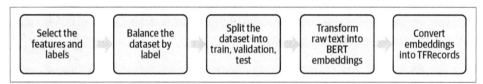

Figure 6-1. Steps in a typical feature engineering pipeline.

Select Training Features Based on Feature Importance

We can use SageMaker Data Wrangler's "Quick Model" analysis to evaluate which columns of our data are most useful when making predictions for a given label, `star_rating` in our case. We simply select the data that we want Data Wrangler to analyze along with the `star_rating` label that we want to predict. Data Wrangler automatically preprocesses the data, trains a "quick model," evaluates the model, and calculates a feature importance score for each feature. Figure 6-2 shows the feature importance results for our Amazon Customer Reviews Dataset using Data Wrangler's Quick Model analysis feature.

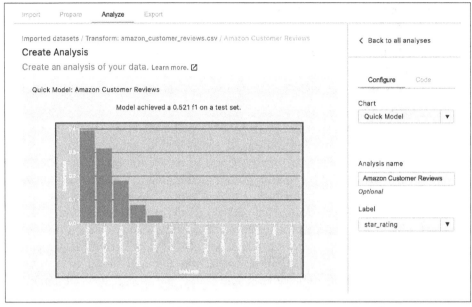

Figure 6-2. Data Wrangler's Quick Model analysis allows us to analyze feature importance.

Following the Quick Model analysis, the most important feature for our dataset is `review_body`, with `review_headline`, `product_title`, and `product_category` being next-most important.

Because we plan to use our model to classify product reviews from social channels and partner websites "in the wild" that only have the raw review text, we have decided to only use the `review_body` column to predict a `star_rating`. In our case, `star_rat ing` is the "label," and a transformed version of the `review_body` is the "feature." The `star_rating` label is the actual `star_rating` value, 1 through 5, from our training dataset. This is the value that our trained model will learn to predict in Chapter 7. The `review_body` feature, transformed from raw text into a series of BERT vectors, is the input for our model-training process. Later in this chapter, we will demonstrate how to transform the raw text into BERT vectors.

We use both the feature and the label to train our model to predict a `star_rating` label from `review_body` text from social channels and partner websites. Following, we view the `star_rating` and `review_body` columns as a pandas DataFrame:

```
df = pd.read_csv('./data/amazon_reviews_us_Digital_Software_v1_00.tsv.gz',
        delimiter='\t',
        quoting=csv.QUOTE_NONE,
        compression='gzip')

df.head(5)
```

star_rating	review_body
1	Poor business decision to strip away user abil...
5	Avast is an easy to use and download. I feel i...
2	Problems from the start. It has been 30 days,...
4	Works well.
3	Hard to use

Since the `star_rating` label is discrete and categorical (1, 2, 3, 4, 5), we will use a "classification" algorithm. We are not treating this as a regression problem since we are using `star_rating` as a categorical feature with only five possible values: 1, 2, 3, 4, or 5. If `star_rating` contained continuous values, such as 3.14, 4.20, or 1.69, then we would potentially use `star_rating` as a continuous feature with a regression model.

Instead of the traditional machine learning classification algorithms, we will use a neural-network-based classification model using the Keras API with TensorFlow 2.x. We will dive deep into model training in the next chapter. Let's move forward and prepare our Amazon Customer Reviews Dataset to train a model that predicts `star_rating` (1–5) from `review_body` text.

Balance the Dataset to Improve Model Accuracy

In the previous chapter, we showed the breakdown of `star_rating` for all reviews in our dataset, and we saw that approximately 62% of all reviews have a `star_rating` of 5, as shown in Figure 6-3.

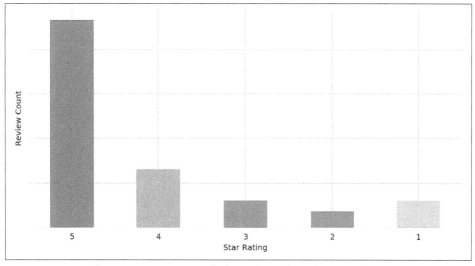

Figure 6-3. Our dataset contains an unbalanced number of reviews by star rating.

If we naively train on this unbalanced dataset, our classifier may simply learn to predict 5 for the star_rating since 62% accuracy is better than 20% random accuracy across the 5 classes: 1, 2, 3, 4, or 5. In other words, an unbalanced training dataset may create a model with artificially high accuracy when, in reality, it learned to just predict 5 every time. This model would not do well in a production setting.

 Some algorithms like XGBoost support a scaling factor to counteract the problem of unbalanced classes. However, in general, it's a good idea to handle class imbalance during the feature engineering process to avoid misusing these features later.

There are two common ways to balance a dataset and prevent bias toward a particular class: undersampling the majority classes (star_rating 5) and oversampling the minority classes (star_rating 2 and 3). When choosing a sampling strategy, we should carefully consider how the sampling affects the overall mean and standard deviation of the feature's data distribution. We see examples of undersampling in Figure 6-4 and oversampling in Figure 6-5.

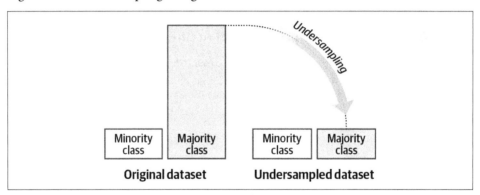

Figure 6-4. Undersampling the majority class down to the minority class.

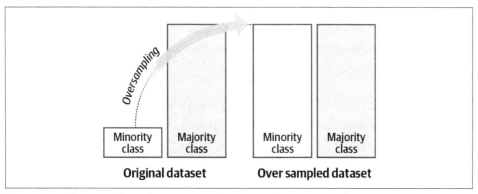

Figure 6-5. Oversampling the minority class up to the majority class.

The idea is to evenly distribute data along a particular label or "class," as it's commonly called. In our case, the class is our categorical star_rating field. Therefore, we want our training dataset to contain a consistent number of reviews for each star_rating: 1, 2, 3, 4, and 5. Here is the code to undersample the original dataset using star_rating:

```
df_grouped_by = df.groupby(["star_rating"])

df_balanced = df_grouped_by.apply(
        lambda x: x.sample(df_grouped_by.size().min())\
        .reset_index(drop=True)
)
```

We now have a balanced dataset, as shown in Figure 6-6.

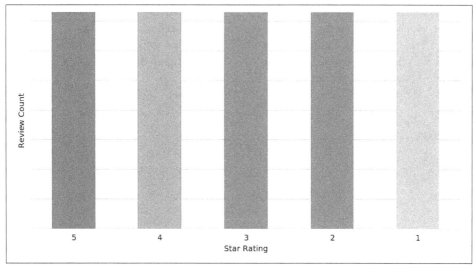

Figure 6-6. Balanced dataset for star_rating class.

One drawback to undersampling is that the training dataset size is sampled down to the size of the smallest category. This can reduce the predictive power and robustness of the trained models by reducing the signal from undersampled classes. In this example, we reduced the number of reviews by 65%, from approximately 100,000 to 35,000.

Oversampling will artificially create new data for the underrepresented class. In our case, star_rating 2 and 3 are underrepresented. One common technique is called the *Synthetic Minority Oversampling Technique*, which uses statistical methods to synthetically generate new data from existing data. They tend to work better when we have a larger dataset, so be careful when using oversampling on small datasets with a low number of minority class examples.

Split the Dataset into Train, Validation, and Test Sets

Model development typically follows three phases: model *training*, model *validating*, and model *testing* (Figure 6-7).

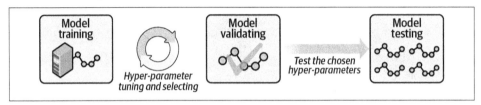

Figure 6-7. Phases of a typical model development life cycle.

To align with these three phases, we split the balanced data into separate train, validation, and test datasets. The train dataset is used for model training. The validation dataset is used to validate the model training configuration called the "hyper-parameters." And the test dataset is used to test the chosen hyper-parameters. For our model, we chose 90% train, 5% validation, and 5% test, as this breakdown, shown in Figure 6-8, works well for our dataset and model.

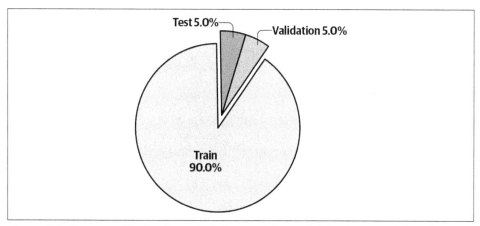

Figure 6-8. Dataset splits for the typical phases of the model development life cycle.

Let's split the data using scikit-learn's `train_test_split` function, with the `stratify` parameter set to the `star_rating` field to preserve our previous balance efforts. If we don't specify the `stratify` parameter, the split function is free to choose any data in the given dataset, causing the splits to become unbalanced:

```
from sklearn.model_selection import train_test_split

# Split all data into 90% train and 10% holdout
df_train, df_holdout = train_test_split(
        df_balanced,
        test_size=0.10,
    stratify=df_balanced['star_rating'])

# Split holdout data into 50% validation and 50% test
df_validation, df_test = train_test_split(
        df_holdout,
        test_size=0.50,
        stratify=df_holdout[ 'star_rating'])
```

In this case, we are not using k-folds cross-validation—a classic machine learning technique that reuses each row of data across different splits, including train, validation, and test. K-folds cross-validation is traditionally applied to smaller datasets, and, in our case, we have a large amount of data so we can avoid the downside of k-folds: data "leakage" between the train, validation, and test phases. Data leakage can lead to artificially inflated model accuracy for our trained models. These models don't perform well on real-world data outside of the lab. In summary, each of the three phases, train, validation, and test, should use separate and independent datasets, otherwise leakage may occur.

On a related note, time-series data is often prone to leakage across splits. Companies often want to validate a new model using "back-in-time" historical information before pushing the model to production. When working with time-series data, make sure the model does not peek into the future accidentally. Otherwise, these models may appear more accurate than they really are.

 Peeking into the future almost ended in disaster for the characters in the movie *Back to the Future*. Similarly, peeking into the future may cause trouble for our modeling efforts as well.

Additionally, we may want to keep all data for the same customer in the same split. Otherwise, an individual's customer data is spread across multiple splits, which could cause problems. In this case, we would group the data by `customer_id` before creating the splits. Our model does not require us to group our data by `customer_id`, so we will skip this step.

When processing large datasets at scale with SageMaker, we can split the data across multiple instances in a cluster. This is called *sharding* and we will demonstrate this later when we transform our data using multiple instances in a SageMaker cluster using scikit-learn, Apache Spark, and TensorFlow.

Transform Raw Text into BERT Embeddings

We will use TensorFlow and a state-of-the-art natural language processing (NLP) and natural language understanding neural network architecture called BERT (*https://oreil.ly/HBic8*). We will dive deep into *BERT* in a bit. At a high level—and unlike previous generations of NLP models, such as Word2Vec (*https://oreil.ly/nKuFP*)—BERT captures the bidirectional (left-to-right and right-to-left) context of each word in a sentence. This allows BERT to learn different meanings of the same word across different sentences. For example, the meaning of the word *bank* is different in these two sentences: "A thief stole money from the *bank* vault" and "Later, he was arrested while fishing on a river *bank*."

For each `review_body`, we use BERT to create a feature vector within a previously learned, high-dimensional vector space of 30,000 words, or "tokens." BERT learned these tokens by training on millions of documents, including Wikipedia and Google Books.

Figure 6-9 shows how BERT converts the raw input text into the final BERT embedding, which is passed through the actual model architecture.

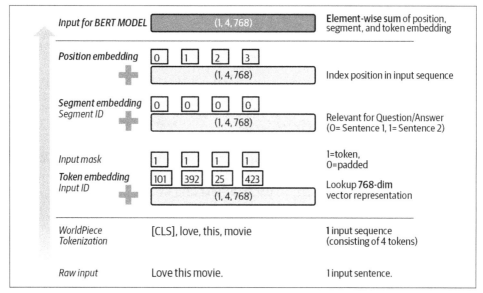

Figure 6-9. BERT converts raw input text into embeddings.

BERT first applies WordPiece tokenization to the raw input text. WordPiece is a technique to segment words to the subword level in NLP tasks with a vocabulary dimension of approximately 30,000 tokens. Note that BERT also adds special tokens at the beginning of the input sequence, such as [CLS] to mark a classification task.

In a next step, BERT creates the token embedding by looking up the 768-dimensional vector representation of any input token. The `input_id` is the actual ID that points to the relevant token embedding vector. An `input_mask` specifies which tokens BERT should pay attention to (0 or 1). In case we pass multiple sentences to BERT, the segment embedding will map each token to the corresponding input sentence (0 refers to the first sentence, 1 refers to the second sentence). Then the position embedding keeps track of the position of each token in the input sequence (0, 1, 2, etc.). We will learn that a very important hyper-parameter for BERT is `max_seq_length`, which defines the maximum number of input tokens we can pass to BERT per sample. As the maximum value for this parameter is 512, the position embedding is a lookup table of dimension (512, 768).

In a final step, BERT creates the element-wise sum of the token embedding, the segment embedding, and the position embedding. The resulting embedding of dimension (n, 768) where n stands for the number of input tokens will be passed as the input embedding for BERT.

Let's use a variant of BERT called DistilBERT (*https://oreil.ly/t90gS*). DistilBERT is a lightweight version of BERT that is 60% faster and 40% smaller while preserving 97% of BERT's language understanding capabilities. We use the popular Hugging Face

Python library called Transformers to perform the transformation. To install this library, simply type `pip install transformers`:

```
from transformers import DistilBertTokenizer

tokenizer = DistilBertTokenizer.from_pretrained('distilbert-base-uncased')

tokens = tokenizer.tokenize("""I needed an antivirus application and know
    the quality of Norton products. This was a no brainer for me and I am
    glad it was so simple to get.""")
```

The tokenizer performs lower-casing and parses the text into a set of words contained in the pre-trained DistilBERT vocabulary. The Transformers library uses another popular library called WordPieces to parse the text into word tokens:

```
print(tokens)

['i', 'needed', 'an', 'anti', '##virus', 'application', 'and', 'know', 'the',
'quality', 'of', 'norton', 'products', '.', 'this', 'was', 'a', 'no',
'brain', '##er', 'for', 'me', 'and', 'i', 'am', 'glad', 'it', 'was', 'so',
'simple', 'to', 'get', '.']
```

Most BERT variants, including DistilBERT, have a concept of a "maximum sequence length" that defines the maximum number of tokens used to represent each text input. In our case, any reviews that end up with `max_seq_length` tokens (after tokenization) will be truncated down to 64. Reviews that end up with less than 64 tokens will be padded to a length of 64. Empirically, we have chosen 64 for the maximum sequence length as 80% of our reviews are under 64 words, as we saw in Chapter 5, and, while not exact, the number of words is a good indication of the number of tokens. Below is a distribution of the number of words per review presented in Chapter 5:

```
10%         2.000000
20%         7.000000
30%        19.000000
40%        22.000000
50%        26.000000
60%        32.000000
70%        43.000000
80%        63.000000 <===
90%       110.000000
100%     5347.000000
```

We must use this same maximum sequence length during feature engineering and model training. So if we want to try a different value, we need to regenerate the BERT embeddings with the updated value. If we aren't sure which value to choose, we may want to generate multiple versions of the embeddings using 128, 256, and 512 as the maximum sequence length. These seem to work well for most BERT tasks. Larger values will likely increase model training time due to higher dimensionality.

We still have some more processing to do, however, as our DistilBERT model uses numeric arrays of length 64 derived from the preceding text-based tokens:

input_ids
> The numeric ID of the token from the BERT vocabulary

input_mask
> Specifies which tokens BERT should pay attention to (0 or 1)

segment_ids
> Always 0 in our case since we are doing a single-sequence NLP task (1 if we were doing a two-sequence NLP task such as next-sentence prediction)

Fortunately, the Transformers tokenizer creates two of the three arrays for us—and even pads and truncates the arrays as needed based on the maximum sequence length!

```
MAX_SEQ_LENGTH = 64

encode_plus_tokens = tokenizer.encode_plus(
    text_input.text,
    pad_to_max_length=True,
    max_length=MAX_SEQ_LENGTH)

# Convert tokens to ids from the pre-trained BERT vocabulary

input_ids = encode_plus_tokens['input_ids']
print(input_ids)
```

Output:

```
[101, 1045, 2734, 2019, 3424, 23350, 4646, 1998, 2113, 1996, 3737, 1997, 10770,
3688, 1012, 2023, 2001, 1037, 2053, 4167, 2121, 2005, 2033, 1998, 1045, 2572,
5580, 2009, 2001, 2061, 3722, 2000, 2131, 1012, 102, 0, 0, 0, 0, 0, 0, 0, 0, 0,
0, 0, 0, 0, 0, 0, 0, 0, 0, 0, 0, 0, 0, 0, 0, 0, 0, 0, 0, 0,
0, 0, 0, 0, 0, 0, 0, 0, 0, 0, 0, 0, 0, 0, 0, 0, 0, 0, 0, 0, 0, 0, 0, 0, 0, 0,
0, 0, 0, 0, 0, 0, 0, 0, 0, 0, 0, 0, 0, 0, 0, 0, 0, 0, 0, 0, 0, 0, 0, 0, 0, 0,
0, 0, 0, 0, 0, 0]
```

```
# Specifies which tokens BERT should pay attention to (0 or 1)
input_mask = encode_plus_tokens['attention_mask']
print(input_mask)
```

Output:

```
[1, 1, 1, 1, 1, 1, 1, 1, 1, 1, 1, 1, 1, 1, 1, 1, 1, 1, 1, 1, 1, 1, 1, 1, 1, 1,
1, 1, 1, 1, 1, 1, 1, 0, 0, 0, 0, 0, 0, 0, 0, 0, 0, 0, 0, 0, 0, 0, 0, 0, 0,
0, 0, 0, 0, 0, 0, 0, 0, 0, 0, 0, 0, 0, 0, 0, 0, 0, 0, 0, 0, 0, 0, 0, 0, 0, 0,
0, 0, 0, 0, 0, 0, 0, 0, 0, 0, 0, 0, 0, 0, 0, 0, 0, 0, 0, 0, 0, 0, 0, 0, 0, 0,
0, 0, 0, 0, 0, 0, 0, 0, 0, 0, 0, 0, 0, 0, 0, 0, 0, 0, 0, 0]
```

The third array, `segment_ids`, is easy to generate on our own since it contains all 0s in our case as we are performing a single-sequence classification NLP task. For two-sequence NLP tasks such as question-and-answer, the `sequence_id` is either 0 (question) or 1 (answer):

```
segment_ids = [0] * MAX_SEQ_LENGTH
print(segment_ids)
```

Output:

```
[0, 0, 0, 0, 0, 0, 0, 0, 0, 0, 0, 0, 0, 0, 0, 0, 0, 0, 0, 0, 0, 0, 0, 0, 0, 0,
 0, 0, 0, 0, 0, 0, 0, 0, 0, 0, 0, 0, 0, 0, 0, 0, 0, 0, 0, 0, 0, 0, 0, 0, 0, 0,
 0, 0, 0, 0, 0, 0, 0, 0, 0, 0, 0, 0, 0, 0, 0, 0, 0, 0, 0, 0, 0, 0, 0, 0, 0, 0,
 0, 0, 0, 0, 0, 0, 0, 0, 0, 0, 0, 0, 0, 0, 0, 0, 0, 0, 0, 0, 0, 0, 0, 0, 0, 0,
 0, 0, 0, 0, 0, 0, 0, 0, 0, 0, 0, 0, 0, 0, 0, 0, 0, 0, 0, 0, 0, 0, 0, 0, 0, 0]
```

Convert Features and Labels to Optimized TensorFlow File Format

The last step in our feature engineering journey is to store our newly engineered features in the `TFRecord` file format (*.tfrecord* file extension). `TFRecord` is a binary, lightweight file format optimized for TensorFlow data processing and is based on protocol buffers ("protobufs"). TFRecords are cross-platform and cross-language—as well as highly efficient for data processing workloads. They are encoded and optimized for sequential, row-based access used during model training. This encoding contains features and labels—as well as any corresponding metadata for each example.

> The term "example" in the machine learning context means a row of data used for model training (including the label) or predicting (predicting the label).

While `TFRecord` is the file format, `tf.train.Example` and `tf.train.Feature` are the most common data structures stored within TFRecords. `tf.train.Feature` stores lists of either `byte`, `float`, or `int64` using `tf.train.BytesList`, `FloatList`, and `Int64List`, respectively.

Here is the code to convert our features into TFRecords using the TensorFlow API:

```
import tensorflow as tf
import collections
tfrecord_writer = tf.io.TFRecordWriter(output_file)

tfrecord_features = collections.OrderedDict()

tfrecord_features['input_ids'] =
    tf.train.Feature(int64_list=tf.train.Int64List(
        value=input_ids))
tfrecord_features['input_mask'] =
```

```
        tf.train.Feature(int64_list=tf.train.Int64List(
            value=input_mask))
    tfrecord_features['segment_ids'] =
        tf.train.Feature(int64_list=tf.train.Int64List(
            value=segment_ids))

    # Target label (star_rating)
    tfrecord_features['label_ids'] =
        tf.train.Feature(int64_list=tf.train.Int64List(
            value=[label_id]))

    tfrecord = tf.train.Example(
            features=tf.train.Features(feature=tfrecord_features))

    tfrecord_writer.write(tfrecord.SerializeToString())

    tfrecord_writer.close()
```

`tf.train.Example.SerializeToString()` produces a serialized, binary, and human-unreadable string, as follows:

```
[b'\n\xfe\x03\n\x96\x01\n\x0bsegment_ids\x12\x86\x01\x1a\x83\x01\n\x80\x01\n\
xb6\x01\n\tinput_ids\x12\xa8\x01\x1a\xa5\x01\n\xa2\x01e\x95\x08\x8d\x10\x8a\
x1d\xd0\x0f\xd3\x10\xf4\x07f\n\x95\x01\n\ninput_mask\x12\x01\x01\x01\x01\x01\
x01\x01\n\tlabel_ids\x12\x05\x1a\x03\n\x01\x04']
```

Scale Feature Engineering with SageMaker Processing Jobs

Up until now, we've been working in a SageMaker Notebook on a sample of the dataset. Let's move our custom Python code into a SageMaker Processing Job and scale our feature engineering to all 150 million reviews in our dataset. SageMaker Processing Jobs will parallelize our custom scripts (aka "Script Mode") or Docker images (aka "Bring Your Own Container") over many SageMaker instances in a cluster, as shown in Figure 6-10.

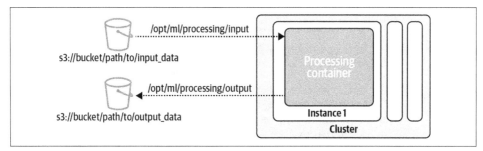

Figure 6-10. SageMaker Processing Jobs can parallelize code and Docker images over many SageMaker instances in a cluster.

In a later chapter, we will automate this step with an end-to-end pipeline. For now, let's just focus on scaling our feature engineering step to a SageMaker cluster using Processing Jobs.

Transform with scikit-learn and TensorFlow

Let's balance, split, and transform the entire dataset across a cluster using TensorFlow, scikit-learn, BERT, and SageMaker Processing Jobs, as shown in Figure 6-11.

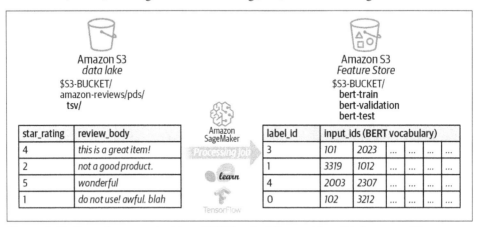

Figure 6-11. Transform raw text into BERT embeddings with scikit-learn and Sage-Maker Processing Jobs.

First we configure the scikit-learn Processing Job with the version of scikit-learn, the instance type, and number of instances for our cluster. Since the transformations are stateless, the more instances we use, the faster the processing will happen. Note that we are only using scikit-learn to balance and split the data. The heavy lifting is done using TensorFlow and Transformers:

```
from sagemaker.sklearn.processing import SKLearnProcessor
from sagemaker.processing import ProcessingInput, ProcessingOutput

processor = SKLearnProcessor(framework_version='<SCIKIT_LEARN_VERSION>',
                             role=role,
                             instance_type='ml.c5.4xlarge',
                             instance_count=2)
```

> We can specify `instance_type='local'` in the SageMaker Processing Job to run the script either inside our notebook or on our local laptop. This lets us "locally" run the processing job on a small subset of data in a notebook before launching a full-scale SageMaker Processing Job.

Next, we start the SageMaker Processing Job by specifying the location of the transformed features and sharding the data across the two instances in our Processing Job cluster to reduce the time needed to transform the data. We specify the S3 location of the input dataset and various arguments, such as the train, validation, and test split percentages. We also provide the max_seq_length that we chose for BERT:

```
processor.run(code='preprocess-scikit-text-to-bert.py',
  inputs=[
    ProcessingInput(input_name='raw-input-data',
                    source=raw_input_data_s3_uri,
                    destination='/opt/ml/processing/input/data/',
                    s3_data_distribution_type='ShardedByS3Key')
  ],
  outputs=[
    ProcessingOutput(output_name='bert-train',
                     s3_upload_mode='EndOfJob',
                     source='/opt/ml/processing/output/bert/train'),
    ProcessingOutput(output_name='bert-validation',
                     s3_upload_mode='EndOfJob',
                     source='/opt/ml/processing/output/bert/validation'),
    ProcessingOutput(output_name='bert-test',
                     s3_upload_mode='EndOfJob',
                     source='/opt/ml/processing/output/bert/test'),
  ],
  arguments=['--train-split-percentage',
             str(train_split_percentage),
             '--validation-split-percentage',
             str(validation_split_percentage),
             '--test-split-percentage',
             str(test_split_percentage),
             '--max-seq-length', str(max_seq_length)],
  logs=True,
  wait=False)
```

When the job completes, we retrieve the S3 output locations as follows:

```
output_config = processing_job_description['ProcessingOutputConfig']

for output in output_config['Outputs']:
  if output['OutputName'] == 'bert-train':
    processed_train_data_s3_uri = output['S3Output']['S3Uri']
  if output['OutputName'] == 'bert-validation':
    processed_validation_data_s3_uri = output['S3Output']['S3Uri']
  if output['OutputName'] == 'bert-test':
    processed_test_data_s3_uri = output['S3Output']['S3Uri']
```

Transform with Apache Spark and TensorFlow

Apache Spark is a powerful data processing and feature transformation engine supported by SageMaker Processing Jobs. While Apache Spark does not support BERT natively, we can use the Python-based BERT Transformers library within a PySpark application to scale our BERT Transformations across a distributed Spark cluster. In this case, we are using Spark as just a distributed processing engine and Transformers as just another Python library installed in the cluster, as shown in Figures 6-12 and 6-13.

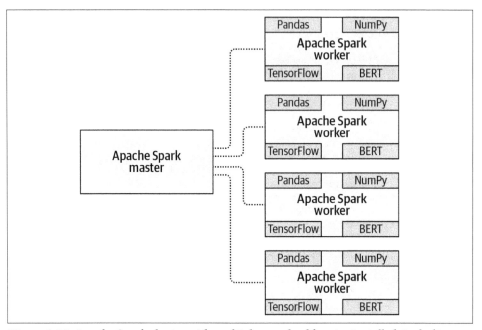

Figure 6-12. Apache Spark cluster with multiple popular libraries installed, including TensorFlow and BERT.

The Apache Spark ML library includes a highly parallel, distributed implementation of term frequency–inverse document frequency (TF-IDF) for text-based feature engineering. TF-IDF, dating back to the 1980s, requires a stateful pre-training step to count the term frequencies and build up a "vocabulary" on the given dataset. This limits TF-IDF's ability to learn a broader language model outside of the given dataset.

On the other hand, BERT has been pre-trained on millions of documents and generally performs better on our natural-language dataset than TF-IDF, so we will use BERT for the feature engineering tasks presented here.

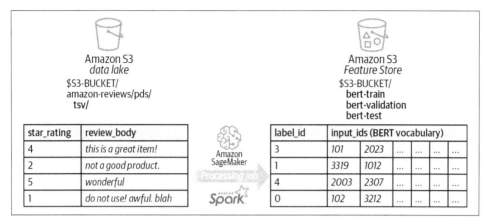

Figure 6-13. Transform raw text into BERT embeddings with Apache Spark.

If we prefer to use Apache Spark because we already have a Spark-based feature engineering pipeline, we can spin up a cloud-native, serverless, pay-for-what-you-use Apache Spark cluster to create the BERT vectors from the raw `review_body` data using SageMaker Processing Jobs.

We just need to provide our PySpark script, specify the instance type, and decide on the cluster instance count—SageMaker will run our Spark job on the cluster. Since Spark performs better with more RAM, we use a high-RAM `r5` instance type:

```
from sagemaker.spark.processing import PySparkProcessor

processor = PySparkProcessor(base_job_name='spark-amazon-reviews-processor',
                             role=role,
                             framework_version='<SPARK_VERSION>',
                             instance_count=2,
                             instance_type='ml.r5.xlarge',
                             max_runtime_in_seconds=7200)
```

Let's run the Processing Job. Since Apache Spark efficiently reads and writes to S3 directly, we don't need to specify the usual `ProcessingInput` and `ProcessingOutput` parameters to our `run()` function. Instead, we use the `arguments` parameter to pass in four S3 locations: one for the raw TSV files and the three S3 locations for the generated BERT vectors for the train, validation, and test splits. We also pass the split percentages and `max_seq_length` for BERT:

```
train_data_bert_output = 's3://{}/{}/output/bert-train'.format(bucket,
                            output_prefix)
validation_data_bert_output = 's3://{}/{}/output/bert-validation'.format(bucket,
                            output_prefix)
test_data_bert_output = 's3://{}/{}/output/bert-test'.format(bucket,
                            output_prefix)
processor.run(submit_app='preprocess-spark-text-to-bert.py',
              arguments=['s3_input_data',
```

```
                            s3_input_data,
                            's3_output_train_data',
                            train_data_bert_output,
                            's3_output_validation_data',
                            validation_data_bert_output,
                            's3_output_test_data',
                            test_data_bert_output,
                            'train_split_percentage',
                            str(train_split_percentage),
                            'validation_split_percentage',
                            str(validation_split_percentage),
                            'test_split_percentage',
                            str(test_split_percentage),
                            'max_seq_length',
                            str(max_seq_length)
                ],
                outputs=[
                  ProcessingOutput(s3_upload_mode='EndOfJob',
                    output_name='bert-train',
                    source='/opt/ml/processing/output/bert/train'),
                  ProcessingOutput(s3_upload_mode='EndOfJob',
                    output_name='bert-validation',
                    source='/opt/ml/processing/output/bert/validation'),
                  ProcessingOutput(s3_upload_mode='EndOfJob',
                    output_name='bert-test',
                    source='/opt/ml/processing/output/bert/test'),
                ],
                logs=True,
                wait=False
    )
```

The preceding code runs in the notebook and launches the *preprocess-spark-text-to-bert.py* script on the SageMaker Processing Job Cluster running Apache Spark. The following code is a snippet from this PySpark script:

```
def transform(spark, s3_input_data, s3_output_train_data,
                s3_output_validation_data, s3_output_test_data):

    schema = StructType([
        StructField('marketplace', StringType(), True),
        StructField('customer_id', StringType(), True),
        StructField('review_id', StringType(), True),
        StructField('product_id', StringType(), True),
        StructField('product_parent', StringType(), True),
        StructField('product_title', StringType(), True),
        StructField('product_category', StringType(), True),
        StructField('star_rating', IntegerType(), True),
        StructField('helpful_votes', IntegerType(), True),
        StructField('total_votes', IntegerType(), True),
        StructField('vine', StringType(), True),
        StructField('verified_purchase', StringType(), True),
        StructField('review_headline', StringType(), True),
```

```
        StructField('review_body', StringType(), True),
        StructField('review_date', StringType(), True)
    ])

    df_csv = spark.read.csv(path=s3_input_data,
                            sep='\t',
                            schema=schema,
                            header=True,
                            quote=None)
```

Here is the Spark user-defined function (UDF) to transform the raw text into BERT embeddings using the Transformers Python library:

```
MAX_SEQ_LENGTH = 64
DATA_COLUMN = 'review_body'
LABEL_COLUMN = 'star_rating'
LABEL_VALUES = [1, 2, 3, 4, 5]

label_map = {}
for (i, label) in enumerate(LABEL_VALUES):
    label_map[label] = i

def convert_input(label, text):
    encode_plus_tokens = tokenizer.encode_plus(
        text,
        pad_to_max_length=True,
        max_length=MAX_SEQ_LENGTH)

    # Convert the text-based tokens to ids from the pre-trained BERT vocabulary
    input_ids = encode_plus_tokens['input_ids']
    # Specifies which tokens BERT should pay attention to (0 or 1)
    input_mask = encode_plus_tokens['attention_mask']
    # Segment ids are always 0 for single-sequence tasks
        # (or 1 if two-sequence tasks)
        segment_ids = [0] * MAX_SEQ_LENGTH

        # Label for our training data (star_rating 1 through 5)
        label_id = label_map[label]

        return {'input_ids': input_ids, 'input_mask': input_mask,
                'segment_ids': segment_ids, 'label_ids': [label_id]}
```

Here is the Spark code that invokes the UDF on each worker in the cluster. Note that we are preparing to write a TFRecord, so we are setting up a PySpark schema that matches the desired TFRecord format:

```
tfrecord_schema = StructType([
    StructField("input_ids", ArrayType(IntegerType(), False)),
    StructField("input_mask", ArrayType(IntegerType(), False)),
    StructField("segment_ids", ArrayType(IntegerType(), False)),
    StructField("label_ids", ArrayType(IntegerType(), False))
])
```

```
bert_transformer = udf(lambda text, label: convert_input(text, label), \
                       tfrecord_schema)
```

Next, we split the data into train, validation, and test and save the splits in S3 in the TFRecord format:

```
train_df, validation_df, test_df = features_df.randomSplit(
        [
          train_split_percentage,
          validation_split_percentage,
          test_split_percentage
        ]
)

train_df.write.format('tfrecord').option('recordType', 'Example')\
                              .save(path=s3_output_train_data)

validation_df.write.format('tfrecord').option('recordType', 'Example')\
                                 .save(path=s3_output_validation_data)

test_df.write.format('tfrecord').option('recordType', 'Example')\
                             .save(path=s3_output_test_data)
```

 We are using format('tfrecord') from an open source library that implements the Apache Spark DataFrameReader and DataFra meWriter interfaces for TFRecord. References to this library are in this book's GitHub repository.

Share Features Through SageMaker Feature Store

Feature engineering requires intuition, patience, trial, and error. As more teams utilize AI and machine learning to solve business use cases, the need arises for a centralized, discoverable, and reusable repository of features. This type of repository is called a *Feature Store*.

Feature stores are data lakes for machine learning features. Since features sometimes require heavy compute processing, as we demonstrated earlier with our BERT features using SageMaker Processing Jobs, we would like to store and reuse these features, if possible, throughout the organization.

It is likely that different transformations are needed for the feature store targeted at machine learning workflows with SageMaker and the data warehouse targeted at business intelligence reports and dashboards with Amazon Redshift. For example, we would store our BERT embeddings in the feature store, while we store cleaned and enriched data in our data warehouse, as shown in Figure 6-14.

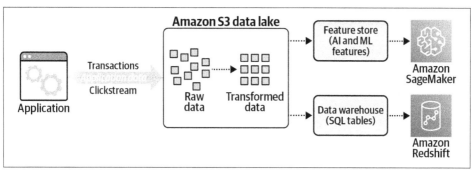

Figure 6-14. Relationship between feature store, data lake, and data warehouse.

Instead of building a feature store ourselves, we can leverage a managed feature store through Amazon SageMaker. SageMaker Feature Store can store both offline and online features. Offline features are stored in repositories optimized for high-throughput and batch-retrieval workloads such as model training. Online features are stored in repositories optimized for low-latency and real-time requests such as model inference.

Since we spent a fair amount of time generating our BERT features, we'd like to share them with other teams in our organization. Perhaps these other teams can discover new and improved combinations of our features that we never explored. We'd like to use our feature store to help us safely "travel in time" and avoid leakage.

Feature stores can cache frequently-accessed features into memory to reduce model-training times. They can also provide governance and access control to regulate and audit our features. Last, a feature store can provide consistency between model training and inference by ensuring the same features are present for both batch training and real-time predicting.

Ingest Features into SageMaker Feature Store

Assume we have the following data frame, `df_records`, which contains the processed BERT features using DistilBERT, with a maximum sequence length of 64:

input_ids	input_mask	segment_ids	label_id	review_id	date	label	split_type
[101, 1045, 2734, 2019, 1000, 3424, 23350, 100...	[1, 1, 1, 1, 1, 1, 1, 1, 1, 1, 1, 1, 1, 1, 1, ...	[0, 0, 0, 0, 0, 0, 0, 0, 0, 0, 0, 0, 0, 0, ...	4	ABCD12345	2021-01-30T20:55:33Z	5	train

input_ids	input_mask	segment_ids	label_id	review_id	date	label	split_type
[101, 1996, 3291, 2007, 10777, 23663, 2003, 20..	[1, 1, 1, 1, 1, 1, 1, 1, 1, 1, 1, 1, 1, 1, 1, ...	[0, 0, 0, 0, 0, 0, 0, 0, 0, 0, 0, 0, 0, 0, 0, ...	2	EFGH12345	2021-01-30T20:55:33Z	3	train
[101, 6659, 1010, 3904, 1997, 2026, 9537, 2499...	[1, 1, 1, 1, 1, 1, 1, 1, 1, 1, 1, 1, 1, 1, 1, ...	[0, 0, 0, 0, 0, 0, 0, 0, 0, 0, 0, 0, 0, 0, 0, ...	0	IJKL2345	2021-01-30T20:55:33Z	1	train

We will now ingest the BERT features, df_records, into our feature store with the feature group name reviews_distilbert_64_max_seq_length:

```
from sagemaker.feature_store.feature_group import FeatureGroup

reviews_feature_group_name = "reviews_distilbert_max_seq_length_64"

reviews_feature_group = FeatureGroup(name=reviews_feature_group_name,
sagemaker_session=sagemaker_session)
```

We need to specify the unique record identifier column, review_id, in our case. In addition, we need to specify an event time that corresponds to the time a record was created or updated in our feature store. In our case, we will generate a timestamp at the time of ingestion. All records must have a unique ID and event time:

```
record_identifier_feature_name = "review_id"
event_time_feature_name = "date"

reviews_feature_group.load_feature_definitions(data_frame=df_records)
```

The SageMaker Feature Store Python SDK will auto-detect the data schema based on input data. Here is the detected schema:

```
FeatureGroup(
    feature_definitions=[
        FeatureDefinition(feature_name='input_ids', \
        feature_type=<FeatureTypeEnum.STRING: 'String'>),
        FeatureDefinition(feature_name='input_mask', \
        feature_type=<FeatureTypeEnum.STRING: 'String'>),
        FeatureDefinition(feature_name='segment_ids', \
        feature_type=<FeatureTypeEnum.STRING: 'String'>),
        FeatureDefinition(feature_name='label_id', \
        feature_type=<FeatureTypeEnum.INTEGRAL: 'Integral'>),
        FeatureDefinition(feature_name='review_id', \
        feature_type=<FeatureTypeEnum.STRING: 'String'>),
        FeatureDefinition(feature_name='date', \
        feature_type=<FeatureTypeEnum.STRING: 'String'>),
        FeatureDefinition(feature_name='label', \
        feature_type=<FeatureTypeEnum.INTEGRAL: 'Integral'>),
```

```
                FeatureDefinition(feature_name=split_type, \
                feature_type=<FeatureTypeEnum.STRING: 'String'>),
                ...
        ]
    )
```

In order to create the feature group, we also need to specify the S3 bucket to store the `df_records` as well as a flag to enable the online feature store option for inference:

```
reviews_feature_group.create(
    s3_uri="s3://{}/{}".format(bucket, prefix),
    record_identifier_name=record_identifier_feature_name,
    event_time_feature_name=event_time_feature_name,
    role_arn=role,
    enable_online_store=True)
```

Now let's ingest the data into the feature store. The data is ingested into both the offline and online repositories unless we specify one or the other:

```
reviews_feature_group.ingest(
    data_frame=df_records, max_workers=3, wait=True)
```

Retrieve Features from SageMaker Feature Store

We can retrieve features from the offline feature store using Athena. We can use these features in our model training, for example:

```
reviews_feature_store_query = reviews_feature_group.athena_query()

reviews_feature_store_table = reviews_feature_store_query.table_name

query_string = """
SELECT review_body, input_ids, input_mask, segment_ids, label_id FROM "{}"
""".format(reviews_feature_store_query)

reviews_feature_store_query.run(query_string=query_string, ...)
```

Here is the output from the feature store query showing our BERT features:

review_body	input_ids	input_mask	segment_ids	label_id
I needed an "antivirus" application and know t...	[101, 1996, 3291, 2007, 10777, 23663, 2003, 20...	[1, 1, 1, 1, 1, 1, 1, 1, 1, 1, 1, 1, 1, 1, 1, ...	[0, 0, 0, 0, 0, 0, 0, 0, 0, 0, 0, 0, 0, 0, 0, ...	2
The problem with ElephantDrive is that it requ...	[101, 6659, 1010, 3904, 1997, 2026, 9537, 2499...	[1, 1, 1, 1, 1, 1, 1, 1, 1, 1, 1, 1, 1, 1, 1, ...	[0, 0, 0, 0, 0, 0, 0, 0, 0, 0, 0, 0, 0, 0, 0, ...	0
Terrible, none of my codes work.	[101, 1045, 2734, 2019, 1000, 3424, 23350, 100...	[1, 1, 1, 1, 1, 1, 1, 1, 1, 1, 1, 1, 1, 1, 1, ...	[0, 0, 0, 0, 0, 0, 0, 0, 0, 0, 0, 0, 0, 0, 0, ...	4

Note that the `label_id` is 0-indexed. In this case, the `label_id` of 0 corresponds to the `star_rating` class 1, 4 represents `star_rating` 5, etc.

We can also query a specific feature in our feature group to use for model predictions by its record identifier as follows:

```
featurestore_runtime = boto3.Session()\
                    .client(
                        service_name='sagemaker-featurestore-runtime',
                        region_name=region)

record_identifier_value = 'IJKL2345'

featurestore_runtime.get_record(
        FeatureGroupName=reviews_feature_group_name,
        RecordIdentifierValueAsString=record_identifier_value)
```

Ingest and Transform Data with SageMaker Data Wrangler

Data Wrangler is SageMaker native, focuses on machine learning use cases, and preserves artifact lineage across the full model development life cycle (MDLC), including data ingestion, feature engineering, model training, model optimization, and model deployment. In addition to analyzing our data in Chapter 5, SageMaker Data Wrangler prepares and transforms our machine-learning features with support for over 300+ built-in transformations—as well as custom SQL, pandas, and Apache Spark code. Data Wrangler is used for many purposes, such as converting column data types, imputing missing data values, splitting datasets into train/validation/test, scaling and normalizing columns, and dropping columns.

The data transformation steps are stored as a Data Wrangler *.flow* definition file and are reused as new data arrives into the system.

We can also export the *.flow* Data Wrangler transformation to a SageMaker Processing Job, Pipeline, Feature Store, or raw Python script. Let's export our Data Wrangler flow to a SageMaker Pipeline to automate the transformation and track the lineage with SageMaker Lineage. We will dive deeper into lineage in the next section and SageMaker Pipelines in Chapter 10. Here is an excerpt of the code that was generated by Data Wrangler when we export the flow to a SageMaker Pipeline:

```
import time
from sagemaker.workflow.parameters import (
    ParameterInteger,
    ParameterString,
)
from sagemaker.workflow.pipeline import Pipeline

with open(flow_file_name) as f:
```

```
    flow = json.load(f)

s3_client = boto3.client("s3")
s3_client.upload_file(flow_file_name, bucket,
     f"{prefix}/{flow_name}.flow")

pipeline_name = f"datawrangler-pipeline-{int(time.time() * 10**7)}"
instance_type = ParameterString(name="InstanceType",
                                default_value="ml.m5.4xlarge")
instance_count = ParameterInteger(name="InstanceCount",
                                default_value=1)

step_process = Step(
    name="DataWranglerProcessingStep",
    step_type=StepTypeEnum.PROCESSING,
    step_args=processing_job_arguments
)

pipeline = Pipeline(
    name=pipeline_name,
    parameters=[instance_type, instance_count],
    steps=[step_process],
    sagemaker_session=sess
)
pipeline.create(role_arn=role)

pipeline.start()
```

Track Artifact and Experiment Lineage with Amazon SageMaker

Humans are naturally curious. When presented with an object, people will likely want to know how that object was created. Now consider an object as powerful and mysterious as a predictive model learned by a machine. We naturally want to know how this model was created. Which dataset was used? Which hyper-parameters were chosen? Which other hyper-parameters were explored? How does this version of the model compare to the previous version? All of these questions can be answered by SageMaker ML Lineage Tracking and SageMaker Experiments.

As a best practice, we should track the lineage of data transformations used in our overall MDLC from feature engineering to model training to model deployment. SageMaker Data Wrangler automatically tracks the lineage of any data it ingests or transforms. Additionally SageMaker Processing Jobs, Training Jobs, and Endpoints track their lineage. We inspect the lineage at any time using either the SageMaker Studio IDE or the SageMaker Lineage API directly. For each step in our workflow, we store the input artifacts, the action, and the generated output artifacts. We can use the Lineage API to inspect the lineage graph and analyze the relationships between steps, actions, and artifacts.

We can leverage the SageMaker Lineage API and lineage graphs for a number of purposes, such as maintaining a history of model experiments, sharing work with colleagues, reproducing workflows to enhance the model, tracing which datasets were used to train each model in production, determining where the model has been deployed, and complying with regulatory standards and audits.

Understand Lineage-Tracking Concepts

The SageMaker Lineage Tracking API utilizes the following key concepts:

Lineage graph
> The connected graph tracing our machine learning workflow end to end.

Artifacts
> Represents a URI addressable object or data. Artifacts are typically inputs or outputs to actions.

Actions
> Represents an action taken, such as a computation, transformation, or job.

Contexts
> Provides a method to logically group other entities.

Associations
> A directed edge in the lineage graph that links two entities. Associations can be of type `Produced`, `DerivedFrom`, `AssociatedWith`, or `ContributedTo`.

Lineage traversal
> Starting from an arbitrary point, trace the lineage graph to discover and analyze relationships between steps in the workflow either upstream or downstream.

Experiments
> Experiment entities including trials and trial components are part of the lineage graph. They are associated with SageMaker Lineage core components, including artifacts, actions, and contexts.

SageMaker automatically creates the lineage tracking entities for every step in a SageMaker Pipeline, including SageMaker Processing Jobs, Training Jobs, Models, Model Packages, and Endpoints. Each pipeline step is associated with input artifacts, actions, output artifacts, and metadata. We will continue to build up our lineage graph as we train, tune, and deploy our model in Chapters 7, 8, and 9. We will then tie everything together in a pipeline with a full end-to-end lineage graph in Chapter 10.

Show Lineage of a Feature Engineering Job

We can show the lineage information that has been captured for the SageMaker Processing Job used to create the BERT embeddings from the raw review text:

```
import time
Import sagemaker
from sagemaker.lineage.visualizer import LineageTableVisualizer

viz = LineageTableVisualizer(sagemaker.session.Session())

viz.show(processing_job_name='<sm_processing_job_name>')
```

The output should look similar to this:

Name/Source	Direction	Type	Association Type	Lineage Type
s3://.../amazon-reviews-pds/tsv/	Input	DataSet	ContributedTo	artifact
68331.../sagemaker-scikit-learn:0.20.0-cpu-py3	Input	Image	ContributedTo	artifact
s3://.../output/bert-test	Output	DataSet	Produced	artifact
s3://.../output/bert-validation	Output	DataSet	Produced	artifact
s3://.../output/bert-train	Output	DataSet	Produced	artifact

SageMaker Lineage Tracking automatically recorded the input data (TSVs), output data (`TFRecords`), and SageMaker container image. The association type shows that the inputs have `ContributedTo` this pipeline step.

The generated training data split into train, validation, and test datasets has been recorded as outputs of this step. The association type correctly classifies them as `Pro duced` artifacts of this step.

Understand the SageMaker Experiments API

SageMaker Experiments is a valuable tool in our data science toolkit that gives us deep insight into the model training and tuning process. With Experiments, we can track, organize, visualize, and compare our AI and machine learning models across all stages of the MDLC, including feature engineering, model training, model tuning, and model deploying. Experiments are seamlessly integrated with SageMaker Studio, Processing Jobs, Training Jobs, and Endpoints. The SageMaker Experiments API is made up of the following key abstractions:

Experiment
> A collection of related Trials. Add Trials to an Experiment that we wish to compare together.

Trial

A description of a multistep machine learning workflow. Each step in the workflow is described by a Trial Component.

Trial Component

A description of a single step in a machine learning workflow, for example, data transformation, feature engineering, model training, model evaluation, etc.

Tracker

A logger of information about a single Trial Component.

While SageMaker Experiments are natively integrated into SageMaker, we can track experiments from any Jupyter notebook or Python script by using the SageMaker Experiments API and just a few lines of code.

Figure 6-15 shows three trials within a single experiment: Trials A, B, and C. All Trials reuse the same feature-engineering Trial Component, "Prepare A," to train three different models using different hyper-parameters. Trial C provides the best accuracy, so we deploy the model and track the deployment Trial Component, "Deploy C."

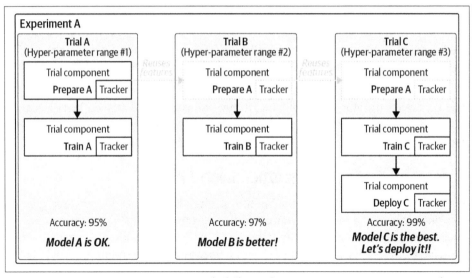

Figure 6-15. Compare training runs with different hyper-parameters using SageMaker Experiments.

Using the SageMaker Experiments API, we create a complete record of every step and hyper-parameter used to re-create Models A, B, and C. At any given point in time, we can determine how a model was trained, including the exact dataset and hyper-parameters used. This traceability is essential for auditing, explaining, and improving our models. We will dive deeper into tracking the model train, optimize, and deploy steps in Chapters 7, 8, and 9, respectively. For now, let's use the SageMaker

Experiment API to track the lineage of our feature-engineering step. First, we create the `Experiment` as follows:

```
import time
from smexperiments.experiment import Experiment

experiment_name = 'Experiment-{}'.format(int(time.time()))

experiment = Experiment.create(
                experiment_name=experiment_name,
                description='Amazon Customer Reviews BERT Experiment',
                sagemaker_boto_client=sm)
```

Next, let's create the `experiment_config` parameter that we will pass to the processor when we create our BERT embeddings. This `experiment_config` is used by the Sage-Maker Processing Job to add a new `TrialComponent` named `prepare` that tracks the S3 locations of the raw-review inputs as well as the transformed train, validation, and test output splits:

```
experiment_config = {
        'ExperimentName': experiment_name,
        'TrialName': trial.trial_name,
        'TrialComponentDisplayName': 'prepare'
}

processor.run(code='preprocess-scikit-text-to-bert.py',
                ...
                experiment_config=experiment_config)
```

We can use the SageMaker Experiments API to display the parameters used in our `prepare` step, as shown in the following. We will continue to track our experiment lineage through model training, hyper-parameter tuning, and model deployment in Chapters 7, 8, and 9, respectively:

```
from sagemaker.analytics import ExperimentAnalytics

lineage_table = ExperimentAnalytics(
    sagemaker_session=sess,
    experiment_name=experiment_name,
    sort_by="CreationTime",
    sort_order="Ascending",
)

lineage_df = lineage_table.dataframe()
lineage_df
```

TrialComponentName	DisplayName	max_seq _length	train_split _percentage	validation_split _percentage	test_split _percentage
bert-transformation-2021-01-09-062410-pxuy	prepare	64.0	0.90	0.05	0.05

Ingest and Transform Data with AWS Glue DataBrew

We can use the built-in Glue DataBrew data transformations to combine, pivot, or transpose the data. The sequence of applied data transformations is captured in a recipe that we can apply to new data as it arrives. SageMaker Data Wrangler is preferred over Glue DataBrew for machine learning use cases as Data Wrangler is integrated with SageMaker and tracks the complete lineage across all phases of the MDLC. While Data Wrangler focuses on the machine learning use cases and the data transformations can be exported as processing code, we can leverage Glue DataBrew for scheduled, initial data cleaning and transformations.

The sequence of applied data transformations is captured in a recipe that we can apply to new data as it arrives. While DataBrew is focused on traditional extract-transform-load workflows, it includes some very powerful statistical functions to analyze and transform data, including the text-based data in the Amazon Reviews Customer Dataset.

Let's create a simple recipe to remove some unused fields from our dataset by creating a recipe called `amazon-reviews-dataset-recipe` in the DataBrew UI. After exporting *recipe.json* from the UI we can programmatically drop the columns using the DataBrew Python SDK. Here is the *recipe.json* that drops unused columns from our dataset:

```
[
    {
        "Action": {
            "Operation": "DELETE",
            "Parameters": {
                "sourceColumns": "[\"marketplace\",\"customer_id\", \
                        \"product_id\",\"product_parent\",\"product_title\", \
                        \""total_votes\",\"vine\",\"verified_purchase\", \
                        \"review_headline\",\"year\"]"
            }
        }
    }
]
```

We need to create a DataBrew project for our dataset and recipe:

```
project_name = 'amazon-customer-reviews-dataset-project'
recipe_name='amazon-customer-reviews-dataset-recipe'

response = db.create_project(
    Name=project_name,
    DatasetName=dataset_name,
    RecipeName=recipe_name,
    Sample={
        'Size': 500,
        'Type': 'FIRST_N'
```

```
        },
        RoleArn=<ROLE_ARN>
    )
```

Now let's call the DataBrew Python SDK to create a transformation job based on the *recipe.json* listed earlier:

```
job_name = 'amazon-customer-reviews-dataset-recipe-job'

response = db.create_recipe_job(
    Name=job_name,
    LogSubscription='ENABLE',
    MaxCapacity=10,
    MaxRetries=0,
    Outputs=[
        {
            'Format': 'CSV',
            'PartitionColumns': [],
            'Location': {
                'Bucket': <S3_BUCKET>,
                'Key': <S3_PREFIX>
            },
            'Overwrite': True
        },
    ],
    ProjectName=project_name,
    RoleArn=<IAM_ROLE>,
    Timeout=2880
)
```

We start the data transformation job as follows:

```
response = db.start_job_run(
    Name=job_name
)
```

DataBrew keeps track of the lineage of each data transformation step, as shown in Figure 6-16.

Once the DataBrew job completes, we have our transformed data in S3. Here is a sample of the data as a pandas DataFrame:

star_rating	review_body
5	After attending a few Qigong classes, I wanted...
4	Krauss traces the remarkable transformation in...
4	Rebecca, a dental hygienist, receives a call a...
5	Good characters and plot line. I spent a pleas...

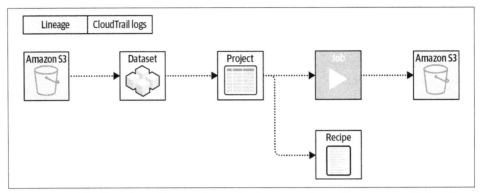

Figure 6-16. Glue DataBrew lineage shows the data transformation steps applied to the dataset.

Summary

In this chapter, we explored feature engineering using a real-world example of transforming raw Amazon Customer Reviews into machine learning features using BERT and TensorFlow. We described how to use SageMaker Data Wrangler to select features and perform transformations on our data to prepare for model training. And we demonstrated how to track and analyze the lineage of transformations using the SageMaker Lineage and Experiment APIs. We also showed how to use Glue DataBrew as another option for data analysis and transformation outside of SageMaker.

In Chapter 7, we will use these features to train a review-classification model to predict the `star_rating` from review text captured in the wild from social channels, partner websites, and other sources of product reviews. We will dive deep into various model-training and deep-learning options, including TensorFlow, PyTorch, Apache MXNet, and even Java! We demonstrate how to profile training jobs, detect model biases, and explain model predictions with SageMaker Debugger.

## CHAPTER 7

Train Your First Model

In the previous chapter, we used SageMaker Processing Jobs to transform a raw data-set into machine-usable features through the "feature engineering" process. In this chapter, we use these features to train a custom review classifier using TensorFlow, PyTorch, BERT (*https://oreil.ly/hmyQz*), and SageMaker to classify reviews "in the wild" from social channels, partner websites, etc. We even show how to train a BERT model with Java!

Along the way, we explain key concepts like the Transformers architecture, BERT, and fine-tuning pre-trained models. We also describe the various training options provided by SageMaker, including built-in algorithms and "bring-your-own" options. Next, we discuss the SageMaker infrastructure, including containers, networking, and security. We then train, evaluate, and profile our models with SageMaker. Profiling helps us debug our models, reduce training time, and reduce cost. Lastly, we provide tips to further reduce cost and increase performance when developing models with SageMaker.

Understand the SageMaker Infrastructure

Largely container based, SageMaker manages the infrastructure and helps us focus on our specific machine learning task. Out of the box, we can directly leverage one of many built-in algorithms that cover use cases such as natural language processing (NLP), classification, regression, computer vision, and reinforcement learning. In addition to these built-in algorithms, SageMaker also offers pre-built containers for many popular AI and machine learning frameworks, such as TensorFlow, PyTorch, Apache MXNet, XGBoost, and scikit-learn. Finally, we can also provide our own Docker containers with the libraries and frameworks of our choice. In this section, we go into more detail about the SageMaker infrastructure, including environment variables, S3 locations, security, and encryption.

We can choose to train on a single instance or on a distributed cluster of instances. Amazon SageMaker removes the burden of managing the underlying infrastructure and handles the undifferentiated heavy lifting for us.

Introduction to SageMaker Containers

When running a training job, SageMaker reads input data from Amazon S3, uses that data to train a model, and finally writes the model artifacts back to Amazon S3. Figure 7-1 illustrates how SageMaker uses containers for training and inference. Starting from the bottom left, training data from S3 is made available to the Model Training instance container, which is pulled from Amazon Elastic Container Registry. The training job persists model artifacts back to the output S3 location designated in the training job configuration. When we are ready to deploy a model, SageMaker spins up new ML instances and pulls in these model artifacts to use for batch or real-time model inference.

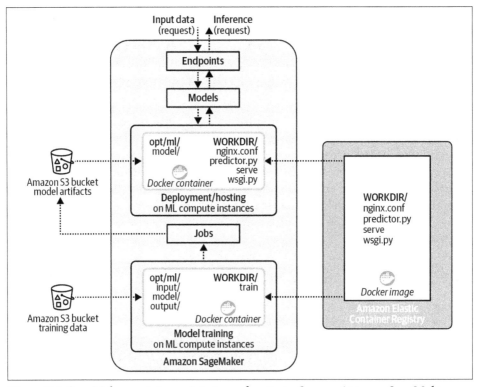

Figure 7-1. SageMaker containers, inputs, and outputs. Source: Amazon SageMaker Workshop (https://oreil.ly/eu9G1).

Much like a software framework, SageMaker provides multiple "hot spots" for our training script to leverage. There are two hot spots worth highlighting: input/output data locations and environment variables.

SageMaker provides our container with locations for our training input and output files. For example, a typical training job reads in data files, trains the model, and writes out a model file. Some AI and machine learning frameworks support model checkpointing in case our training job fails or we decide to use a previous checkpoint with better predictive performance than our latest model. In this case, the job can restart from where it left off. These input, output, and checkpoint files must move in and out of the ephemeral Docker container from/to more durable storage like S3. Otherwise, when the training job ends and the Docker container goes away, the data is lost.

While seemingly simple, this mapping is a very critical piece in the training performance puzzle. If this layer mapping is not optimized, our training times will suffer greatly. Later, we will discuss a SageMaker feature called Pipe Mode that specifically optimizes the movement of data at this layer. Figure 7-2 shows the mapping of the file location inside the Docker container to the S3 location outside the container.

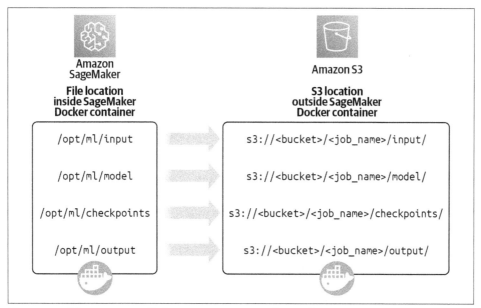

Figure 7-2. The container file locations are mapped to S3 locations.

SageMaker automatically provides our container with many predefined environment variables, such as the number of GPUs available to the container and the log level. Our training script can use these SageMaker-injected environment variables to modify the behavior of our training job accordingly. Here is a subset of the environment variables that SageMaker passes through to our script from a Jupyter notebook, script, pipeline, etc.:

SM_MODEL_DIR
> Directory containing the training or processing script as well as dependent libraries and assets (*/opt/ml/model*)

SM_INPUT_DIR
> Directory containing input data (*/opt/ml/input*)

SM_INPUT_CONFIG_DIR
> Directory containing the input configuration (*/opt/ml/input/config*)

SM_CHANNELS
> S3 locations for splits of data, including "train," "validation," and "test"

SM_OUTPUT_DATA_DIR
> Directory to store evaluation results and other nontraining-related output assets (*/opt/ml/output/data*)

SM_HPS
> Model hyper-parameters used by the algorithm

SM_CURRENT_HOST
> Unique hostname for the current instance

SM_HOSTS
> Hostnames of all instances in the cluster

SM_NUM_GPUS
> Number of GPUs of the current instance

SM_NUM_CPUS
> Number of CPUs of the current instance

SM_LOG_LEVEL
> Logging level used by the training scripts

SM_USER_ARGS
> Additional arguments specified by the user and parsed by the training or processing script

The _DIR variables map are the local filepaths internal to the Docker container running our training code. These map to external input and output file locations in S3, for example, provided by SageMaker and specified by the user when the training job is started. However, our training script references the local paths when reading input or writing output.

Increase Availability with Compute and Network Isolation

Network isolation is also important from a high-availability standpoint. While we usually discuss high availability in terms of microservices and real-time systems, we should also strive to increase the availability of our training jobs.

Our training scripts almost always include `pip installing` Python libraries from PyPI or downloading pre-trained models from third-party model repositories (or "model zoos") on the internet. By creating dependencies on external resources, our training job now depends on the availability of those third-party services. If one of these services is temporarily down, our training job may not start.

 At Netflix, we "burned" all dependencies into our Docker images and Amazon Machine Images (AMIs) to remove all external dependencies and achieve higher availability. It was absolutely critical to reduce external dependencies during rapid scale-out events and failover scenarios.

To improve availability, it is recommended that we reduce as many external dependencies as possible by copying these resources into our Docker image or into our own S3 bucket. This has the added benefit of reducing network latency and starting our training jobs faster. The following IAM policy will not start SageMaker Training Jobs with network isolation disabled. If we do not enable network isolation, the training job will fail immediately, which is exactly what we want to enforce:

```
{
  "Sid": "SageMakerNetworkIsolation",
  "Effect": "Deny",
  "Action": [
    "sagemaker:CreateTrainingJob"
  ],
  "Resource": "*",
  "Condition": {
    "Bool": {
      "sagemaker:NetworkIsolation": "false"
    }
  }
}
```

Computer and network isolation also improve security and reduce the risk of attackers gaining access to our data. As a security best practice, all SageMaker components should be used in a Virtual Private Cloud (VPC) without direct internet connectivity. This requires that we carefully configure IAM roles, VPC Endpoints, subnets, and security groups for least-privilege access policies for Amazon S3, SageMaker, Redshift, Athena, CloudWatch, and any other AWS service used by our data science workflows. In Chapter 12, we will dive deeper into using compute isolation, network isolation, VPC Endpoints, and IAM policies to secure our data science environments.

Deploy a Pre-Trained BERT Model with SageMaker JumpStart

SageMaker JumpStart provides access to pre-built machine learning solutions and pre-trained models from AWS, TensorFlow Hub, and PyTorch Hub across many use cases and tasks, such as fraud detection, predictive maintenance, demand forecasting, NLP, object detection, and image classification, as shown in Figure 7-3.

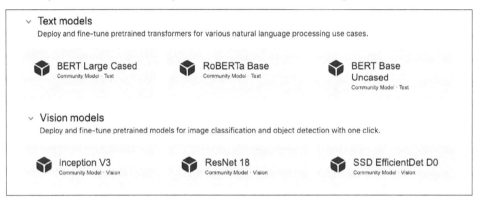

Figure 7-3. Deploy pre-trained models with SageMaker JumpStart.

SageMaker JumpStart is useful when we want to quickly test a solution or model on our dataset and generate a baseline set of evaluation metrics. We can quickly rule out models that do not work well with our data and, conversely, dive deeper into the solutions and models that do work well.

Let's fine-tune a pre-trained BERT model with the Amazon Customer Reviews Dataset and deploy the model to production in just a few clicks within SageMaker Studio, as shown in Figure 7-4.

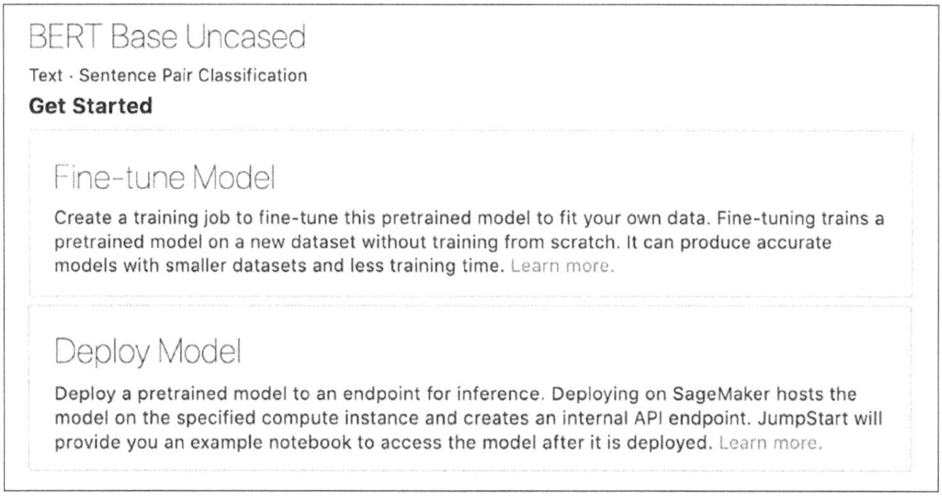

*Figure 7-4. SageMaker JumpStart lets us fine-tune and deploy a pre-trained BERT
model with just a few clicks.*

After fine-tuning the chosen BERT model with the Amazon Customer Reviews Dataset, SageMaker JumpStart deploys the model so we can start making predictions right
away:

```
import json
import boto3

text1 = 'i simply love this product'
text2 = 'worst product ever'

label_map = {0: "1", 1: "2", 2: "3", 3: "4", 4: "5"}

def query_endpoint(encoded_text):
    endpoint_name = 'jumpstart-tf-tc-bert-en-uncased-l-12-h-768-a-12-2'
    client = boto3.client('runtime.sagemaker')
    response = client.invoke_endpoint(
                  EndpointName = endpoint_name,
                  ContentType = 'application/x-text',
                  Body = encoded_text)
    model_predictions = json.loads(response['Body'].read())['predictions'][0]
    return model_predictions

for text in [text1, text2]:
    model_predictions = query_endpoint(text.encode('utf-8'))
    class_index = model_predictions.index(max(model_predictions))
```

The output will look similar to this:

```
Review text:  'i simply love this product'
Predicted star_rating:  5

Review text:  'worst product ever'
Predicted star_rating:  1
```

Develop a SageMaker Model

Just as Amazon.com provides many options to customers through the Amazon.com Marketplace, Amazon SageMaker provides many options for building, training, tuning, and deploying models. We will dive deep into model tuning in Chapter 8 and deploying in Chapter 9. There are three main options depending on the level of customization needed, as shown in Figure 7-5.

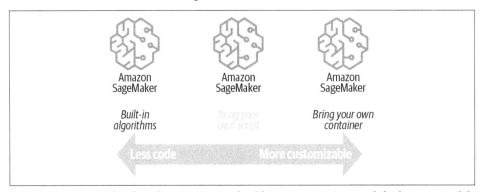

Figure 7-5. SageMaker has three options to build, train, optimize, and deploy our model.

Built-in Algorithms

SageMaker provides built-in algorithms that are ready to use out of the box across a number of different domains, such as NLP, computer vision, anomaly detection, and recommendations. Simply point these highly optimized algorithms at our data and we will get a fully trained, easily deployed machine learning model to integrate into our application. These algorithms, shown in the following chart, are targeted toward those of us who don't want to manage a lot of infrastructure but rather want to reuse battle-tested algorithms designed to work with very large datasets and used by tens of thousands of customers. Additionally, they provide conveniences such as large-scale distributed training to reduce training times and mixed-precision floating-point support to improve model-prediction latency.

Classification	Computer vision	Working with text
• Linear learner	• Image classification	• BlazingText
• XGBoost	• Object detection	• Supervised
• KNN	• Semantic segmentation	• Unsupervised

Regression	Anomaly detection	Topic modeling
• Linear learner	• Random cut forests	• LDA
• XGBoost	• IP insights	• NTM
• KNN		

Sequence translation	Recommendation	Clustering
• Seq2Seq	• Factorization machines	• KMeans

Feature reduction	Forecasting
• PCA	• DeepAR
• Object2Vec	

Bring Your Own Script

SageMaker offers a more customizable option to "bring your own script," often called *Script Mode*. Script Mode lets us focus on our training script, while SageMaker provides highly optimized Docker containers for each of the familiar open source frameworks, such as TensorFlow, PyTorch, Apache MXNet, XGBoost, and scikit-learn, as shown in Figure 7-6.

Figure 7-6. Popular AI and machine learning frameworks supported by Amazon SageMaker.

This option is a good balance of high customization and low maintenance. Most of the remaining SageMaker examples in this book will utilize Script Mode with TensorFlow and BERT for NLP and natural language understanding (NLU) use cases, as shown in Figure 7-7.

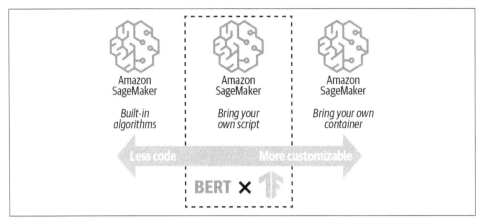

Figure 7-7. SageMaker Script Mode with BERT and TensorFlow is a good balance of high customization and low maintenance.

Bring Your Own Container

The most customizable option is "bring your own container." This option lets us build and deploy our own Docker container to SageMaker. This Docker container can contain any library or framework. While we maintain complete control over the details of the training script and its dependencies, SageMaker manages the low-level infrastructure for logging, monitoring, injecting environment variables, injecting hyper-parameters, mapping dataset input and output locations, etc. This option is targeted toward a more low-level machine learning practitioner with a systems back-ground—or scenarios where we need to use our own Docker container for compliance and security reasons. Converting an existing Docker image to run within SageMaker is simple and straightforward—just follow the steps listed in this AWS open source project (*https://oreil.ly/7Rn86*).

A Brief History of Natural Language Processing

In the previous chapter, we transformed raw Amazon Customer Reviews into BERT feature vectors to ultimately build a review classifier model to predict the `star_rating` from `review_body` text. Before we build our natural language model, we want to provide some background on NLP.

In 1935, a famous British linguist, J. R. Firth, said the following: "The complete meaning of a word is always contextual, and no study of meaning apart from context can be taken seriously." Fast forward 80 years to 2013: word vectors, or "word embeddings," began to dominate language representations, as shown in Figure 7-8. These word embeddings capture the contextual relationships between words in a set of documents, or "corpus," as it is commonly called.

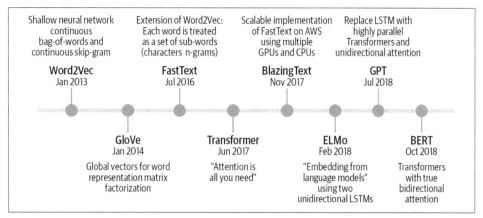

Figure 7-8. Evolution of NLP algorithms and architectures.

Word2Vec and GloVe are two of the popular NLP algorithms from the past decade. They both use contextual information to create vector representations of our text data in a vector space that lets us perform mathematical computations such as word similarity and word differences.

FastText continues the innovation of contextual NLP algorithms and builds word embeddings using subword tokenization. This allows FastText to learn non-English language models with relatively small amounts of data compared to other models. Amazon SageMaker offers a built-in, pay-as-you-go SageMaker algorithm called *BlazingText* that uses an implementation of FastText optimized for AWS. This algorithm was shown in "Built-in Algorithms" on page 214.

There are some drawbacks to this generation of NLP models, however, as they are all forms of static word embeddings. While static embeddings capture the semantic meanings of words, they don't actually understand high-level language concepts. In fact, once the embeddings are created, the actual model is often discarded after training (i.e., Word2Vec, GloVe) and simply preserve the word embeddings to use as features for classical machine learning algorithms such as logistic regression and XGBoost.

ELMo preserves the trained model and uses two long short-term memory (LSTM) network branches: one to learn from left to right and one to learn from right to left. The context is captured in the LSTM state and updated after every word in both network branches. Therefore ELMo does not learn a true bidirectional contextual representation of the words and phrases in the corpus, but it performs very well nonetheless.

An LSTM is a special type of recurrent neural network (RNN) that selectively chooses which information to remember and which information to forget. This allows the LSTM to utilize memory and compute efficiently, avoid the vanishing gradient problem, and maintain very good predictive power. A gated recurrent unit is another variant of an RNN that is simpler than LSTM and performs very well. However, ELMo specifically uses LSTM.

GPT and the newer GPT-2 and GPT-3 models (GPT-n) preserve the trained model and use a neural network architecture called the "Transformer" to learn the contextual word representations. Transformers were popularized along with their attention-mechanism counterpart in the 2017 paper titled "Attention Is All You Need" (*https://oreil.ly/mHHL0*). Transformers offer highly parallel computation to enable higher throughput, better performance, and more-efficient utilization of compute resources. LSTM and ELMo do not support parallel computations.

The GPT-n transformer uses a directional, left-to-right "masked self-attention" mechanism to learn the left-to-right contextual representation, as shown in Figure 7-9. This prevents the model from peeking ahead to see the next words in the sentence. Even with this limitation, GPT-n performs very well on text generation tasks because of this left-to-right mechanism.

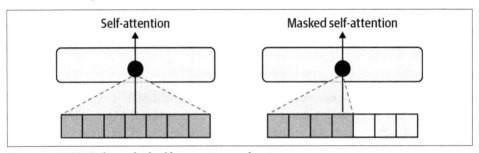

Figure 7-9. GPT-n's masked self-attention mechanism.

In 2018, a new neural network-based algorithm for NLP was released called *Bidirectional Encoder Representations from Transformers* (BERT). BERT has revolutionized the field of NLP and NLU and is now widely used throughout the industry at Facebook, LinkedIn, Netflix, Amazon, and many other AI-first companies. BERT builds on the highly parallelizable Transformer architecture and adds true bidirectional self-attention that looks both forward and backward. BERT's self-attention mechanism improves upon the GPT-n backward-looking, masked self-attention mechanism.

BERT Transformer Architecture

At its core, the BERT Transformer architecture uses an attention mechanism to "pay attention" to specific and interesting words or phrases as it traverses the corpus. Specifically, the BERT transformer uses "self-attention" to attend every token in the data to all other tokens in the input sequence. Additionally, BERT uses "multiheaded attention" to handle ambiguity in the meanings of words, also called *polysemy* (Greek *poly* = many, *sema* = sign). An example of attention is shown in Figure 7-10 where the word *it* attends highly to the word *movie* as well as the words *funny* and *great*, though to a lesser degree than the word *movie*.

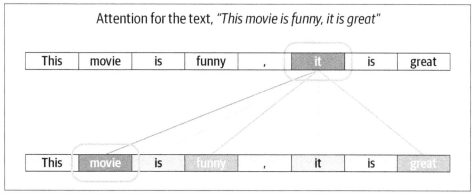

Figure 7-10. The "self-attention" mechanism attends every token in the data to all other tokens in the input sequence.

Without this bidirectional attention, an algorithm would potentially create the same embedding for the word *bank* for the following two sentences: "A thief stole money from the *bank* vault" and "Later, he was arrested while fishing on a river *bank*." Note that the word *bank* has a different meaning in each sentence. This is easy for humans to distinguish because of our lifelong, natural "pre-training," but this is not easy for a machine without similar pre-training. BERT distinguishes between these two words (tokens) by learning different vectors for each token in the context of a specific (sequence). The learned token vector is called the "input token vector representation," and the learned sentence vector is called the "pooled text vector representation."

BERT's transformer-based sequence model consists of several transformer blocks stacked upon each other. The pre-trained BERT$_{Base}$ model consists of 12 such transformer blocks, while the BERT$_{Large}$ model consists of 24 transformer blocks. Each transformer block implements a multihead attention layer and a fully connected feedforward layer. Each layer is wrapped with a skip connection (residual connection) and a layer normalization module.

We add another layer to fine-tune the model to a specific NLP task. For text classification, we would add a classifier layer. After the training data is processed by all transformer blocks, the data passes through the fine-tuning layer and learns parameters specific to our NLP task and dataset. Figure 7-11 shows the BERT architecture.

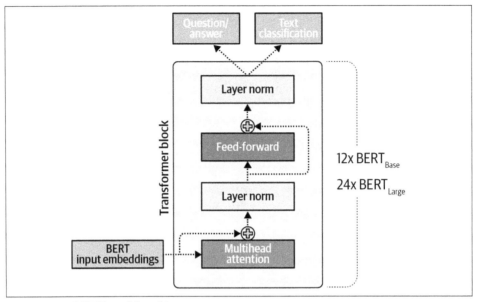

Figure 7-11. BERT model architecture.

Let's have a closer look at how BERT implements attention. We can think of attention as the process of assigning a weight to the input tokens based on their importance to the NLP task to solve. In more mathematical terms, attention is a function that takes an input sequence X and returns another sequence Y, composed of vectors of the same length of those in X. Each vector in Y is a weighted average of the vectors in X, as shown in Figure 7-12.

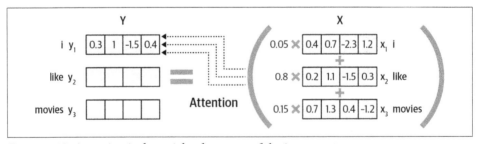

Figure 7-12. Attention is the weighted average of the input vectors.

The weights express how much the model attends to each input vector in X when computing the weighted average. So how does BERT calculate the attention weights?

A compatibility function assigns a score to each pair of words indicating how strongly they *attend* to one another. In a first step, the model creates a query vector (for the word that is paying attention) and a key vector (for the word being paid attention to) as linear transformations from the actual value vector. The compatibility score is then calculated as the dot product of the query vector of one word and the key vector of the other. The score is then normalized by applying the softmax function. The result is the attention weight, as shown in Figure 7-13.

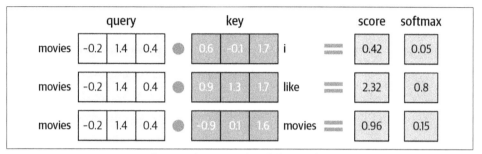

Figure 7-13. Attention weights are the normalized dot product of the query and key vectors.

Training BERT from Scratch

While we can use BERT as is without training from scratch, it's useful to know how BERT uses word masking and next sentence prediction—in parallel—to learn and understand language.

Masked Language Model

As BERT sees new text, it masks 15% of the words in each sentence, or "sequence," in BERT terminology. BERT then predicts the masked words and corrects itself (aka "updates the model weights") when it predicts incorrectly. This is called the *Masked Language Model* or Masked LM. Masking forces the model to learn the surrounding words for each sequence, as shown in Figure 7-14.

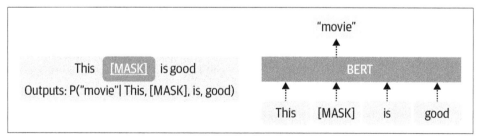

Figure 7-14. BERT Masked LM masks 15% of input tokens and learns by predicting the masked tokens—correcting itself when it predicts the wrong word.

To be more concrete, BERT is trained by forcing it to predict masked words (actually tokens) in a sentence. For example, if we feed in the contents of this book, we can ask BERT to predict the missing word in the following sentence: "This book is called Data ____ on AWS." Obviously, the missing word is "Science." This is easy for a human who has been pre-trained on millions of documents since birth, but is not easy for a machine—not without training, anyway.

Next Sentence Prediction

At the same time BERT is masking and predicting input tokens, it is also performing next sentence prediction (NSP) on pairs of input sequences. Both of these training tasks are optimized together to create a single accuracy score for the combined training efforts. This results in a more robust model capable of performing word- and sentence-level predictive tasks.

To perform NSP, BERT randomly chooses 50% of the sentence pairs and replaces one of the two sentences with a random sentence from another part of the document. BERT then predicts if the two sentences are a valid sentence pair or not, as shown in Figure 7-15. BERT will correct itself when it predicts incorrectly.

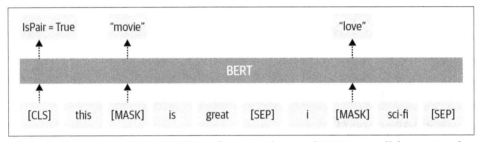

Figure 7-15. During training, BERT performs masking and NSP in parallel on pairs of input sequences.

For more details on BERT, check out the 2018 paper, "BERT: Pre-training of Deep Bidirectional Transformers for Language Understanding" (*https://oreil.ly/LP4yX*).

In most cases, we don't need to train BERT from scratch. Neural networks are designed to be reused and continuously trained as new data arrives into the system. Since BERT has already been pre-trained on millions of public documents from Wikipedia and the Google Books Corpus, the vocabulary and learned representations are transferable to a large number of NLP and NLU tasks across a wide variety of domains.

Training BERT from scratch requires a lot of data and compute, but it allows BERT to learn a representation of the custom dataset using a highly specialized vocabulary. Companies like Amazon and LinkedIn have pre-trained internal versions of BERT from scratch to learn language representations specific to their domain. LinkedIn's variant of BERT, for example, has learned a language model specific to job titles, resumes, companies, and business news.

Fine Tune a Pre-Trained BERT Model

ELMo, GPT/GPT-2, and BERT preserve certain trained models known as "pre-trained models." Pre-trained on millions of documents across many different domains, these models are good at not only predicting missing words, but also at learning the meaning of words, sentence structure, and sentence correlations. Their ability to generate meaningful, relevant, and realistic text is phenomenal and scary. Let's dive deeper into BERT's pre-trained models.

BERT's pre-trained models are, like most neural network models, just point-in-time snapshots of the model weights learned from the data seen to date. And like most models, BERT becomes even more valuable with more data.

The core BERT pre-trained models come in "base" and "large" variants that differ by number of layers, attention heads, hidden units, and parameters, as shown in the following table. We see very good performance with the smaller model with only 12 attention heads and 110 million parameters.

	Layers	Hidden units	Parameters
BERT base	12	768	110M
BERT large	24	1024	340M

Additionally, the community has created many pre-trained versions of BERT using domain and language-specific datasets, including PatentBERT (US patent data), ClinicalBERT (healthcare data), CamemBERT (French language), GermanBERT (German language), and BERTje (Dutch language).

These BERT variants were pre-trained from scratch because the default BERT models, trained on English versions of Wikipedia and Google Books, do not share the same vocabulary as the custom datasets—e.g., French for CamemBERT, and healthcare terminology for ClinicalBERT. When training from scratch, we can reuse BERT's neural network transformer architecture but throw out the pre-trained base model weights learned from Wikipedia and Google Books.

For our Amazon Customer Reviews Dataset, we can safely reuse the default BERT models because they share a similar vocabulary and language representation. There is no doubt that training BERT from scratch to learn the specific Amazon.com product catalog would improve accuracy on some tasks, such as entity recognition. However, the default BERT models perform very well on our review text, so we will keep things simple and "fine-tune" a default BERT model to create a custom text classifier using our Amazon Customer Reviews Dataset.

Let's reuse the language understanding and semantics learned by the pre-trained BERT model to learn a new, domain-specific NLP task using the Amazon Customer Reviews Dataset. This process, called "fine-tuning," is shown in Figure 7-16.

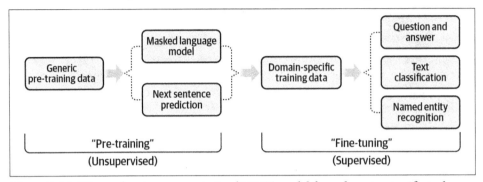

Figure 7-16. We can fine-tune a pre-trained BERT model for a domain-specific task using a custom dataset.

The simplicity and bidirectional nature of the BERT self-attention mechanism allow us to fine-tune the base BERT models to a wide range of out-of-the-box, "downstream" NLP/NLU tasks, including text classification to analyze sentiment, entity recognition to detect a product name, and next sentence prediction to provide answers to natural language questions, as shown in Figure 7-17.

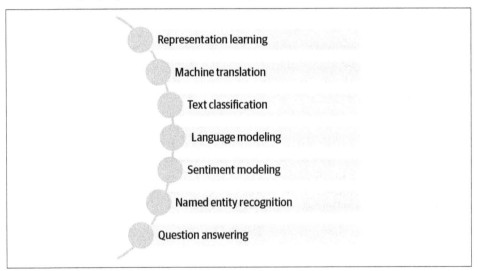

Figure 7-17. We can fine-tune the default BERT models to many "downstream" NLP and NLU tasks.

Since fine-tuning is a supervised training process (versus pre-training, which is unsupervised), masking and next sentence prediction do not happen during fine-tuning—

only during pre-training. As a result, fine-tuning is very fast and requires a relatively small number of samples, or reviews, in our case. This translates to lower processing power, lower cost, and faster training/tuning iterations.

Remember that we can use SageMaker JumpStart to try out these pre-trained models quickly and establish their usefulness as a solution for our machine learning task. By quickly fine-tuning the pre-trained BERT model to our dataset, we can determine if BERT is a good fit or not.

Since we already generated the BERT embeddings from the raw `review_body` text in Chapter 6, we are ready to go! Let's fine-tune BERT to create a custom text classifier that predicts `star_rating` from `review_body` using our dataset, as shown in Figure 7-18.

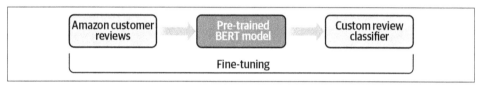

Figure 7-18. We can fine-tune a BERT model to create a custom text classifier with our reviews dataset.

We can use this classifier to predict the sentiment of an incoming customer service email or Twitter comment, for example. So when a new email or comment enters the system, we first classify the email as negative (`star_rating` 1), neutral (`star_rating` 3), or positive (`star_rating` 5). This can help us determine the urgency of the response—or help us route the message to the right person, as shown in Figure 7-19.

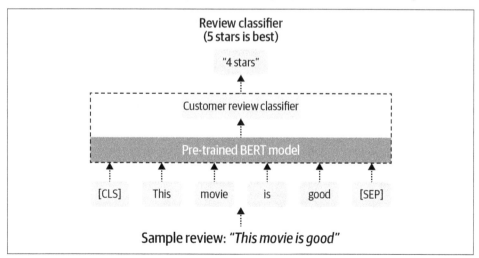

Figure 7-19. We can fine-tune BERT to classify review text into `star_rating` categories of 1 (worst) through 5 (best).

Create the Training Script

Let's create a training script called *tf_bert_reviews.py* that creates our classifier using TensorFlow and Keras. We will then pass the features generated from the previous chapter into our classifier for model training.

Setup the Train, Validation, and Test Dataset Splits

In the last chapter, we used SageMaker Processing Jobs to transform raw Amazon Customer Reviews into BERT embeddings, as shown in Figure 7-20.

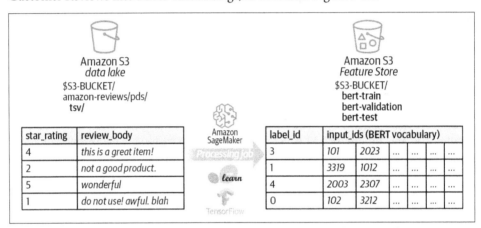

Figure 7-20. BERT embeddings as inputs for model training with TensorFlow.

In this section, we load the train, validation, and test datasets to feed into our model for training. We will use TensorFlow's `TFRecordDataset` implementation to load the `TFRecords` in parallel and shuffle the data to prevent the model from learning the pattern in which the data is presented to the model.

> In AI and machine learning, randomness is celebrated. Proper shuffling of the training data will provide enough randomness to prevent the model from learning any patterns about how the data is stored on disk and/or presented to the model. "Bootstrapping" is a common technique to describe random sampling with replacement. Bootstrapping adds bias, variance, confidence intervals, and other metrics to the sampling process.

In Chapter 6, we created a SageMaker Processing Job to transform the raw `review_body` column into BERT embeddings using the Hugging Face Transformers library. This Processing Job stores the embeddings in S3 using a TensorFlow-optimized `TFRecord` file format, which we will use in our training job. Let's create a helper function to load, parse, and shuffle the TFRecords. We should recognize the input_ids, input_mask, segment_ids, and label_ids field names from the previous chapter:

```
def file_based_input_dataset_builder(channel,
                                     input_filenames,
                                     pipe_mode,
                                     is_training,
                                     drop_remainder,
                                     batch_size,
                                     epochs,
                                     steps_per_epoch,
                                     max_seq_length):

    dataset = tf.data.TFRecordDataset(input_filenames)
    dataset = dataset.repeat(epochs * steps_per_epoch * 100)
    dataset = dataset.prefetch(tf.data.experimental.AUTOTUNE)

    name_to_features = {
      "input_ids": tf.io.FixedLenFeature([max_seq_length], tf.int64),
      "input_mask": tf.io.FixedLenFeature([max_seq_length], tf.int64),
      "segment_ids": tf.io.FixedLenFeature([max_seq_length], tf.int64),
      "label_ids": tf.io.FixedLenFeature([], tf.int64),
    }

    def _decode_record(record, name_to_features):
        """Decodes a record to a TensorFlow example."""
        record = tf.io.parse_single_example(record, name_to_features)
        return record

    dataset = dataset.apply(
        tf.data.experimental.map_and_batch(
          lambda record: _decode_record(record, name_to_features),
          batch_size=batch_size,
          drop_remainder=drop_remainder,
          num_parallel_calls=tf.data.experimental.AUTOTUNE))

    dataset.cache()

    if is_training:
        dataset = dataset.shuffle(seed=42,
                                  buffer_size=steps_per_epoch * batch_size,
                                  reshuffle_each_iteration=True)

    return dataset
```

If is_training is true, we are in the training phase. During the training phase, we want to shuffle the data between iterations. Otherwise, the model may pick up on patterns about how the data is stored on disk and presented to the model—i.e., first all the 5s, then all the 4s, 3s, 2s, 1s, etc. To discourage the model from learning this pattern, we shuffle the data. If `is_training` is false, then we are in either the valida-tion or test phase, and we can avoid the shuffle overhead and iterate sequentially.

Let's read in the training, validation, and test datasets using the helper function cre-ated earlier:

```
# Training Dataset
train_data_filenames = glob(os.path.join(train_data,
                                         '*.tfrecord'))
train_dataset = file_based_input_dataset_builder(
    channel='train',
    input_filenames=train_data_filenames,
    pipe_mode=pipe_mode,
    is_training=True,
    drop_remainder=False,
    batch_size=train_batch_size,
    epochs=epochs,
    steps_per_epoch=train_steps_per_epoch,
    max_seq_length=max_seq_length)\
        .map(select_data_and_label_from_record)

# Validation Dataset
validation_data_filenames = glob(os.path.join(validation_data,
                                              '*.tfrecord'))
validation_dataset = file_based_input_dataset_builder(
    channel='validation',
    input_filenames=validation_data_filenames,
    pipe_mode=pipe_mode,
    is_training=False,
    drop_remainder=False,
    batch_size=validation_batch_size,
    epochs=epochs,
    steps_per_epoch=validation_steps,
    max_seq_length=max_seq_length)\
        .map(select_data_and_label_from_record)
```

We will soon pass these train, validation, and test datasets to our model training pro-cess. But first, let's set up the custom reviews classifier using TensorFlow, Keras, BERT, and Hugging Face.

Set Up the Custom Classifier Model

Soon, we will feed the `review_body` embeddings and `star_rating` labels into a neural network to fine-tune the BERT model and train the custom review classifier, as shown in Figure 7-21. Note that the words shown in the figure may be broken up into smaller word tokens during tokenization. For illustrative purposes, however, we show them as full words.

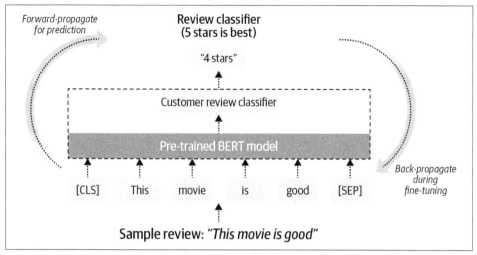

Figure 7-21. Classify reviews into star rating 1 (worst) through 5 (best) using our custom classifier.

For this, we use the Keras API with TensorFlow 2.x to add a neural classifier layer on top of the pre-trained BERT model to learn the `star_rating` (1–5). Remember that we are using a relatively lightweight variant of BERT called DistilBERT, which requires less memory and compute but maintains very good accuracy on our dataset. To reduce the size of the model, DistilBERT, a student neural network, was trained by a larger teacher neural network in a process called *knowledge distillation*, as shown in Figure 7-22.

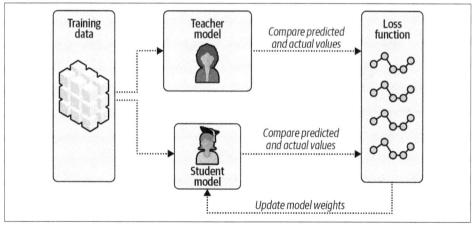

Figure 7-22. Knowledge distillation trains a student model from a teacher model.

Let's load `DistilBertConfig`, map our 1-indexed `star_rating` labels to the 0-indexed internal classes, and load our pre-trained DistilBERT model as follows:

```
from transformers import DistilBertConfig
from transformers import TFDistilBertForSequenceClassification

CLASSES=[1, 2, 3, 4, 5]

config = DistilBertConfig.from_pretrained('distilbert-base-uncased',
                                          num_labels=len(CLASSES),
                                          id2label={
                                          0: 1, 1: 2, 2: 3, 3: 4, 4: 5
                                          },
                                          label2id={
                                          1: 0, 2: 1, 3: 2, 4: 3, 5: 4
                                          })

transformer_model = TFDistilBertForSequenceClassification.from_pretrained(
                "distilbert-base-uncased", config=config
            )
```

It's important to highlight that the from_pretrained() function calls will download a large model from the Hugging Face service. We should consider downloading this model to our own S3 bucket and pass the S3 URI to the from_pretrained() function calls. This small change will decouple us from the Hugging Face service, remove a potential single point of failure, enable network isolation, and reduce the start time of our model training jobs. Next, let's set up our inputs and model layers:

```
input_ids = tf.keras.layers.Input(shape=(max_seq_length,),
            name='input_ids',
            dtype='int32')
input_mask = tf.keras.layers.Input(shape=(max_seq_length,),
            name='input_mask',
            dtype='int32')

embedding_layer = transformer_model.distilbert(input_ids,
            attention_mask=input_mask)[0]
X = tf.keras.layers.Bidirectional(tf.keras.layers.LSTM(50,
            return_sequences=True,
            dropout=0.1,
            recurrent_dropout=0.1))(embedding_layer)
X = tf.keras.layers.GlobalMaxPool1D()(X)
X = tf.keras.layers.Dense(50, activation='relu')(X)
X = tf.keras.layers.Dropout(0.2)(X)
X = tf.keras.layers.Dense(len(CLASSES), activation='softmax')(X)

model = tf.keras.Model(inputs=[input_ids, input_mask], outputs = X)

for layer in model.layers[:3]:
    layer.trainable = not freeze_bert_layer
```

We have chosen not to train the BERT layers by specifying trainable=False. We do this on purpose to keep the underlying BERT model from changing—focusing only on training our custom classifier. Training the BERT layer will likely improve our accuracy, but the training job will take longer. Since our accuracy is pretty good without training the underlying BERT model, we focus only on training the classifier layer. Next, let's add a Keras-based neural classifier to complete our neural network and prepare for model training:

```
loss=tf.keras.losses.SparseCategoricalCrossentropy(from_logits=True)
metric=tf.keras.metrics.SparseCategoricalAccuracy('accuracy')

optimizer=tf.keras.optimizers.Adam(learning_rate=learning_rate, epsilon=epsilon)

model.compile(optimizer=optimizer, loss=loss, metrics=[metric])

model.summary()
```

Here is the output of the model summary showing the breakdown of trainable and nontrainable parameters:

Layer (type)	Output Shape	Param #
input_ids (InputLayer)	[(None, 64)]	0
input_mask (InputLayer)	[(None, 64)]	0
distilbert (TFDistilBertMainLay	((None, 64, 768),)	66362880
bidirectional (Bidirectional)	(None, 64, 100)	327600
global_max_pooling1d (GlobalMax	(None, 100)	0
dense (Dense)	(None, 50)	5050
dropout_19 (Dropout)	(None, 50)	0
dense_1 (Dense)	(None, 5)	255

```
Total params: 66,695,785
Trainable params: 332,905
Non-trainable params: 66,362,880
```

Train and Validate the Model

At this point, we have prepared our train, validation, and test datasets as input data and defined our custom classifier model. Let's pull everything together and invoke the fit() function on our model using the train_dataset and validation_dataset.

By passing validation_dataset, we are using the Keras API with TensorFlow 2.x to perform both training and validation simultaneously:

```
train_and_validation_history = model.fit(train_dataset,
                                          shuffle=True,
                                          epochs=5,
                                          ...
                                          validation_data=validation_dataset)
```

We set `shuffle=True` to shuffle our dataset and `epochs=5` to run through our dataset five times. The number of `epochs` (pronounced "eh-puhks") is configurable and tunable. We will explore model tuning in the next chapter.

Save the Model

Now, let's save the model with the TensorFlow `SavedModel` format used by our predictive applications:

```
model.save('./tensorflow/', save_format='tf')
```

In Chapter 9, we will use the model saved in *./tensorflow/* with TensorFlow Serving to deploy our models and serve review-classification predictions at scale using SageMaker Batch Transform (offline, batch) and SageMaker Endpoints (online, real time).

Launch the Training Script from a SageMaker Notebook

Let's walk through the steps needed to run our training script from a SageMaker Notebook. Later, we will run this same script from an automated pipeline. For now, we run the script from the notebook. First, we will set up the metrics needed to monitor the training job. We'll then configure our algorithm-specific hyper-parameters. Next, we'll select the instance type and number of instances in our cluster. And finally, we will launch our training job.

Define the Metrics to Capture and Monitor

We can create a metric from anything that our training script prints or logs to the console. Let's assume that our TensorFlow model emits the following log lines with the training loss and training accuracy (`loss`, `accuracy`) as well as the validation loss and validation accuracy (`val_loss`, `val_accuracy`):

```
5000/10000 [>...................] - loss: 0.1420 - accuracy: 0.800103
6000/10000 [>...................] - loss: 0.1081 - accuracy: 0.939455
...
10000/10000 [>...................] - val_loss: 0.1420 - val_accuracy: 0.512193
```

Next, we define four regular expressions to populate four metrics by parsing the values from the log lines. If we upgrade the framework—or switch to a new framework—these regular expressions may need adjusting. We will know when this happens because we will no longer see the correct model metrics in our CloudWatch dashboards:

```
metrics_definitions = [
    {'Name': 'train:loss', 'Regex': 'loss: ([0-9\\.]+)'},
    {'Name': 'train:accuracy', 'Regex': 'accuracy: ([0-9\\.]+)'},
    {'Name': 'validation:loss', 'Regex': 'val_loss: ([0-9\\.]+)'},
    {'Name': 'validation:accuracy', 'Regex': 'val_accuracy: ([0-9\\.]+)'},
]
```

Configure the Hyper-Parameters for Our Algorithm

It's important to note that "parameters" (aka "weights") are *what* the model learns during training and that "hyper-parameters" are *how* the model learns the parameters. Every algorithm supports a set of hyper-parameters that alter the algorithm's behavior while learning the dataset. Hyper-parameters can be anything from the depth of a decision tree to the number of layers in our neural network.

Hyper-parameter selection involves the usual trade-offs between latency and accuracy. For example, a deeper neural network with lots of layers may provide better accuracy than a shallow neural network, but the deeper network may lead to higher latency during inference as prediction time increases with each layer in the network.

While most hyper-parameters have suitable defaults based on empirical testing, they are highly tunable. In fact, there's an entire subfield within machine learning dedicated to hyper-parameter tuning/hyper-parameter optimization.

We will dive deep into the art and science of hyper-parameter selection and optimization in Chapter 8 to find the best combination of hyper-parameters. For now, we set these hyper-parameters manually using our experience and intuition—as well as some lightweight, ad hoc empirical testing with our specific dataset and algorithm:

```
epochs=500
learning_rate=0.00001
epsilon=0.00000001
train_batch_size=128
validation_batch_size=128
train_steps_per_epoch=100
validation_steps=100
test_steps=100
train_volume_size=1024
use_xla=True
use_amp=True
freeze_bert_layer=True
```

When evaluating an algorithm, we should seek to understand all of the available hyper-parameters. Setting these hyper-parameters to suboptimal values can make or break a data science project. This is why the subfield of hyper-parameter optimization is so important.

Select Instance Type and Instance Count

The choice of instance type and instance count depends on our workload and budget. Fortunately AWS offers many different instance types, including AI/ML-optimized instances with ultra-fast GPUs, terabytes of RAM, and gigabits of network bandwidth. In the cloud, we can easily scale up our training jobs to larger instances with more memory and compute or scale out to tens, hundreds, or even thousands of instances with just one line of code.

Let's train with a `p4d.24xlarge` instance type with 8 NVIDIA Tesla A100 GPUs, 96 CPUs, 1.1 terabytes of RAM, 400 gigabits per second of network bandwidth, and 600 gigabytes per second of inter-GPU communication using NVIDIA's NVSwitch "mesh" network hardware, as shown in Figure 7-23.

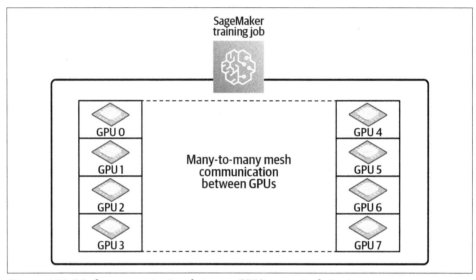

Figure 7-23. Mesh communication between GPUs on a single instance.

To save cost, we would normally start small and slowly ramp up the compute resources needed for our specific workload to find the lowest-cost option. This is commonly called "right-sizing our cluster." Empirically, we found that this instance type works well with our specific model, dataset, and cost budget. We only need one of these instances for our example, so we set the `train_instance_count` to 1, as follows:

```
train_instance_type='ml.p4.24xlarge'
train_instance_count=1
```

We can specify `instance_type='local'` in our SageMaker Training Job to run the script either inside our notebook or on our local laptop. See "Reduce Cost and Increase Performance" on page 268 for more information.

It's important to choose parallelizable algorithms that benefit from multiple cluster instances. If our algorithm is not parallelizable, we should not add more instances because they will not be used. And adding too many instances may actually slow down our training job by creating too much communication overhead between the instances. Most neural-network-based algorithms like BERT are parallelizable and benefit from a distributed cluster when training or fine-tuning on large datasets.

Putting It All Together in the Notebook

Here is our Jupyter notebook that sets up and invokes the TensorFlow training job using SageMaker Script Mode:

```python
from sagemaker.tensorflow import TensorFlow

epochs=500
learning_rate=0.00001
epsilon=0.00000001
train_batch_size=128
validation_batch_size=128
test_batch_size=128
train_steps_per_epoch=100
validation_steps=100
test_steps=100
train_instance_count=1
train_instance_type='ml.p4d.24xlarge'
train_volume_size=1024
use_xla=True
use_amp=True
freeze_bert_layer=False
enable_sagemaker_debugger=True
enable_checkpointing=False
enable_tensorboard=True
input_mode='File'
run_validation=True
run_test=True
run_sample_predictions=True
max_seq_length=64

hyperparameters={'epochs': epochs,
                 'learning_rate': learning_rate,
                 'epsilon': epsilon,
                 'train_batch_size': train_batch_size,
                 'validation_batch_size': validation_batch_size,
                 'test_batch_size': test_batch_size,
                 'train_steps_per_epoch': train_steps_per_epoch,
```

```
                    'validation_steps': validation_steps,
                    'test_steps': validation_steps,
                    'use_xla': use_xla,
                    'use_amp': use_amp,
                    'max_seq_length': max_seq_length,
                    'freeze_bert_layer': freeze_bert_layer,
                    'run_validation': run_validation,
                    'run_sample_predictions': run_sample_predictions}

estimator = TensorFlow(entry_point='tf_bert_reviews.py',
                    instance_count=train_instance_count,
                    instance_type=train_instance_type,
                    volume_size=train_volume_size,
                    py_version='<PYTHON_VERSION>',
                    framework_version='<TENSORFLOW_VERSION>',
                    hyperparameters=hyperparameters,
                    metric_definitions=metrics_definitions,
                    max_run=7200 # seconds)
```

Lastly, we call the `estimator.fit()`method with the train, validation, and test dataset splits to start the training job from the notebook as follows:

```
from sagemaker.inputs import TrainingInput

s3_input_train_data =
        TrainingInput(s3_data=processed_train_data_s3_uri,
                    distribution='ShardedByS3Key')

s3_input_validation_data =
        TrainingInput(s3_data=processed_validation_data_s3_uri,
                    distribution='ShardedByS3Key')

s3_input_test_data =
        TrainingInput(s3_data=processed_test_data_s3_uri,
                    distribution='ShardedByS3Key')

estimator.fit(inputs={'train': s3_input_train_data,
                    'validation': s3_input_validation_data,
                    'test': s3_input_test_data
                },
            wait=False)
```

Download and Inspect Our Trained Model from S3

Let's use the AWS CLI to download our model from S3 and inspect it with Tensor-Flow's `saved_model_cli` script:

```
aws s3 cp s3://$bucket/$training_job_name/output/model.tar.gz \
        ./model.tar.gz
mkdir -p ./model/
tar -xvzf ./model.tar.gz -C ./model/
saved_model_cli show --all --dir ./model/tensorflow/saved_model/0/
```

```
### OUTPUT ###

signature_def['serving_default']:
  The given SavedModel SignatureDef contains the following input(s):
    inputs['input_ids'] tensor_info:
        dtype: DT_INT32
        shape: (-1, 64)
        name: serving_default_input_ids:0
    inputs['input_mask'] tensor_info:
        dtype: DT_INT32
        shape: (-1, 64)
        name: serving_default_input_mask:0
  The given SavedModel SignatureDef contains the following output(s):
    outputs['dense_1'] tensor_info:
        dtype: DT_FLOAT
        shape: (-1, 5)
        name: StatefulPartitionedCall:0
```

We see that the model expects two input vectors of size 64, the `max_seq_length` for the `input_ids` and `input_mask` vectors, and returns one output vector of size 5, the number of classes for the `star_rating` 1–5. The output represents a confidence distribution over the five classes. The most-confident prediction will be our `star_rating` prediction.

Let's use `saved_model_cli` to make a quick prediction with sample data (all zeros) to verify that the model inputs are sufficient. The actual input and output values do not matter here. We are simply testing the network to make sure the model accepts two vectors of the expected input size and returns one vector of the expected output size:

```
saved_model_cli run --dir '$tensorflow_model_dir' \
      --tag_set serve \
      --signature_def serving_default \
      --input_exprs \ 'input_ids=np.zeros((1,64));input_mask=np.zeros((1,64))'

### OUTPUT ###

Result for output key dense_1:
[[0.5148565  0.50950885 0.514237   0.5389632  0.545161  ]]
```

Show Experiment Lineage for Our SageMaker Training Job

Once the hyper-parameter tuning job has finished, we can analyze the results directly in our notebook or through SageMaker Studio.

Let's summarize the experiment lineage up to this point. In Chapter 8, we will tune our hyper-parameters and extend our experiment lineage to include hyper-parameter optimization. In Chapter 9, we will deploy the model and further extend our experiment lineage to include model deployment. We will then tie everything together in an end-to-end pipeline with full lineage tracking in Chapter 10:

```
from sagemaker.analytics import ExperimentAnalytics

lineage_table = ExperimentAnalytics(
    sagemaker_session=sess,
    experiment_name=experiment_name,
    metric_names=['validation:accuracy'],
    sort_by="CreationTime",
    sort_order="Ascending",
)


lineage_table.dataframe()
```

TrialComponentName	DisplayName	max_seq_length	learning_rate	train_accuracy	...
TrialComponent-2021-01-09-062410-pxuy	prepare	64.0	NaN	NaN	...
tensorflow-training-2021-01-09-06-24-12-989	train	64.0	0.00001	0.9394	...

Show Artifact Lineage for Our SageMaker Training Job

We can show the artifact lineage information that has been captured for our Sage-Maker Training Job used to fine-tune our product review classifier:

```
import time
Import sagemaker
from sagemaker.lineage.visualizer import LineageTableVisualizer

viz = LineageTableVisualizer(sagemaker.session.Session())
df = viz.show(training_job_name='<TRAINING_JOB_NAME>')
```

The output should look similar to this:

Name/source	Direction	Type	Association type	Lineage type
s3://.../output/bert-test	Input	DataSet	ContributedTo	artifact
s3://.../output/bert-validation	Input	DataSet	ContributedTo	artifact
s3://.../output/bert-train	Input	DataSet	ContributedTo	artifact
76310.../tensorflow-training:2.3.1-gpu-py37	Input	Image	ContributedTo	artifact
s3://.../output/model.tar.gz	Output	Model	Produced	artifact

SageMaker Lineage Tracking automatically recorded the input data, output artifacts, and SageMaker container image. The Association Type shows that the inputs have ContributedTo this pipeline step. Let's continue to build up our model lineage graph as we tune and deploy our model in Chapters 8 and 9. We will then tie everything together in an end-to-end pipeline with full lineage tracking in Chapter 10.

Evaluate Models

After we have trained and validated our model, we can use the remaining holdout dataset—the test dataset—to perform our own predictions and measure the model's performance. Testing the model with the test dataset helps us evaluate how well the model generalizes on unseen data. Therefore, we should never use the holdout test dataset for training or validation. Based on the test results, we may need to modify our algorithm, hyper-parameters, or training data. Additionally, more training data—and more diverse feature engineering—may help improve our evaluation results.

Following is the code to evaluate the model using Keras API within TensorFlow—similar to how we trained and validated the model in the previous section:

```
test_batch_size = 128
test_steps = 1000

test_data_filenames = glob(os.path.join(test_data, '*.tfrecord'))

test_dataset = file_based_input_dataset_builder(
                channel='test',
                input_filenames=test_data_filenames,
                pipe_mode=pipe_mode,
                is_training=False,
                drop_remainder=False,
                batch_size=test_batch_size,
                epochs=epochs,
                steps_per_epoch=test_steps,
                max_seq_length=max_seq_length)\
            .map(select_data_and_label_from_record)

test_history = model.evaluate(test_dataset,
                              steps=test_steps,
                              callbacks=callbacks)
print(test_history)
```

The test_history contains the test_loss and test_accuracy, respectively:

```
[0.17315794393, 0.50945542373]
```

Run Some Ad Hoc Predictions from the Notebook

We can also run some cursory predictions from the notebook to quickly satisfy our curiosity about the model's health. Here's a snippet of relevant code to run sample predictions:

```
import pandas as pd
import numpy as np

from transformers import DistilBertTokenizer

tokenizer =
```

```
    DistilBertTokenizer.from_pretrained('distilbert-base-uncased')

def predict(text):
    encode_plus_tokens = tokenizer.encode_plus(
                             text,
                             pad_to_max_length=True,
                             max_length=max_seq_length,
                             truncation=True,
                             return_tensors='tf')


    input_ids = encode_plus_tokens['input_ids']

    input_mask = encode_plus_tokens['attention_mask']

    outputs = model.predict(x=(input_ids, input_mask))

    prediction = [{"label": config.id2label[item.argmax()], \
                   "score": item.max().item()} for item in outputs]

    return prediction[0]

predict('This is great!')
predict('This is OK.')
predict('This is terrible.')
```

The following output shows the predicted label (1–5) as well as the confidence for each predicted label. In this case, the model is 92% confident that the label is 5 for the review text "This is great!":

```
{'label': 5, 'score': 0.92150515}
{'label': 3, 'score': 0.2807838}
{'label': 1, 'score': 0.48466408}
```

Analyze Our Classifier with a Confusion Matrix

A confusion matrix is a visual way of evaluating a classifier's performance. Let's create a confusion matrix to visually inspect the test results by comparing the predicted and actual values. We start by reading in the holdout test dataset that includes the raw review_body text:

```
import csv

df_test_reviews = pd.read_csv(
    './data/holdout_test.tsv.gz',
    delimiter='\t',
    quoting=csv.QUOTE_NONE,
    compression='gzip')[['review_body', 'star_rating']]

df_test_reviews = df_test_reviews.sample(n=100,000)
```

Next, we use the `predict` function to calculate the predicted `y_test` dataset. We'll compare this to the observed values, `y_actual`, using the following code:

```
y_test = df_test_reviews['review_body'].map(predict)

y_actual = df_test_reviews['star_rating']
```

This results in the confusion matrix shown in Figure 7-24.

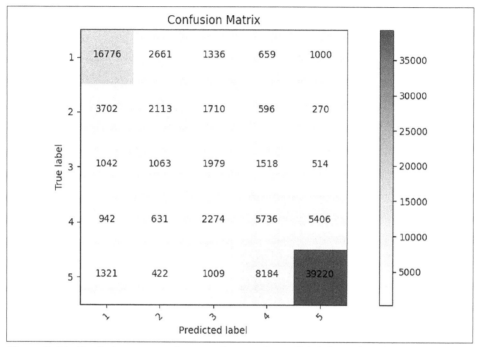

Figure 7-24. Confusion matrix showing the true (actual) labels and predicted labels.

Visualize Our Neural Network with TensorBoard

TensorBoard is an open source visualization and exploration tool maintained by the TensorFlow community to provide insight into TensorFlow model training. Sage-Maker captures and saves the TensorBoard metrics in S3 during model training. We can then visualize these metrics directly from our SageMaker Studio notebook using the S3 location of the saved TensorBoard metrics, as shown in Figure 7-25.

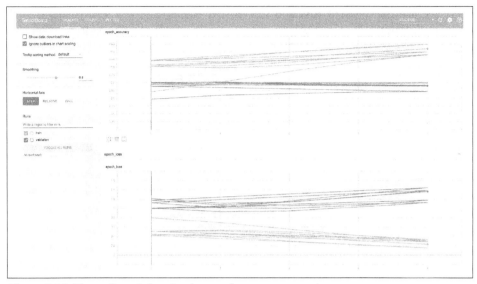

Figure 7-25. TensorBoard showing loss and accuracy over time.

We can also inspect our neural network, as shown in Figure 7-26.

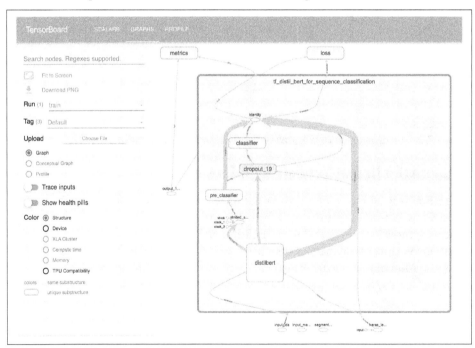

Figure 7-26. TensorBoard showing the TensorFlow graph for BERT.

To run TensorBoard from a SageMaker Notebook, simply install it with `pip install tensorboard`, point to the TensorBoard logs in S3, and start the process from a notebook terminal as follows:

```
S3_REGION=<REGION> tensorboard --port 6006 \
        --logdir s3://$bucket/$training_job_name/debug-output/events
```

Using our browser, we can securely navigate to TensorBoard running in our Sage-Maker Notebook as follows:

https://<NOTEBOOK_NAME>.notebook.<REGION>.sagemaker.aws/proxy/6006/

The 6006 port was chosen by one of the Google engineers who created TensorBoard. The port is the term "goog" upside down!

Monitor Metrics with SageMaker Studio

After training, we should evaluate a model's performance using metrics such as accuracy to determine if the model achieves our business objective. In our example, we want to measure if our model correctly predicts the `star_rating` from the `review_body`. Note that we performed training and validation in the same Keras step.

We can visualize our training and validation metrics directly with SageMaker Studio throughout the training process, as shown in Figure 7-27. We visually see overfitting happening very early, so we likely want to stop the training job early to save money.

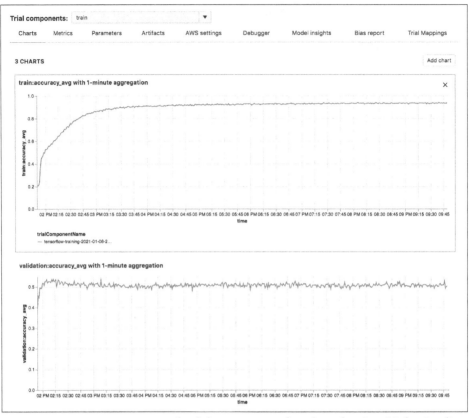

Figure 7-27. Monitor training and validation metrics directly within SageMaker Studio.

Monitor Metrics with CloudWatch Metrics

We can also visualize our model metrics in CloudWatch alongside system metrics like CPU, GPU, and memory utilization. Figure 7-28 shows the train and validation accuracy metrics alongside the system metrics in CloudWatch.

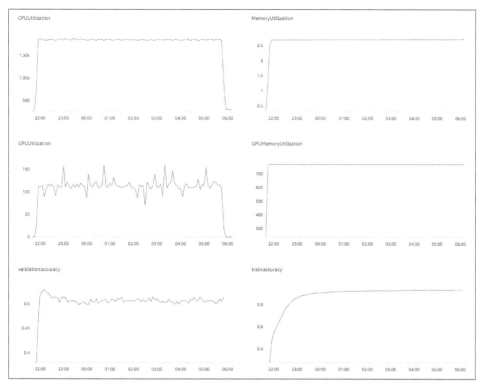

Figure 7-28. Dashboard of training and validation accuracy metrics in CloudWatch.

Debug and Profile Model Training with SageMaker Debugger

During training, we can use SageMaker Debugger to provide full insight into model training by monitoring, recording, and analyzing the state of each model training job —without any code changes. We can use SageMaker Debugger to stop our training job early to save money when we detect certain conditions like overfitting.

With SageMaker Debugger, we can interactively and visually explore the data captured during training, including tensor, gradient, and resource utilization. SageMaker Debugger captures this debugging and profiling information for both single-instance training jobs as well as multi-instance, distributed training clusters.

Detect and Resolve Issues with SageMaker Debugger Rules and Actions

Combined with CloudWatch Events, SageMaker Debugger can trigger an alert if a particular rule condition is met, such as bad training data, vanishing gradients, and exploding gradients. Bad data includes NaNs and nulls. Vanishing gradients occur when really small values are multiplied by other really small values and the result is too small for our `float` data type to store. Exploding gradients are the opposite of vanishing gradients. They occur when really large values are multiplied by other really large values and the result can't be represented by the 32 bits of our `float` data type. Both vanishing and exploding gradients can occur in deep neural networks given the number of matrix multiplications happening throughout the layers. As small numbers are multiplied by other small numbers, they will eventually approach zero and no longer be representable with a 32-bit `float`.

If SageMaker Debugger triggers an alert at 3 a.m., for example, SageMaker can automatically stop the training job. SageMaker can also send an email or text message to the on-call data scientist to investigate the issue. The data scientist would then use SageMaker Debugger to analyze the training run, visualize the tensors, review the CPU and GPU system metrics, and determine the root cause of the alert.

In addition to vanishing and exploding gradients, SageMaker Debugger also supports built-in rules for common debugging scenarios, such as `loss_not_decreasing`, `overfit`, `overtraining`, and `class_imbalance`. SageMaker launches an evaluation job for each SageMaker rule specified. We can also provide our own rules by providing a Docker image and implementation of the `Rule` framework.

Following is the code to create two rules to detect when the training loss stops decreasing at an adequate rate (`loss_not_decreasing`) and when the model starts to overtrain as the validation loss increases after a number of steps of normally decreasing behavior. These are both signals to "early stop" the training job, reduce the cost of the overall training job, avoid overfitting our model to the training dataset, and allow the model to generalize better on new, unseen data. Rules are configured with thresholds to define when the rules should trigger—as well as the Action to take when the rules are triggered:

```
from sagemaker.debugger import Rule
from sagemaker.debugger import rule_configs
from sagemaker.debugger import CollectionConfig
from sagemaker.debugger import DebuggerHookConfig

actions=rule_configs.ActionList(
    rule_configs.StopTraining(),
    rule_configs.Email("<EMAIL_ADDRESS>"),
    rule_configs.SMS("<PHONE_NUMBER>")
)
```

```
rules=[
    Rule.sagemaker(
        base_config=rule_configs.loss_not_decreasing(),
        rule_parameters={
            'collection_names': 'losses,metrics',
            'use_losses_collection': 'true',
            'num_steps': '10',
            'diff_percent': '50'
        },
        collections_to_save=[
            CollectionConfig(name='losses',
                            parameters={
                                'save_interval': '10',
                            }),
            CollectionConfig(name='metrics',
                            parameters={
                                'save_interval': '10',
                            })
        ],
        actions=actions
    ),
    Rule.sagemaker(
        base_config=rule_configs.overtraining(),
        rule_parameters={
            'collection_names': 'losses,metrics',
            'patience_train': '10',
            'patience_validation': '10',
            'delta': '0.5'
        },
        collections_to_save=[
            CollectionConfig(name='losses',
                            parameters={
                                'save_interval': '10',
                            }),
            CollectionConfig(name='metrics',
                            parameters={
                                'save_interval': '10',
                            })
        ],
        actions=actions
    )
]
```

We also need to create a debugger hook to use with the Keras API within TensorFlow 2.x as follows:

```
hook_config = DebuggerHookConfig(
    hook_parameters={
        'save_interval': '10', # number of steps
        'export_tensorboard': 'true',
        'tensorboard_dir': 'hook_tensorboard/',
    })
```

Then we need to set the rules and debugger hook in our Estimator as follows:

```
from sagemaker.tensorflow import TensorFlow
estimator = TensorFlow(entry_point='tf_bert_reviews.py',
                       ...
                       rules=rules,
                       debugger_hook_config=hook_config,
                       ...
)
```

Profile Training Jobs

Let's configure some `ProfileRules` to analyze CPU, GPU, network, and disk I/O metrics—as well as generate a `ProfilerReport` for our training job. Here, we are adding more to our existing `rules` list from the debugging section:

```
from sagemaker.debugger import Rule
from sagemaker.debugger import rule_configs
from sagemaker.debugger import ProfilerRule

rules=[
Rule.sagemaker(...),
        ProfilerRule.sagemaker(rule_configs.ProfilerReport()),
        ProfilerRule.sagemaker(rule_configs.BatchSize()),
        ProfilerRule.sagemaker(rule_configs.CPUBottleneck()),
        ProfilerRule.sagemaker(rule_configs.GPUMemoryIncrease()),
        ProfilerRule.sagemaker(rule_configs.IOBottleneck()),
        ProfilerRule.sagemaker(rule_configs.LoadBalancing()),
        ProfilerRule.sagemaker(rule_configs.LowGPUUtilization()),
        ProfilerRule.sagemaker(rule_configs.OverallSystemUsage()),
        ProfilerRule.sagemaker(rule_configs.StepOutlier())
    ]
```

We then need to create a `ProfilerConfig` and pass it to our Estimator as follows:

```
from sagemaker.debugger import ProfilerConfig, FrameworkProfile

profiler_config = ProfilerConfig(
    system_monitor_interval_millis=500,
    framework_profile_params=FrameworkProfile(
        local_path="/opt/ml/output/profiler/",
        start_step=5,
        num_steps=10)
)

from sagemaker.tensorflow import TensorFlow

estimator = TensorFlow(entry_point='tf_bert_reviews.py',
                       source_dir='src',
                       ...
                       py_version='<PYTHON_VERSION>',
                       framework_version='<TENSORFLOW_VERSION>',
                       hyperparameters={...},
```

```
        rules=rules,
        debugger_hook_config=hook_config,
        profiler_config=profiler_config,
```

Figure 7-29 shows a profile report generated by SageMaker Debugger during our training run. This report includes a suggestion to increase our batch size to improve GPU utilization, speed up our training job, and reduce cost.

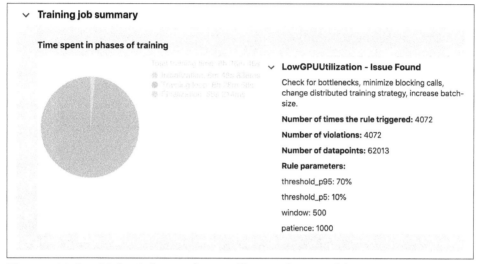

Figure 7-29. SageMaker Debugger deep profiling analyzes model training jobs.

Interpret and Explain Model Predictions

We can also use SageMaker Debugger to track gradients, layers, and weights during the training process. We will use this to monitor the BERT attention mechanism during model training. By understanding how the model is learning, we can better identify model bias and potentially explain model predictions. To do this, we need to capture tensors, including the attention scores, query vectors, and key vectors as SageMaker Debugger "collections." This information can then be used to plot the attention heads and individual neurons in the query and key vectors. Let's create our DebuggerHookConfig and a CollectionConfig using regex to capture the attention tensors at a particular interval during training:

```
debugger_hook_config = DebuggerHookConfig(
    s3_output_path=s3_bucket_for_tensors,
    collection_configs=[
    CollectionConfig(
    name="all",
    parameters={
        "include_regex":
          ".*multiheadattentioncell0_output_1|.*key_output|.*query_output",
        "train.save_steps": "0",
```

```
        "eval.save_interval": "1"}
    )]
)
```

We also add the following lines in the training script's validation loop to record the string representation of input tokens:

```
if hook.get_collections()['all'].save_config\
        .should_save_step(modes.EVAL, hook.mode_steps[modes.EVAL]):

    hook._write_raw_tensor_simple("input_tokens", input_tokens)
```

To visualize the results, we create a trial pointing to the captured tensors:

```
from smdebug.trials import create_trial
trial = create_trial( path )
```

We will use a script that plots the attention head using Bokeh (*https://oreil.ly/ZTxLN*), an interactive visualization library:

```
from utils import attention_head_view, neuron_view
from ipywidgets import interactive
```

Let's get the tensor names of the attention scores:

```
tensor_names = []

for tname in sorted(trial.tensor_names(regex='.*multiheadattentioncell0_output_1'):
    tensor_names.append(tname)
```

The tensor names should look similar to this since we are using a BERT model with 12 attention heads:

```
['bertencoder0_transformer0_multiheadattentioncell0_output_1',
 'bertencoder0_transformer10_multiheadattentioncell0_output_1',
 'bertencoder0_transformer11_multiheadattentioncell0_output_1',
 'bertencoder0_transformer1_multiheadattentioncell0_output_1',
 'bertencoder0_transformer2_multiheadattentioncell0_output_1',
 'bertencoder0_transformer3_multiheadattentioncell0_output_1',
 'bertencoder0_transformer4_multiheadattentioncell0_output_1',
 'bertencoder0_transformer5_multiheadattentioncell0_output_1',
 'bertencoder0_transformer6_multiheadattentioncell0_output_1',
 'bertencoder0_transformer7_multiheadattentioncell0_output_1',
 'bertencoder0_transformer8_multiheadattentioncell0_output_1',
 'bertencoder0_transformer9_multiheadattentioncell0_output_1']
```

Next we iterate over the available tensors and retrieve the tensor values:

```
steps = trial.steps(modes.EVAL)
tensors = {}

for step in steps:
    print("Reading tensors from step", step)
    for tname in tensor_names:
        if tname not in tensors:
            tensors[tname]={}
        tensors[tname][step] = trial.tensor(tname).value(step, modes.EVAL)
num_heads = tensors[tname][step].shape[1]
```

Next, we retrieve the query and key output tensor names:

```
ayers = []
layer_names = {}

for index, (key, query) in enumerate(
        zip(trial.tensor_names(regex='.*key_output_'),
            trial.tensor_names(regex='.*query_output_'))):

    layers.append([key,query])
    layer_names[key.split('_')[1]] = index
```

We also retrieve the string representation of the input tokens:

```
input_tokens = trial.tensor('input_tokens').value(0, modes.EVAL)
```

We are now ready to plot the attention head showing the attention scores between different tokens. The thicker the line, the higher the score. Let's plot the first 20 tokens using the following code, summarized in Figure 7-30:

```
n_tokens = 20
view = attention_head_view.AttentionHeadView(input_tokens,
                                    tensors,
                                    step=trial.steps(modes.EVAL)[0],
layer='bertencoder0_transformer0_multiheadattentioncell0_output_1',
                                    n_tokens=n_tokens)
```

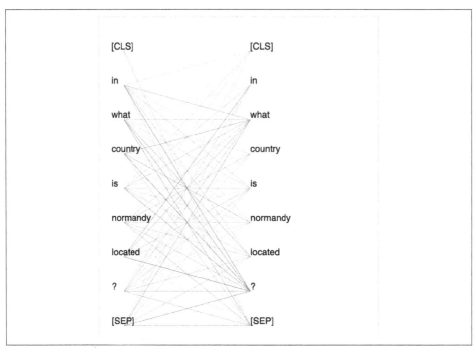

Figure 7-30. Attention-head view for the first 20 tokens. Source: "Visualizing Attention in Transformer-Based Language Representation Models" (https://oreil.ly/v6a5S).

Next, we retrieve the query and key vector tensors:

```
queries = {}
steps = trial.steps(modes.EVAL)

for step in steps:
    print("Reading tensors from step", step)

    for tname in trial.tensor_names(regex='.*query_output'):
        query = trial.tensor(tname).value(step, modes.EVAL)
        query = query.reshape((query.shape[0], query.shape[1], num_heads, -1))
        query = query.transpose(0,2,1,3)
        if tname not in queries:
            queries[tname] = {}
        queries[tname][step] = query

keys = {}
steps = trial.steps(modes.EVAL)

for step in steps:
    print("Reading tensors from step", step)

    for tname in trial.tensor_names(regex='.*key_output'):
        key = trial.tensor(tname).value(step, modes.EVAL)
```

```
key = key.reshape((key.shape[0], key.shape[1], num_heads, -1))
key = key.transpose(0,2,1,3)
if tname not in keys:
    keys[tname] = {}
keys[tname][step] = key
```

With the tensor values at hand, we can plot a detailed neuron view:

```
view = neuron_view.NeuronView(input_tokens,
                              keys=keys,
                              queries=queries,
                              layers=layers,
                              step=trial.steps(modes.EVAL)[0],
                              n_tokens=n_tokens,
                              layer_names=layer_names)
```

The resulting visualization is shown in Figure 7-31.

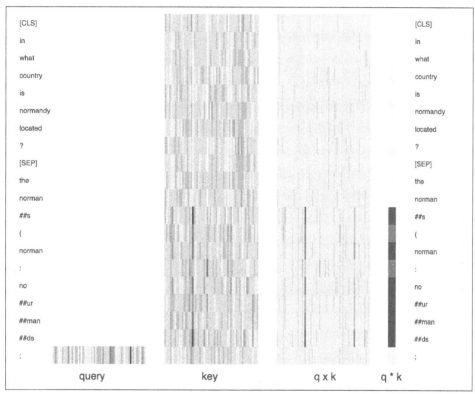

Figure 7-31. Neuron view of query and key vectors. Source: "Visualizing Attention in Transformer-Based Language Representation Models" (https://oreil.ly/v6a5S).

The darker the color in this visualization, the more the neurons influenced the attention scores.

As mentioned, the visualization of BERT attention can help to identify the root cause for incorrect model predictions. There is an active debate in the industry right now whether or not attention can be used for model explainability. A more popular approach to model explainability is gradient-based toolkits that generate saliency maps, such as AllenNLP Interpret (*https://oreil.ly/wJLRh*). The saliency maps identify which input tokens had the biggest influence on a model prediction and might be a more straightforward approach to NLP model explainability. Let's use the AllenNLP demo website (*https://oreil.ly/WzARH*) to create a saliency map when predicting the sentiment of the following review text: "a very well-made, funny and entertaining picture." Figure 7-32 shows the top 10 most important words that led to the "Positive" prediction.

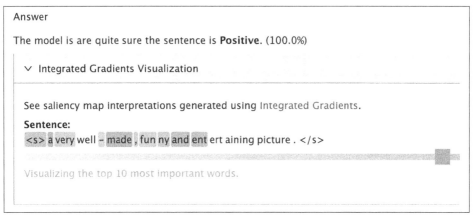

Figure 7-32. Visualization of the top 10 most important words to a sentiment analysis prediction using AllenNLP Interpret (https://oreil.ly/wJLRh).

We can integrate AllenNLP saliency maps into our Python applications by installing AllenNLP using `pip install allennlp`. In the following, we are calculating the integrated gradients, a measure of the influence that each token has on a prediction. We are specifically using a variant of BERT called RoBERTa, but AllenNLP supports many variants of BERT:

```
from pprint import pprint
from allennlp.predictors.predictor import Predictor
from allennlp.interpret.saliency_interpreters import IntegratedGradient

predictor = Predictor.from_path(
"https://.../allennlp-public-models/sst-roberta-large-2020.06.08.tar.gz"
)

integrated_gradient_interpreter = IntegratedGradient(predictor)

sentence = "a very well-made, funny and entertaining picture."
```

```
integrated_gradient_interpretation = \
    integrated_gradient_interpreter.saliency_interpret_from_json(inputs)

pprint(integrated_gradient_interpretation)
```

The output looks as follows:

```
{'instance_1': {'grad_input_1': [0.10338538634781776,
                                 0.19893729477254535,
                                 0.008472852427212439,
                                 0.0005615125409780962,
                                 0.01615882936970941,
                                 0.19841675479930443,
                                 0.06983715792756516,
                                 0.02557800239689324,
                                 0.06044705677145928,
                                 0.16507210055696683,
                                 0.1531329783765724]}}
```

Detect Model Bias and Explain Predictions

Even with an unbiased dataset, there is still the potential to train a biased model. This sounds surprising, but there are certain hyper-parameters that may favor particular facets of input features differently than other facets of the same feature. Additionally, we should be careful when fine-tuning with pre-trained models that are biased. BERT, for example, is biased because of the type of data that it was trained on. Due to the model's ability to learn from context, BERT picks up the statistical properties of the Wikipedia training data, including any expressed bias and social stereotypes. As we are fighting to reduce bias and stereotypes in our society, we should also implement mechanisms to detect and stop this bias from propagating into our models.

SageMaker Clarify helps us to detect bias and evaluate model fairness in each step of our machine learning pipeline. We saw in Chapter 5 how to use SageMaker Clarify to detect bias and class imbalances in our dataset. We now use SageMaker Clarify to analyze our trained model.

For post-training bias analysis, SageMaker Clarify integrates with SageMaker Experiments. SageMaker Clarify will look into the training data, the labels, and the model predictions and run a set of algorithms to calculate common data and model bias metrics. We can also use SageMaker Clarify to explain model predictions by analyzing feature importances.

Detect Bias with a SageMaker Clarify Processing Job

Similar to the pre-training bias analysis, we can run SageMaker Clarify as a Processing Job to calculate post-training data and model bias metrics. Calculating post-training bias metrics does require a trained model because the analysis now includes the data, labels, and model predictions. We define our trained model in ModelConfig and specify the model prediction format in ModelPredictedLabelConfig. SageMaker Clarify performs the post-training bias analysis by comparing the model predictions against the labels in the training data with respect to the chosen facet.

The provided training data must match the model's expected inference inputs plus the label column. We have chosen to train our model with just review_body as the single input feature. However, for this example, we have added product_category as a second feature and retrained our model. We use product_category as the facet to analyze for bias and imbalance across gift cards, digital software, and digital video games:

```
from sagemaker import clarify

clarify_processor = clarify.SageMakerClarifyProcessor(
        role=role,
        instance_count=1,
        instance_type='ml.c5.2xlarge',
        sagemaker_session=sess)

bias_report_output_path = 's3://{}/clarify'.format(bucket)

data_config = clarify.DataConfig(
        s3_data_input_path=train_dataset_s3_uri,
        s3_output_path=bias_report_output_path,
        label='star_rating',
        headers=['product_category', 'review_body'],
        dataset_type='text/csv')

bias_config = clarify.BiasConfig(
        label_values_or_threshold=[5,4]
        facet_name='product_category',
        facet_values_or_threshold=['Gift Card'],
        group_name='product_category')
```

In ModelConfig we define our trained model and specify the instance type and count for a shadow endpoint, which SageMaker Clarify creates:

```
model_config = clarify.ModelConfig(
        model_name=model_name,
        instance_type='ml.m5.4xlarge',
        instance_count=1,
        content_type='text/csv',
        accept_type='application/jsonlines')
```

ModelPredictedLabelConfig defines how to parse and read the model predictions. We can specify label, probability, probability_threshold, and label_headers. If our model returns a JSON output such as {"predicted_label": 5}, we could parse the prediction result by setting label='predicted_label'. If the model output matches the provided label type and format from the training data, we can simply leave it as is:

```
predictions_config = clarify.ModelPredictedLabelConfig(label='predicted_label')

clarify_processor.run_post_training_bias(
                    data_config=data_config,
                    data_bias_config=bias_config,
                    model_config=model_config,
                    model_predicted_label_config=predictions_config,
                    methods=['DPPL', 'DI', 'DCA', 'DCR', 'RD', \
                        'DAR', 'DRR', 'AD', 'CDDPL', 'TE'],
                    wait=True)
```

In methods we can select which post-training bias metrics to calculate.

In our example, we could analyze whether our model predicts more negative star ratings for a specific product category (facet) value, such as Digital Software, compared to another facet value, such as Gift Cards. One of the corresponding bias metrics to check would be difference in conditional rejection (DCR), which compares the labels to the predicted labels for each facet (product_category) for negative classifications (rejections). In this case, we could define star_rating==5 and star_rating==4 as the positive outcomes and the other classes as negative outcomes.

Post-training metrics include difference in positive proportions in predicted labels, disparate impact, difference in conditional acceptance, difference in conditional rejection, recall difference, difference in acceptance rate, difference in rejection rates, accuracy difference, treatment equality, conditional demographic disparity in predicted labels, and counterfactual fliptest.

SageMaker Clarify starts the post-training bias analysis by validating the provided configuration inputs and output parameters. SageMaker Clarify then creates an ephemeral, shadow SageMaker model endpoint and deploys the trained model. The processing job then calculates the defined bias metrics. Table 7-1 shows the calculated post-training bias metrics for our model. Once the job completes, SageMaker Clarify generates the output files and deletes the shadow endpoint.

Table 7-1. Post-training bias metrics analysis results

name	description	value
AD	Accuracy difference (AD)	-0.25
CDDPL	Conditional demographic disparity in predicted labels (CDDPL)	-0.333333
DAR	Difference in acceptance rates (DAR)	-0.444444
DCA	Difference in conditional acceptance (DCA)	-0.333333
DCR	Difference in conditional rejection (DCR)	-1.27273
DI	Disparate impact (DI)	2.22222
DPPL	Difference in positive proportions in predicted labels (DPPL)	-0.55

name	description	value
DRR	Difference in rejection rates (DRR)	-0.909091
RD	Recall difference (RD)	-0.166667
TE	Treatment equality (TE)	-0.25

In addition, SageMaker Clarify generates *analysis.json* with bias metrics and *report.ipynb* to visualize the bias metrics and share with our colleagues. The processing job also generates a bias baseline that we will use with SageMaker Model Monitor to detect drifts in bias on live model endpoints. We will describe this in more detail in Chapter 9.

Feature Attribution and Importance with SageMaker Clarify and SHAP

SageMaker Clarify also supports SHAP, a concept from game theory applied to machine learning content, to determine the contribution that each feature makes to a model's prediction. We can use this information to select features or create new feature combinations. Following is the code to perform feature attribution and model explainability with a SageMaker Clarify Processing Job:

```
from sagemaker import clarify

shap_config = clarify.SHAPConfig(
        baseline=[shap_dataset.iloc[0].values.tolist()],
        num_samples=15,
        agg_method='mean_abs')

explainability_output_path = 's3://{}/clarify'.format(bucket)

explainability_data_config = clarify.DataConfig(
        s3_data_input_path=train_dataset_s3_uri,
        s3_output_path=explainability_output_path,
        label='star_rating',
        headers=['product_category', 'review_body'],
        dataset_type='text/csv')

clarify_processor.run_explainability(
        data_config=explainability_data_config,
        model_config=model_config,
        model_score='predicted_label',
        explainability_config=shap_config)
```

In addition to *analysis.json* and *report.ipynb*, the processing job generates *explanations_shap/out.csv* with SHAP values for each feature and predicted label in the dataset. Here is a relevant snippet from *analysis.json* for the feature attributions and explanations:

```
"explanations": {
    "kernel_shap": {
        "star_rating": {
            "global_shap_values": {
                "product_category": 0.04999999999999998,
                "review_body": 1.3833333333333333
            },
            "expected_value": 2.0
        }
    }
}
```

We can also see the aggregated SHAP value for each feature visualized in SageMaker Studio, as shown in Figure 7-33. This represents the importance of each feature toward the prediction.

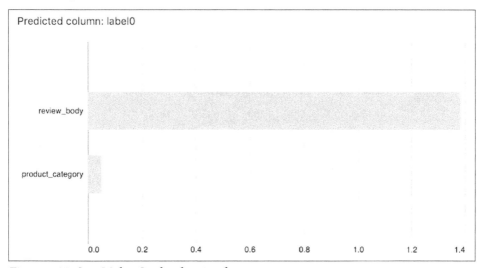

Figure 7-33. SageMaker Studio showing feature importance.

The processing job also generates an explainability baseline that we will use with SageMaker Model Monitor to detect drifts in feature attribution and model explainability on live model endpoints. We will describe this in more detail in Chapter 9.

More Training Options for BERT

While this book uses a lot of TensorFlow examples, SageMaker supports other popular AI and machine learning frameworks, including PyTorch and Apache MXNet, as we will discuss in the next few sections. We will also demonstrate how to train deep learning models with Java using AWS's open source Deep Java Library (*https://djl.ai*). This is useful for enterprises looking to integrate deep learning into their Java-based applications.

Convert TensorFlow BERT Model to PyTorch

In some cases, we may want to try out a different framework to see if we see better training or inference performance. Since we are using the popular Transformers library for BERT, we can convert our model from TensorFlow to PyTorch in just a few lines of code:

```
# Import the PyTorch version of DistilBert (without the TF prefix)
from transformers import DistilBertForSequenceClassification

# Using from_tf=True to load the model from TensorFlow to PyTorch
loaded_pytorch_model =
  DistilBertForSequenceClassification.from_pretrained(
      tensorflow_model_path, from_tf=True)

# Save the model as PyTorch
loaded_pytorch_model.save_pretrained(pytorch_models_dir)
```

 We can also convert a PyTorch model to TensorFlow. This is a feature of the Transformers library and will not work for non-Transformers-based PyTorch and TensorFlow models.

After converting the model, we have a PyTorch version of the same model that we trained with TensorFlow—using the same weights. We will deploy this PyTorch model using the TorchServe runtime in Chapter 9. TorchServe was built and optimized by AWS, Facebook, and the PyTorch Community to serve PyTorch model predictions and scale across AWS's elastic infrastructure:

```
print(loaded_pytorch_model)

### OUTPUT ###

DistilBertForSequenceClassification(
  (distilbert): DistilBertModel(
    (embeddings): Embeddings(
      (word_embeddings): Embedding(30522, 768, padding_idx=0)
      (position_embeddings): Embedding(512, 768)
      (LayerNorm): LayerNorm((768,), eps=1e-12, elementwise_affine=True)
      (dropout): Dropout(p=0.1, inplace=False)
    )
    (transformer): Transformer(
      (layer): ModuleList(
        (0): TransformerBlock(
          (attention): MultiHeadSelfAttention(
            (dropout): Dropout(p=0.1, inplace=False)
            (q_lin): Linear(in_features=768, out_features=768, bias=True)
            (k_lin): Linear(in_features=768, out_features=768, bias=True)
            (v_lin): Linear(in_features=768, out_features=768, bias=True)
```

```
            (out_lin): Linear(in_features=768, out_features=768, bias=True)
        )
        (sa_layer_norm): LayerNorm((768,), eps=1e-12, \
  elementwise_affine=True)
        (ffn): FFN(
          (dropout): Dropout(p=0.1, inplace=False)
          (lin1): Linear(in_features=768, out_features=3072, bias=True)
          (lin2): Linear(in_features=3072, out_features=768, bias=True)
        )
        (output_layer_norm): LayerNorm((768,), eps=1e-12, \
  elementwise_affine=True)
      )
      ...
    )
  )
)
(pre_classifier): Linear(in_features=768, out_features=768, bias=True)
(classifier): Linear(in_features=768, out_features=5, bias=True)
...
)
```

Train PyTorch BERT Models with SageMaker

PyTorch is a popular deep-learning framework with a large community of contributors from many companies like Facebook and AWS. PyTorch is natively supported by SageMaker, including distributed model training, debugging, profiling, hyperparameter tuning, and model inference endpoints. Following are snippets of code that train a DistilBERT PyTorch model on SageMaker and save the code to S3 to deploy in Chapter 9. The complete code is available in the GitHub repository for this book:

```
from sagemaker.pytorch import PyTorch

estimator = PyTorch(
    entry_point='train.py',
    source_dir='src',
    role=role,
    instance_count=train_instance_count,
    instance_type=train_instance_type,
    volume_size=train_volume_size,
    py_version='<PYTHON_VERSION>',
    framework_version='<PYTORCH_VERSION>',
    hyperparameters=hyperparameters,
    metric_definitions=metric_definitions,
    input_mode=input_mode,
    debugger_hook_config=debugger_hook_config
)

estimator.fit(inputs={'train': s3_input_train_data,
                      'validation': s3_input_validation_data,
                      'test': s3_input_test_data
```

```
        },
        experiment_config=experiment_config,
        wait=False)
```

Following is the Python *train.py* script that sets up the network and trains the model. Notice that we are using the PyTorch DistilBertForSequenceClassification and not the TensorFlow TFDistilBertForSequenceClassification, which uses a TF prefix to differentiate the implementation:

```
import torch
import torch.distributed as dist
import torch.nn as nn
import torch.optim as optim
import torch.utils.data

PRE_TRAINED_MODEL_NAME = 'distilbert-base-uncased'

tokenizer = DistilBertTokenizer.from_pretrained(
        PRE_TRAINED_MODEL_NAME)

config = DistilBertConfig.from_pretrained(PRE_TRAINED_MODEL_NAME,
                num_labels=len(CLASS_NAMES),
                id2label={0: 1, 1: 2, 2: 3, 3: 4, 4: 5},
                label2id={1: 0, 2: 1, 3: 2, 4: 3, 5: 4}
)
config.output_attentions=True

model = DistilBertForSequenceClassification.from_pretrained(
        PRE_TRAINED_MODEL_NAME, config=config)

device = torch.device('cuda' if use_cuda else 'cpu')
model.to(device)

ds_train = ReviewDataset(
        reviews=df_train.review_body.to_numpy(),
        targets=df_train.star_rating.to_numpy(),
        tokenizer=tokenizer,
        max_seq_len=max_seq_len
)

train_data_loader = DataLoader(
    ds_train,
    batch_size=batch_size,
    shuffle=True
)

loss_function = nn.CrossEntropyLoss()
optimizer = optim.Adam(params=model.parameters(), lr=args.lr)
for epoch in range(args.epochs):
for i, (sent, label) in enumerate(train_data_loader):
    model.train()
    optimizer.zero_grad()
```

```
    sent = sent.squeeze(0)
    if torch.cuda.is_available():
        sent = sent.cuda()
        label = label.cuda()
    output = model(sent)[0]
    _, predicted = torch.max(output, 1)

    loss = loss_function(output, label)
    loss.backward()
    optimizer.step()
...
torch.save(model.state_dict(), save_path)
```

Train Apache MXNet BERT Models with SageMaker

MXNet is another popular deep-learning framework used heavily within Amazon and AWS for many different use cases, including demand forecast, shipping logistics, infrastructure resource optimization, natural language processing, computer vision, fraud detection, and much more. MXNet is natively supported by SageMaker, including distributed training, debugging, profiling, hyper-parameter tuning, and model inference endpoints. Following is the code to train a BERT model with MXNet:

```
from sagemaker.mxnet import MXNet

estimator = MXNet(
    entry_point='train.py',
    source_dir='src',
    role=role,
    instance_count=train_instance_count,
    instance_type=train_instance_type,
    volume_size=train_volume_size,
    py_version='<PYTHON_VERSION>',
    framework_version='<MXNET_VERSION>',
    hyperparameters=hyperparameters,
    metric_definitions=metric_definitions,
    input_mode=input_mode,
    debugger_hook_config=debugger_hook_config
)

estimator.fit(inputs={'train': s3_input_train_data,
                      'validation': s3_input_validation_data,
                      'test': s3_input_test_data
                     },
              experiment_config=experiment_config,
              wait=False)
```

Train BERT Models with PyTorch and AWS Deep Java Library

While Python and C are the dominant languages for data science, there are scenarios that require integration with the billions of lines of Java code that have been written since Java's inception in the 1990s. Additionally, a lot of big data frameworks such as Apache Hadoop, Spark, and ElasticSearch are implemented in Java. Following are a series of code snippets that demonstrate how to train a BERT model with PyTorch using AWS Deep Learning Java that invokes TensorFlow, PyTorch, and Apache MXNet libraries from Java using the Java Native Interface. These examples are derived from the Deep Java Library GitHub repository (*https://oreil.ly/eVeQY*).

First, let's define a sizable amount of imports:

```
import ai.djl.*;
import ai.djl.engine.Engine;
import ai.djl.basicdataset.CsvDataset;
import ai.djl.basicdataset.utils.DynamicBuffer;
import ai.djl.modality.nlp.SimpleVocabulary;
import ai.djl.modality.nlp.bert.BertFullTokenizer;
import ai.djl.ndarray.NDArray;
import ai.djl.ndarray.NDList;
import ai.djl.repository.zoo.*;
import ai.djl.training.*;
import ai.djl.training.dataset.Batch;
import ai.djl.training.dataset.RandomAccessDataset;
import ai.djl.training.evaluator.Accuracy;
import ai.djl.training.listener.CheckpointsTrainingListener;
import ai.djl.training.listener.TrainingListener;
```

Next, we define a Java class to transform raw text into BERT embeddings:

```
final class BertFeaturizer implements CsvDataset.Featurizer {
    private final BertFullTokenizer tokenizer;
    private final int maxLength; // the cut-off length

    public BertFeaturizer(BertFullTokenizer tokenizer, int maxLength) {
        this.tokenizer = tokenizer;
        this.maxLength = maxLength;
    }

    @Override
    public void featurize(DynamicBuffer buf, String input) {
        SimpleVocabulary vocab = tokenizer.getVocabulary();
        // convert sentence to tokens (toLowerCase for uncased model)
        List<String> tokens = tokenizer.tokenize(input.toLowerCase());
        // trim the tokens to maxLength
        tokens = tokens.size() > maxLength ?
        tokens.subList(0, maxLength) : tokens;
        // BERT embedding convention "[CLS] Your Sentence [SEP]"
        buf.put(vocab.getIndex("[CLS]"));
        tokens.forEach(token -> buf.put(vocab.getIndex(token)));
        buf.put(vocab.getIndex("[SEP]"));
    }
}
```

Let's define a function to retrieve our Amazon Customer Reviews Dataset. For this example, we use the `Digital_Software` product category:

```
CsvDataset getDataset(int batchSize, BertFullTokenizer tokenizer, int maxLength){
    String amazonReview =
            "https://s3.amazonaws.com/amazon-reviews-
pds/tsv/amazon_reviews_us_Digital_Software_v1_00.tsv.gz";
    float paddingToken = tokenizer.getVocabulary().getIndex("[PAD]");
    return CsvDataset.builder()
            .optCsvUrl(amazonReview) // load from Url
            .setCsvFormat(CSVFormat.TDF.withQuote(null).withHeader())
            .setSampling(batchSize, true) // make sample size and random access
            .addFeature(
                    new CsvDataset.Feature(
                            "review_body", new BertFeaturizer(tokenizer,
                                                        maxLength)))
            .addLabel(
                    new CsvDataset.Feature(
                            "star_rating", (buf, data) ->
                                    buf.put(Float.parseFloat(data) - 1.0f)))
            .optDataBatchifier(
                    PaddingStackBatchifier.builder()
                            .optIncludeValidLengths(false)
                            .addPad(0, 0, (m) ->
                                    m.ones(new Shape(1)).mul(paddingToken))
                            .build())
            .build();
}
```

Now we retrieve a pre-trained DistilBERT PyTorch model from the Deep Java Library model zoo:

```
String modelUrls =
    "https://resources.djl.ai/test-models/traced_distilbert_wikipedia_uncased.zip";
}

Criteria<NDList, NDList> criteria = Criteria.builder()
        .optApplication(Application.NLP.WORD_EMBEDDING)
        .setTypes(NDList.class, NDList.class)
        .optModelUrls(modelUrls)
        .optProgress(new ProgressBar())
        .build();
ZooModel<NDList, NDList> embedding = ModelZoo.loadModel(criteria);
```

Let's construct our model to fine-tune DistilBERT with our Amazon Customer Reviews Dataset:

```
Predictor<NDList, NDList> embedder = embedding.newPredictor();
Block classifier = new SequentialBlock()
        // text embedding layer
        .add(
            ndList -> {
                NDArray data = ndList.singletonOrThrow();
```

```
                NDList inputs = new NDList();
                long batchSize = data.getShape().get(0);
                float maxLength = data.getShape().get(1);

                if ("PyTorch".equals(Engine.getInstance().getEngineName())) {
                    inputs.add(data.toType(DataType.INT64, false));
                    inputs.add(data.getManager().full(data.getShape(), 1,
                                                    DataType.INT64));
                    inputs.add(data.getManager().arange(maxLength)
                                .toType(DataType.INT64, false)
                                .broadcast(data.getShape()));
                } else {
                    inputs.add(data);
                    inputs.add(data.getManager().full(new Shape(batchSize),
                            maxLength));
                }
                // run embedding
                try {
                    return embedder.predict(inputs);
                } catch (TranslateException e) {
                    throw new IllegalArgumentException("embedding error", e);
                }
            })
        // classification layer
        .add(Linear.builder().setUnits(768).build()) // pre classifier
        .add(Activation::relu)
        .add(Dropout.builder().optRate(0.2f).build())
        .add(Linear.builder().setUnits(5).build()) // 5 star rating
        .addSingleton(nd -> nd.get(":,0")); // Take [CLS] as the head
Model model = Model.newInstance("AmazonReviewRatingClassification");
model.setBlock(classifier);
```

Finally, let's tie everything together, transform our dataset into BERT embeddings, set up a Checkpoint callback listener, and train our BERT-based review classifier with Java!

```
// Prepare the vocabulary
SimpleVocabulary vocabulary = SimpleVocabulary.builder()
        .optMinFrequency(1)
        .addFromTextFile(embedding.getArtifact("vocab.txt"))
        .optUnknownToken("[UNK]")
        .build();
// Prepare dataset
int maxTokenLength = 64; // cutoff tokens length
int batchSize = 128;

BertFullTokenizer tokenizer = new BertFullTokenizer(vocabulary, true);

CsvDataset amazonReviewDataset = getDataset(batchSize, tokenizer, maxTokenLength);

RandomAccessDataset[] datasets = amazonReviewDataset.randomSplit(0.9, 0.1);
RandomAccessDataset trainingSet = datasets[0];
```

```
RandomAccessDataset validationSet = datasets[1];

CheckpointsTrainingListener listener =
        new CheckpointsTrainingListener("build/model");
        listener.setSaveModelCallback(
            trainer -> {
                TrainingResult result = trainer.getTrainingResult();
                Model model = trainer.getModel();
                // track for accuracy and loss
                float accuracy = result.getValidateEvaluation("Accuracy");
                model.setProperty("Accuracy", String.format("%.5f", accuracy));
                model.setProperty("Loss", String.format("%.5f",
                        result.getValidateLoss()));
            });
DefaultTrainingConfig config =
  new DefaultTrainingConfig(Loss.softmaxCrossEntropyLoss())
        .addEvaluator(new Accuracy())
        .optDevices(Device.getDevices(1)) // train using single GPU
        .addTrainingListeners(TrainingListener.Defaults.logging("build/model"))
        .addTrainingListeners(listener);

int epoch = 2;

Trainer trainer = model.newTrainer(config);
trainer.setMetrics(new Metrics());
Shape encoderInputShape = new Shape(batchSize, maxTokenLength);
// initialize trainer with proper input shape
trainer.initialize(encoderInputShape);
EasyTrain.fit(trainer, epoch, trainingSet, validationSet);
System.out.println(trainer.getTrainingResult());

model.save(Paths.get("build/model"), "amazon-review.param");
```

We can run some sample predictions using a custom `Translator` class that uses a DistilBERT tokenizer to transform raw text into BERT embeddings:

```
class MyTranslator implements Translator<String, Classifications> {

    private BertFullTokenizer tokenizer;
    private SimpleVocabulary vocab;
    private List<String> ranks;

    public MyTranslator(BertFullTokenizer tokenizer) {
        this.tokenizer = tokenizer;
        vocab = tokenizer.getVocabulary();
        ranks = Arrays.asList("1", "2", "3", "4", "5");
    }

    @Override
    public Batchifier getBatchifier() {return new StackBatchifier();}

    @Override
    public NDList processInput(TranslatorContext ctx, String input) {
```

```
        List<String> tokens = tokenizer.tokenize(input);
        float[] indices = new float[tokens.size() + 2];
        indices[0] = vocab.getIndex("[CLS]");
        for (int i = 0; i < tokens.size(); i++) {
            indices[i+1] = vocab.getIndex(tokens.get(i));
        }
        indices[indices.length - 1] = vocab.getIndex("[SEP]");
        return new NDList(ctx.getNDManager().create(indices));
    }

    @Override
    public Classifications processOutput(TranslatorContext ctx, NDList list)
    {
        return new Classifications(ranks, list.singletonOrThrow().softmax(0));
    }
}

String review = "It works great, but takes too long to update";
Predictor<String, Classifications> predictor =
        model.newPredictor(new MyTranslator(tokenizer));

System.out.println(predictor.predict(review));

### OUTPUT ###

4
```

Reduce Cost and Increase Performance

In this section, we provide tips on how to improve performance and reduce costs by using hardware- and infrastructure-level optimizations such as reduced precision and Spot Instances. Additionally, we describe how to stop training jobs early when they stop improving.

Use Small Notebook Instances

As a best practice, we should do all of our heavy GPU-based computations in a Sage-Maker Processing, Training, or Batch Transform Job instead of our notebook. This helps us save money since we can use a smaller instance type for our longer-running notebook instance. If we find ourselves using a GPU instance type for our SageMaker Notebooks, we can likely save money by switching to a cheaper notebook instance type and moving our GPU-based computations into a SageMaker Training or Processing Job so that we only pay for the GPU for the duration of the Training or Processing Job.

Test Model-Training Scripts Locally in the Notebook

We can specify `instance_type='local'` in our SageMaker Training Job to run the script either inside a SageMaker Notebook—or on our local laptop. This lets us "locally" run the training job on a small subset of data in a notebook before launching a full-scale SageMaker Training Job. If we run in the notebook, we should remember that we are limited to the memory and compute resources of the notebook instance. Therefore, we should only run for one or two epochs using a small batch size on a subset of the training dataset when training inside of a notebook instance.

Profile Training Jobs with SageMaker Debugger

Profiler provides valuable insight into bottlenecks of our training jobs and provides useful recommendations to fix those bottlenecks. Oftentimes, we are not actually compute bound but rather I/O bound. SageMaker Debugger helps identify these less-intuitive bottlenecks with actual data to help us increase resource utilization, decrease training times, and reduce cost. In this example, SageMaker Debugger identified a CPU bottleneck and suggests that we add more data loaders or enable more aggressive data prefetching:

```
CPUBottleneck - Issue Found
CPU bottlenecks can happen when data preprocessing is very compute intensive.
You should consider increasing the number of data-loader processes or apply
pre-fetching.
Number of times the rule triggered: 16
Number of violations: 8090
Number of datapoints: 62020
Rule parameters:
threshold: 50%
cpu_threshold: 90%
gpu_threshold: 10%
patience: 1000
```

SageMaker Debugger also suggests using a smaller instance or increasing the batch size since our GPU utilization is low:

```
BatchSize - Issue Found
Run on a smaller instance type or increase batch size
Number of times the rule triggered: 4072
Number of violations: 4072
Number of datapoints: 62012
Rule parameters:
cpu_threshold_p95: 70%
gpu_threshold_p95: 70%
gpu_memory_threshold_p95: 70%
patience: 1000
window: 500
LowGPUUtilization - Issue Found
Check for bottlenecks, minimize blocking calls, change distributed training
```

```
strategy, increase batch-size.
Number of times the rule triggered: 4072
Number of violations: 4072
Number of datapoints: 62013
Rule parameters:
threshold_p95: 70%
threshold_p5: 10%
window: 500
patience: 1000
```

Start with a Pre-Trained Model

Fine-tuning a pre-trained model like BERT can save us lots of time and money by letting us avoid tasks that have already been done for us. In some cases where our domain uses a vastly different language model than an option like BERT, we may need to train a model from scratch. However, we should try these pre-trained models first and see how far they get us.

Use 16-Bit Half Precision and bfloat16

Most models store parameters and perform calculations using full 32-bit numerical precision. Intuitively, if we reduce the precision to 16-bit or "reduced" or "half" precision, we would not only reduce the footprint of the stored parameters by half but also increase computation performance by 2x as the chip can perform two 16-bit calculations on the same 32-bit hardware.

Another reduced precision 16-bit float, bfloat16, is a truncated version of float32 that preserves the 8-bit exponent portion of a float32 but leaves only 7 bits for the fraction. Note that bfloat is not IEEE compliant; however it is natively supported in modern chips from ARM, Intel, Google, and Amazon. Figure 7-34 shows a comparison of float16, float32, and bfloat16, including the number of bits used to represent the exponent and fraction.

There are downsides to reduced precision, however. While the training times go toward zero in this perfect world, so can accuracy and numeric instability. By reducing the numerical precision to 16 bits, our model may not learn as well as a 32-bit model. Additionally, we may experience more frequent vanishing gradients as the model only has 16 bits to represent the parameters and gradients. So the chance of the value going to 0 is much higher than using 32 bits. bfloat16 reduces the chance of vanishing gradients by preserving the dynamic range of a float32 through the 8-bit exponent. We can also use loss-scaling policies to reduce the potential for vanishing gradients.

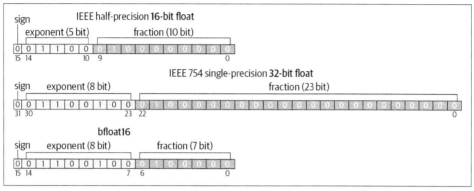

Figure 7-34. Comparison of float16, float32, *and* bfloat. *Source: Wikipedia (https://oreil.ly/8W544).*

When deploying models to tiny devices with limited memory, we may need to reduce precision to 8 bit, 4 bit, or even 1 bit for our floats. The challenge is preserving accuracy at this lower precision.

Mixed 32-Bit Full and 16-Bit Half Precision

The choice of 32 bit or 16 bit is yet another hyper-parameter to optimize. Some algorithms and datasets may be more sensitive to reduced precision than others. However, there is a middle ground called "mixed" precision that stores the parameters in 32 bits with "full precision" to maintain numerical stability but performs the calculations using 16-bit operations in "half precision." Ideally, half precision would lead to 2x speed-up in operations utilizing half the memory. However, in practice we see less-than-ideal improvements due to overhead.

TensorFlow and Keras offer native mixed-precision support at the network-layer level. Here, we set the global policy for all layers using an automatic mixed-precision "policy" that allows the framework to decide which layers and operations should utilize 16-bit half precision:

```
import tf.keras.mixed_precision.Policy

policy = mixed_precision.Policy('mixed_float16')
mixed_precision.set_policy(policy)
```

This is effectively a "turbo button" for model training; however, we should treat this like any other hyper-parameter and tune it for our specific dataset and algorithm.

Quantization

In the future chapter on model deployment, we will describe how to reduce the precision of a model from 32 bit to 16 bit after training to reduce the size of the model and speed up the computations. The quantization process uses statistical methods—rooted in audio signal processing—to preserve the dynamic range of the parameter values. While not required, we can modify our training script to be "quantization-aware" and prepare the model for the post-training quantization. This helps to preserve model accuracy after quantizing.

Use Training-Optimized Hardware

AWS Trainium is a training-optimized chip designed to accelerate model-training workloads for popular deep learning frameworks, including TensorFlow, PyTorch, and Apache MXNet. AWS Trainium uses the AWS Neuron SDK and supports autocasting of 32-bit full-precision floating points to 16-bit bfloats to increase throughput and reduce cost.

Spot Instances and Checkpoints

If we are using an algorithm that supports checkpointing, such as TensorFlow, PyTorch, and Apache MXNet, we can use Spot Instances with SageMaker Training Jobs to save cost. Spot Instances are cheaper than on-demand instances. To train with Spot Instances, we specify use_spot_instances=True in our estimator, as shown here:

```
checkpoint_s3_uri = 's3://<BUCKET>/<CHECKPOINT_PREFIX/'

estimator = TensorFlow(entry_point='tf_bert_reviews.py',
                       source_dir='src'
                       use_spot_instances=True,
                       max_wait=120, # seconds,
                       checkpoint_s3_uri=checkpoint_s3_uri,
                       ...
```

Spot Instances may be terminated while the training job is running. Using the max_wait parameter, SageMaker will wait max_wait seconds for new Spot Instances to replace the previously terminated Spot Instances. After max_wait seconds, the job will end. The latest checkpoint is used to begin training from the point in time when the Spot Instances were terminated.

Figure 7-35 shows an example of one Spot Instance replaced at Time 0 and three Spot Instances replaced at Time 1. However, the replacement cadence is driven by supply and demand of Spot Instances and is somewhat difficult to predict. Single-instance training jobs that use checkpoints can also benefit from Spot Instance savings.

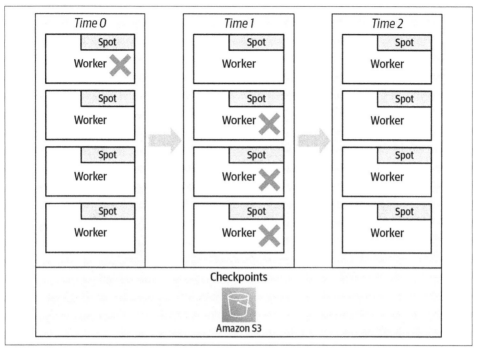

Figure 7-35. Use checkpoints to continue training when spot instances are replaced.

Our script then leverages the provided checkpoint location to save a checkpoint using a Keras `ModelCheckpoint` as follows:

```
checkpoint_path = '/opt/ml/checkpoints'

checkpoint_callback = ModelCheckpoint(
            filepath=os.path.join(checkpoint_path, 'tf_model_{epoch:05d}.h5'),
            save_weights_only=False,
            verbose=1,
            monitor='val_accuracy')

callbacks.append(checkpoint_callback)
```

To load the model, our script uses the checkpoint location to load the model as follows:

```
def load_checkpoint_model(checkpoint_path):
    import glob
    import os

    glob_pattern = os.path.join(checkpoint_path, '*.h5')
    print('glob pattern {}'.format(glob_pattern))

    list_of_checkpoint_files = glob.glob(glob_pattern)
    print('List of checkpoint files {}'.format(list_of_checkpoint_files))
```

```
latest_checkpoint_file = max(list_of_checkpoint_files)
loaded_model = TFDistilBertForSequenceClassification.from_pretrained(
                   latest_checkpoint_file,
                   config=config)

if os.listdir(checkpoint_path):
    model = load_checkpoint_model(checkpoint_path)
```

Early Stopping Rule in SageMaker Debugger

SageMaker Debugger supports a number of built-in actions to execute when a rule fires. For example, the `StopTraining()` action reduces cost by stopping a training job when the objective metric (e.g., accuracy) plateaus and no longer improves with additional training. The plateau is detected by a rule such as `overfit`. We configure the rule in terms of relative change over a given time or number of steps. For example, if our accuracy does not improve by 1% over one thousand steps, we want to stop the training job and save some money.

The `StopTraining()` action will end the training job abruptly when the rule is triggered. Similar to using Spot Instances, we should use checkpoints, specifically the last checkpoint before the job was stopped early.

Summary

In this chapter, we trained our first model using the Keras API within TensorFlow 2.x, BERT, and Amazon SageMaker. We dove deep into the SageMaker infrastructure, model development SDKs, and SageMaker Training Jobs. We trained a model using SageMaker, described security best practices, and explored some cost-saving and performance-improvement tips.

We also learned how BERT's Transformer neural-network architecture has revolutionized the field of NLP and NLU by using a bidirectional approach to learn a contextual representation of the words in a corpus. We demonstrated how to fine-tune a pre-trained BERT model to build a domain-specific text classifier for product reviews. This is in contrast to the previous generation of NLP models such as Word2Vec, GloVe, and ELMo that either (1) learn only in one direction at a time, (2) throw away the original model and preserve only the learned embeddings, or (3) use complex recurrent neural network (RNNs) architectures that require a large amount of memory and compute.

In Chapter 8, we will retrain our model using different configurations and hyperparameters in a process called hyper-parameter optimization or hyper-parameter tuning. Through this process, we will find the best model and hyper-parameter combination that provides the highest accuracy. We will optimize models even further to take advantage of hardware optimizations provided by our target deployment hardware, such as NVIDIA GPUs or AWS Inferentia chips. In Chapter 9, we will deploy and monitor our model in production. In Chapter 10, we build an end-to-end pipeline for our model with SageMaker Pipelines, AWS Step Functions, Apache Airflow, Kubeflow, and other open source options.

## CHAPTER 8

Train and Optimize Models at Scale

Peter Drucker, one of Jeff Bezos's favorite business strategists, once said, "If you can't measure it, you can't improve it." This quote captures the essence of this chapter, which focuses on measuring, optimizing, and improving our predictive models.

In the previous chapter, we trained a single model with a single set of hyper-parameters using Amazon SageMaker. We also demonstrated how to fine-tune a pre-trained BERT model to build a review-text classifier model to predict the sentiment of product reviews in the wild from social channels, partner websites, etc.

In this chapter, we will use SageMaker Experiments to measure, track, compare, and improve our models at scale. We also use SageMaker Hyper-Parameter Tuning to choose the best hyper-parameters for our specific algorithm and dataset. We also show how to perform distributed training using various communication strategies and distributed file systems. We finish with tips on how to reduce cost and increase performance using SageMaker Autopilot's hyper-parameter-selection algorithm, SageMaker's optimized pipe to S3, and AWS's enhanced-networking hardware.

Automatically Find the Best Model Hyper-Parameters

Now that we understand how to track and compare model-training runs, we can automatically find the best hyper-parameters for our dataset and algorithm using a scalable process called hyper-parameter tuning (HPT) or hyper-parameter optimization (HPO). SageMaker natively supports HPT jobs. These tuning jobs are the building blocks for SageMaker Autopilot, discussed in Chapter 3.

We have already learned that hyper-parameters control *how* our machine learning algorithm learns the model parameters during model training. When tuning our hyper-parameters, we need to define an objective to optimize, such as model accuracy. In other words, we need to find a set of hyper-parameters that meets or exceeds our given objective.

After each HPT run, we evaluate the model performance and adjust the hyper-parameters until the objective is reached. Doing this manually is very time-consuming as model tuning often requires tens or hundreds of training jobs to converge on the best combination of hyper-parameters for our objective. SageMaker's HPT jobs speed up and scale out the optimization process by running multiple training jobs in parallel using a given tuning strategy, as shown in Figure 8-1.

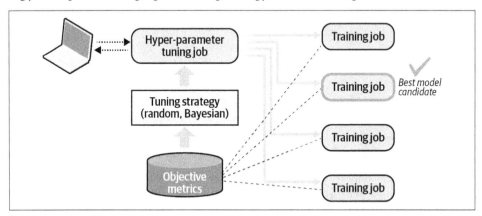

Figure 8-1. SageMaker HPT supports common tuning strategies.

SageMaker supports the random-search and Bayesian hyper-parameter optimization strategies. With random search, we randomly keep picking combinations of hyper-parameters until we find a well-performing combination. This approach is very fast and very easy to parallelize, but we might miss the best set of hyper-parameters as we are picking randomly from the hyper-parameter space. With Bayesian optimization, we treat the task as a regression problem.

Similar to how our actual model learns the model weights that minimize a loss function, Bayesian optimization iterates to find the best hyper-parameters using a surrogate model and acquisition function that performs an informed search over the hyper-parameter space using prior knowledge learned during previous optimization runs. Bayesian optimization is usually more efficient than manual, random, or grid search but requires that we perform some optimizations sequentially (versus in parallel) to build up the prior knowledge needed to perform the informed search across the hyper-parameter space.

What about grid search? With grid search, we would evaluate a grid of every possible hyper-parameter combination in our hyper-parameter space. This approach is often inefficient and takes orders of magnitude longer to complete relative to the random search and Bayesian optimization strategies. At the time of this writing, SageMaker

HPT does not support the inefficient grid search optimization strategy. Instead, we recommend using the random-search and Bayesian optimization strategies.

Set Up the Hyper-Parameter Ranges

Let's use SageMaker HPT to find the best hyper-parameters for our BERT-based review classifier from the previous chapter. First, let's create an `optimize` experiment tracker and associate it with our experiment:

```
from smexperiments.tracker import Tracker

tracker_optimize = Tracker.create(display_name='optimize-1',
                                  sagemaker_boto_client=sm)

optimize_trial_component_name =
        tracker_optimize.trial_component.trial_component_name

trial.add_trial_component(tracker_optimize.trial_component)
```

To keep this example simple and avoid a combinatorial explosion of trial runs, we will freeze most hyper-parameters and explore only a limited set for this particular optimization run. In a perfect world with unlimited resources and budget, we would explore every combination of hyper-parameters. For now, we will manually choose some of the following hyper-parameters and explore the rest in our HPO run:

```
epochs=500
epsilon=0.00000001
train_batch_size=128
validation_batch_size=128
test_batch_size=128
train_steps_per_epoch=100
validation_steps=100
test_steps=100
use_xla=True
use_amp=True
freeze_bert_layer=True
```

Next, let's set up the hyper-parameter ranges that we wish to explore. We are choosing these hyper-parameters based on intuition, domain knowledge, and algorithm documentation. We may also find research papers useful—or other prior work from the community. At this point in the life cycle of machine learning and predictive analytics, we can almost always find relevant information on the problem we are trying to solve.

If we still can't find a suitable starting point, we should explore ranges logarithmically (versus linearly) to help gain a sense of the scale of the hyper-parameter. There is no point in exploring the set [1, 2, 3, 4] if our best hyper-parameter is orders of magnitude away in the 1,000s, for example.

SageMaker Autopilot is another way to determine a baseline set of hyper-parameters for our problem and dataset. SageMaker Autopilot's hyper-parameter selection process has been refined on many thousands of hours of training jobs across a wide range of datasets, algorithms, and use cases within Amazon.

SageMaker HPT supports three types of parameter ranges: categorical, continuous, and integer. `Categorical` is used for discrete sets of values (e.g., `product_category`). `Continuous` is used for floats, and `Integer` is used for integers. We can also specify the scaling type for each type of hyper-parameter ranges. The scaling type can be set to `Linear`, `Logarithmic`, `ReverseLogarithmic`, or `Auto`, which allows SageMaker to decide. Certain hyper-parameters are better suited to certain scaling types. Here, we are specifying that the SageMaker Tuning Job should explore the continuous hyper-parameter, `learning_rate`, between the given range using a linear scale:

```
from sagemaker.tuner import ContinuousParameter

hyperparameter_ranges = {
    'learning_rate': ContinuousParameter(0.00001, 0.00005,
                                         scaling_type='Linear'),
}
```

If we do not have a suitable range for exploring a particular hyper-parameter—even after researching other algorithms that address the problem similar to ours—we can start with the `Logarithmic` scaling type for that hyper-parameter and narrow in on a range to subsequently explore linearly with the `Linear` scaling type.

Finally, we need to define the objective metric that the HPT job is trying to optimize —in our case, validation accuracy. Remember that we need to provide the regular expression (regex) to extract the metric from the SageMaker container logs. We chose to also collect the training loss, training accuracy, and validation loss for informational purposes:

```
objective_metric_name = 'validation:accuracy'

metrics_definitions = [
    {'Name': 'train:loss', 'Regex': 'loss: ([0-9\\.]+)'},
    {'Name': 'train:accuracy', 'Regex': 'accuracy: ([0-9\\.]+)'},
    {'Name': 'validation:loss', 'Regex': 'val_loss: ([0-9\\.]+)'},
    {'Name': 'validation:accuracy', 'Regex': 'val_accuracy: ([0-9\\.]+)'}]
```

Run the Hyper-Parameter Tuning Job

We start by creating our TensorFlow estimator as in the previous chapter. Note that we are not specifying the `learning_rate` hyper-parameter in this case. We will pass this as a hyper-parameter range to the `HyperparameterTuner` in a moment:

```
from sagemaker.tensorflow import TensorFlow

hyperparameters={'epochs': epochs,
                 'epsilon': epsilon,
                 'train_batch_size': train_batch_size,
                 'validation_batch_size': validation_batch_size,
                 'test_batch_size': test_batch_size,
                 'train_steps_per_epoch': train_steps_per_epoch,
                 'validation_steps': validation_steps,
                 'test_steps': test_steps,
                 'use_xla': use_xla,
                 'use_amp': use_amp,
                 'max_seq_length': max_seq_length,
                 'freeze_bert_layer': freeze_bert_layer,
}

estimator = TensorFlow(entry_point='tf_bert_reviews.py',
                       source_dir='src',
                       role=role,
                       instance_count=train_instance_count,
                       instance_type=train_instance_type,
                       py_version='<PYTHON_VERSION>',
                       framework_version='<TENSORFLOW_VERSION>',
                       hyperparameters=hyper_parameters,
                       metric_definitions=metrics_definitions,
                       )
```

Next, we can create our HPT job by passing the TensorFlow estimator, hyper-parameter range, objective metric, tuning strategy, number of jobs to run in parallel/total, and an early stopping strategy. SageMaker will use the given optimization strategy (i.e., "Bayesian" or "Random") to explore the values within the given ranges:

```
objective_metric_name = 'validation:accuracy'

tuner = HyperparameterTuner(
    estimator=estimator,
    objective_type='Maximize',
    objective_metric_name=objective_metric_name,
    hyperparameter_ranges=hyperparameter_ranges,
    metric_definitions=metrics_definitions,
    max_jobs=100,
    max_parallel_jobs=10,
    strategy='Bayesian',
    early_stopping_type='Auto'
)
```

In this example, we are using the Bayesian optimization strategy with 10 jobs in parallel and 100 total. By only doing 10 at a time, we give the Bayesian strategy a chance to learn from previous runs. In other words, if we did all 100 in parallel, the Bayesian strategy could not use prior information to choose better values within the ranges provided.

By setting `early_stopping_type` to `Auto`, SageMaker will stop the tuning job if the tuning job is not going to improve upon the objective metric. This helps save time, reduces the potential for overfitting to our training dataset, and reduces the overall cost of the tuning job.

Let's start the tuning job by calling `tuner.fit()` using the train, validation, and test dataset splits:

```
s3_input_train_data =
        TrainingInput(s3_data=processed_train_data_s3_uri,
                      distribution='ShardedByS3Key')

s3_input_validation_data =
        TrainingInput(s3_data=processed_validation_data_s3_uri,
                      distribution='ShardedByS3Key')

s3_input_test_data =
        TrainingInput(s3_data=processed_test_data_s3_uri,
                      distribution='ShardedByS3Key')

tuner.fit(inputs={'train': s3_input_train_data,
                  'validation': s3_input_validation_data,
                  'test': s3_input_test_data
          },
          include_cls_metadata=False)
```

Analyze the Best Hyper-Parameters from the Tuning Job

Following are results of the tuning job to determine the best hyper-parameters. This tuning job resulted in a final training accuracy of 0.9416 for the best candidate, which is higher than 0.9394, the accuracy from Chapter 7 using a set of manually chosen hyper-parameter values:

```
from sagemaker.analytics import HyperparameterTuningJobAnalytics

hp_results = HyperparameterTuningJobAnalytics(
    sagemaker_session=sess,
    hyperparameter_tuning_job_name=tuning_job_name
)

df_results = hp_results.dataframe()
df_results
```

freeze_bert_ layer	learning_ rate	train_batch_ size	TrainingJob Name	TrainingJob Status	FinalObjective Value	TrainingElapsed TimeSeconds
"False"	0.000017	"128"	tensorflow-training-210109-0222-003-cf95cdaa	Completed	0.9416	11245.0
...						
"False"	0.000042	"128"	tensorflow-training-210109-0222-004-48da4bab	Stopped	0.8056	693.0

Given the results of this tuning job, the best combination of hyper-parameters is
learning_rate 0.000017, train_batch_size 128, and freeze_bert_layer False.
SageMaker stopped a job early because its combination of hyper-parameters was not
improving the training-accuracy objective metric. This is an example of SageMaker
saving us money by intelligently stopping jobs early when they are not adding value
to our business objective.

Show Experiment Lineage for Our SageMaker Tuning Job

Once the HPT job has finished, we can analyze the results directly in our notebook or
through SageMaker Studio.

First, let's update the experiment lineage to include the best hyper-parameters and
objective metrics found by our HPT job:

```
best_learning_rate = df_results.sort_values('FinalObjectiveValue',
        ascending=0).head(1)['learning_rate']

tracker_optimize.log_parameters({
        'learning_rate': best_learning_rate
})

best_accuracy = df_results.sort_values('FinalObjectiveValue',
        ascending=0).head(1)['FinalObjectiveValue']

tracker_optimize.log_metrics({
        'train:accuracy': best_accuracy
})

tracker_optimize.trial_component.save()
```

Now, let's summarize the experiment lineage up to this point. In Chapter 9, we will
deploy the model and further extend our experiment lineage to include model
deployment. We will then tie everything together in an end-to-end pipeline with full
lineage tracking in Chapter 10:

```
from sagemaker.analytics import ExperimentAnalytics

lineage_table = ExperimentAnalytics(
    sagemaker_session=sess,
    experiment_name=experiment_name,
    metric_names=['train:accuracy'],
    sort_by="CreationTime",
    sort_order="Ascending",
)

lineage_table.dataframe()
```

TrialComponentName	DisplayName	max_seq_length	learning_rate	train_accuracy	...
TrialComponent-2021-01-09-062410-pxuy	prepare	64.0	NaN	NaN	...
tensorflow-training-2021-01-09-06-24-12-989	train	64.0	0.00001	0.9394	...
TrialComponent-2020-06-12-193933-bowu	optimize-1	64.0	0.000017	0.9416	...

In this example, we have optimized the hyper-parameters of our TensorFlow BERT classifier layer. SageMaker HPT also supports automatic HPT across multiple algorithms by adding a list of algorithms to the tuning job definition. We can specify different hyper-parameters and ranges for each algorithm. Similarly, SageMaker Autopilot uses multialgorithm tuning to find the best model across different algorithms based on our problem type, dataset, and objective function.

Use Warm Start for Additional SageMaker Hyper-Parameter Tuning Jobs

Once we have our best candidate, we can choose to perform yet another round of hyper-parameter optimization using a technique called "warm start." Warm starting reuses the prior results from a previous HPT job—or set of jobs—to speed up the optimization process and reduce overall cost. Warm start creates a many-to-many parent–child relationship. In our example, we perform a warm start with a single parent, the previous tuning job, as shown in Figure 8-2.

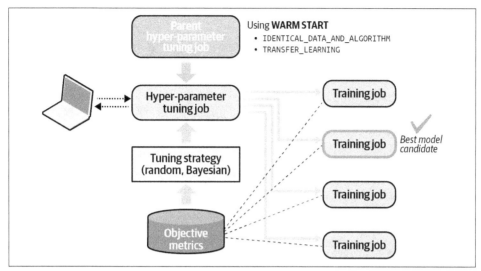

Figure 8-2. Use warm start to start an additional HPT job from a previous tuning job.

Warm start is particularly useful when we want to change the tunable hyper-parameter ranges from the previous job or add new hyper-parameters. Both scenarios use the previous tuning job to find the best model faster. The two scenarios are implemented with two warm start types: IDENTICAL_DATA_AND_ALGORITHM and TRANSFER_LEARNING.

If we choose IDENTICAL_DATA_AND_ALGORITHM, the new tuning job uses the same input data and training image as the parent job. We are allowed to update the tunable hyper-parameter ranges and the maximum number of training jobs. We can also add previously fixed hyper-parameters to the list of tunable hyper-parameters and vice versa—as long as the overall number of fixed plus tunable hyper-parameters remains the same. Upon completion, a tuning job with this strategy will return an additional field, OverallBestTrainingJob, containing the best model candidate, including this tuning job as well as the completed parent tuning jobs.

If we choose TRANSFER_LEARNING, we can use updated training data and a different version of the training algorithm. Perhaps we collected more training data since the last optimization run—and now we want to rerun the tuning job with the updated dataset. Or perhaps a newer version of the algorithm has been released and we want to rerun the optimization process.

Run HPT Job Using Warm Start

We need to configure the tuning job with WarmStartConfig using one or more of the previous HPT jobs as parents. The parent HPT jobs must have finished with one of the following success or failure states: Completed, Stopped, or Failed. Recursive parent–child relationships are not supported. We also need to specify the WarmStart Type. In our example, we will use IDENTICAL_DATA_AND_ALGORITHM as we plan to only modify the hyper-parameter ranges and not use an updated dataset or algorithm version.

Let's start with the setup of WarmStartConfig:

```
from sagemaker.tuner import WarmStartConfig
from sagemaker.tuner import WarmStartTypes

warm_start_config = WarmStartConfig(
        warm_start_type=WarmStartTypes.IDENTICAL_DATA_AND_ALGORITHM,
        parents={tuning_job_name})
```

Let's define the fixed hyper-parameters that we are not planning to tune:

```
epochs=500
epsilon=0.00000001
train_batch_size=128
validation_batch_size=128
test_batch_size=128
train_steps_per_epoch=100
validation_steps=100
test_steps=100
use_xla=True
use_amp=True
freeze_bert_layer=False

from sagemaker.tensorflow import TensorFlow

hyperparameters={'epochs': epochs,
                 'epsilon': epsilon,
                 'train_batch_size': train_batch_size,
                 'validation_batch_size': validation_batch_size,
                 'test_batch_size': test_batch_size,
                 'train_steps_per_epoch': train_steps_per_epoch,
                 'validation_steps': validation_steps,
                 'test_steps': test_steps,
                 'use_xla': use_xla,
                 'use_amp': use_amp,
                 'max_seq_length': max_seq_length,
                 'freeze_bert_layer': freeze_bert_layer
}

estimator = TensorFlow(entry_point='tf_bert_reviews.py',
                       source_dir='src',
                       role=role,
```

```
                    instance_count=train_instance_count,
                    instance_type=train_instance_type,
                    volume_size=train_volume_size,
                    py_version='<PYTHON_VERSION>',
                    framework_version='<TENSORFLOW_VERSION>',
                    hyperparameters=hyperparameters,
                    metric_definitions=metrics_definitions,
                    )
```

While we can choose to tune more hyper-parameters in this warm-start tuning job, we will simply modify the range of our `learning_rate` to narrow in on the best value found in the parent tuning job:

```
from sagemaker.tuner import IntegerParameter
from sagemaker.tuner import ContinuousParameter
from sagemaker.tuner import CategoricalParameter

hyperparameter_ranges = {
    'learning_rate': ContinuousParameter(0.00015, 0.00020,
                                    scaling_type='Linear')}
```

Now let's define the objective metric, create the `HyperparameterTuner` with the preceding `warm_start_config`, and start the tuning job:

```
objective_metric_name = 'validation:accuracy'

tuner = HyperparameterTuner(
    estimator=estimator,
    objective_type='Maximize',
    objective_metric_name=objective_metric_name,
    hyperparameter_ranges=hyperparameter_ranges,
    metric_definitions=metrics_definitions,
    max_jobs=50,
    max_parallel_jobs=5,
    strategy='Bayesian',
    early_stopping_type='Auto',
    warm_start_config=warm_start_config
)
```

Finally, let's configure the dataset splits and start our tuning job:

```
s3_input_train_data =
        TrainingInput(s3_data=processed_train_data_s3_uri,
                    distribution='ShardedByS3Key')

s3_input_validation_data =
        TrainingInput(s3_data=processed_validation_data_s3_uri,
                    distribution='ShardedByS3Key')

s3_input_test_data =
        TrainingInput(s3_data=processed_test_data_s3_uri,
                    distribution='ShardedByS3Key')
```

```
tuner.fit({'train': s3_input_train_data,
            'validation': s3_input_validation_data,
            'test': s3_input_test_data},
        },
        include_cls_metadata=False)
```

Analyze the Best Hyper-Parameters from the Warm-Start Tuning Job

Following are results of the tuning job to determine the best hyper-parameters. The tuning job resulted in a best-candidate training accuracy of 0.9216, which is lower than 0.9416, the best-candidate training accuracy of the parent HPT job. After updating our experiment lineage with the warm-start HPT results, we will move forward with the hyper-parameters of the candidate that generated the highest training accuracy of 0.9416 from the parent tuning job.

TrialComponentName	DisplayName	max_seq_length	learning_rate	train_accuracy	...
TrialComponent-2021-01-09-062410-pxuy	prepare	64.0	NaN	NaN	...
tensorflow-training-2021-01-09-06-24-12-989	train	64.0	0.00001	0.9394	...
TrialComponent-2021-01-09-193933-bowu	optimize-1	64.0	0.000017	0.9416	...
TrialComponent-2021-01-09-234445-dep	optimize-2	64.0	0.000013	0.9216	...

In this example, we have optimized the hyper-parameters of our TensorFlow BERT classifier layer. SageMaker HPT also supports automatic HPT across multiple algorithms by adding a list of algorithms to the tuning job definition. We can specify different hyper-parameters and ranges for each algorithm. Similarly, SageMaker Autopilot uses multialgorithm tuning to find the best model across different algorithms based on our problem type, dataset, and objective function.

The warm-start tuning job did not beat the accuracy of the parent tuning job's best candidate. Therefore, the hyper-parameter found from the parent tuning is still the best candidate in this example.

Scale Out with SageMaker Distributed Training

Most modern AI and machine learning frameworks support some form of distributed processing to scale out the computation. Without distributed processing, the training job is limited to the resources of a single instance. While individual instance types are constantly growing in capabilities (RAM, CPU, and GPU), our modern world of big data requires a cluster to power continuous data ingestion, real-time analytics, and data-hungry machine learning models.

Let's run a distributed training job to build our reviews classifier model using the TensorFlow 2.x Keras API, BERT, and SageMaker's native distributed-training support for TensorFlow.

While we do not include a PyTorch example in this chapter, Sage-Maker absolutely supports distributed PyTorch. Review our Git-Hub repository for the PyTorch and BERT examples. Additionally, the Hugging Face Transformers library natively supports SageMaker's distributed training infrastructure for both TensorFlow and PyTorch.

Choose a Distributed-Communication Strategy

Any distributed computation requires that the cluster instances communicate and share information with each other. This cluster communication benefits from higher-bandwidth connections between the instances. Therefore, the instances should be physically close to each other in the cloud data center, if possible. Fortunately, Sage-Maker handles all of this heavy lifting for us so we can focus on creating our review classifier and address our business problem of classifying product reviews in the wild. SageMaker supports distributed computations with many distributed-native frameworks, including Apache Spark, TensorFlow, PyTorch, and APache MXNet.

While most modern AI and machine learning frameworks like TensorFlow, PyTorch, and Apache MXNet are designed for distributed computations, many classic data science libraries such as scikit-learn and pandas do not natively support distributed communication protocols or distributed datasets. Dask is a popular runtime to help scale certain scikit-learn models to multiple nodes in a cluster.

"Parameter server" is a primitive distributed training strategy supported by most distributed machine learning frameworks. Remember that parameters are what the algorithm is learning. Parameter servers store the learned parameters and share them with every instance during the training process. Since parameter servers store the state of the parameters, SageMaker runs a parameter server on every instance for higher availability, as shown in Figure 8-3.

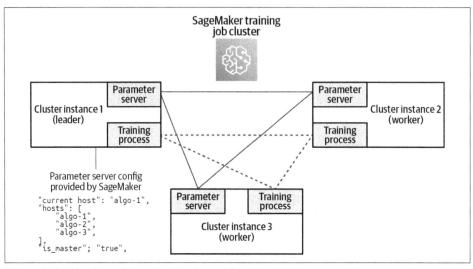

Figure 8-3. Distributed communication with parameter servers.

Running stateful parameter servers on every instance helps SageMaker recover from failure situations or when Spot Instances are terminated and replaced during the training process.

Another common distributed communication strategy rooted in parallel computing and message-passing interfaces (MPI) is "all-reduce." All-reduce uses a ring-like communication pattern, as shown in Figure 8-4, and increases overall training efficiency for very large clusters where the communication overhead between parameter servers becomes overwhelming.

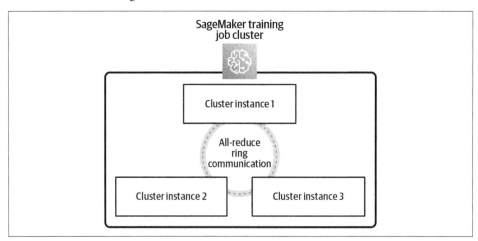

Figure 8-4. All-reduce distributed communication strategy.

SageMaker's all-reduce distributed training strategy is compatible with Horovod, a popular all-reduce and MPI implementation commonly used to scale TensorFlow and PyTorch training jobs to multiple instances in a cluster. If we are currently using Horovod for distributed training, we can easily transition to SageMaker's all-reduce strategy. For our example, we will use SageMaker's built-in distributed all-reduce communication strategy.

Choose a Parallelism Strategy

There are two main types of parallelism when performing distributed computations: data parallelism and model parallelism. Most of us are already familiar with data parallelism from classical map-reduce data-processing tools like Apache Spark that split up the dataset into "shards" and place them on separate instances. Each instance processes its split separately in the "map" phase, then combines the results in the "reduce" phase. Data parallelism is required when our dataset cannot fit on a single instance, as in the case with most modern big data processing and distributed machine learning. Figure 8-5 shows how data parallelism splits up the data onto different instances for the model to process separately.

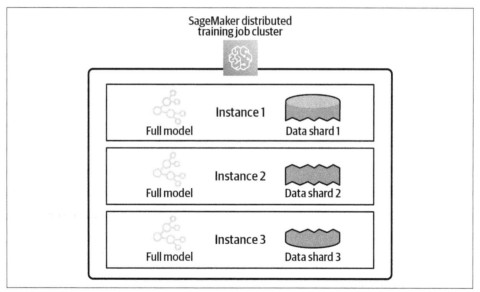

Figure 8-5. Sharding a dataset across multiple instances for distributed training with data parallelism.

Model parallelism does the opposite and splits the processing onto separate instances and processes the entire dataset separately on each instance. It is quite a bit more complicated and is typically required when our model is too large to fit into the resources of a single instance due to memory constraints. Figure 8-6 shows how model parallelism splits up the model onto different instances and processes the full dataset with each "model shard."

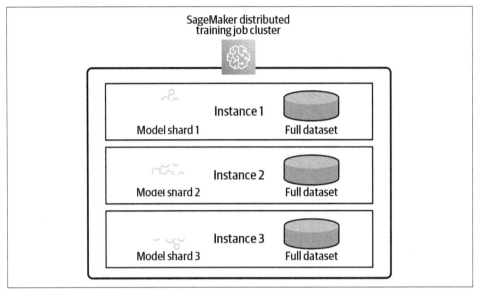

Figure 8-6. Sharding a model across multiple instances for distributed training with model parallelism.

SageMaker natively supports both data parallelism and model parallelism. For our BERT model, we will use data parallelism since our model fits into a single instance, so we will shard our dataset across the different instances, train on each shard, and combine the results through the all-reduce communication strategy built in to Sage-Maker distributed training.

Choose a Distributed File System

Typically, our distributed training clusters communicate directly with S3 to read and write our data. However, some frameworks and tools are not optimized for S3 natively—or only support POSIX-compatible filesystems. For these scenarios, we can use FSx for Lustre (Linux) or Amazon FSx for Windows File Server to expose a POSIX-compatible filesystem on top of S3. This extra layer also provides a crucial cache-performance benefit that reduces training times to reasonable levels for larger datasets.

Amazon FSx for Lustre is a high-performance, POSIX-compatible filesystem that natively integrates with S3. FSx for Lustre is based on the open source Lustre filesystem designed for highly scalable, highly distributed, and highly parallel training jobs with petabytes of data, terabytes per second of aggregate I/O throughput, and consistent low latency.

There is also Amazon FSx for Windows File Server, which provides a Windows-compatible filesystem that natively integrates with S3 as well. However, we have chosen to focus on FSx for Lustre as our examples are Linux based. Both filesystems are optimized for machine learning, analytics, and high-performance computing workloads using S3. And both filesystems offer similar features.

FSx for Lustre is a fully managed service that simplifies the complexity of setting up and managing the Lustre filesystem. Mounting an S3 bucket as a filesystem in minutes, FSx for Lustre lets us access data from any number of instances concurrently and caches S3 objects to improve performance of iterative machine learning workloads that pass over the dataset many times to fit a high-accuracy model. Figure 8-7 shows how SageMaker uses FSx for Lustre to provide fast, shared access to our S3 data and accelerate our training and tuning jobs.

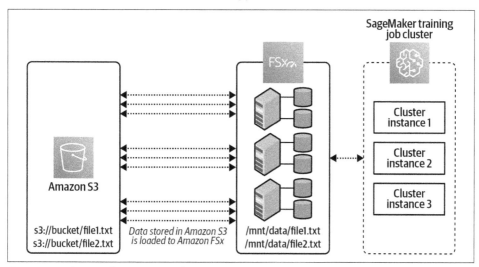

Figure 8-7. SageMaker uses FSx for Lustre to increase training and tuning job performance.

Our SageMaker training cluster instances access a file in FSx for Lustre using */mnt/data/file1.txt*. FSx for Lustre translates this request and issues a `GetObject` request to S3. The file is cached and returned to the cluster instance. If the file has not changed, subsequent requests will return from FSx for Lustre's cache. Since training data does not typically change during a training job run, we see huge performance gains as we iterate through our dataset over many training epochs.

Once we have set up the FSx for Lustre filesystem, we can pass the location of the FSx for Lustre filesystem into the training job as follows:

```
estimator = TensorFlow(entry_point='tf_bert_reviews.py',
                       source_dir='src',
                       instance_count=train_instance_count,
```

```
                      instance_type=train_instance_type,
                      subnets=['subnet-1', 'subnet-2']
                      security_group_ids=['sg-1'])

    fsx_data = FileSystemInput(file_system_id='fs-1',
                               file_system_type='FSxLustre',
                               directory_path='/mnt/data,
                               file_system_access_mode='ro')

    estimator.fit(inputs=fsx_data)
```

Note that we need to specify the `subnets` and `security_group_ids` used when we
created our FSx for Lustre filesystem. We will dive deep into networking and security
in Chapter 12.

Another option for distributed training is Amazon Elastic File System (Amazon EFS).
Amazon EFS is compatible with industry-standard Network File System protocols
but optimized for AWS's cloud-native and elastic environment, including networking,
access control, encryption, and availability. In this section, we adapt our distributed
training job to use both FSx for Lustre (Linux) and Amazon EFS. Amazon EFS provides centralized, shared access to our training datasets across thousands of instances
in a distributed training cluster, as shown in Figure 8-8.

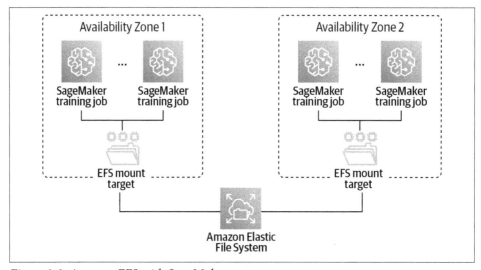

Figure 8-8. Amazon EFS with SageMaker.

  SageMaker Studio uses Amazon EFS to provide centralized, shared,
and secure access to code and notebooks across all team members
with proper authorization.

Data stored in Amazon EFS is replicated across multiple Availability Zones, which provides higher availability and read/write throughput. The Amazon EFS filesystem will scale out automatically as new data is ingested.

Assuming we have mounted and populated the Amazon EFS filesystem with training data, we can pass the Amazon EFS mount into the training job using two different implementations: FileSystemInput and FileSystemRecordSet.

This example shows how to use the FileSystemInput implementation:

```
estimator = TensorFlow(entry_point='tf_bert_reviews.py',
                       source_dir='src',
                       instance_count=train_instance_count,
                       instance_type=train_instance_type,
                       subnets=['subnet-1', 'subnet-2']
                       security_group_ids=['sg-1'])

efs_data = FileSystemInput(file_system_id='fs-1',
                           file_system_type='EFS',
                           directory_path='/mnt/data,
                           file_system_access_mode='ro')

estimator.fit(inputs=efs_data)
```

Note that we need to specify the subnets and security_group_ids used when we created our Amazon EFS filesystem. We will dive deep into networking and security in Chapter 12.

For our example, we will use FSx for Lustre because of its S3-caching capabilities, which greatly increases our training performance.

Launch the Distributed Training Job

SageMaker, following cloud-native principles, is inherently distributed and scalable in nature. In the previous chapter, we were using a single instance by specifying train_instance_count=1. Here, we will increase the train_instance_count and specify the distribution parameter in our TensorFlow estimator to enable Sage-Maker distributed training, as shown in the following:

```
train_instance_count=3
train_instance_type='ml.p4d.24xlarge'

from sagemaker.tensorflow import TensorFlow

estimator = TensorFlow(entry_point='tf_bert_reviews.py',
                       source_dir='src',
                       instance_count=train_instance_count,
                       instance_type=train_instance_type,
                       ...
                       py_version='<PYTHON_VERSION>',
```

```
                  framework_version='<TENSORFLOW_VERSION>',
                  distribution={'smdistributed':{
                          'dataparallel':{
                                  'enabled': True
                          }
                  }
          )
```

SageMaker automatically passes the relevant cluster information to TensorFlow to enable the all-reduce strategy and use distributed TensorFlow.

 SageMaker also passes the same cluster information to enable distributed PyTorch and Apache MXNet, but we are only showing TensorFlow in this example.

Reduce Cost and Increase Performance

In this section, we discuss various ways to increase cost-effectiveness and performance using some advanced SageMaker features, including SageMaker Autopilot for baseline hyper-parameter selection, ShardedByS3Key to distribute input files across all training instances, and Pipe mode to improve I/O throughput. We also highlight AWS's enhanced networking capabilities, including the Elastic Network Adapter (ENA) and Elastic Fabric Adapter (EFA) to optimize network performance between instances in our training and tuning cluster.

Start with Reasonable Hyper-Parameter Ranges

By researching the work of others, we can likely find a range of hyper-parameters that will narrow the search space and speed up our SageMaker HPT jobs. If we don't have a good starting point, we can use the Logarithmic scaling strategy to determine the scale within which we should explore. Just knowing the power of 10 can make a big difference in reducing the time to find the best hyper-parameters for our algorithm and dataset.

Shard the Data with ShardedByS3Key

When training at scale, we need to consider how each instance in the cluster will read the large training datasets. We can use a brute-force approach and copy all of the data to all of the instances. However, with larger datasets, this may take a long time and potentially dominate the overall training time. For example, after performing feature engineering, our tokenized training dataset has approximately 45 TFRecord "part" files, as shown in the following:

```
part-algo-1-amazon_reviews_us_Apparel_v1_00.tfrecord
...
part-algo-2-amazon_reviews_us_Digital_Software_v1_00.tfrecord
part-algo-4-amazon_reviews_us_Digital_Video_Games_v1_00.tfrecord
...
part-algo-9-amazon_reviews_us_Sports_v1_00.tfrecord
```

Rather than load all 45 part files onto all instances in the cluster, we can improve startup performance by placing only 15 part files onto each of the 3 cluster instances for a total of 45 part files spread across the cluster. This is called "sharding." We will use a SageMaker feature called ShardedByS3Key that evenly distributes the part files across the cluster, as shown in Figure 8-9.

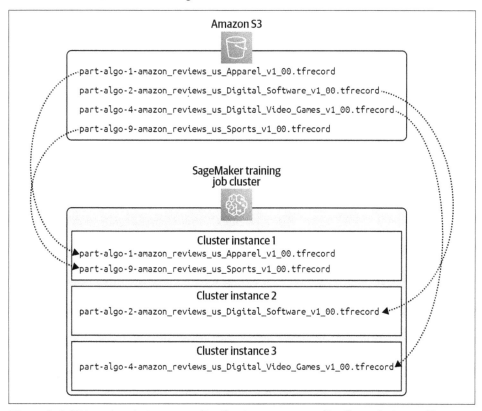

Figure 8-9. Using ShardedByS3Key distribution strategy to distribute the input files across the cluster instances.

Here we set up the ShardedByS3Key distribution strategy for our S3 input data including the train, validation, and test datasets:

```
s3_input_train_data =
    sagemaker.s3_input(s3_data=processed_train_data_s3_uri,
                       distribution='ShardedByS3Key')
```

```
s3_input_validation_data =
    sagemaker.s3_input(s3_data=processed_validation_data_s3_uri,
                       distribution='ShardedByS3Key')

s3_input_test_data =
    sagemaker.s3_input(s3_data=processed_test_data_s3_uri,
                       distribution='ShardedByS3Key')
```

Next, we call `fit()` with the input map for each of our dataset splits, including train, validation, and test:

```
estimator.fit(inputs={'train': s3_input_train_data,
                      'validation': s3_input_validation_data,
                      'test': s3_input_test_data
            })
```

In this case, each instance in our cluster will receive approximately 15 files for each of the dataset splits.

Stream Data on the Fly with Pipe Mode

In addition to sharding, we can also use a SageMaker feature called `Pipe` mode to load the data on the fly and as needed. Up until now, we've been using the default `File` mode, which copies all of the data to all the instances when the training job starts. This creates a long pause at the start of the training job as the data is copied. `Pipe` mode provides the most significant performance boost when using large datasets in the 10, 100, or 1,000 GB range. If our dataset is smaller, we should use `File` mode.

`Pipe` mode streams data in parallel from S3 directly into the training processes running on each instance, which provides significantly higher I/O throughput than `File` mode. By streaming only the data that is needed when it's needed, our training and tuning jobs start quicker, complete faster, and use less disk space overall. This directly leads to lower cost for our training and tuning jobs.

`Pipe` mode works with S3 to pull the rows of training data as needed. Under the hood, `Pipe` mode is using Unix first-in, first-out (FIFO) files to read data from S3 and cache it locally on the instance shortly before the data is needed by the training job. These FIFO files are one-way readable. In other words, we can't back up or skip ahead randomly.

Here is how we configure our training job to use `Pipe` mode:

```
estimator = TensorFlow(entry_point='tf_bert_reviews.py',
                       source_dir='src',
                       instance_count=train_instance_count,
                       instance_type=train_instance_type,
```

```
        ...
        input_mode='Pipe')
```

Since `Pipe` mode wraps our TensorFlow Dataset Reader, we need to change our TensorFlow code slightly to detect `Pipe` mode and use the `PipeModeDataset` wrapper:

```
if input_mode == 'Pipe':
    from sagemaker_tensorflow import PipeModeDataset

    dataset = PipeModeDataset(channel=channel,
                              record_format='TFRecord')
else:
    dataset = tf.data.TFRecordDataset(input_filenames)
```

Enable Enhanced Networking

Training at scale requires super-fast communication between instances in the cluster. Be sure to select an instance type that utilizes ENA and EFA to provide high network bandwidth and consistent network latency between the cluster instances.

ENA works well with the AWS deep learning instance types, including the C, M, P, and X series. These instance types offer a large number of CPUs, so they benefit greatly from efficient sharing of the network adapter. By performing various network-level optimizations such as hardware-based checksum generation and software-based routing, ENA reduces overhead, improves scalability, and maximizes consistency. All of these optimizations are designed to reduce bottlenecks, offload work from the CPUs, and create an efficient path for the network packets.

EFA uses custom-built, OS-level bypass techniques to improve network performance between instances in a cluster. EFA natively supports MPI, which is critical to scaling high-performance computing applications that scale to thousands of CPUs. EFA is supported by many of the compute-optimized instance types, including the C and P series.

While not much concrete data exists to verify, some practitioners have noticed a performance improvement when running distributed SageMaker jobs in a Virtual Private Cloud (VPC). This is likely attributed to reduced network latency between cluster instances running in the same VPC. If our training jobs are particularly latency-sensitive, we might want to try running our training jobs in a VPC. We dive deep into VPCs and SageMaker in Chapter 12.

Summary

In this chapter, we used SageMaker Experiments and HPT to track, compare, and choose the best hyper-parameters for our specific algorithm and dataset. We explored various distributed communication strategies, such as parameter servers and all-reduce. We demonstrated how to use FSx for Lustre to increase S3 performance and how to configure our training job to use the Amazon EFS. Next, we explored a few ways to reduce cost and increase performance using SageMaker Autopilot's hyper-parameter selection feature and SageMaker's optimized data loading strategies like `ShardedByS3Key` and `Pipe` mode. Last, we discussed the enhanced networking features for compute-optimized instance types, including the ENA and EFA.

In Chapter 9, we will deploy our models into production using various rollout, A/B testing, and multiarmed bandit strategies. We will discuss how to integrate model predictions into applications using real-time REST endpoints, offline batch jobs, and edge devices. We demonstrate how to auto-scale our endpoints based on built-in and custom CloudWatch metrics. We also dive deep into using SageMaker Model Monitor to detect drifts in data distributions, model bias, and model explainability of our live SageMaker Endpoints.

## CHAPTER 9

Deploy Models to Production

In previous chapters, we demonstrated how to train and optimize models. In this chapter, we shift focus from model development in the research lab to model deployment in production. We demonstrate how to deploy, optimize, scale, and monitor models to serve our applications and business use cases.

We deploy our model to serve online, real-time predictions and show how to run offline, batch predictions. For real-time predictions, we deploy our model via SageMaker Endpoints. We discuss best practices and deployment strategies, such as canary rollouts and blue/green deployments. We show how to test and compare new models using A/B tests and how to implement reinforcement learning with multiarmed bandit (MAB) tests. We demonstrate how to automatically scale our model hosting infrastructure with changes in model-prediction traffic. We show how to continuously monitor the deployed model to detect concept drift, drift in model quality or bias, and drift in feature importance. We also touch on serving model predictions via serverless APIs using Lambda and how to optimize and manage models at the edge. We conclude the chapter with tips on how to reduce our model size, reduce inference cost, and increase our prediction performance using various hardware, services, and tools, such as the AWS Inferentia hardware, SageMaker Neo service, and TensorFlow Lite library.

Choose Real-Time or Batch Predictions

We need to understand the application and business context to choose between realtime and batch predictions. Are we trying to optimize for latency or throughput? Does the application require our models to scale automatically throughout the day to handle cyclic traffic requirements? Do we plan to compare models in production through A/B tests?

If our application requires low latency, then we should deploy the model as a real-time API to provide super-fast predictions on single prediction requests over HTTPS, for example. We can deploy, scale, and compare our model prediction servers with SageMaker Endpoints using the REST API protocol with HTTPS and JSON, as shown in Figure 9-1.

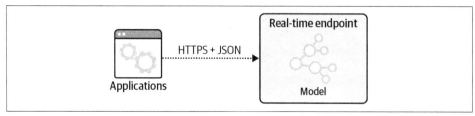

Figure 9-1. Deploy model as a real-time REST endpoint.

For less-latency-sensitive applications that require high throughput, we should deploy our model as a batch job to perform batch predictions on large amounts of data in S3, for example. We will use SageMaker Batch Transform to perform the batch predictions along with a data store like Amazon RDS or DynamoDB to productionize the predictions, as shown in Figure 9-2.

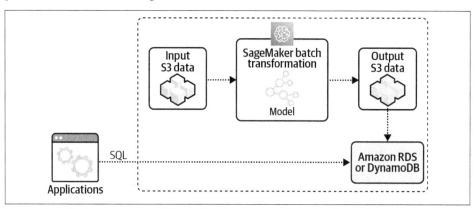

Figure 9-2. Deploying our model as a batch job to perform batch predictions on large amounts of data in S3 using SageMaker Batch Transform.

Real-Time Predictions with SageMaker Endpoints

In 2002, Jeff Bezos, founder of Amazon, wrote a memo to his employees later called the "Bezos API Mandate." The mandate dictated that all teams must expose their services through APIs—and communicate with each other through these APIs. This mandate addressed the "deadlock" situation that Amazon faced back in the early 2000s in which everybody wanted to build and use APIs, but nobody wanted to spend the time refactoring their monolithic code to support this idealistic best practice. The mandate released the deadlock and required all teams to build and use APIs within Amazon.

 Seen as the cornerstone of Amazon's success early on, the Bezos API Mandate is the foundation of Amazon Web Services as we know it today. APIs helped Amazon reuse their internal ecosystem as scalable managed services for other organizations to build upon.

Following the Bezos API Mandate, we will deploy our model as a REST API using SageMaker Endpoints. SageMaker Endpoints are, by default, distributed containers. Applications invoke our models through a simple RESTful interface, as shown in Figure 9-3, which shows the model deployed across multiple cluster instances and Availability Zones for higher availability.

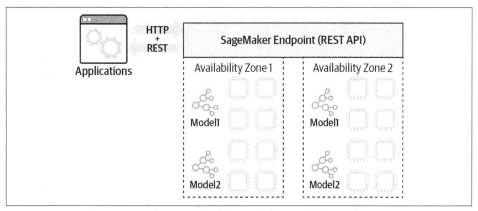

Figure 9-3. Application invoking our highly available model hosted on a REST endpoint.

Deploy Model Using SageMaker Python SDK

There are two ways to deploy the model using the SageMaker Python SDK. We can call `deploy()` on a model object, or we can call `deploy()` on the SageMaker estimator object that we used to train the model.

 We can also deploy models to SageMaker that were not trained using SageMaker. This is often called "bring your own model."

Following is the code for deploying our TensorFlow-and-BERT-based review classifier model trained with SageMaker:

```
from sagemaker.tensorflow.model import TensorFlowModel

tensorflow_model = TensorFlowModel(
    name=tensorflow_model_name,
    source_dir='code',
    entry_point='inference.py',
    model_data=<TENSORFLOW_MODEL_S3_URI>,
    role=role,
    framework_version='<TENSORFLOW_VERSION>')

tensorflow_model.deploy(endpoint_name=<ENDPOINT_NAME>,
                        initial_instance_count=1,
                        instance_type='ml.m5.4xlarge',
                        wait=False)
```

Next is the *inference.py* specified earlier. This Python script contains the `input_han
dler()` and `output_handler()` functions that convert raw JSON to and from Tensor-
Flow tensors. These functions are critical pieces of the prediction request/response
process.

The `input_handler()` function converts the JSON containing raw review text into
BERT-embedding tensors using `DistilBertTokenizer`. These embeddings are con-
verted to tensors and used as inputs to the TensorFlow model:

```
def input_handler(data, context):
    data_str = data.read().decode('utf-8')

    jsonlines = data_str.split("\n")

    transformed_instances = []

    for jsonline in jsonlines:
        review_body = json.loads(jsonline)["features"][0]
        encode_plus_tokens = tokenizer.encode_plus(
            review_body,
            pad_to_max_length=True,
            max_length=max_seq_length,
            truncation=True)

        input_ids = encode_plus_tokens['input_ids']

        input_mask = encode_plus_tokens['attention_mask']

        transformed_instance = {
            "input_ids": input_ids,
            "input_mask": input_mask
        }

        transformed_instances.append(transformed_instance)

    transformed_data = {
        "signature_name":"serving_default",
```

```
        "instances": transformed_instances
    }

    transformed_data_json = json.dumps(transformed_data)

    return transformed_data_json
```

The output_handler() converts the TensorFlow response from a tensor into a JSON response with the predicted label (star_rating) and the prediction confidence:

```
def output_handler(response, context):
    response_json = response.json()

    outputs_list = response_json["predictions"]

    predicted_classes = []

    for outputs in outputs_list:
        predicted_class_idx = tf.argmax(outputs, axis=-1, output_type=tf.int32)
        predicted_class = classes[predicted_class_idx]

        prediction_dict = {}
        prediction_dict["predicted_label"] = predicted_class

        jsonline = json.dumps(prediction_dict)

        predicted_classes.append(jsonline)

    predicted_classes_jsonlines = "\n".join(predicted_classes)

    response_content_type = context.accept_header

    return predicted_classes_jsonlines, response_content_type
```

Track Model Deployment in Our Experiment

We also want to track the deployment within our experiment for data lineage:

```
from smexperiments.trial import Trial
trial = Trial.load(trial_name=trial_name)

from smexperiments.tracker import Tracker
tracker_deploy = Tracker.create(display_name='deploy',
                                sagemaker_boto_client=sm)

deploy_trial_component_name = tracker_deploy.trial_component.trial_component_name

# Attach the 'deploy' Trial Component and Tracker to the Trial
trial.add_trial_component(tracker_deploy.trial_component)

# Track the Endpoint Name
tracker_deploy.log_parameters({
    'endpoint_name': endpoint_name,
```

```
})

# Must save after logging
tracker_deploy.trial_component.save()
```

Analyze the Experiment Lineage of a Deployed Model

Let's use the Experiment Analytics API to show us the lineage of our model in production, including feature engineering, model training, hyper-parameter optimization, and model deployment. We will tie everything together in an end-to-end
pipeline with full lineage tracking in Chapter 10, but let's analyze the experiment lineage up to this point:

```
from sagemaker.analytics import ExperimentAnalytics

lineage_table = ExperimentAnalytics(
  sagemaker_session=sess,
  experiment_name=experiment_name,
  metric_names=['validation:accuracy'],
  sort_by="CreationTime",
  sort_order="Ascending",
)

lineage_table.dataframe()
```

TrialComponentName	DisplayName	max_seq_length	learning_rate	train_accuracy	endpoint_name
TrialComponent-2021-01-09-062410-pxuy	prepare	64.0	NaN	NaN	
tensorflow-training-2021-01-09-06-24-12-989	train	64.0	0.00001	0.9394	
TrialComponent-2021-01-09-193933-bowu	optimize-1	64.0	0.000017	0.9416	
TrialComponent-2021-01-09214921-dgtu	deploy	NaN	NaN	NaN	tensorflow-training-2021-01-09-06-24-12-989

Invoke Predictions Using the SageMaker Python SDK

Here is some simple application code to invoke our deployed model endpoint and
classify raw product reviews into star_rating 1–5:

```
import json
from sagemaker.tensorflow.model import TensorFlowPredictor
from sagemaker.serializers import JSONLinesSerializer
from sagemaker.deserializers import JSONLinesDeserializer

predictor =
    TensorFlowPredictor(endpoint_name=tensorflow_endpoint_name,
```

```
                        sagemaker_session=sess,
                        model_name='saved_model',
                        model_version=0,
                        content_type='application/jsonlines',
                        accept_type='application/jsonlines',
                        serializer=JSONLinesSerializer(),
                        deserializer=JSONLinesDeserializer())

inputs = [
    {"features": ["This is great!"]},
    {"features": ["This is OK."]}
    {"features": ["This is bad."]}
]

predicted_classes = predictor.predict(inputs)

for predicted_class in predicted_classes:
    print(predicted_class)

### OUTPUT ###

{"predicted_label": 5}
{"predicted_label": 3}
{"predicted_label": 1}
```

Now let's predict on a sample batch of raw product reviews using a pandas Data-Frame:

```
import pandas as pd

df_reviews = pd.read_csv('./data/amazon_reviews_us_Digital_Software_v1_00.tsv.gz',
                        delimiter='\t',
                        quoting=csv.QUOTE_NONE,
                        compression='gzip')
df_sample_reviews = df_reviews[['review_body']].sample(n=100)

def predict(review_body):
    inputs = [
        {"features": [review_body]}
    ]
    predicted_classes = predictor.predict(inputs)
    return predicted_classes[0]['predicted_label']

df_sample_reviews['predicted_class'] = \
df_sample_reviews['review_body'].map(predict)
```

The output shows the predicted class for star_rating 1–5.

review_body	predicted_class
"This is great!"	5
"This is OK."	3
"This is terrible."	1

Invoke Predictions Using HTTP POST

When we productionize models as microservices, we need to decide how to make our predictions available to client applications. Assuming we have the proper authentication credentials and HTTP headers, we can invoke a model as a SageMaker Endpoint directly using the following HTTP request/response syntax.

HTTP request syntax:

```
POST /endpoints/<EndpointName>/invocations HTTP/1.1
Content-Type: ContentType
Accept: Accept
X-Amzn-SageMaker-Custom-Attributes: <CustomAttributes>
X-Amzn-SageMaker-Target-Model: <TargetModel>
X-Amzn-SageMaker-Target-Variant: <TargetVariant>
X-Amzn-SageMaker-Inference-Id: <InferenceId>

This is great!
```

HTTP response syntax:

```
HTTP/1.1 200
Content-Type: ContentType
x-Amzn-Invoked-Production-Variant: <InvokedProductionVariant>
X-Amzn-SageMaker-Custom-Attributes: <CustomAttributes>

{'label': 5, 'score': 0.92150515}
```

In this example, we implemented the `input_handler()` and `output_handler()` functions using a single *inference.py* script. For more complex request and response handling, we can deploy each function in its own container using SageMaker Inference Pipelines, as we see in the next section.

Create Inference Pipelines

An inference pipeline is a sequence of steps deployed on a single endpoint. Following our example, we could deploy the request handler as its own scikit-learn container (`step1`), followed by the TensorFlow/BERT model in its own TensorFlow Serving container (`step2`), and succeeded by the response handler as its own scikit-learn container (`step3`), as shown in Figure 9-4.

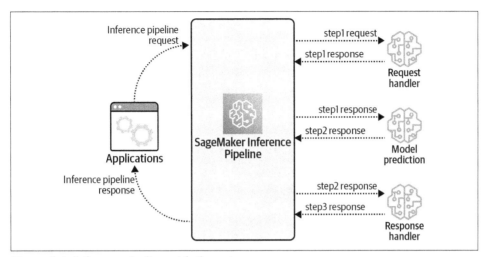

Figure 9-4. Inference pipeline with three steps.

We can also deploy ensembles of models across different AI and machine learning frameworks, including TensorFlow, PyTorch, scikit-learn, Apache Spark ML, etc. Each step is a sequence of HTTPS requests between the containers controlled by SageMaker. One step's response is used as the prediction request for the next step and so on. The last step returns the final response back to the inference pipeline, which returns the response back to the calling application. The inference pipeline is fully managed by SageMaker and can be used for real-time predictions as well as batch transforms.

To deploy an inference pipeline, we create a `PipelineModel` with a sequence of steps, including the request handler, model prediction, and response handler. We can then call `deploy()` on the `PipelineModel`, which deploys the inference pipeline and returns the endpoint API:

```
# Define model name and endpoint name
model_name = 'inference-pipeline-model'
endpoint_name = 'inference-pipeline-endpoint'

# Create a PipelineModel with a list of models to deploy in sequence
pipeline_model = PipelineModel(
    name=model_name,
    role=sagemaker_role,
    models=[
        request_handler,
        model,
        response_handler])

# Deploy the PipelineModel
pipeline_model.deploy(
    initial_instance_count=1,
```

```
    instance_type='ml.c5.xlarge',
    endpoint_name=endpoint_name)
```

`pipeline_model.deploy()` returns a predictor, as shown in the single-model example. Whenever we make an inference request to this predictor, make sure we pass the data that the first container expects. The predictor returns the output from the last container.

If we want to run a batch transform job with the `PipelineModel`, just follow the steps of creating a `pipeline_model.transformer()` object and call `transform()`:

```
transformer = pipeline_model.transformer(
    instance_type='ml.c5.xlarge',
    instance_count=1,
    strategy='MultiRecord',
    max_payload=6,
    max_concurrent_transforms=8,
    accept='text/csv',
    assemble_with='Line',
    output_path='<S3_OUTPUT_PATH>')

transformer.transform(
    data='<S3_PATH_TO_DATA>',
    content_type='text/csv',
    split_type='Line')
```

The preceding example demonstrates how to create steps from a series of Python scripts. With SageMaker Inference Pipelines, we can also provide our own Docker containers for each step.

Invoke SageMaker Models from SQL and Graph-Based Queries

AWS provides deep integration between the Amazon AI, machine learning, and analytics services. Amazon Redshift, Athena, and Aurora can execute predictive SQL queries with models deployed as SageMaker Endpoints. Neptune can execute graph-based queries with SageMaker Endpoints, as well.

Auto-Scale SageMaker Endpoints Using Amazon CloudWatch

While we can manually scale using the `InstanceCount` parameter in `EndpointCon fig`, we can configure our endpoint to automatically scale out (more instances) or scale in (less instances) based on a given metric like requests per second. As more requests come in, SageMaker will automatically scale our model cluster to meet the demand.

In the cloud, we talk about "scaling in" and "scaling out" in addition to the typical "scaling down" and "scaling up." Scaling in and out refers to removing and adding instances of the same type, respectively. Scaling down and up refers to using smaller or bigger instance types, respectively. Larger instances have more CPUs, GPUs, memory, and network bandwidth, typically.

It's best to use homogenous instance types when defining our cluster. If we mix instance types, we may have difficulty tuning the cluster and defining scaling policies that apply consistently to every instance in the heterogeneous cluster. When trying new instance types, we recommend creating a new cluster with only that instance type and comparing each cluster as a single unit.

Define a Scaling Policy with AWS-Provided Metrics

In this example, we use `SageMakerVariantInvocationsPerInstance`, the AWS-provided CloudWatch metric, to automatically scale our model endpoint when we reach a certain threshold of invocations per instance. In the next section, we will use a custom auto-scaling metric:

```
autoscale = boto3.Session().client(
                        service_name='application-autoscaling',
                        region_name=region)

autoscale.register_scalable_target(
    ServiceNamespace='sagemaker',
    ResourceId="endpoint/" + tensorflow_endpoint_name + "/variant/AllTraffic",
    ScalableDimension='sagemaker:variant:DesiredInstanceCount',
    MinCapacity=1,
    MaxCapacity=2,
    RoleARN=role,
    SuspendedState={
        'DynamicScalingInSuspended': False,
        'DynamicScalingOutSuspended': False,
        'ScheduledScalingSuspended': False
    }
)

autoscale.put_scaling_policy(
    PolicyName='bert-reviews-autoscale-policy',
    ServiceNamespace='sagemaker',
    ResourceId="endpoint/" + tensorflow_endpoint_name + "/variant/AllTraffic",
    ScalableDimension='sagemaker:variant:DesiredInstanceCount',
    PolicyType='TargetTrackingScaling',
    TargetTrackingScalingPolicyConfiguration={
        'TargetValue': 1000.0,
        'PredefinedMetricSpecification': {
            'PredefinedMetricType': 'SageMakerVariantInvocationsPerInstance',
        },
        'ScaleOutCooldown': 60,
        'ScaleInCooldown': 300,
    }
)
```

We can see a spike in the `InvocationsPerInstance` metric in CloudWatch after we send a large amount of traffic to our endpoint, as shown in Figure 9-5, as well as a spike in CPU and memory utilization, as shown in Figure 9-6.

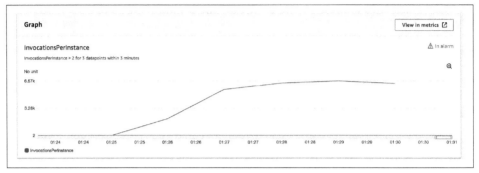

Figure 9-5. Spike in the `InvocationsPerInstance` metric.

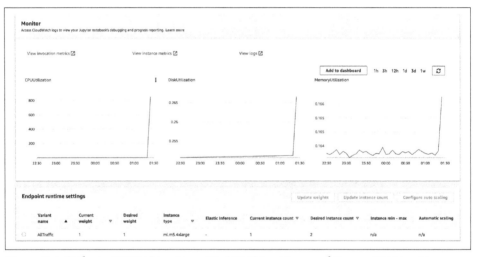

Figure 9-6. Spike in `CPUUtilization`, `DiskUtilization`, and `MemoryUtilization` from increased prediction traffic.

This causes an alarm that triggers a scale-out event from one instance to two instances to handle the spike in prediction traffic by sharing the traffic across two instances. Figure 9-7 shows the positive effect of adding an additional instance to the endpoint cluster. As the number of `InvocationsPerInstance` decreases, so does the CPU and memory utilization.

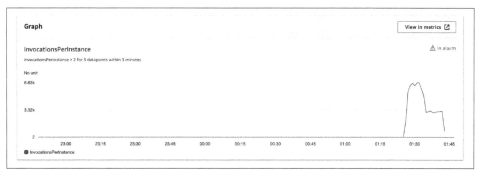

Figure 9-7. The number of `InvocationsPerInstance` *decreases when we add a second instance to the endpoint cluster.*

Define a Scaling Policy with a Custom Metric

Netflix is known to use a custom auto-scaling metric called "starts per second" or SPS. A start is recorded every time a user clicks "play" to watch a movie or TV show. This was a key metric for auto-scaling because the more "Starts per Second," the more traffic we would start receiving on our streaming control plane.

Assuming we are publishing the `StartsPerSecond` metric, we can use this custom metric to scale out our cluster as more movies are started. This metric is called a "target tracking" metric, and we need to define the metric name, target value, model name, variant name, and summary statistic. The following scaling policy will begin scaling out the cluster if the aggregate `StartsPerSecond` metric exceeds an average of 50% across all instances in our model-serving cluster:

```
{
  "TargetValue": 50,
  "CustomizedMetricSpecification":
  {
    "MetricName": "StartsPerSecond",
    "Namespace": "/aws/sagemaker/Endpoints",
    "Dimensions": [
      {"Name": "EndpointName", "Value": "ModelA" },
      {"Name": "VariantName","Value": "VariantA"}
    ],
    "Statistic": "Average",
    "Unit": "Percent"
  }
}
```

When using custom metrics for our scaling policy, we should pick a metric that measures instance utilization, decreases as more instances are added, and increases as instances are removed.

Tuning Responsiveness Using a Cooldown Period

When our endpoint is auto-scaling in or out, we likely want to specify a "cooldown" period in seconds. A cooldown period essentially reduces the responsiveness of the scaling policy by defining the number of seconds between iterations of the scale events. We may want to scale out quickly when a spike of traffic comes in, but we should scale in slowly to make sure we handle any temporary dips in traffic during rapid scale-out events. The following scaling policy will take twice as long to scale in as it does to scale out, as shown in the `ScaleInCooldown` and `ScaleOutCooldown` attributes:

```
{
  "TargetValue": 60.0,
  "PredefinedMetricSpecification":
  {
    "PredefinedMetricType":
        "SageMakerVariantInvocationsPerInstance"
  },
  "ScaleInCooldown": 600,
  "ScaleOutCooldown": 300
}
```

Auto-Scale Policies

There are three main types of scaling policies to choose from when setting up auto-scaling for our SageMaker Endpoints:

Target tracking
> Specify a single metric and AWS auto-scales as needed; for example, "keep `InvocationsPerInstance` = 1000." This strategy requires the least configuration.

Simple
> Trigger on a metric at a given threshold with a fixed amount of scaling; for example, "when `InvocationsPerInstance` > 1000, add 1 instance." This strategy requires a bit of configuration but provides more control over the target-tracking strategy.

Step scaling
> Trigger on a metric at various thresholds with configurable amounts of scaling at each threshold; for example, "when `InvocationsPerInstance` > 1000, add 1 instance, `InvocationsPerInstance` > 2000, add 5 instances," etc. This strategy requires the most amount of configuration but provides the most amount of control for situations such as spiky traffic.

Strategies to Deploy New and Updated Models

We can test and deploy new and updated models behind a single SageMaker Endpoint with a concept called "production variants." These variants can differ by hardware (CPU/GPU), by data (comedy/drama movies), or by region (US West or Germany North). We can safely shift traffic between the model variants in our endpoint for canary rollouts, blue/green deployments, A/B tests, and MAB tests. Using these deployment strategies, we can minimize the risks involved when pushing new and updated models to production.

Split Traffic for Canary Rollouts

Since our data is continuously changing, our models need to evolve to capture this change. When we update our models, we may choose to do this slowly using a "canary rollout," named after the antiquated and morbid process of using a canary to detect whether a human could breathe in a coal mine. If the canary survives the coal mine, then the conditions are good and we can proceed. If the canary does not survive, then we should make adjustments and try again later with a different canary. Similarly, we can point a small percentage of traffic to our "canary" model and test if the model services. Perhaps there is a memory leak or other production-specific issue that we didn't catch in the research lab.

The combination of the cloud instance providing compute, memory, and storage and the model container application is called a "production variant." The production variant defines the instance type, instance count, and model. By default, the SageMaker Endpoint is configured with a single production variant, but we can add multiple variants as needed.

Here is the code to setup a single variant, VariantA, at a single endpoint receiving 100% of the traffic across 20 instances:

```
endpoint_config = sm.create_endpoint_config(
    EndpointConfigName='my_endpoint_config_name',
    ProductionVariants=[
        {
         'VariantName': 'VariantA',
         'ModelName': 'ModelA',
         'InstanceType':'ml.m5.large',
         'InitialInstanceCount': 20,
         'InitialVariantWeight': 100,
        }
    ])
```

After creating a new production variant for our canary, we can create a new endpoint and point a small amount of traffic (5%) to the canary and point the rest of the traffic (95%) to our existing variant, as shown in Figure 9-8.

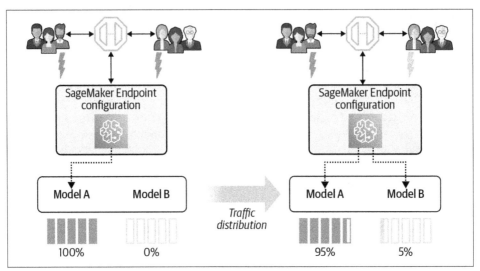

Figure 9-8. Splitting 5% traffic to a new model for a canary rollout.

Following is the code to create a new endpoint, including the new canary `VariantB` accepting 5% of the traffic. Note that we are specifying `'InitialInstanceCount': 1` for the new canary, `VariantB`. Assuming that 20 instances handle 100% of the current traffic, then each instance likely handles approximately 5% of the traffic. This 5% matches the amount of traffic we wish to send to the new canary instance. If we wished to send 10% traffic to the new canary, for example, we would choose `'Initia lInstanceCount': 2` to support 10% of the canary traffic. This assumes that we are using the same instance type for the new canary. If choosing a different instance type, we may need more or less instances to handle the % traffic load:

```
updated_endpoint_config=[
    {
    'VariantName': 'VariantA',
    'ModelName': 'ModelA',
    'InstanceType':'ml.m5.large',
    'InitialInstanceCount': 20,
    'InitialVariantWeight': 95,
    },
    {
    'VariantName': 'VariantB',
    'ModelName': 'ModelB',
    'InstanceType':'ml.m5.large',
    'InitialInstanceCount': 1,
    'InitialVariantWeight': 5,
    }
])

sm.update_endpoint(
    EndpointName='my_endpoint_name',
```

```
          EndpointConfigName='my_endpoint_config_name'
)
```

Canary rollouts release new models safely to a small percentage of users for initial production testing in the wild. They are useful if we want to test in live production without affecting the entire user base. Since the majority of traffic goes to the existing model, the cluster size of the canary model can be relatively small since it's only receiving 5% of the traffic. In the preceding example, we are only using a single instance for the canary variant.

Shift Traffic for Blue/Green Deployments

If the new model performs well, we can proceed with a blue/green deployment to shift all traffic to the new model, as shown in Figure 9-9. Blue/green deployments help to reduce downtime in case we need to roll back to the old deployment. With a blue/green deployment, we spin up a full clone of the existing model-server cluster using the new canary model. We then shift all the traffic from the old cluster (blue) over to the new cluster (green), as shown in Figure 9-9. Blue/green deployments prevent the partial-deployment scenario where some of the instances are running the new canary model and some are running the existing model. This partial-deployment scenario is very hard to debug and manage at scale.

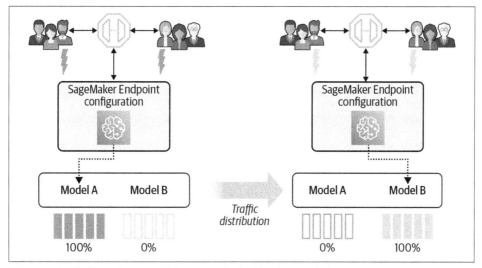

Figure 9-9. Shift traffic to model variant B for blue/green deployments.

Following is the code to update our endpoint and shift 100% of the traffic to the successful canary model, VariantB. Note that we have also increased the size of the new cluster to match the existing cluster since the new cluster is now handling all of the traffic:

```
updated_endpoint_config=[
    {
     'VariantName': 'VariantA',
     'ModelName': 'ModelA',
     'InstanceType':'ml.m5.large',
     'InitialInstanceCount': 20,
     'InitialVariantWeight': 0,
    },
    {
     'VariantName': 'VariantB',
     'ModelName': 'ModelB',
     'InstanceType':'ml.m5.large',
     'InitialInstanceCount': 20,
     'InitialVariantWeight': 100,
    }
])

sm.update_endpoint_weights_and_capacities(
    EndpointName='my_endpoint_name',
    DesiredWeightsAndCapacities=updated_endpoint_config
)
```

We will keep the old cluster with VariantA idle for 24 hours, let's say, in case our canary fails unexpectedly and we need to roll back quickly to the old cluster. After 24 hours, we can remove the old environment and complete the blue/green deployment. Here is the code to remove the old model, VariantA, by removing VariantA from the endpoint configuration and updating the endpoint:

```
updated_endpoint_config=[
    {
     'VariantName': 'VariantB',
     'ModelName': 'ModelB',
     'InstanceType':'ml.m5.large',
     'InitialInstanceCount': 20,
     'InitialVariantWeight': 100,
    }
])

sm.update_endpoint(
    EndpointName='my_endpoint_name',
    EndpointConfigName='my_endpoint_config_name'
)
```

While keeping the old cluster idle for a period of time—24 hours, in our example—may seem wasteful, consider the cost of an outage during the time needed to roll back and scale out the previous model, VariantA. Sometimes the new model cluster works fine for the first few hours, then degrades or crashes unexpectedly after a nighttime cron job, early morning product catalog refresh, or other untested scenario. In these cases, we were able to immediately switch traffic back to the old cluster and conduct business as usual.

Testing and Comparing New Models

We can test new models behind a single SageMaker Endpoint using the same "production variant" concept described in the previous section on model deployment. In this section, we will configure our SageMaker Endpoint to shift traffic between the models in our endpoint to compare model performance in production using A/B and MAB tests.

When testing our models in production, we need to define and track the business metrics that we wish to optimize. The business metric is usually tied to revenue or user engagement, such as orders purchased, movies watched, or ads clicked. We can store the metrics in any database, such as DynamoDB, as shown in Figure 9-10. Analysts and scientists will use this data to determine the winning model from our tests.

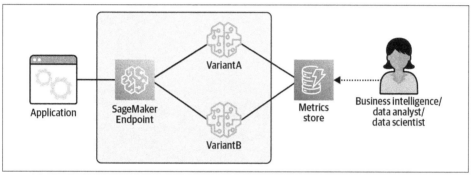

Figure 9-10. Tracking business metrics to determine the best model variant.

Continuing with our text-classifier example, we will create a test to maximize the number of successfully labeled customer service messages. As customer service receives new messages, our application will predict the message's `star_rating` (1–5) and route 1s and 2s to a high-priority customer service queue. If the representative agrees with the predicted `star_rating`, they will mark our prediction as successful (positive feedback); otherwise they will mark the prediction as unsuccessful (negative feedback). Unsuccessful predictions could be routed to a human-in-the-loop workflow using Amazon A2I and SageMaker Ground Truth, which we discuss in more detail in Chapter 10. We will then choose the model variant with the most successful number of `star_rating` predictions and start shifting traffic to this winning variant. Let's dive deeper into managing the experiments and shifting the traffic.

Perform A/B Tests to Compare Model Variants

Similar to canary rollouts, we can use traffic splitting to direct subsets of users to different model variants for the purpose of comparing and testing different models in live production. The goal is to see which variants perform better. Often, these tests need to run for a long period of time (weeks) to be statistically significant. Figure 9-11 shows two different recommendation models deployed using a random 50/50 traffic split between the two variants.

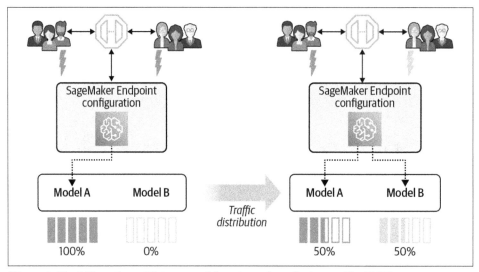

Figure 9-11. A/B testing with two model variants by splitting traffic 50/50.

While A/B testing seems similar to canary rollouts, they are focused on gathering data about different variants of a model. A/B tests are targeted to larger user groups, take more traffic, and run for longer periods of time. Canary rollouts are focused more on risk mitigation and smooth upgrades.

 For fine-grained traffic routing based on IP address, HTTP headers, query string, or payload content, use an Application Load Balancer in front of the SageMaker Endpoints.

One example for a model A/B test could be streaming music recommendations. Let's assume we are recommending a playlist for Sunday mornings. We might want to test if we can identify specific user groups that are more likely to listen to powerful wake-up beats (model A) or that prefer smooth lounge music (model B). Let's implement this A/B test using Python. We start with creating a SageMaker Endpoint configuration that defines a separate production variant for Model A and Model B. We initialize both production variants with the identical instance types and instance counts:

```
import time
timestamp = '{}'.format(int(time.time()))

endpoint_config_name = '{}-{}'.format(training_job_name, timestamp)

variantA = production_variant(model_name='ModelA',
                              instance_type="ml.m5.large",
                              initial_instance_count=1,
                              variant_name='VariantA',
                              initial_weight=50)

variantB = production_variant(model_name='ModelB',
                              instance_type="ml.m5.large",
                              initial_instance_count=1,
                              variant_name='VariantB',
                              initial_weight=50)

endpoint_config = sm.create_endpoint_config(
    EndpointConfigName=endpoint_config_name,
    ProductionVariants=[variantA, variantB]
)

endpoint_name = '{}-{}'.format(training_job_name, timestamp)

endpoint_response = sm.create_endpoint(
    EndpointName=endpoint_name,
    EndpointConfigName=endpoint_config_name)
```

After we have monitored the performance of both models for a period of time, we can shift 100% of the traffic to the better-performing model, Model B in our case. Let's shift our traffic from a 50/50 split to a 0/100 split, as shown in Figure 9-12.

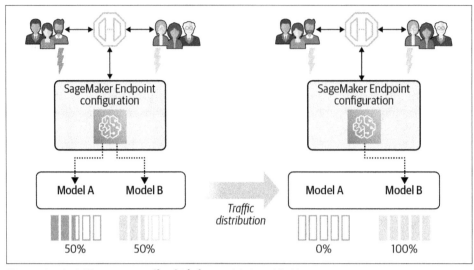

Figure 9-12. A/B testing traffic shift from 50/50 to 0/100.

Following is the code to shift all traffic to `VariantB` and ultimately remove `VariantA` when we are confident that `VariantB` is working correctly:

```
updated_endpoint_config = [
  {
    'VariantName': 'VariantA',
    'DesiredWeight': 0,
  },
  {
    'VariantName': 'VariantB',
    'DesiredWeight': 100,
  }
]

sm.update_endpoint_weights_and_capacities(
  EndpointName='my_endpoint_name',
  DesiredWeightsAndCapacities=updated_endpoint_config
)

updated_endpoint_config=[
    {
      'VariantName': 'VariantB',
      'ModelName': 'ModelB',
      'InstanceType':'ml.m5.large',
      'InitialInstanceCount': 2,
      'InitialVariantWeight': 100,
    }
])

sm.update_endpoint(
```

```
        EndpointName='my_endpoint_name',
        EndpointConfigName='my_endpoint_config_name'
)
```

Reinforcement Learning with Multiarmed Bandit Testing

A/B tests are static and must run for a period of time—sometimes weeks or months—before they are considered statistically significant. During this time, we may have deployed a bad model variant that is negatively affecting revenue. However, if we stop the test early, we ruin the statistical significance of the experiment and cannot derive much meaning from the results. In other words, our model may have performed poorly initially but may actually have been a better model overall if the experiment had run longer. A/B tests are static and do not allow us to dynamically shift traffic during an experiment to minimize the "regret" caused by a poor-performing model. They also do not allow us to add or remove model variants during the lifetime of the experiment.

A more dynamic method for testing different model variants is called MABs. Named after a slot machine that can quickly take our money, these mischievous bandits can actually earn us quite a bit of money by dynamically shifting traffic to the winning model variants much sooner than with an A/B test. This is the "exploit" part of the MAB. At the same time, the MAB continues to "explore" the nonwinning model variants just in case the early winners were not the overall best model variants. This dynamic pull between "exploit and explore" is what give MABs their power. Based on reinforcement learning (RL), MABs rely on the feedback positive-negative mechanism to choose an "action."

In our case, the MAB chooses the model variant based on the current reward metrics and the chosen exploit-explore strategy. The RL-based MAB acts as the primary Sage-Maker Endpoint and dynamically routes prediction traffic to the available BERT-based SageMaker Endpoints, as shown in Figure 9-13.

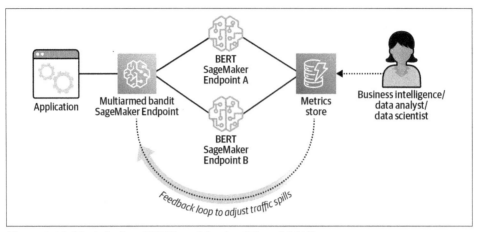

Figure 9-13. Find the best BERT model using RL and MABs.

There are various MAB exploration strategies, including epsilon greedy, Thompson sampling, bagging, and online cover. Epsilon greedy uses a fixed exploit-explore threshold, while Thompson sampling uses a more sophisticated and dynamic threshold based on prior information—a technique rooted in Bayesian statistics. Bagging uses an ensemble approach by training on random subsets of data to generate a set of policies to ensemble. Online cover is, in theory, the optimal exploration algorithm based on the paper "Taming the Monster: A Fast and Simple Algorithm for Contextual Bandits" (*https://oreil.ly/ZNyKH*). Like bagging, online cover trains a set of policies on different subsets of the dataset. Unlike bagging, however, online cover trains the set of policies to result in a diverse set of predictions for a more sophisticated and complete exploration strategy.

SageMaker natively supports popular RL libraries, including Vowpal Wabbit, Ray, Coach, Unity, and others. Additionally, we can use any other reinforcement library by building our own Docker image for SageMaker to deploy and manage. In our example, we will use Vowpal Wabbit and the online-cover exploration strategy. Our Vowpal Wabbit–based MAB is continuously trained on the latest reward metrics and will adjust the prediction traffic to send more traffic to the winning BERT-based model, as shown in Figure 9-14, where Model 2 starts to receive more traffic as it accumulates more rewards.

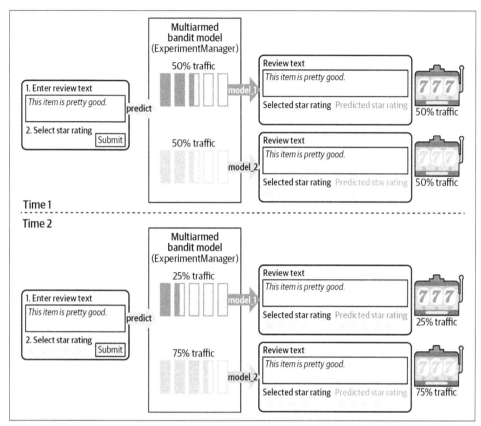

Figure 9-14. MAB dynamically shifting traffic to the "winning" model variant.

Figure 9-15 shows a complete, end-to-end production implementation of MABs in AWS using the Vowpal Wabbit RL framework, SageMaker, Amazon Kinesis Firehose, S3 for persistent storage, and Athena for application queries.

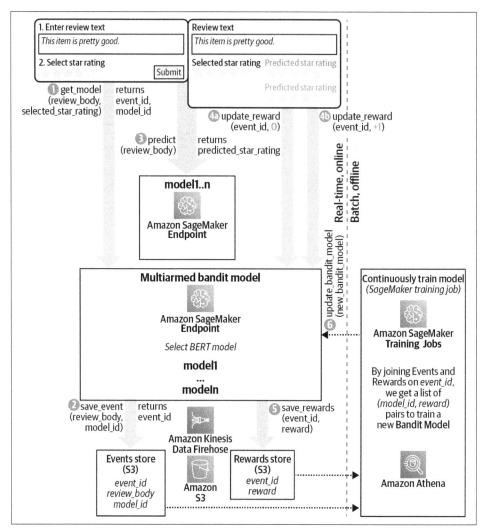

Figure 9-15. Complete, end-to-end implementation of MABs and RL on AWS.

We are continuously training our MAB with the Vowpal Wabbit RL framework as new reward data flows into the system from our applications. New versions of the MAB models are continuously deployed as SageMaker Endpoints. We can dynamically add and remove model variants from testing because of the dynamic nature of MABs. This is something that we cannot do with traditional A/B tests, where we need to keep all model variants fixed for the lifetime of the experiment.

Following is a subset of the configuration for our MAB model using the native Vowpal Wabbit integration with SageMaker, DynamoDB, and Kinesis. This configuration also highlights the hyper-parameters used by the online-cover exploration strategy, including the number of subpolicies to train as well as the counterfactual analysis (CFA) strategy to use:

```
resource:
  shared_resource:
    experiment_db:
      table_name: "BanditsExperimentTable" # Status of an experiment
    model_db:
      table_name: "BanditsModelTable" # Status of trained models
    join_db:
      table_name: "BanditsJoinTable" # Status of reward ingestion
image: "sagemaker-rl-vw-container:vw-<VW_VERSION>"
<VOWPAL_WABBIT_VERSION>-<CPU_OR_GPU>" # Vowpal Wabbit container
algor: # Vowpal Wabbit algorithm parameters
  algorithms_parameters:
    exploration_policy: "cover"
    num_policies: 3 # number of online cover policies to create
    num_arms: 2
    cfa_type: "dr" # supports "dr", "ips"
```

We have chosen to train three subpolicies when deciding which action to take (which BERT model to invoke)—as well as the doubly robust (DR) CFA method. For more information on these hyper-parameters, see the Vowpal Wabbit documentation (*https://oreil.ly/lDikQ*) and the GitHub repository associated with this book.

Following is a snippet from the SageMaker Training Job logs as the bandit model is continuously trained on new reward data arriving to the system. In this case, six hundred new rewards were picked up:

```
/usr/bin/python train-vw.py --cfa_type dr --epsilon 0.1 --exploration_policy
cover --num_arms 2 --num_policies 3
INFO:root:channels ['pretrained_model', 'training']
INFO:root:hps: {'cfa_type': 'dr', 'epsilon': 0.1, 'exploration_policy':
'cover', 'num_arms': 2, 'num_policies': 3}
INFO:root:Loading model from /opt/ml/input/data/pretrained_model/vw.model
INFO:VW CLI:creating an instance of VWModel
INFO:VW CLI:successfully created VWModel
INFO:VW CLI:command: ['vw', '--cb_explore', '2', '--cover', '3', '-i',
'/opt/ml/input/data/pretrained_model/vw.model', '-f', '/opt/ml/model/vw.model',
'--save_resume', '-p', '/dev/stdout']
INFO:VW CLI:Started VW process!
INFO:root:Processing training data: [PosixPath('/opt/ml/input/data/training/local-
joined-data-1605218616.csv')]
finished run
number of examples = 600
INFO:root:Model learned using 600 training experiences.
INFO       Reporting training SUCCESS
```

Let's assume we want to compare two BERT models: BERT Model 1 and BERT Model 2. We will reuse the model we trained in Chapter 7 for BERT Model 1. This model had a training accuracy of close to 93% and a validation accuracy around 50%. Given that random chance to predict the five categories is 20%, 50% is not that bad. For BERT Model 2, we train a model that achieves slightly less training and validation accuracy around 40%.

We deploy the two BERT models and a fresh MAB. After running these models in production, we analyze the latest probabilities used by the MAB to choose either Model 1 or Model 2. Action probability is a measurement of the probability that selecting either Model 1 or Model 2 is the best choice given the current reward information and context. The mean action probability for BERT Model 1 is 0.743 and for BERT Model 2 is 0.696. BERT Model 1 is favored in this case as measured by the higher action probability. Figure 9-16 shows the plot of the action probability used by the MAB for all predictions.

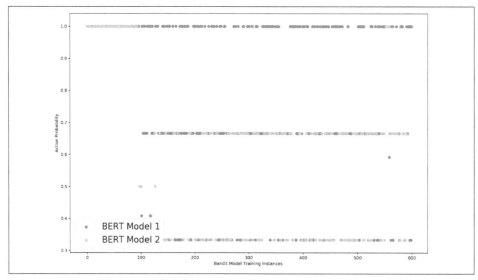

Figure 9-16. MAB action probability.

Sample probability is a measurement of the probability that the bandit will choose Model 1 or Model 2 given the exploration policy, current reward information, and context. The combination of the action probability and sample probability determines which BERT Model the bandit will use to classify the review test. The mean sample probability our bandit uses for BERT Model 1 is 0.499, and for BERT Model 2 it is 0.477. BERT Model 1 is favored in this case as measured by the higher sample probability.

Figure 9-17 shows the sample probability used by the MAB to choose between BERT Model 1 and BERT Model 2 across all predictions.

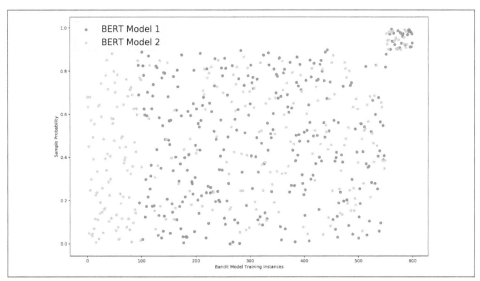

Figure 9-17. MAB sample probability.

We also notice a shift in traffic between the two variants, as shown in Figure 9-18. Model 2 starts with all of the traffic but slowly receives less traffic as the MAB begins to favor Model 1 due to higher rewards, which leads to a higher sample probability.

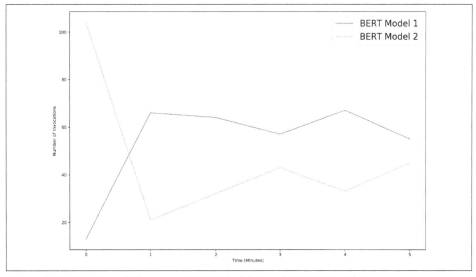

Figure 9-18. Traffic split between BERT Model 1 and BERT Model 2.

We see that BERT Model 1, the incumbent model, has an advantage over the challenger model, BERT Model 2. In this case, we choose to keep Model 1 in production and not replace it with BERT Model 2.

Let's analyze reward versus regret and make sure our model is exploiting and exploring appropriately and not giving up too much during the exploration process. We assign a reward of 1 if the model predicts the `star_rating` correctly and a reward of 0 if the model predicts incorrectly. Therefore, the reward is tied to model accuracy. The mean reward is 0.472, which is, not coincidentally, a blend of the validation accuracies of BERT Model 1 and BERT Model 2 that we trained in Chapter 7. Figure 9-19 shows a plot of the rolling one hundred mean reward across all predictions.

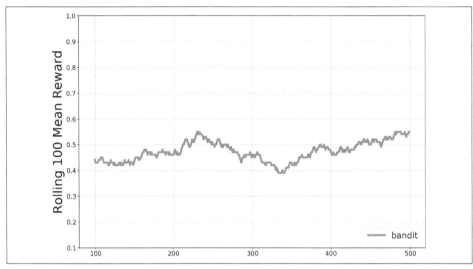

Figure 9-19. Rolling one hundred mean reward of our experiment.

All of these plots indicate that the bandit initially explores the action space by sending traffic to both BERT Model 1 and BERT Model 2, finds an early winner, and exploits BERT Model 2 up to around 230 predictions. It then starts exploring again until around 330 predictions, when it begins to exploit up BERT Model 2 again up to the 500th prediction, where it likely would have begun exploring again.

This trade-off between exploit and explore is controlled by the chosen exploration policy and is the key differentiator between A/B and MAB tests. With an aggressive exploration policy, we will see the bandit explore the space and reduce the mean reward. Here, we are using the self-tuning online-cover exploration policy.

Bandits help us minimize the regret of deploying a poor-performing model in production and give us near-real-time insight into our BERT model performance on real-world data. If one of our BERT models is performing poorly, we can remove the model from the experiment—or even add new model variants that the bandit will begin exploring using the exploration policy that we selected.

We can tune our Vowpal Wabbit bandit model using the hyper-parameters described in the framework's documentation. For more information on the Vowpal Wabbit hyper-parameters for the online-cover exploration policy, see the Vowpal Wabbit documentation (*https://oreil.ly/lDikQ*).

We can also provide historical data to pre-train the RL model before initially deploying to production. This seeds our model with action and sample probabilities that may potentially reduce the regret caused by the initial exploration phase when the RL model is learning the action and sample space from scratch.

Remember that this is just an example of predictions over a few minutes. We likely want to run the experiment longer to gain more insight into which model is better for our application and use case.

Monitor Model Performance and Detect Drift

The world continues to change around us. Customer behavior changes relatively quickly. The application team is releasing new features. The Netflix catalog is swelling with new content. Fraudsters are finding clever ways to hack our credit cards. A continuously changing world requires continuous retraining and redeploying of our predictive models to adjust for these real-world drift scenarios.

In Chapter 5, we discussed various types of drift that may cause model performance to degrade. By automatically recording SageMaker Endpoint inputs (features) and outputs (predictions), SageMaker Model Monitor automatically detects and measures drift against a provided baseline. SageMaker Model Monitor then notifies us when the drift reaches a user-specified threshold from a baseline learned on our trained model and specified during model deployment.

SageMaker Model Monitor calculates drift using statistical methods such as Kullback–Leibler divergence and L-infinity norm. For L-infinity norm, for example, SageMaker Model Monitor supports `linf_simple` and `linf_robust`. The `linf_simple` method is based on the maximum absolute difference between the cumulative distribution functions of two distributions. The `linf_robust` method is based on `linf_simple` but is used when there are not enough samples. The `linf_robust` formula is based on the two-sample Kolmogorov–Smirnov test.

Enable Data Capture

SageMaker Model Monitor analyzes our model predictions (and their inputs) to detect drift in data quality, model quality, model bias, or feature attribution. In a first step, we need to enable data capture for a given endpoint, as shown in Figure 9-20.

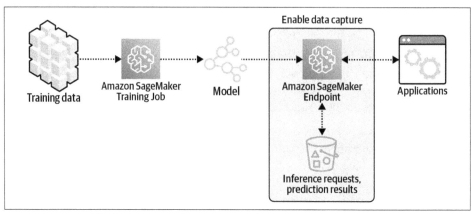

Figure 9-20. Enable data capture for a given endpoint.

Following is the code to enable data capture. We can define all configuration options in the `DataCaptureConfig` object. We can choose to capture the request payload, the response payload, or both with this configuration. The capture config applies to all model production variants of the endpoint:

```
from sagemaker.model_monitor import DataCaptureConfig

data_capture_config = DataCaptureConfig(
            enable_capture=True,
            sampling_percentage=100,
            destination_s3_uri='<S3_PATH>')
```

Next, we pass the DataCaptureConfig in the model.deploy()call:

```
predictor = model.deploy(
    initial_instance_count=1,
    instance_type='ml.m5.xlarge',
    endpoint_name=endpoint_name,
    data_capture_config=data_capture_config)
```

We are now capturing all inference requests and prediction results in the specified S3 destination.

Understand Baselines and Drift

In Chapter 5, we explored our dataset and visualized the distribution of reviews for each `product_category` and `star_rating`. We will use this data to create baseline distribution metrics to compare with live distributions seen by our SageMaker Model Endpoints. Figure 9-21 shows the number of reviews per product category.

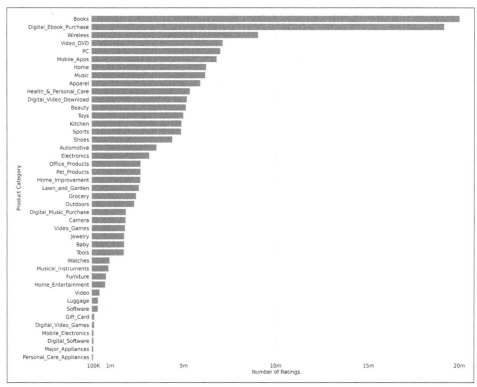

Figure 9-21. The number of reviews per product category in our data is an example baseline for input feature distribution.

This represents the baseline distribution of the `product_category` input features used to train our model. SageMaker Model Monitor captures the actual model-input distribution seen by our SageMaker Model Endpoints, compares against that baseline distribution used during training, and produces a drift metric that measures the covariate shift in our model-input distribution.

If the measure drift exceeds a threshold that we specify, SageMaker Model Monitor would notify us and potentially retrain and redeploy an updated version of the model trained on the latest distribution of input data. Figure 9-22 shows the baseline distribution of data for each `product_category` and `star_rating` from Chapter 5.

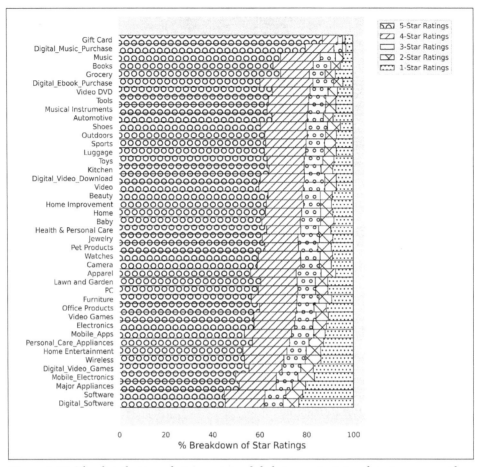

Figure 9-22. The distribution of `star_rating` *labels in our training data is an example baseline for target distribution.*

We can detect covariate shifts in model-input distribution using SageMaker Model Monitor's data-quality monitoring feature. And we can also detect concept shifts using SageMaker Model Monitor's model-quality monitoring feature that compares live predictions against ground truth labels for the same model inputs captured by SageMaker Model Monitor on live predictions. These ground truth labels are provided by humans in an offline human-in-the-loop workflow using, for example, Amazon A2I and SageMaker Ground Truth, as described in Chapter 3.

In addition, SageMaker Model Monitor's model-quality feature can monitor, measure, and detect drifts in model bias, feature importance, and model explainability. Each drift is measured relative to a baseline generated from our trained model. These baselines are provided to each SageMaker Endpoint deployed with SageMaker Model Monitor enabled.

Monitor Data Quality of Deployed SageMaker Endpoints

Our model learns and adapts the statistical characteristics of our training data. If the statistical characteristics of the data that our online model receives drifts from that baseline, the model quality will degrade. We can create a data-quality baseline using Deequ, as discussed in Chapter 5. Deequ analyzes the input data and creates schema constraints and statistics for each input feature. We can identify missing values and detect covariate shifts relative to that baseline. SageMaker Model Monitor uses Deequ to create baselines for data-quality monitoring.

Create a Baseline to Measure Data Quality

A data-quality baseline helps us detect drift in the statistical characteristics of online model inputs from the provided baseline data. We typically use our training data to create the first baseline, as shown in Figure 9-23.

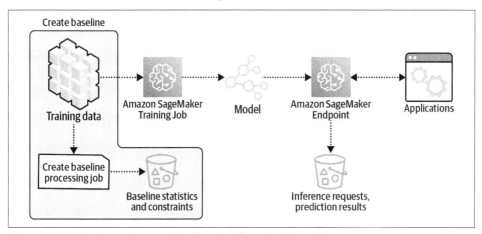

Figure 9-23. Create a data-quality baseline from training data.

The training dataset schema and the inference dataset schema must match exactly, including the number of features and the order in which they are passed in for inference. We can now start a SageMaker Processing Job to suggest a set of baseline constraints and generate statistics of the data as follows:

```
from sagemaker.model_monitor import DefaultModelMonitor
from sagemaker.model_monitor.dataset_format import DatasetFormat

my_default_monitor = DefaultModelMonitor(
    role=role,
    instance_count=1,
    instance_type='ml.m5.xlarge',
    volume_size_in_gb=20,
    max_runtime_in_seconds=3600,
```

```
)
my_default_monitor.suggest_baseline(
baseline_dataset='s3://my_bucket/path/some.csv',
    dataset_format=DatasetFormat.csv(header=True),
    output_s3_uri='s3://my_bucket/output_path/',
    wait=True
)
```

After the baseline job has finished, we can explore the generated statistics:

```
import pandas as pd

baseline_job = my_default_monitor.latest_baselining_job

statistics = pd.io.json.json_normalize(
baseline_job.baseline_statistics().body_dict["features"])
```

Here is an example set of statistics for our `review_body` prediction inputs:

```
"name" : "Review Body",
  "inferred_type" : "String",
  "numerical_statistics" : {
  "common" : {
   "num_present" : 1420,
   "num_missing" : 0
  }, "data" : [ [ "I love this item.", "This item is OK", … ] ]
```

We can explore the generated constraints as follows:

```
constraints = pd.io.json.json_normalize(
baseline_job.suggested_constraints().body_dict["features"])
```

Here is an example of the constraints defined for our `review_body` prediction inputs:

```
{
  "name" : "Review Body",
  "inferred_type" : "String",
  "completeness" : 1.0
}
```

In this example, the constraint would raise an alarm if there are missing values for `review_body`. With the baseline, we can now create and schedule data-quality monitoring jobs.

Schedule Data-Quality Monitoring Jobs

SageMaker Model Monitor gives us the ability to continuously monitor the data collected from the endpoints on a schedule. We can create the schedule with the `Create MonitoringSchedule` API defining a periodic interval. Similar to the data-quality baseline job, SageMaker Model Monitor starts a SageMaker Processing Job, which compares the dataset for the current analysis with the baseline statistics and constraints. The result is a violation report. In addition, SageMaker Model Monitor sends metrics for each feature to CloudWatch, as shown in Figure 9-24.

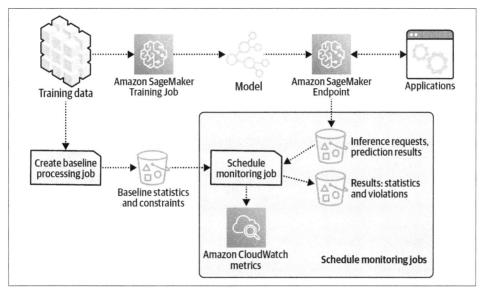

Figure 9-24. SageMaker Model Monitor gives us the ability to continuously monitor the data collected from the endpoints on a schedule.

We can use `my_default_monitor.create_monitoring_schedule()` to create a model monitoring schedule for an endpoint. In the configuration of the monitoring schedule, we point to the baseline statistics and constraints and define a cron schedule:

```
from sagemaker.model_monitor import DefaultModelMonitor
from sagemaker.model_monitor import CronExpressionGenerator

mon_schedule_name = 'my-model-monitor-schedule'

my_default_monitor.create_monitoring_schedule(
  monitor_schedule_name=mon_schedule_name,
  endpoint_input=predictor.endpoint,
  output_s3_uri=s3_report_path,
  statistics=my_default_monitor.baseline_statistics(),
  constraints=my_default_monitor.suggested_constraints(),
  schedule_cron_expression=CronExpressionGenerator.hourly(),
  enable_cloudwatch_metrics=True,
)
```

SageMaker Model Monitor now runs at the scheduled intervals and analyzes the captured data against the baseline. The job creates a violation report and stores the report in Amazon S3, along with a statistics report for the collected data.

Once the monitoring job has started its executions, we can use `list_executions()` to view all executions:

```
executions = my_monitor.list_executions()
```

The SageMaker Model Monitor jobs should exit with one of the following statuses:

Completed
> The monitoring execution completed and no violations were found.

CompletedWithViolations
> The monitoring execution completed, but constraint violations were found.

Failed
> The monitoring execution failed, maybe due to incorrect role permissions or infrastructure issues.

Stopped
> The job exceeded the specified maximum runtime or was manually stopped.

 We can create our own custom monitoring schedules and procedures using preprocessing and postprocessing scripts. We can also build our own analysis container.

Inspect Data-Quality Results

With the monitoring data collected and continuously compared against the data-quality baseline, we are now in a much better position to make decisions about how to improve the model. Depending on the model monitoring results, we might decide to retrain and redeploy the model. In this final step, we visualize and interpret the data-quality monitoring results, as shown in Figure 9-25.

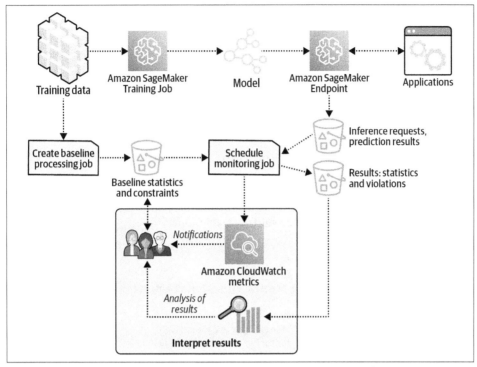

Figure 9-25. Visualize and interpret the data-quality monitoring results.

Let's query for the location for the generated reports:

```
report_uri=latest_execution.output.destination
print('Report Uri: {}'.format(report_uri))
```

Next, we can list the generated reports:

```
from urllib.parse import urlparse

s3uri = urlparse(report_uri)
report_bucket = s3uri.netloc
report_key = s3uri.path.lstrip('/')

print('Report bucket: {}'.format(report_bucket))
print('Report key: {}'.format(report_key))

s3_client = boto3.Session().client('s3')

result = s3_client.list_objects(Bucket=report_bucket,
    Prefix=report_key)

report_files = [report_file.get("Key") for report_file in
    result.get('Contents')]
```

```
print("Found Report Files:")
print("\n ".join(report_files))
```

Output:

```
s3://<bucket>/<prefix>/constraint_violations.json
s3://<bucket>/<prefix>/constraints.json
s3://<bucket>/<prefix>/statistics.json
```

We already looked at *constraints.json* and *statistics.json*, so let's analyze the violations:

```
violations =
my_default_monitor.latest_monitoring_constraint_violations()

violations = pd.io.json.json_normalize(
    violations.body_dict["violations"])
```

Here are example violations for our `review_body` inputs:

```
{
  "feature_name" : "review_body",
  "constraint_check_type" : "data_type_check",
  "description" : "Value: 1.0 meets the constraint requirement"
}, {
  "feature_name" : "review_body",
  "constraint_check_type" : "baseline_drift_check",
  "description" : "Numerical distance: 0.2711598746081505 exceeds
    numerical threshold: 0"
}
```

To find the root cause of this data-quality drift, we want to examine the model inputs and examine any upstream application bugs (or features) that may have been recently introduced. For example, if the application team adds a new set of product categories that our model was not trained on, the model may predict poorly for those particular product categories. In this case, SageMaker Model Monitor would detect the covariate shift in model inputs, notify us, and potentially retrain and redeploy the model.

As an extreme example, let's say that the application team started to feature emojis as the primary review mechanism. Given that our review classifier has not been trained on a vocabulary that includes emojis, the model may predict poorly on reviews that contain emojis. In this case, SageMaker Model Monitor would notify us of the change in review-language distribution. We could then retrain and redeploy an updated model that understands the emoji language.

Monitor Model Quality of Deployed SageMaker Endpoints

We can also use SageMaker Model Monitor to detect drift in model quality metrics such as accuracy. SageMaker Model Monitor compares the online model predictions with provided ground truth labels. Model-quality monitoring can be used to detect concept drift.

Input data is captured by SageMaker Model Monitor using the real-time data capture feature. This data is saved into S3 and labeled by humans offline. A Model Quality Job then compares the offline data at a schedule that we define. If the model quality decays, SageMaker Model Monitor will notify us and potentially retrain and redeploy the model, including the ground truth data labeled by humans. Note that the availability of the ground truth labels might be delayed because of the required human interaction. Figure 9-26 shows the high-level overview of model-quality drift detection using offline, ground-truth labels provided by a human workforce.

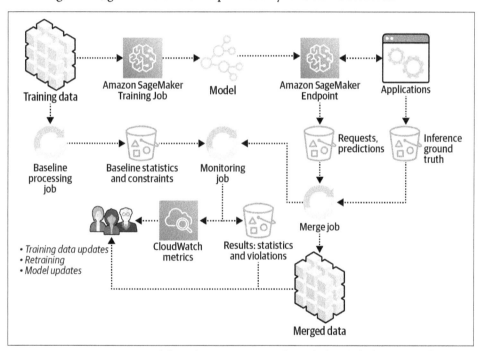

Figure 9-26. Comparing model predictions to ground-truth data labels generated from a human workforce.

Here, the Model Quality Job compares the actual, ground truth `star_rating` chosen by the human with the predicted `star_rating` from the model endpoint. The job calculates a confusion matrix and the standard multiclass classification metrics, including accuracy, precision, recall, etc.:

```
"multiclass_classification_metrics" : {
    "confusion_matrix" : {
      ...
    },
    "accuracy" : {
      "value" : 0.6288167938931297,
      "standard_deviation" : 0.00375663881299405
    },
    ...
}
```

Before we start monitoring the model quality, we need to create a baseline.

Create a Baseline to Measure Model Quality

The model quality baseline job compares the model's predictions with provided ground truth labels we store in S3. The baseline job then calculates the relevant model quality metrics and suggests applicable constraints to identify drift.

We start with the creation of a `ModelQualityMonitor` as follows:

```
from sagemaker.model_monitor import ModelQualityMonitor

model_quality_monitor = ModelQualityMonitor(
    role=role,
    instance_count=1,
    instance_type='ml.m5.xlarge',
    volume_size_in_gb=20,
    max_runtime_in_seconds=1800,
    sagemaker_session=sess
)
```

Then, we can start the baseline job with `suggest_baseline` as follows:

```
job = model_quality_monitor.suggest_baseline(
    job_name=baseline_job_name,
    baseline_dataset=baseline_dataset_uri,
    dataset_format=DatasetFormat.csv(header=True),
    output_s3_uri = baseline_results_uri,
    problem_type='MulticlassClassification',
    inference_attribute= 'prediction',
    probability_attribute= 'probability',
    ground_truth_attribute= 'star_rating')
```

Once the job completes, we can review the suggested constraints in the *constraints.json* file in the specified S3 output path. In our example, the file will contain the suggested constraints for our multiclass classification model. Make sure to review the constraints and adjust them if needed. We will then pass the constraints as a parameter when we schedule the model-quality monitoring job:

```
{
  "version" : 0.0,
```

```
"multiclass_classification_constraints" : {
  "weighted_recall" : {
    "threshold" : 0.5714285714285714,
    "comparison_operator" : "LessThanThreshold"
  },
  "weighted_precision" : {
    "threshold" : 0.6983172269629505,
    "comparison_operator" : "LessThanThreshold"
  },
  ...
}
```

Schedule Model-Quality Monitoring Jobs

Model-quality monitoring jobs follow the same scheduling steps as data-quality monitoring jobs. One difference to keep in mind is that the model-quality monitoring jobs assume the availability of ground truth labels for the captured predictions. As humans need to provide the ground truth labels, we need to deal with potential delays. Therefore, model-quality monitor jobs provide additional `StartOffset` and `EndOffset` parameters, which subtract the specified offset from the job's start and end time, respectively.

For example, if we start providing the ground truth labels one day after the data capture, we could grant a window of three days for the ground truth data to be labeled by specifying a `StartOffset` with -P3D and an `EndOffset` with -P1D for the monitoring job. Assuming the ground truth data is labeled in that time, the job will analyze data starting three days ago up to one day ago. The job then merges the ground truth labels with the captured model predictions and calculates the distribution drift.

We can create the model-quality monitoring job as follows:

```
sm = boto3.Session().client(service_name='sagemaker', region_name=region)

sm.create_model_quality_job_definition(
    JobDefinitionName=<NAME>,
    ModelQualityBaselineConfig={...},
    ModelQualityAppSpecification={...},
    ModelQualityJobInput={...
        'EndpointInput': {...},
        'GroundTruthS3Input': {...},
    ModelQualityJobOutputConfig={...},
    JobResources={...}
    NetworkConfig={...},
    RoleArn=<IAM_ROLE_ARN>)
```

And we define the monitoring schedule for our `ModelQualityMonitor` as follows:

```
model_quality_monitor.create_monitoring_schedule(
    endpoint_input=<ENDPOINT_NAME>,
    ground_truth_input=<S3_INPUT_PATH>,
```

```
    problem_type='MulticlassClassification',
    record_preprocessor_script=<S3_PRE_SCRIPT_PATH>,
    post_analytics_processor_script=<S3_POST_SCRIPT_PATH>,
    output_s3_uri=<S3_OUTPUT_PATH>,
    constraints=<S3_CONSTRAINTS_PATH>,
    monitor_schedule_name=<NAME>,
    schedule_cron_expression=<SCHEDULE>,
    enable_cloudwatch_metrics=True)
```

The `ModelQualityMonitor` now runs at the scheduled intervals and compares the model-quality metrics based on the captured data and ground truth labels against the baseline. We can inspect the constraint violation reports in Amazon S3.

Inspect Model-Quality Monitoring Results

`ModelQualityMonitor` stores the constraint violations in Amazon S3. We can compare the baseline and observed model-quality metrics directly in SageMaker Studio, as shown in Figure 9-27, or programmatically inspect the constraint violations using the following code. The baseline average accuracy is on top, and the current average accuracy is on bottom.

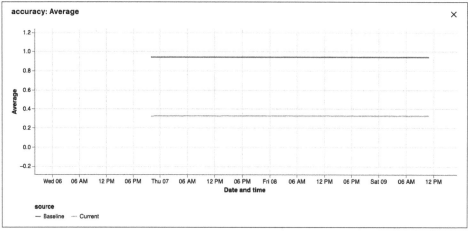

Figure 9-27. SageMaker Studio Endpoint details show charts of model-quality metrics such as average accuracy.

```
import pandas as pd

latest_exec = model_quality_monitor.list_executions()[-1]

report_uri = \
    latest_exec.describe()\
    ["ProcessingOutputConfig"]["Outputs"][0]["S3Output"]["S3Uri"]

pd.options.display.max_colwidth = None
```

```
violations =
    latest_exec.constraint_violations().body_dict["violations"]
pd.json_normalize(violations)
```

Monitor Bias Drift of Deployed SageMaker Endpoints

Even though we cleared our training data of bias and took action to mitigate bias in our trained models, bias can still be introduced in deployed models. This happens if the data that our model sees has a different distribution compared to the training data. New data can also cause our model to assign different weights to input features. SageMaker Clarify integrates with SageMaker Model Monitor to help us to detect bias drift in our deployed models.

Create a Baseline to Detect Bias

SageMaker Clarify continuously monitors the bias metrics of our deployed models and raises an alarm if those metrics exceed defined thresholds. We start with the creation of a ModelBiasMonitor as follows:

```
from sagemaker.model_monitor import ModelBiasMonitor

model_bias_monitor = ModelBiasMonitor(
    role=role,
    sagemaker_session=sagemaker_session,
    max_runtime_in_seconds=1800,
)
```

Similar to detecting post-training model bias with SageMaker Clarify in Chapter 7, we need to specify the DataConfig, the BiasConfig, and the ModelConfig, which points to the model used for inference. The ModelPredictedLabelConfig specifies again how to parse the model predictions:

```
from sagemaker import clarify

data_config = clarify.DataConfig(
        s3_data_input_path=validation_dataset,
        s3_output_path=model_bias_baselining_job_result_uri,
        label='star_rating',
        headers=['review_body', 'product_category', ...],
        dataset_type='text/csv')

bias_config = clarify.BiasConfig(
        label_values_or_threshold=[5, 4]
        facet_name='product_category',
        facet_values_or_threshold=['Gift Card'],
        group_name='product_category')
```

```
model_config = clarify.ModelConfig(
    model_name=model_name,
    instance_type='ml.m5.4xlarge',
    instance_count=1,
    content_type='text/csv',
    accept_type='application/jsonlines')

predictions_config = clarify.ModelPredictedLabelConfig(label='predicted_label')
```

With this configuration, we can create and start the model bias baselining job:

```
model_bias_monitor.suggest_baseline(
    model_config=model_config,
    data_config=data_config,
    bias_config=bias_config,
    model_predicted_label_config=model_predicted_label_config,
)
```

By calling `suggest_baseline()` we start a SageMaker Clarify Processing Job to generate the constraints. Once the job completes and we have our bias baseline, we can create a bias-drift monitoring job and schedule.

Schedule Bias-Drift Monitoring Jobs

The monitor will automatically pick up the results from the baseline job as its model bias analysis configuration. We can also create the analysis configuration manually if we haven't run a baseline job:

```
model_bias_monitor.create_monitoring_schedule(
    analysis_config=analysis_config,
    output_s3_uri=s3_report_path,
    endpoint_input=EndpointInput(
        endpoint_name=endpoint_name,
        destination="/opt/ml/processing/input/endpoint",
        start_time_offset="-PT1H",
        end_time_offset="-PT0H",
        probability_threshold_attribute=<THRESHOLD>,
    ),
    ground_truth_input=ground_truth_upload_path,
    schedule_cron_expression=schedule_expression,
)
```

Note that the model bias monitor makes use of the provided ground truth label data as well. The bias monitoring job merges the ground truth labels with the captured model predictions and uses the combined data as its validation dataset. The bias drift monitor results are stored in Amazon S3 again.

Inspect Bias-Drift Monitoring Results

We inspect the bias and drift results for each monitored endpoint in SageMaker Studio, as shown in Figure 9-28, or programmatically with the following code:

```
schedule_desc = model_bias_monitor.describe_schedule()

exec_summary = schedule_desc.get("LastMonitoringExecutionSummary")

if exec_summary and exec_summary["MonitoringExecutionStatus"] in
    ["Completed", "CompletedWithViolations"]:

    last_exec = model_bias_monitor.list_executions()[-1]
    last_exec_report_uri = last_exec.output.destination
    last_exec_report_files =
        sorted(S3Downloader.list(last_exec_report_uri))

    last_exec = None
```

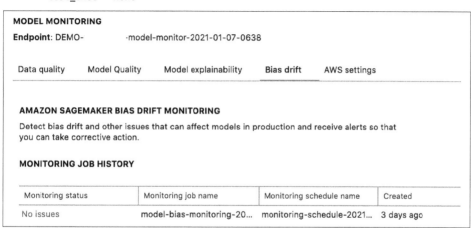

Figure 9-28. SageMaker Studio Endpoint details show bias-drift monitoring results.

If the bias-drift monitor detected any violations compared to its baseline, we can list the violations as follows:

```
if last_exec:
    model_bias_violations = last_exec.constraint_violations()
if model_bias_violations:
    print(model_bias_violations.body_dict)
```

Monitor Feature Attribution Drift of Deployed SageMaker Endpoints

Similarly to model bias drift, SageMaker Clarify monitors the features contributing to the predictions over time. Feature attributions help to explain model predictions. If the ranking of feature attributions changes, SageMaker Clarify raises a feature attribution drift alarm. SageMaker Clarify implements a model-agnostic method called *SHAP* to analyze global and local feature importances. SHAP has been inspired by game theory and generates multiple datasets that differ by just one feature. SHAP uses the trained model to receive the model predictions for each of the generated datasets. The algorithm compares the results against pre-calculated baseline statistics to infer the importance of each feature toward the prediction target.

Create a Baseline to Monitor Feature Attribution

The feature attribution baseline job can leverage the same dataset used for the model bias baseline job:

```
model_explainability_data_config = DataConfig(
        s3_data_input_path=validation_dataset,
        s3_output_path=model_explainability_baselining_job_result_uri,
        label='star_rating',
        headers=['review_body', product_category', ...],
        dataset_type='text/csv')
```

SageMaker Clarify implements SHAP for model explanation. Hence, we need to provide a `SHAPConfig` as follows:

```
# Using the mean value of test dataset as SHAP baseline
test_dataframe = pd.read_csv(test_dataset, header=None)
shap_baseline = [list(test_dataframe.mean())]

shap_config = SHAPConfig(
    baseline=shap_baseline,
    num_samples=100,
    agg_method="mean_abs",
    save_local_shap_values=False,
)
```

`shap_baseline` needs to contain a list of rows to be used as the baseline dataset, or an S3 object URI to the baseline dataset. The data should only contain the feature columns and no label column. `num_samples` specifies the number of samples used in the Kernel SHAP algorithm. `agg_method` defines the aggregation method for global SHAP values. We can choose between `mean_abs` (mean of absolute SHAP values), `median` (median of all SHAP values), and `mean_sq` (mean of squared SHAP values).

We can then start the feature attribution baselining job as follows:

```
model_explainability_monitor.suggest_baseline(
        data_config=model_explainability_data_config,
        model_config=model_config,
        explainability_config=shap_config,
)
```

By calling `suggest_baseline()` we start a SageMaker Clarify Processing Job to generate the constraints. Once the baselining job completes, we can view the suggested constraints as follows:

```
model_explainability_constraints =
    model_explainability_monitor.suggested_constraints()
```

We can now create a feature attribution drift monitoring job and schedule.

Schedule Feature Attribution Drift Monitoring Jobs

The monitor will automatically pick up the results from the baseline job as its feature attribution analysis configuration. We can also create the analysis configuration manually if we haven't run a baseline job:

```
model_explainability_monitor.create_monitoring_schedule(
    output_s3_uri=s3_report_path,
    endpoint_input=endpoint_name,
    schedule_cron_expression=schedule_expression,
)
```

Inspect Feature Attribution Drift Monitoring Results

We can inspect the feature attribution drift monitoring results as follows:

```
schedule_desc = model_explainability_monitor.describe_schedule()

exec_summary = schedule_desc.get("LastMonitoringExecutionSummary")

if exec_summary and exec_summary["MonitoringExecutionStatus"] in \
    ["Completed", "CompletedWithViolations"]:

    last_exec = model_explainability_monitor.list_executions()[-1]
    last_exec_report_uri = last_exec.output.destination

    last_exec_report_files = sorted(S3Downloader.list(last_exec_report_uri))

else:
    last_exec = None
```

If the feature attribution drift monitor detected any violations compared to its baseline, we can list the violations as follows:

```
if last_exec:
    explainability_violations = last_exec.constraint_violations()
```

```
if explainability_violations:
    print(explainability_violations.body_dict)
```

We can also find the explainability results for each monitored endpoint in SageMaker Studio in the endpoint details, as shown in Figure 9-29. In addition, we can see a chart that visualizes the change in the top 10 features, as shown in Figure 9-30.

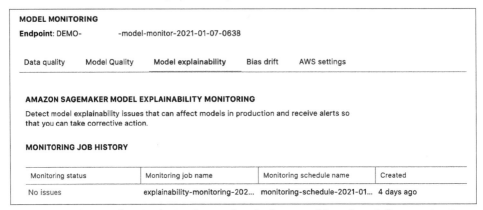

Figure 9-29. SageMaker Studio Endpoint details show model explainability monitoring results showing "No Issues" when generating the report.

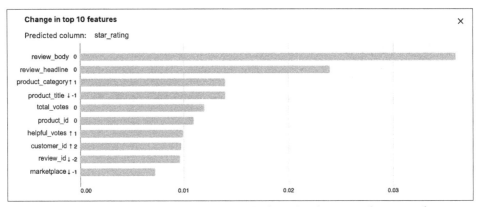

Figure 9-30. SageMaker Studio Endpoint details show the change in the top 10 features, with review_body, review_headline, product_category, product_title, *and* total_votes *as the top 5.*

Now that we have detailed monitoring of our models in place, we can build additional automation. We could leverage the SageMaker Model Monitor integration into CloudWatch to trigger actions on baseline drift alarms, such as model updates, training data updates, or an automated retraining of our model.

Perform Batch Predictions with SageMaker Batch Transform

Amazon SageMaker Batch Transform allows us to make predictions on batches of data in S3 without setting up a REST endpoint. Batch predictions are also called "off-line" predictions since they do not require an online REST endpoint. Typically meant for higher-throughput workloads that can tolerate higher latency and lower freshness, batch prediction servers typically do not run 24 hours per day like real-time prediction servers. They run for a few hours on a batch of data, then shut down—hence the term "batch." SageMaker Batch Transform manages all of the resources needed to perform the inferences, including the launch and termination of the cluster after the job completes.

For example, if our movie catalog only changes a few times a day, we can likely just run one batch prediction job each night that uses a new recommendation model trained with the day's new movies and user activity. Since we are only updating the recommendations once in the evening, our recommendations will be a bit stale throughout the day. However, our overall cost is minimized and, even more importantly, stays predictable.

The alternative is to continuously retrain and redeploy new recommendation models throughout the day with every new movie that joins or leaves our movie catalog. This could lead to excessive model training and deployment costs that are difficult to control and predict. These types of continuous updates typically fall under the "trending now" category of popular websites like Facebook and Netflix that offer real-time content recommendations. We explore these types of continuous models when we discuss streaming data analytics.

Select an Instance Type

Similar to model training, the choice of instance type often involves a balance between latency, throughput, and cost. Always start with a small instance type and then increase only as needed. Batch predictions may benefit from GPUs more than real-time endpoint predictions since GPUs perform much better with large batches of data. However, we recommend trying CPU instances first to set the baseline for latency, throughput, and cost. Here, we are using a cluster of high-CPU instances:

```
instance_type='ml.c5.18xlarge'
instance_count=5
```

Set Up the Input Data

Let's specify the input data. In our case, we are using the original TSVs that are stored as *gzip* compressed text files:

```
# Specify the input data
input_csv_s3_uri = \
    's3://{}/amazon-reviews-pds/tsv/'.format(bucket)
```

We specify `MultiRecord` for our strategy to take advantage of our multiple CPUs. We specify `Gzip` as the compression type since our input data is compressed using *gzip*. We're using TSVs, so `text/csv` is a suitable `accept_type` and `content_type`. And since our rows are separated by line breaks, we use `Line` for `assemble_with` and `split_type`:

```
strategy='MultiRecord'
compression_type='Gzip'
accept_type='text/csv'
content_type='text/csv'
assemble_with='Line'
split_type='Line'
```

Tune the SageMaker Batch Transform Configuration

When we start the batch transform job, our code runs in an HTTP server inside the TensorFlow Serving inference container. Note that TensorFlow Serving natively supports batches of data on a single request.

Let's leverage TensorFlow Serving's built-in batching feature to batch multiple records to increase prediction throughput—especially on GPU instances that perform well on batches of data. Set the following environment variables to enable batching:

```
batch_env = {
  # Configures whether to enable record batching.
  'SAGEMAKER_TFS_ENABLE_BATCHING': 'true',

  # Name of the model - this is important in multi-model deployments
  'SAGEMAKER_TFS_DEFAULT_MODEL_NAME': 'saved_model',

  # Configures how long to wait for a full batch, in microseconds.
  'SAGEMAKER_TFS_BATCH_TIMEOUT_MICROS': '50000', # microseconds

  # Corresponds to "max_batch_size" in TensorFlow Serving.
  'SAGEMAKER_TFS_MAX_BATCH_SIZE': '10000',

  # Number of seconds for the SageMaker web server timeout
  'SAGEMAKER_MODEL_SERVER_TIMEOUT': '3600', # Seconds

  # Configures number of batches that can be enqueued.
  'SAGEMAKER_TFS_MAX_ENQUEUED_BATCHES': '10000'
}
```

Prepare the SageMaker Batch Transform Job

We can inject preprocessing and postprocessing code directly into the Batch Transform Container to customize the prediction flow. The preprocessing code is specified in *inference.py* and will transform the request from raw data (i.e., review_body text) into machine-readable features (i.e., BERT tokens). These features are then fed to the model for inference. The model prediction results are then passed through the postprocessing code from *inference.py* to convert the model prediction into human-readable responses before saving to S3. Figure 9-31 shows how SageMaker Batch Transform works in detail.

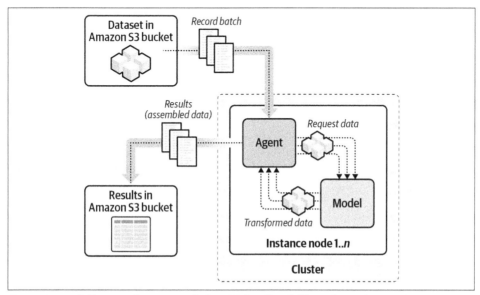

Figure 9-31. Offline predictions with SageMaker Batch Transform. Source: Amazon SageMaker Developer Guide.

Let's set up the batch transformer to use our *inference.py* script that we will show in a bit. We are specifying the S3 location of the classifier model that we trained in a previous chapter:

```
batch_model = Model(entry_point='inference.py',
                    source_dir='src_tsv',
                    model_data=<TENSORFLOW_MODEL_S3_URI>,
                    role=role,
                    framework_version='<TENSORFLOW_VERSION>',
                    env=batch_env)

batch_predictor = batch_model.transformer(
    strategy=strategy,
    instance_type=instance_type,
    instance_count=instance_count,
```

```
        accept=accept_type,
        assemble_with=assemble_with,
        max_concurrent_transforms=max_concurrent_transforms,
        max_payload=max_payload, # This is in Megabytes
        env=batch_env)
```

Following is the *inference.py* script used by the Batch Transform Job defined earlier. This script has an `input_handler` for request processing and `output_handler` for response processing, as shown in Figure 9-32.

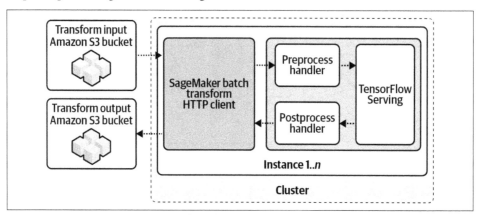

Figure 9-32. Preprocessing request handler and postprocessing response handler.

The preprocessing handler, `input_handler`, and the postprocessing handler, `out put_handler`, are similar to the functions used for the SageMaker REST Endpoint earlier. The `input_handler` function converts batches of raw text into BERT tokens using the Transformer library. SageMaker then passes this batched output from the `input_handler` into our model, which produces batches of predictions. The predictions are passed through the `output_handler` function, which converts the prediction into a JSON response. SageMaker then joins each prediction within a batch to its specific line of input. This produces a single, coherent line of output for each row that was passed in.

Run the SageMaker Batch Transform Job

Next we will specify the input data and start the actual Batch Transform Job. Note that our input data is compressed using *gzip* as Batch Transform Jobs support many types of compression:

```
batch_predictor.transform(data=input_csv_s3_uri,
                          split_type=split_type,
                          compression_type=compression_type,
                          content_type=content_type,
                          join_source='Input',
```

```
                    experiment_config=experiment_config,
                    wait=False)
```

We specify `join_source='Input'` to force SageMaker to join our prediction with the original input before writing to S3. And while not shown here, SageMaker lets us specify the exact input features to pass into this batch transformation process using `InputFilter` and the exact data to write to S3 using `OutputFilter`. This helps to reduce overhead, reduce cost, and improve batch prediction performance.

If we are using `join_source='Input'` and `InputFilter` together, SageMaker will join the original inputs—including the filtered-out inputs—with the predictions to keep all of the data together. We can also filter the outputs to reduce the size of the prediction files written to S3. The whole flow is shown in Figure 9-33.

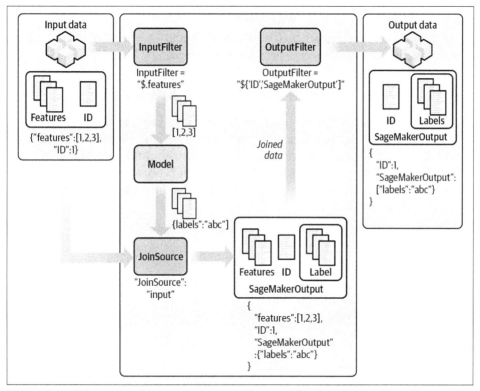

Figure 9-33. Filtering and joining inputs to reduce overhead and improve performance.

Review the Batch Predictions

Once the Batch Transform Job completes, we can review the generated comma-separated *.out* files that contain our `review_body` inputs and `star_rating` predictions as shown here:

```
amazon_reviews_us_Digital_Software_v1_00.tsv.gz.out
amazon_reviews_us_Digital_Video_Games_v1_00.tsv.gz.out
```

Here are a few sample predictions:

```
'This is the best movie I have ever seen', 5, 'Star Wars'
'This is an ok, decently-funny movie.', 3, 'Spaceballs'
'This is the worst movie I have ever seen', 1, 'Star Trek'
```

At this point, we have performed a large number of predictions and generated comma-separated output files. With a little bit of application code (SQL, Python, Java, etc.), we can use these predictions to power natural-language-based applications to improve the customer service experience, for example.

AWS Lambda Functions and Amazon API Gateway

We can also deploy our models as serverless APIs with Lambda. When a prediction request arrives, the Lambda function loads the model and executes the inference function code. Models can be loaded directly from within the Lambda function or from a data store like Amazon S3 and EFS. Lambda functions are callable from many AWS services, including Amazon Simple Queue Service and S3, to effectively implement event-based predictions.

We can use the "provisioned concurrency" feature of Lambda to pre-load the model into the function and greatly improve prediction latency. Amazon API Gateway provides additional support for application authentication, authorization, caching, rate-limiting, and web application firewall rules. Figure 9-34 shows how we implement serverless inference with Lambda and API Gateway.

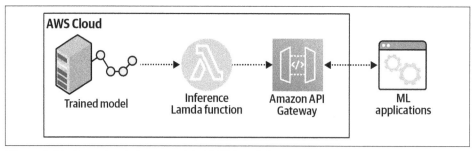

Figure 9-34. Serverless inference with AWS Lambda.

Optimize and Manage Models at the Edge

We can leverage Amazon SageMaker Neo Compilation Jobs to optimize our model for specific hardware platforms such as AWS Inferentia, NVIDIA GPUs, Intel CPUs, and ARM CPUs. SageMaker Neo frees us from manually tuning our models to specific hardware and software configurations found in different CPU and GPU architectures, or edge device platforms with limited compute and storage resources. The SageMaker Neo compiler converts models into efficient and compact formats using device-specific instruction sets. These instructions perform low-latency machine learning inference on the target device directly.

> In 2019, AWS made SageMaker Neo (*https://oreil.ly/CkO1f*) open source to allow processor vendors, device manufacturers, and software developers to collaborate and bring ML models to a diverse set of hardware-optimized platforms.

Once the model is compiled by SageMaker Neo, SageMaker Edge Manager cryptographically signs the model, packages the model with a lightweight runtime, and uploads the model package to an S3 bucket in preparation for deployment. SageMaker Edge Manager manages models across all registered edge devices, tracks model versions, collects health metrics, and periodically captures model inputs and outputs to detect model drift and degradation.

Deploy a PyTorch Model with TorchServe

TorchServe is an open source collaboration between AWS, Facebook, and the PyTorch community. With TorchServe, we can serve PyTorch models in production as REST endpoints similar to TensorFlow Serving. SageMaker provides native TorchServe integration, which allows us to focus on the business logic of the prediction request versus the infrastructure code.

Similar to the TensorFlow Serving–based SageMaker Endpoint we created earlier, we need to provide a Python-based request and response handler called *inference.py* to transform raw review text from the REST request from JSON to PyTorch input BERT vectors. Additionally, *inference.py* needs to transform the PyTorch `star_rating` classification response back into JSON to return to the calling application. The following is a relevant snippet from *inference.py*:

```
def model_fn(model_dir):
    model_path = '{}/{}'.format(model_dir, MODEL_NAME)
    device = torch.device(
      'cuda' if torch.cuda.is_available() else 'cpu')
    config = DistilBertConfig.from_json_file(
      '/opt/ml/model/code/config.json')
```

```
        model = DistilBertForSequenceClassification.from_pretrained(
          model_path,config=config)
        model.to(device)
        return model

    def predict_fn(input_data, model):
        model.eval()
        data_str = input_data.decode('utf-8')
        jsonlines = data_str.split("\n")

        predicted_classes = []

        for jsonline in jsonlines:
            review_body = json.loads(jsonline)["features"][0]

            encode_plus_token = tokenizer.encode_plus(
                review_body,
                max_length=max_seq_length,
                add_special_tokens=True,
                return_token_type_ids=False,
                pad_to_max_length=True,
                return_attention_mask=True,
                return_tensors='pt',
                truncation=True)

            input_ids = encode_plus_token['input_ids']
            attention_mask = encode_plus_token['attention_mask']

            output = model(input_ids, attention_mask)

            softmax_fn = nn.Softmax(dim=1)
            softmax_output = softmax_fn(output[0])
            print("softmax_output: {}".format(softmax_output))

            _, prediction = torch.max(softmax_output, dim=1)

            predicted_class_idx = prediction.item()
            predicted_class = classes[predicted_class_idx]

            prediction_dict = {}
            prediction_dict['predicted_label'] = predicted_class

            jsonline = json.dumps(prediction_dict)

            predicted_classes.append(jsonline)

        predicted_classes_jsonlines = '\n'.join(predicted_classes)

        return predicted_classes_jsonlines
```

Let's deploy our model as a SageMaker Endpoint with our *inference.py* request/
response handler:

```
class StarRatingPredictor(Predictor):
    def __init__(self, endpoint_name, sagemaker_session):
        super().__init__(endpoint_name,
                         sagemaker_session=sagemaker_session,
                         serializer=JSONLinesSerializer(),
                         deserializer=JSONLinesDeserializer())

model = PyTorchModel(model_data=<PYTORCH_MODEL_S3_URI>,
                     name=pytorch_model_name,
                     role=role,
                     entry_point='inference.py',
                     source_dir='code-pytorch',
                     framework_version='<PYTORCH_VERSION>',
                     predictor_cls=StarRatingPredictor)

predictor = model.deploy(initial_instance_count=1,
                         instance_type='ml.m5.4xlarge',
                         endpoint_name=pytorch_endpoint_name,
                         wait=False)
```

Now we can make a prediction by passing review text to our review classifier endpoint:

```
import json

inputs = [
    {"features": ["This is great!"]},
    {"features": ["This is OK."]}
    {"features": ["This is bad."]}
]

predicted_classes = predictor.predict(inputs)

for predicted_class in predicted_classes:
    print(predicted_class)

### OUTPUT ###

{'predicted_label': 5}
{'predicted_label': 3}
{'predicted_label': 1}
```

TensorFlow-BERT Inference with AWS Deep Java Library

Let's import the required Java libraries from AWS Deep Java Library (DJL):

```
import ai.djl.*;
import ai.djl.engine.*;
import ai.djl.inference.*;
import ai.djl.modality.*;
import ai.djl.modality.nlp.*;
import ai.djl.modality.nlp.bert.*;
import ai.djl.ndarray.*;
import ai.djl.repository.zoo.*;
import ai.djl.translate.*;
import ai.djl.training.util.*;
import ai.djl.util.*;
```

Next, let's download the pre-trained DistilBERT TensorFlow model:

```
String modelUrl =
"https://resources.djl.ai/demo/tensorflow/amazon_review_rank_classification.zip";
DownloadUtils.download(modelUrl,
            "build/amazon_review_rank_classification.zip",
                    new ProgressBar());
Path zipFile = Paths.get("build/amazon_review_rank_classification.zip");
Path modelDir = Paths.get("build/saved_model");
if (Files.notExists(modelDir)) {
    ZipUtils.unzip(Files.newInputStream(zipFile), modelDir);
}
```

Next, we set up the BERT Tokenizer and define the Translator to transform raw text into BERT embeddings:

```
// Prepare the vocabulary
Path vocabFile = modelDir.resolve("vocab.txt");
SimpleVocabulary vocabulary = SimpleVocabulary.builder()
        .optMinFrequency(1)
        .addFromTextFile(vocabFile)
        .optUnknownToken("[UNK]")
        .build();
BertFullTokenizer tokenizer = new BertFullTokenizer(vocabulary, true);
int maxTokenLength = 64; // cutoff tokens length

class MyTranslator implements Translator<String, Classifications> {

    private BertFullTokenizer tokenizer;
    private SimpleVocabulary vocab;
    private List<String> ranks;
    private int length;

    public MyTranslator(BertFullTokenizer tokenizer, int length) {
        this.tokenizer = tokenizer;
        this.length = length;
        vocab = tokenizer.getVocabulary();
```

```java
            ranks = Arrays.asList("1", "2", "3", "4", "5");
        }

        @Override
        public Batchifier getBatchifier() {
            return new StackBatchifier();
        }

        @Override
        public NDList processInput(TranslatorContext ctx, String input) {
            List<String> tokens = tokenizer.tokenize(input);
            long[] indices = new long[length];
            long[] mask = new long[length];
            long[] segmentIds = new long[length];
            int size = Math.min(length, tokens.size());
            for (int i = 0; i < size; i++) {
                indices[i + 1] = vocab.getIndex(tokens.get(i));
            }
            Arrays.fill(mask,  0, size, 1);
            NDManager m = ctx.getNDManager();
            return new NDList(m.create(indices),
                        m.create(mask),
                        m.create(segmentIds));
        }

        @Override
        public Classifications processOutput(TranslatorContext ctx, NDList list) {
            return new Classifications(ranks, list.singletonOrThrow().softmax(0));
        }
    }
}
```

Last, we load the model and make some predictions with BERT and Java!

```java
MyTranslator translator = new MyTranslator(tokenizer, maxTokenLength);

Criteria<String, Classifications> criteria = Criteria.builder()
        .setTypes(String.class, Classifications.class)
        .optModelPath(modelDir) // Load model form model directory
        .optTranslator(translator) // use custom translaotr
        .build();

ZooModel<String, Classifications> model = ModelZoo.loadModel(criteria);

String review = "It works great, but it takes too long to update";

Predictor<String, Classifications> predictor = model.newPredictor();
predictor.predict(review);

### OUTPUT ###

5
```

Reduce Cost and Increase Performance

In this section, we describe multiple ways to reduce cost and increase performance by packing multiple models into a single SageMaker deployment container, utilizing GPU-based Elastic Inference Accelerators, optimizing our trained model for specific hardware, and utilizing inference-optimized hardware such as the AWS Inferentia chip.

Delete Unused Endpoints and Scale In Underutilized Clusters

SageMaker Endpoints are long-running resources and are easy to leave running after a successful blue/green deployment, for example. We should remove unused resources as soon as possible. We can set up CloudWatch alerts to notify us when a Sage-Maker Endpoint is not receiving invocations. Similarly, we should remember to scale in a SageMaker Endpoint cluster if the cluster is overprovisioned and underutilized.

Deploy Multiple Models in One Container

If we have a large number of similar models that we can serve through a shared serving container—and don't need to access all the models at the same time—we can deploy multiple models within a single SageMaker Endpoint. When there is a long tail of ML models that are infrequently accessed, using one endpoint can efficiently serve inference traffic and enable significant cost savings.

Each of the SageMaker Endpoints can automatically load and unload models based on traffic and resource utilization. For example, if traffic to Model 1 goes to zero and Model 2 traffic spikes, SageMaker will dynamically unload Model 1 and load another instance of Model 2. We can invoke a specific model variant by specifying the target model name as a parameter in our prediction request, as shown in Figure 9-35.

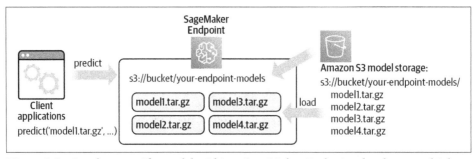

Figure 9-35. Invoke a specific model within a SageMaker Endpoint that hosts multiple models.

This lets us train two different category-specific TensorFlow models—Digital_Soft ware and Gift_Card, for example—and deploy them to a single endpoint for convenience and cost-savings purposes. Here is code to deploy the two models into a single SageMaker Endpoint.

For TensorFlow, we need to package the models as follows:

```
└── multi
    ├── model1
    │   └── <version number>
    │       ├── saved_model.pb
    │       └── variables
    │           └── ...
    └── model2
        └── <version number>
            ├── saved_model.pb
            └── variables
                └── ...

from sagemaker.tensorflow.serving import Model, Predictor

# For endpoints with multiple models, we should set the default
#  model name in this environment variable.
# If it isn't set, the endpoint will work, but the model
#  it will select as default is unpredictable.
env = {
  'SAGEMAKER_TFS_DEFAULT_MODEL_NAME': 'model1' # <== This must match the directory
}

model_data = '{}/multi.tar.gz'.format(multi_model_s3_uri)
model = Model(model_data=model_data,
              role=role,
              framework_version='<TENSORFLOW_VERSION>',
              env=env)
```

Attach a GPU-Based Elastic Inference Accelerator

Elastic Inference Accelerator (EIA) is a low-cost, dynamically attached, GPU-powered add-on for SageMaker instances. While standalone GPU instances are a good fit for model training on large datasets, they are typically oversized for smaller-batch inference requests, which consume small amounts of GPU resources.

While AWS offers a wide range of instance types with different GPU, CPU, network bandwidth, and memory combinations, our model may use a custom combination. With EIAs, we can start by choosing a base CPU instance and add GPUs until we find the right balance for our model inference needs. Otherwise, we may be forced to optimize one set of resources like CPU and RAM but underutilize other resources like GPU and network bandwidth.

Here is the code to deploy our same model but with EIA:

```
import time
timestamp = '{}'.format(int(time.time()))
```

```
endpoint_config_name = '{}-{}'.format(training_job_name, timestamp)

variantA = production_variant(model_name='ModelA',
                              instance_type="ml.m5.large",
                              initial_instance_count=1,
                              variant_name='VariantA',
                              initial_weight=50,
                              accelerator_type='ml.eia2.medium')

variantB = production_variant(model_name='ModelB',
                              instance_type="ml.m5.large",
                              initial_instance_count=1,
                              variant_name='VariantB',
                              initial_weight=50)

endpoint_config = sm.create_endpoint_config(
  EndpointConfigName=endpoint_config_name,
  ProductionVariants=[variantA, variantB]
)

endpoint_name = '{}-{}'.format(training_job_name, timestamp)

endpoint_response = sm.create_endpoint(
  EndpointName=endpoint_name,
  EndpointConfigName=endpoint_config_name)
```

Optimize a Trained Model with SageMaker Neo and TensorFlow Lite

SageMaker Neo takes a trained model and performs a series of hardware-specific optimizations, such as 16-bit quantization, graph pruning, layer fusing, and constant folding for up to 2x model-prediction speedups with minimal accuracy loss. Sage-Maker Neo works across popular AI and machine learning frameworks, including TensorFlow, PyTorch, Apache MXNet, and XGBoost.

SageMaker Neo parses the model, optimizes the graph, quantizes tensors, and generates hardware-specific code for a variety of target environments, including Intel x86 CPUs, NVIDIA GPUs, and AWS Inferentia, as shown in Figure 9-36.

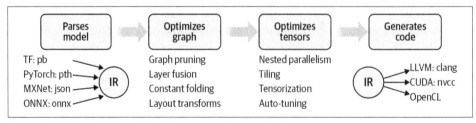

Figure 9-36. SageMaker Neo delivers model compilation as a service.

SageMaker Neo supports TensorFlow Lite (TFLite), a lightweight, highly optimized TensorFlow runtime interpreter and code generator for small devices with limited memory and compute resources. SageMaker Neo uses the TFLite converter to perform hardware-specific optimizations for the TensorFlow Lite runtime interpreter, as shown in Figure 9-37.

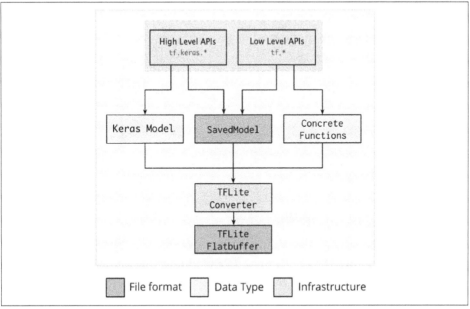

Figure 9-37. TFLite interpreter. Source: TensorFlow (https://oreil.ly/QWiV8).

We can choose to optimize for small size (`tf.lite.Optimize.OPTIMIZE_FOR_SIZE`), optimize for low latency (`tf.lite.OPTIMIZE_FOR_LATENCY`), or balance size and performance (`tf.lite.Optimize.DEFAULT`). Here is the TFLite code that performs 16-bit quantization on a TensorFlow model with a balance between size and performance:

```
import tensorflow as tf

converter = tf.lite.TocoConverter.from_saved_model('./tensorflow/')
converter.post_training_quantize = True
converter.optimizations = [tf.lite.Optimize.DEFAULT]
tflite_model = converter.convert()
tflite_model_path = './tflite/tflite_optimized_model.tflite'
model_size = open(tflite_model_path, "wb").write(tflite_model)
```

Here is the prediction code that leads to an order-of-magnitude speedup in prediction time due to the quantization:

```
import numpy as np
import tensorflow as tf
```

```
# Load TFLite model and allocate tensors.
interpreter = tf.lite.Interpreter(model_path=tflite_model_path)
interpreter.allocate_tensors()

# Get input and output tensors.
input_details = interpreter.get_input_details()
output_details = interpreter.get_output_details()

# Test model on random input data.
input_shape = input_details[0]['shape']
input_data = np.array(np.random.random_sample(input_shape),
dtype=np.float32)

interpreter.set_tensor(input_details[0]['index'], input_data)
interpreter.invoke()

output_data = interpreter.get_tensor(output_details[0]['index'])
print('Prediction: %s' % output_data)

### OUTPUT ###
5
```

Use Inference-Optimized Hardware

AWS Inferentia, is an inference-optimized chip used by the Amazon "Inf" instance
types. The chip accelerates 16-bit and 8-bit floating-point operations generated by the
AWS Neuron compiler to optimize our model for the AWS Inferentia chip and Sage-
Maker Neo and Neuron runtimes (see in Figure 9-38).

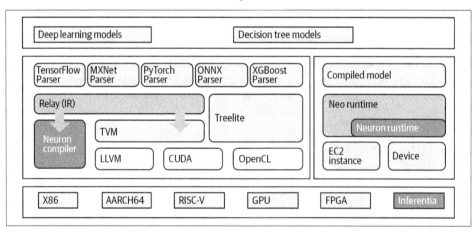

Figure 9-38. SageMaker Neuron compiler and Neo runtime for the AWS Inferentia chip.

Summary

In this chapter, we moved our models out of the research lab and into the end-user application domain. We showed how to measure, improve, and deploy our models using real-world, production-ready fundamentals such as canary rollouts, blue/green deployments, and A/B tests. We demonstrated how to perform data-drift, model-drift, and feature-attribution-drift detection. In addition, we performed batch transformations to improve throughput for offline model predictions. We closed out with tips on how to reduce cost and improve performance using SageMaker Neo, Tensor-Flow Lite, SageMaker Multimodel Endpoints, and inference-optimized hardware such as EIA and AWS Inferentia.

In Chapter 10, we bring the feature engineering, model training, model validation, and model deploying steps into a single, unified, and end-to-end automated pipeline using SageMaker Pipelines, AWS Step Functions, Apache Airflow, Kubeflow, and various other open source options.

Pipelines and MLOps

In previous chapters, we demonstrated how to perform each individual step of a typical ML pipeline, including data ingestion, analysis, and feature engineering—as well as model training, tuning, and deploying.

In this chapter, we tie everything together into repeatable and automated pipelines using a complete machine learning operations (MLOps) solution with SageMaker Pipelines. We also discuss various pipeline-orchestration options, including AWS Step Functions, Kubeflow Pipelines, Apache Airflow, MLFlow, and TensorFlow Extended (TFX).

We will then dive deep into automating our SageMaker Pipelines when new code is committed, when new data arrives, or on a fixed schedule. We describe how to rerun a pipeline when we detect statistical changes in our deployed model, such as data drift or model bias. We will also discuss the concept of human-in-the-loop workflows, which can help to improve our model accuracy.

Machine Learning Operations

The complete model development life cycle typically requires close collaboration between the application, data science, and DevOps teams to successfully production-ize our models, as shown in Figure 10-1.

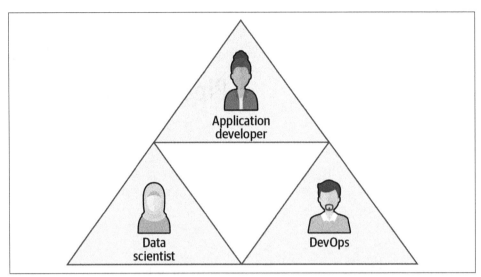

Figure 10-1. Productionizing machine learning applications requires collaboration between teams.

Typically, the data scientist delivers the trained model, the DevOps engineer manages the infrastructure that hosts the model as a REST API, and the application developer integrates the REST API into their applications. Each team must understand the needs and requirements of the other teams in order to implement an efficient workflow and smooth hand-off process.

MLOps has evolved through three stages of maturity:

MLOps v1.0
    Manually build, train, tune, and deploy models

MLOps v2.0
    Manually build and orchestrate model pipelines

MLOps v3.0
    Automatically run pipelines when new data arrives or code changes from deterministic triggers such as GitOps or when models start to degrade in performance based on statistical triggers such as drift, bias, and explainability divergence

In this chapter, we describe how SageMaker supports the complete MLOps strategy, including pipeline orchestration, deterministic automation from changes in data or code, and statistical automation from changes in drift, bias, or explainability.

Software Pipelines

In the early 2000s, software practitioners started to use continuous integration (CI) and continuous delivery (CD) to automatically build, test, and deploy their software modules directly and safely to production. CI and CD facilitated a low-friction collaboration between the DevOps engineers and software engineers. Prior to CI and CD, software engineers would hand their code "over the wall" to the DevOps engineer, who pushed the software to production after confirming successful integration test results in preproduction staging environments and coordinating with quality assurance (QA) teams, etc. An example software pipeline is shown in Figure 10-2.

Figure 10-2. Simple application deployment pipeline.

Jenkins is a popular open source tool for managing software pipelines. With its rich plug-in architecture, Jenkins can orchestrate complex CI/CD software pipelines and provide in-depth reports on the health of the pipeline at any point during the pipeline execution. For large code bases, pipeline execution can span many days, and components can fail for a variety of reasons. Jenkins provides mechanisms to restart any failed components and keep the pipeline running. Human intervention is often required, however. Jenkins supports manual, human-in-the-loop feedback as well.

In addition to restarts, sophisticated pipeline orchestration engines such as Jenkins support component caching strategies as well to improve pipeline execution performance. For example, if our pipeline fails during the integration test step because a remote system is unavailable, the orchestration engine can detect which pipeline steps have already run, reuse the cached results if no dependencies have changed, retry the failed step, and continue the pipeline to completion.

Machine Learning Pipelines

While CI and CD pipelines were built primarily to automate the software development cycle and improve the quality of application releases, they can also improve machine learning releases. ML engineers and data scientists seek to consistently and repeatedly train, test, and deploy models into production with little friction. This lets us spend more time on building and experimenting with new models versus manually retraining and redeploying existing models with the latest datasets.

Similar to CI and CD to efficiently update and improve software in production, machine learning pipelines automatically perform continuous training and CD for machine learning to efficiently update and improve models in production. Automated, reproducible, and parameterized pipelines help to maintain and track framework versions, container runtimes, and hardware throughout the entire process, from feature ingestion and feature engineering to model training and deployment.

Using automated ML pipelines instead of manual, one-off Python scripts will help to reduce subtle bugs that may creep into any step of the pipeline. For example, small changes to an upstream application may introduce data-quality issues such as star ratings outside the bounded and discrete value range between 1 (worst) and 5 (best).

While the model may appear to train successfully with poor-quality data, the model could negatively affect our business if pushed to production. By automating the data-quality checks before model training, we could raise a pipeline exception, notify the application team of the bad data, and save the cost of training a bad model.

We can also combine ML pipelines with artifact and experiment tracking for model reproducibility and auditing. Artifact tracking provides the lineage of deployed models all the way back to the original dataset version used during model training. Experiment tracking records the hyper-parameters used during training as well as the training results, such as model accuracy. The SageMaker Experiments and Lineage APIs are integrated throughout SageMaker to handle these scenarios.

Verifiable ML pipelines can help solve the problem of model degradation. Model degradation is a relatively common and underengineered scenario due to the complexity of monitoring models in production. Degrading model predictions results in poorly classified reviews and missed business opportunities.

By continually monitoring our model predictions with SageMaker Model Monitor and Clarify, we can detect shifts in data distributions, model bias, and model explainability—triggering a pipeline to retrain and deploy a new review-classifier model.

Figure 10-3 shows a sample machine learning pipeline mapped to AWS services, including S3, Data Wrangler, and SageMaker.

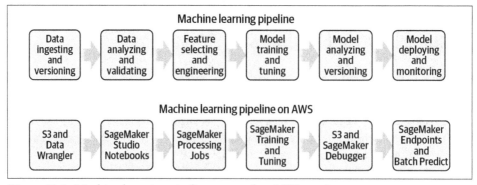

Figure 10-3. Machine learning pipeline mapped to AWS services.

Once the pipeline is running smoothly, we can increase velocity of experimentation by adding simultaneous pipelines to deploy multiple versions of the same model into production, as shown in Figure 10-4. This could be used for online A/B/C or multi-armed bandit (MAB) tests.

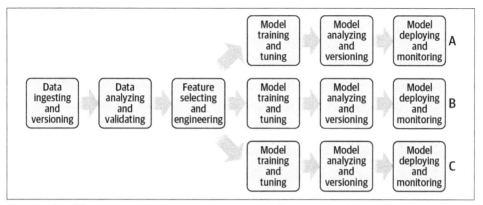

Figure 10-4. Training, tuning, and deploying multiple versions of the same model to improve experimentation velocity.

Components of Effective Machine Learning Pipelines

There are still many machine learning pipelines that include a high-friction step where the data scientist hands their model "over the wall" to the DevOps engineer or ML engineer to deploy. Machine learning pipelines are ripe for the type of revolution that stunned the software engineering community in the early 2000s.

Effective machine learning pipelines hide the details of the pipeline implementation and allow data science practitioners to focus on their business-specific, data science problem. Machine learning is continuous. The more we automate the process, the more we are free to solve additional business problems. Otherwise, we find ourselves manually rerunning one-off scripts every time new data arrives. While running a script is fairly simple, monitoring or restarting the script requires cognitive load that we could likely apply to higher-value tasks.

The ability to go from "ad hoc Jupyter notebook" to "repeatable machine learning pipeline" to "production cluster" is still a complex, error-prone, and underengineered workflow. However, we will provide some options on how to minimize the complexity and reduce errors with AWS.

Effective ML pipelines should include the following:

- Data-focused tasks such as data ingestion, data versioning, data-quality checking, data preprocessing, and feature engineering
- Model-building tasks such as model training, model-quality checking, and model versioning
- Automated model deployment, model scaling, model explaining, and bias detection
- Experiment and lineage tracking to work backward and reproduce any model version from scratch
- Automatic pickup of new data as it arrives (S3 `PutObject` event) and retraining—or perhaps automation using a cron-like timer (every night at midnight)
- Feedback mechanism to continuously improve the model in accordance with our business objectives and key results, such as increasing customer satisfaction by 10% in the next 12 months

In our experience, data-quality issues are the number-one cause of bad ML pipelines. In Chapter 5, we demonstrated how to use the AWS Deequ open source library to perform data-quality checks on our data as "step 0" of the ML pipeline. Without consistent and expected quality, our ML pipeline will, at best, fail quickly and minimize cost. At worst, poor-quality data will produce poor-quality models that may include bias and negatively impact our business.

In the beginning phases of ML exploration, we may not need a pipeline. The rigidity of a pipeline may seem too limiting. Pipelines are often deployed when we are ready to start training models regularly. If we are rapidly experimenting with many different types of features, models, and hyper-parameters, we may want to stay in the research lab until we are ready to automate for the long term and gain the benefits of regular pipeline executions, including data-quality checking, lineage tracking, and infrastructure scaling. However, even the simplest pipeline can help improve our model exploration.

Steps of an Effective Machine Learning Pipeline

The following is a collection of steps that make up an effective, modern machine learning pipeline. We will demonstrate how to perform each of these steps in AWS using SageMaker Pipelines, AWS Step Functions, Airflow, Kubeflow, and other open source options in the upcoming sections.

Data ingestion and versioning

Read the raw dataset from a data source such as a database, S3, or stream. Transform the dataset into a format that will be used in the next steps of the pipeline (i.e., CSV, Parquet, etc.) and version both the raw and transformed datasets.

Data analysis and validation

Analyze the quality and bias of the ingested dataset. Validate that the data is ready for the next pipeline steps.

Feature engineering

Transform the dataset into features such as BERT embeddings used by the next pipeline steps. Balance and split the dataset into train, validation, and test splits. Publish the features to a feature store to be used for both training and inference by the entire organization.

Model training and tuning

Train a model using the features created in the previous pipeline step as well as a set of hyper-parameters specific to the model's algorithm, analyze the accuracy of the model and hyper-parameters using the known validation dataset split, and repeat with different sets of hyper-parameters until the model accuracy is sufficient.

Model evaluation

Test the trained model using the known test dataset split, calculate additional metrics such as a confusion matrix and area under the curve, validate the model bias on different segments of the test dataset split (e.g., different product categories), and retrain and retune to reduce or remove bias.

Model version and deployment

Version the trained model along with the hyper-parameters and dataset splits and deploy the model into production as a real-time endpoint or batch prediction job.

Model feedback and skew detection

Analyze the model performance against business metrics (e.g., revenue increases, successful fraud detections, etc.), detect training-serving skew by analyzing the model inputs and outputs (predictions) relative to the training data baseline, and retrain the model if skew is detected.

Pipeline Orchestration with SageMaker Pipelines

SageMaker Pipelines is the most complete way to implement AI and machine learning pipelines on AWS. Let's build a pipeline for our BERT-based review classifier and perform many of the steps described in previous chapters, including data ingestion, feature engineering, model training, and model deployment, as shown in Figure 10-5.

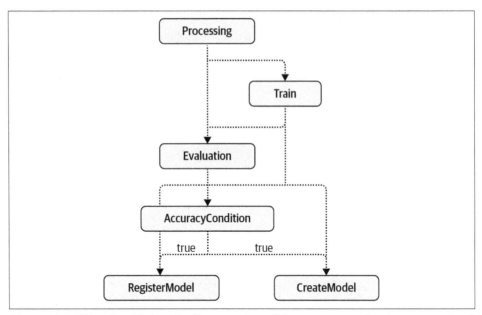

Figure 10-5. Using SageMaker Pipeline to train, validate, create, and register our trained BERT model.

Let's set up the pipeline programmatically using the SageMaker Python SDK to define each of the steps discussed earlier.

Create an Experiment to Track Our Pipeline Lineage

First, we create an experiment and trial to track and compare our pipeline runs:

```
import time
from smexperiments.experiment import Experiment

experiment_name = 'Experiment-{}'.format(int(time.time()))

experiment = Experiment.create(
                experiment_name=experiment_name,
                description='Amazon Customer Reviews BERT Pipeline Experiment',
                ...)

trial_name = 'trial-{}'.format(int(time.time()))

trial = Trial.create(trial_name=trial_name,
                    experiment_name=experiment_name,
                    ...)
```

Define Our Pipeline Steps

The first step of our pipeline is to transform the raw review text into BERT features using a SageMaker Processing Job. We will reuse the same `processor` from Chapter 6 but wrap it in a `ProcessingStep` from the SageMaker Pipeline Python SDK:

```
experiment_config_prepare = {
    'ExperimentName': experiment_name,
    'TrialName': trial_name,
    'TrialComponentDisplayName': 'prepare'
}

from sagemaker.processing import ProcessingInput, ProcessingOutput
from sagemaker.workflow.steps import ProcessingStep

processing_step = ProcessingStep(
    name='Processing',
    code='preprocess-scikit-text-to-bert-feature-store.py',
    processor=processor,
    inputs=processing_inputs,
    outputs=processing_outputs,
    job_arguments=['--train-split-percentage', \
                   str(train_split_percentage.),
                   '--validation-split-percentage', \
                   str(validation_split_percentage.),
                   '--test-split-percentage', \
                   str(test_split_percentage.),
                   '--max-seq-length', \
                   str(max_seq_length.),
                   '--balance-dataset', \
                   str(balance_dataset.),
                   '--feature-store-offline-prefix', \
                   str(feature_store_offline_prefix.),
                   '--feature-group-name', \
                   str(feature_group_name)
                   ]
)
```

Now let's train our model using the output from the previous feature-engineering processing step. We will use the same `estimator` from Chapter 7 but wrap it in a `TrainingStep` from the SageMaker Pipeline Python SDK:

```
from sagemaker.inputs import TrainingInput
from sagemaker.workflow.steps import TrainingStep

experiment_config_train = {
    'ExperimentName': experiment_name,
    'TrialName': trial_name,
    'TrialComponentDisplayName': 'train'
}

training_step = TrainingStep(
```

```python
    name='Train',
    estimator=estimator,
    inputs={
        'train': TrainingInput(
            s3_data=\
            processing_step.properties.ProcessingOutputConfig.Outputs[
                'bert-train'
            ].S3Output.S3Uri,
            content_type='text/csv'
        ),
        'validation': TrainingInput(
            s3_data=\
            processing_step.properties.ProcessingOutputConfig.Outputs[
                'bert-validation'
            ].S3Output.S3Uri,
            content_type='text/csv'
        ),
        'test': TrainingInput(
            s3_data=\
            processing_step.properties.ProcessingOutputConfig.Outputs[
                'bert-test'
            ].S3Output.S3Uri,
            content_type='text/csv'
        )
    }
)
```

Next, let's add a step to evaluate our model using a SageMaker Processing Job to calculate the model test accuracy with *evaluate_model_metrics.py* and write the results to a file called *evaluation.json* in S3. This file will be used by the next steps to conditionally register and prepare the model for deployment:

```python
from sagemaker.workflow.properties import PropertyFile

experiment_config_evaluate = {
    'ExperimentName': experiment_name,
    'TrialName': trial_name,
    'TrialComponentDisplayName': 'evaluate'
}

evaluation_report = PropertyFile(
    name='EvaluationReport',
    output_name='metrics',
    path='evaluation.json'
)

from sagemaker.sklearn.processing import SKLearnProcessor

evaluation_processor = SKLearnProcessor(
    framework_version='<SCIKIT_LEARN_VERSION>',
    role=role,
    ...)
```

```
evaluation_step = ProcessingStep(
    name='Evaluation',
    processor=evaluation_processor,
    code='evaluate_model_metrics.py',
    inputs=[
        ProcessingInput(
            source=\
            training_step.properties.ModelArtifacts.S3ModelArtifacts,
            destination='/opt/ml/processing/input/model'
        ),
        ProcessingInput(
            source=raw_input_data_s3_uri,
            destination='/opt/ml/processing/input/data'
        )
    ],
    outputs=[
        ProcessingOutput(output_name='metrics',
                         s3_upload_mode='EndOfJob',
                         source='/opt/ml/processing/output/metrics/'),
    ],
    job_arguments=[
                    '--max-seq-length', \
                    str(max_seq_length.default_value),
                    ],
    property_files=[evaluation_report],
    experiment_config=experiment_config_evaluate
)
```

The *evaluate_model_metrics.py* file downloads the model, runs a set of test predictions, and writes the results to *evaluation.json*, as shown in the following code:

```
def predict(text):
    encode_plus_tokens = tokenizer.encode_plus(
        text,
        pad_to_max_length=True,
        max_length=args.max_seq_length,
        truncation=True,
        return_tensors='tf')

    input_ids = encode_plus_tokens['input_ids']

    input_mask = encode_plus_tokens['attention_mask']
    outputs = model.predict(x=(input_ids, input_mask))
    scores = np.exp(outputs) / np.exp(outputs).sum(-1, keepdims=True)

    prediction = [{"label": config.id2label[item.argmax()],
                   "score": item.max().item()} for item in scores]

    return prediction[0]['label']
...

df_test_reviews = pd.read_csv(
```

```
        test_data_path,
        delimiter='\t',
        quoting=csv.QUOTE_NONE,
        compression='gzip')[['review_body', 'star_rating']]

    y_test = df_test_reviews['review_body'].map(predict)
    y_actual = df_test_reviews['star_rating']

    accuracy = accuracy_score(y_true=y_test, y_pred=y_actual)

    metrics_path = os.path.join(args.output_data, 'metrics/')

    os.makedirs(metrics_path, exist_ok=True)

    report_dict = {
        "metrics": {
            "accuracy": {
                "value": accuracy,
            },
        },
    }

    evaluation_path = "{}/evaluation.json".format(metrics_path)
    with open(evaluation_path, "w") as f:
        f.write(json.dumps(report_dict))
```

Let's register our trained model with the SageMaker Model Registry. Once the model is registered, our pipeline requires a manual-approval step to deploy the model to staging. We first need to capture the evaluation metrics generated from the previous evaluation step in a ModelMetrics Python object named model_metrics, as shown in the following:

```
from sagemaker.model_metrics import MetricsSource, ModelMetrics

model_metrics = ModelMetrics(
    model_statistics=MetricsSource(
        s3_uri="{}/evaluation.json".format(
            evaluation_step.arguments["ProcessingOutputConfig"]\
["Outputs"][0]["S3Output"]["S3Uri"]
        ),
        content_type="application/json"
    )
)
```

Let's pass model_metrics and create the RegisterModel step using the estimator from the previous TrainingStep. We can limit the instance types for both SageMaker Endpoints and Batch Transform Jobs by specifying lists for inference_instances and transform_instances, respectively:

```
from sagemaker.workflow.step_collections import RegisterModel

inference_image_uri = sagemaker.image_uris.retrieve(
```

```
        framework="tensorflow",
        region=region,
        version="<TENSORFLOW_VERSION>",
        py_version="<PYTHON_VERSION>",
        instance_type=deploy_instance_type,
        image_scope="inference"
)

register_step = RegisterModel(
    name="RegisterModel",
    estimator=estimator,
    image_uri=inference_image_uri,
     model_data=
         training_step.properties.ModelArtifacts.S3ModelArtifacts,
    content_types=["application/jsonlines"],
    response_types=["application/jsonlines"],
    inference_instances=["ml.m5.4xlarge"],
    transform_instances=["ml.c5.18xlarge"],
    model_package_group_name=model_package_group_name,
    model_metrics=model_metrics
)
```

Now we will write the `CreateModelStep` to wrap the SageMaker `Model` used by both our SageMaker Endpoint and Batch Transform Jobs:

```
from sagemaker.model import Model

model = Model(
    name=<MODEL_NAME>,
    image_uri=inference_image_uri,
    model_data=
        training_step.properties.ModelArtifacts.S3ModelArtifacts,
    ...
)

from sagemaker.inputs import CreateModelInput

create_inputs = CreateModelInput(
    instance_type="ml.m5.4xlarge",
)

from sagemaker.workflow.steps import CreateModelStep

create_step = CreateModelStep(
    name="CreateModel",
    model=model,
    inputs=create_inputs,
)
```

Let's add a `ConditionStep` to compare the evaluation accuracy metrics against a threshold. Our pipeline will register, create, and prepare the model for deployment only if the model accuracy exceeds the given threshold of 95%, as shown here:

```
from sagemaker.workflow.conditions import ConditionGreaterThanOrEqualTo

from sagemaker.workflow.condition_step import (
    ConditionStep,
    JsonGet,
)

minimum_accuracy_condition = ConditionGreaterThanOrEqualTo(
    left=JsonGet(
        step=evaluation_step,
        property_file=evaluation_report,
        json_path="metrics.accuracy.value",
    ),
    right=0.95 # 95% accuracy
)

minimum_accuracy_condition_step = ConditionStep(
    name="AccuracyCondition",
    conditions=[minimum_accuracy_condition],
     # success, continue with model registration
    if_steps=[register_step, create_step],
    # fail, end the pipeline
    else_steps=[],
)
```

Configure the Pipeline Parameters

Before creating our pipeline, we must define parameter placeholders to use across all steps in our pipeline with `ParameterInteger`, `ParameterString`, and `Parameter Float` from the SageMaker Pipelines Python SDK. These are merely placeholders for now because we are defining the pipeline. When we start the pipeline, we will specify the exact value to use for each parameter—or use the `default_value` if a value is not provided:

```
from sagemaker.workflow.parameters import (
    ParameterInteger,
    ParameterString,
    ParameterFloat,
)

input_data = ParameterString(
    name="InputData",
    default_value=raw_input_data_s3_uri,
)
...
max_seq_length = ParameterInteger(
    name="MaxSeqLength",
    default_value=64,
)
...
learning_rate = ParameterFloat(
```

```
    name="LearningRate",
    default_value=0.00001,
)
...
```

Create the Pipeline

Next, we create the pipeline using all of the previously defined steps. This includes the processing_step, training_step, evaluation_step, as well as the minimum_accuracy_condition_step, which conditionally calls the register_step and create_step if the model achieves a minimum accuracy of 95% during model evaluation:

```
pipeline = Pipeline(
    name=<PIPELINE_NAME>,
    parameters=[
        input_data, # InputData
        ...
        max_seq_length, # MaxSeqLength
        ...
        learning_rate, # LearningRate
        ...
    ],
    steps=[processing_step, training_step, evaluation_step, \
            minimum_accuracy_condition_step]
)

pipeline.create(role_arn=role)
```

Start the Pipeline with the Python SDK

Finally, we start the Pipeline by providing the desired parameter values, including the S3 location of the reviews dataset, maximum sequence length of the BERT tokens, and learning rate of the TensorFlow gradient-descent optimizer:

```
execution = pipeline.start(
    InputData=raw_input_data_s3_uri,
    MaxSeqLength=64,
    LearningRate=0.000012,
    ...
)
```

Start the Pipeline with the SageMaker Studio UI

We can also trigger a SageMaker Pipeline execution through the SageMaker Studio UI, as shown in Figure 10-6. The Studio UI presents input fields for each of the parameters defined in our Pipeline object.

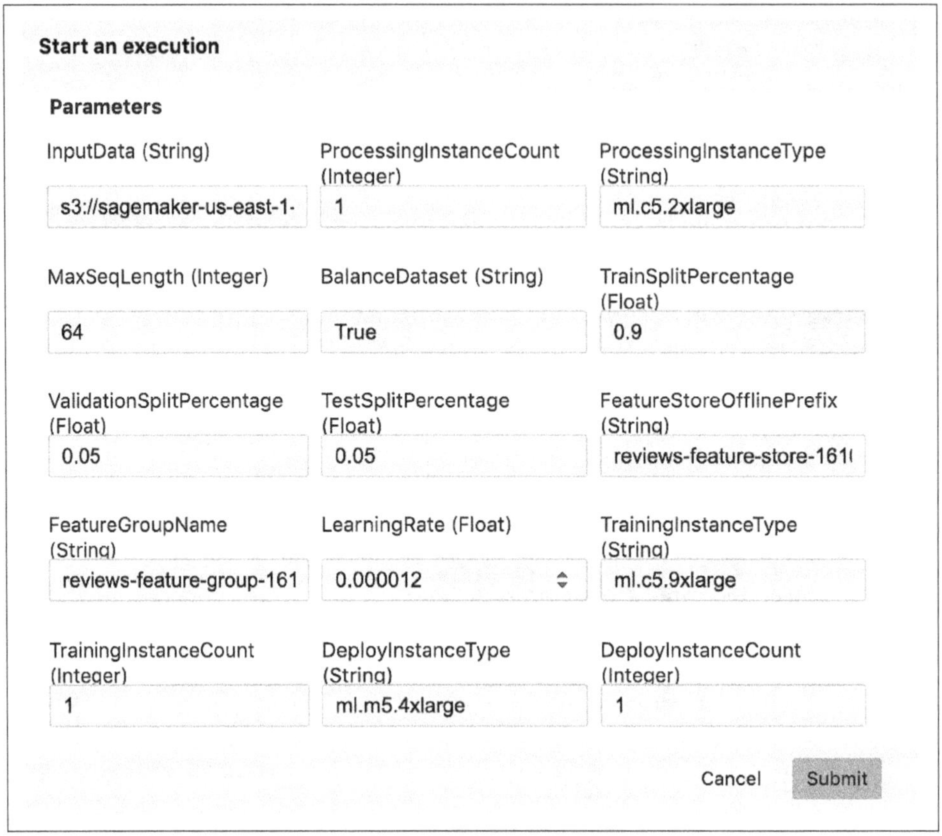

Figure 10-6. Start a pipeline execution through SageMaker Studio UI.

Approve the Model for Staging and Production

We can approve models through the SageMaker Model Registry either manually through the SageMaker Studio UI or programmatically through our notebook. Approving the model will automatically deploy the model to a staging environment for testing. Our pipeline then requires a separate approval to move the model from staging to production if testing is successful. We can programmatically approve the model to staging using the following code:

```
for execution_step in execution.list_steps():
    if execution_step['StepName'] == 'RegisterModel':
        model_package_arn =
            execution_step['Metadata']['RegisterModel']['Arn']
        break

model_package_update_response = sm.update_model_package(
    ModelPackageArn=model_package_arn,
```

```
        ModelApprovalStatus="Approved",
)
```

Review the Pipeline Artifact Lineage

We can review the artifact lineage directly either through the SageMaker Studio UI or programmatically in our notebook with the Python SDK. Following is the code to list the artifacts across all steps, including feature engineering, model training, evaluation, approval, and deployment:

```
import time
from sagemaker.lineage.visualizer import LineageTableVisualizer

viz = LineageTableVisualizer(sagemaker.session.Session())
for execution_step in reversed(execution.list_steps()):
    if execution_step['StepName'] == 'Processing':
        processing_job_name=
            execution_step['Metadata']['ProcessingJob']['Arn']\
            .split('/')[-1]
        display(viz.show(processing_job_name=processing_job_name))
    else:
        display(viz.show(pipeline_execution_step=execution_step))
        time.sleep(5)
```

The output is similar to the following table:

	Name/source	Direction	Type	Association type	Lineage type
0	preprocess-scikit-text-to-bert-feature-store.py	Input	DataSet	ContributedTo	artifact
1	s3://.../amazon-reviews-pds/tsv/	Input	DataSet	ContributedTo	artifact
2	68331...om/sagemaker-scikit-learn:0.23-1-cpu-py3	Input	Image	ContributedTo	artifact
3	s3://.../output/bert-test	Output	DataSet	Produced	artifact
4	s3://.../output/bert-validation	Output	DataSet	Produced	artifact
5	s3://.../output/bert-train	Output	DataSet	Produced	artifact
6	s3://.../output/bert-test	Input	DataSet	ContributedTo	artifact
7	s3://.../output/bert-validation	Input	DataSet	ContributedTo	artifact
8	s3://.../output/bert-train	Input	DataSet	ContributedTo	artifact
9	76310.../tensorflow-training:2.3.1-cpu-py37	Input	Image	ContributedTo	artifact
10	model.tar.gz	Output	Model	Produced	artifact
11	model.tar.gz	Input	Model	ContributedTo	artifact
12	76310.../tensorflow-inference:2.1.0-cpu	Input	Image	ContributedTo	artifact
13	bert-reviews-1610437484-1-Approved-1610443150-aws-model-group	Input	Approval	ContributedTo	action
14	bert-reviews-1610437484-1-Approved-1610443150-aws-endpoint	Output	ModelDeployment	ContributedTo	action
15	bert-reviews-1610437484-1-aws-model-group	Output	ModelGroup	AssociatedWith	context

Review the Pipeline Experiment Lineage

Using the SageMaker Experiments API, we can show the experiment lineage of our pipeline through all steps of the pipeline, including feature engineering, model training, evaluation, and deployment, as shown in the following:

```
from sagemaker.analytics import ExperimentAnalytics

experiment_analytics = ExperimentAnalytics(
    experiment_name=experiment_name,
)

experiment_analytics.dataframe()
```

TrialComponentName	DisplayName	max_seq_ length	learning_ rate	train_ accuracy	test_ accuracy	endpoint_ name
pipelines-0tsa93mahu8v-processing-kch2vw03qc-aws-processing-job	prepare	64.0	NaN	NaN	NaN	
pipelines-0tsa93mahu8v-Train-tlvC7YdBl9-aws-training-job	train	64.0	0.000017	0.9416	NaN	
pipelines-1daa23hlku3v-processing-hkc9wOvOq-aws-processing-job	evaluate	64.0	NaN	NaN	0.9591	
TrialComponent-2021-01-09214921-dgtu	deploy	NaN	NaN	NaN	NaN	bert-reviews-1610437484-endpoint

Automation with SageMaker Pipelines

There are two main ways to automatically start a pipeline: event-based triggers and time-based triggers. Event-based triggers will start a pipeline when a particular event occurs, for example, when a new *train.py* is committed to our Git-based code repository. This is often called "GitOps" automation. We can also start a new pipeline when new data arrives into S3 from a `PutObject` event. Time-based triggers will start the pipeline on a schedule, such as every week, every two days, or every four hours. Let's discuss how to implement GitOps, S3, and time-based triggers to automatically start a SageMaker Pipeline.

GitOps Trigger When Committing Code

SageMaker implements GitOps pipeline automation through SageMaker Projects. SageMaker Projects come with pre-built MLOps templates that automate the model-building and deployment pipelines. We can customize the templates, or create our own templates, as needed.

We can create our own project by selecting one of the pre-built MLOps templates provided by SageMaker or by using our own custom template that we provide. The MLOps templates use AWS CloudFormation to automatically set up all required components for our GitOps automation workflow with SageMaker Pipelines. The MLOps template also sets up a trigger to run the pipeline each time we commit new code to the code repositories.

There are two main components of our MLOps template for SageMaker Pipelines: `modelbuild` and `modeldeploy`. The `modelbuild` component builds and registers the model. The `modeldeploy` component deploys the model to staging and production. Deploying the model to production requires a second manual approval step, as shown in Figure 10-7.

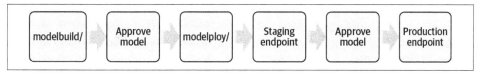

Figure 10-7. MLOps pipeline to deploy models to both staging and production with manual approvals.

The separation of `modelbuild` and `modeldeploy` allows for a separation of responsibility and access control. For example, the data scientist may be responsible for the `modelbuild` phase to push the model into staging, while the DevOps team is responsible for the `modeldeploy` phase to push the model into production.

S3 Trigger When New Data Arrives

As new data arrives into the system—directly from an application or through data streaming services like Kinesis Streams and Managed Streaming for Apache Kafka—we may want to continuously run our pipeline and update our models to include the new data. While it's perfectly acceptable to manually run our pipelines every week, day, or even hour, we can easily automate the pipeline as new data lands in S3 from an upstream application, as shown in Figure 10-8.

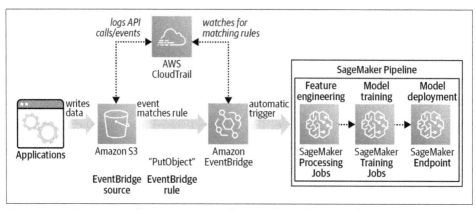

Figure 10-8. Automatically start a SageMaker Pipeline when new data arrives in S3.

First, we need to be notified when new data arrives in S3 by enabling AWS CloudTrail data-event logging on our S3 bucket:

```
watched_bucket_arn=<S3_BUCKET_ARN_TO_WATCH>

event_selector=\
'\'[{ "ReadWriteType": "WriteOnly", "IncludeManagementEvents":true, \
    "DataResources": \
        [{ "Type": "AWS::S3::Object", \
            "Values": ["' + watched_bucket_arn + '"]
        }]
    }]\''

!aws cloudtrail put-event-selectors \
    --trail-name $trail_name \
    --event-selectors $event_selector
```

Next, we will create an Amazon EventBridge rule to trigger the SageMaker Pipeline every time new files are uploaded to the S3 bucket using an EventBridge rule that matches both the S3 `PutObject` and `CompleteMultipartUpload`. Here is the Python code to enable this behavior:

```
events = boto3.client('events')
watched_bucket=<S3_BUCKET_NAME_TO_WATCH>

pattern = {
  "source": [
    "aws.s3"
  ],
  "detail-type": [
    "AWS API Call via CloudTrail"
  ],
  "detail": {
    "eventSource": [
      "s3.amazonaws.com"
```

```
        ],
        "eventName": [
          "PutObject",
          "CompleteMultipartUpload",
          "CopyObject"
        ],
        "requestParameters": {
          "bucketName": [
            "{}".format(watched_bucket)
          ]
        }
      }
    }
  }

response = events.put_rule(
    Name='S3-Trigger',
    EventPattern=json.dumps(pattern),
    State='ENABLED',
    Description='Triggers an event on S3 PUT',
    EventBusName='default'
)
```

Lastly, we associate the rule with an AWS Lambda function to start our pipeline when the rule is matched:

```
response = events.put_targets(
    Rule='S3-Trigger',
    EventBusName='default',
    Targets=[
        {
            'Id': '1',
            'Arn': lambda_arn,
            'RoleArn': iam_role_eventbridge_arn,
        }
    ]
)
```

Here is an excerpt of the AWS Lambda function used to trigger our SageMaker pipeline:

```
sm = boto3.client('sagemaker', region_name=region)

timestamp = int(time.time())

def lambda_handler(event, context):
    response = sm.start_pipeline_execution(
        PipelineName=<PIPELINE_NAME>,
        PipelineExecutionDisplayName='<PIPELINE_EXECUTION_DISPLAY_NAME>',
        PipelineParameters=[
                ...
        ]
    )
```

Anytime a new file is uploaded to this S3 bucket, EventBridge will trigger the rule and start our pipeline execution. We can use the lambda_handler function's event variable to find out the exact file that was uploaded and, perhaps, incrementally train our model on just that new file. Depending on our use case, we may not want to start a new pipeline for every file uploaded to S3. However, this is a good starting point to build our own rules and triggers from many AWS services.

 At the time of this writing, there was no native integration between EventBridge and SageMaker Pipelines, so we need to use a Lambda function shim. However, there will likely be native integration by the time this book is published, so we may be able to skip the Lambda function and integrate EventBridge directly with Sage-Maker Pipelines.

Time-Based Schedule Trigger

We may want to trigger our pipeline on batches of data over a specific period of time, such as hourly, daily, monthly, etc. Similar to configuring a cron job, we can create an EventBridge rule to run our pipeline on a schedule. We can specify the schedule using familiar cron syntax or by defining a fixed rate, such as every hour. Or we can programmatically define the schedule using the AWS Python SDK for EventBridge. The following code triggers the pipeline to run every hour:

```
events = boto3.client('events')

response = events.put_rule(
        Name='Hourly_Time_Based_Trigger',
        ScheduleExpression='rate(1 hour)',
        State='ENABLED',
        Description='Hourly Time-Based Trigger',
        EventBusName='default'
)
```

Statistical Drift Trigger

We can also start a new pipeline if SageMaker Model Monitor detects data-quality drift, model-quality drift, bias drift, or explainability drift relative to a given baseline or ground truth set of predicted labels. We can create baselines for data quality, model quality, model bias, and feature importances and monitor our deployed models with SageMaker Model Monitor, as discussed in Chapter 9.

Model Monitor captures the real-time model predictions and analyzes the data distributions for model inputs and model outputs in comparison to the baseline thresholds learned from the training data. This helps us to detect statistical changes such as covariate shift or concept drift that may trigger a new pipeline execution to retrain the model.

Model Monitor integrates with SageMaker Clarify. With Clarify, SageMaker continuously monitors the deployed models for changes in model bias and feature importances. We define a confidence range of bias metrics for our models based on the offline training data. We continually monitor the confidence intervals seen in the model's online predictions. If the observed confidence interval doesn't overlap with the defined confidence range, SageMaker Clarify will trigger a bias-drift alert that we can use to start a new pipeline. Similarly, if the changes in feature importances cross a defined threshold, SageMaker Clarify will trigger a feature attribution drift alert, which we can use to start a new pipeline.

More Pipeline Options

While SageMaker Pipelines is the standard way to implement AI and machine learning pipelines on AWS, we also present AWS Step Functions and various open source options such as Kubeflow Pipelines, Apache Airflow, TFX, and MLflow. These tools provide great support for AWS data stores, including Amazon S3, Athena, EMR, EFS, and FSx for Lustre.

AWS Step Functions and the Data Science SDK

Step Functions is a great option for building complex workflows without having to build and maintain our own infrastructure. While Step Functions were not specifically designed for machine learning, they provide great flexibility and deep integration with many AWS services, and expose the Step Functions Data Science SDK.

Figure 10-9 shows a Step Function Pipeline that was built to orchestrate the same BERT-based review-classifier pipeline shown in the SageMaker Pipelines section.

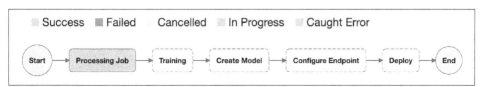

Figure 10-9. Step Function Pipeline to orchestrate our BERT-based pipeline on SageMaker.

Here is an excerpt from the Step Function configuration for the training step of our pipeline. The complete code is in the GitHub repository associated with this book:

```
"Training": {
  "AlgorithmSpecification": {
    "TrainingImage": "<TENSORFLOW_IMAGE_URI>".format(region),
    "TrainingInputMode": "{}".format(input_mode)
  },
  "HyperParameters": {
    "epochs": "{}".format(epochs),
```

```
        "learning_rate": "{}".format(learning_rate),
        "epsilon": "{}".format(epsilon),
        ...
    }
      }
    }
```

Kubeflow Pipelines

Kubeflow is a popular machine learning ecosystem built on Kubernetes that includes an orchestration subsystem called *Kubeflow Pipelines*. While Kubeflow requires us to build and maintain our own Amazon EKS clusters, it is well supported in AWS, as shown in Figure 10-10.

Figure 10-10. Kubeflow is well supported on AWS due to tight integration with Amazon EKS.

With Kubeflow, we can run distributed training jobs, analyze training metrics, track pipeline lineage, restart failed pipelines, and schedule pipeline runs. The conventions used in Kubeflow are well defined and well supported by a large community of open source contributors across many organizations. If we are already using Kubernetes, Kubeflow may be a good option to manage our pipelines.

While managing Kubernetes is fun to some folks—including the authors of this book
—it is a distraction from everyday data science and engineering tasks. The authors of
this book have spent many nights and weekends troubleshooting Kubernetes-level
issues—time that could have been spent engineering more features and training better models.

Because of Kubeflow's tight integration with Kubernetes, almost every question about
managing and scaling a Kubeflow cluster can be answered by reviewing Kubernetes
and Amazon EKS features. Here are some examples:

Question: "How do I monitor the GPUs in my Kubeflow training jobs?"

Answer: "The same way you monitor other system resources in Kubernetes on AWS:
Prometheus, Grafana, and CloudWatch."

Question: "How do I auto-scale my Kubeflow REST endpoints?"

Answer: "The same way you auto-scale other Kubernetes resources on AWS: Horizontal Pod Autoscaling, Cluster Autoscaling, and CloudWatch."

Question: "Does Kubeflow support Spot Instances?"

Answer: "Yes, because Amazon EKS supports Spot Instances."

It's worth noting that when using Spot Instances to train a model
with Kubeflow, we must use a framework that tolerates the Spot
Instances leaving the cluster (during a training job) as they are
replaced when new Spot Instances become available. When the
Spot Instances are replaced, they are removed from the cluster and
appear as failed instances to the training job. Modern frameworks
such as TensorFlow, PyTorch, and Apache MXNet support instance
failures but require extra code and configuration to perform the
checkpointing needed to efficiently recover from the failure and
continue training. We demonstrated the TensorFlow code and
SageMaker configuration for checkpointing in Chapter 8.

Let's create an open source Kubeflow pipeline that trains a BERT model using managed Amazon SageMaker and the same Amazon Customer Reviews Dataset from the
previous chapters, as shown in Figure 10-11.

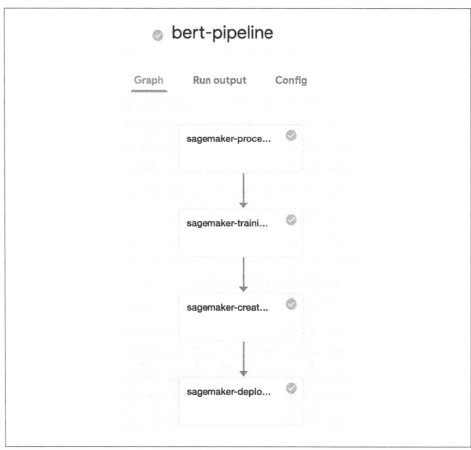

Figure 10-11. Kubeflow pipeline orchestrating our BERT-based pipeline on SageMaker.

First, we import the SageMaker Components for Kubeflow Pipelines Python library and supporting assets to use in our Kubeflow Pipeline. The following YAML can be found on GitHub (*https://oreil.ly/Uh4Ls*):

```
sagemaker_process_op = components.load_component_from_url( \
        'components/aws/sagemaker/process/component.yaml')

sagemaker_train_op = components.load_component_from_url(
        'components/aws/sagemaker/train/component.yaml')

sagemaker_model_op = components.load_component_from_url(
        'components/aws/sagemaker/model/component.yaml')

sagemaker_deploy_op = components.load_component_from_url(
        'components/aws/sagemaker/deploy/component.yaml')
```

Now let's set up the S3 locations of the raw training data:

```
def processing_input(input_name,
                     s3_uri,
                     local_path,
                     s3_data_distribution_type):
    return {
        "InputName": input_name,
        "S3Input": {
            "LocalPath": local_path,
            "S3Uri": s3_uri,
            "S3DataType": "S3Prefix",
            "S3DataDistributionType": s3_data_distribution_type,
            "S3InputMode": "File",
        },
    }
```

Let's define the S3 locations of the transformed features:

```
def processing_output(output_name, s3_uri,
                      local_path, s3_upload_mode):
    return {
        "OutputName": output_name,
        "S3Output": {
            "LocalPath": local_path,
            "S3Uri": s3_uri,
            "S3UploadMode": s3_upload_mode
        },
    }
```

Let's define the actual Kubeflow Pipeline using the Kubeflow Pipelines Python SDK:

```
@dsl.pipeline(
    name="BERT Pipeline",
    description="BERT Pipeline",
)
def bert_pipeline(role=role,
                  bucket=bucket,
                  region=region,
                  raw_input_data_s3_uri=<RAW_DATA_S3_URI>):
```

Let's transform the raw input data to BERT features:

```
    # Training input and output location based on bucket name
    process = sagemaker_process_op(
        ...
        container_arguments=['--train-split-percentage',
                             str(train_split_percentage),
                             '--validation-split-percentage',
                             str(validation_split_percentage),
                             '--test-split-percentage',
                             str(test_split_percentage),
                             '--max-seq-length',
                             str(max_seq_length),
                             '--balance-dataset',
                             str(balance_dataset)])
```

Let's train the model:

```
hyperparameters={
    'epochs': '{}'.format(epochs),
    'learning_rate': '{}'.format(learning_rate),
    'epsilon': '{}'.format(epsilon),
    ...
}
hyperparameters_json = json.dumps(hyperparameters)

training = sagemaker_train_op(
    hyperparameters=hyperparameters_json,
    ...
).after(process)
```

Deploy the BERT model as a REST-based SageMaker Endpoint:

```
create_model = sagemaker_model_op(
    model_name=training.outputs["job_name"],
    model_artifact_url=training.outputs["model_artifact_url"],
    ...
)

deploy_model = sagemaker_deploy_op(
    variant_name_1='AllTraffic',
    model_name_1=create_model.output,
    instance_type_1=deploy_instance_type,
    initial_instance_count_1=deploy_instance_count
)
```

Let's compile and run the Kubeflow Pipeline, which results in a deployed SageMaker Endpoint with our BERT model:

```
kfp.compiler.Compiler().compile(bert_pipeline, 'bert-pipeline.zip')

client = kfp.Client()

experiment = client.create_experiment(name='kubeflow')

my_run = client.run_pipeline(experiment.id,
                             'bert-pipeline',
                             'bert-pipeline.zip')
```

Let's invoke the SageMaker Endpoint and get a star rating prediction from the review text:

```
sm_runtime =
boto3.Session(region_name=region).client('sagemaker-runtime')

review = "This is great!".encode('utf-8')

response = sm_runtime.invoke_endpoint(
    EndpointName=endpoint_name,
    ContentType='application/jsonlines',
```

```
    Body=review)

json.loads(response['Body'].read().decode())

### OUTPUT ###
{'predicted_label': 5}
```

Apache Airflow

Apache Airflow is a very mature and popular option initially developed to orchestrate data engineering and extract-transform-load (ETL) pipelines for analytics workloads. However, Airflow has expanded into the machine-learning space as a viable pipeline orchestrator. Amazon supports Amazon Managed Workflows for Apache Airflow to reduce the operational burden of running Airflow clusters on AWS.

With a large library of third-party plug-ins and native integration with many AWS services, Amazon MWAA is a great option for managing pipelines on AWS with Airflow. If we are already using Airflow for our data engineering and ETL pipelines, Airflow may be a good option to orchestrate our machine learning pipelines. Figure 10-12 shows our BERT-based review-classifier pipeline implemented as an Apache Airflow directed acyclic graph (DAG) using Amazon MWAA and SageMaker.

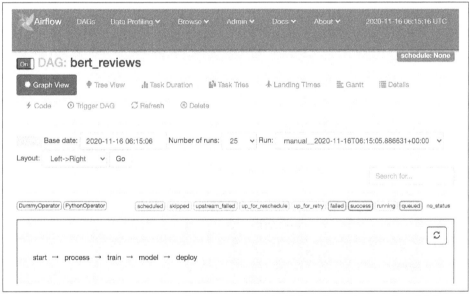

Figure 10-12. Amazon MWAA orchestrating our BERT-based pipeline on SageMaker.

Let's demonstrate how to build an Airflow DAG with SageMaker to orchestrate our BERT-based machine learning pipeline. First, we need to define the Airflow DAG:

```
import airflow
from airflow import DAG

default_args = {
    'owner': 'airflow',
    'provide_context': True
}

dag = DAG('bert_reviews',
          default_args=default_args,
          schedule_interval='@once')
```

Next, let's transform the raw data into BERT features:

```
from airflow.contrib.operators.sagemaker_processing_operator \
        import SageMakerProcessingOperator
from sagemaker.workflow.airflow import processing_config

process_config = processing_config(estimator=estimator,
                                   inputs=input_data_s3_uri,
                                   outputs=output_data_s3_uri)

process_op = SageMakerProcessingOperator(
    task_id='process',
    config=process_config,
    wait_for_completion=True,
    dag=dag)
```

Let's train the model:

```
import sagemaker
from sagemaker.tensorflow import TensorFlow

estimator = TensorFlow(
    entry_point='tf_bert_reviews.py',
    source_dir='src',
    role=role,
    instance_count=train_instance_count,
    instance_type=train_instance_type,
    volume_size=train_volume_size,
    use_spot_instances=True,
    # Seconds to wait for spot instances to become available
    max_wait=7200,
    checkpoint_s3_uri=checkpoint_s3_uri,
    py_version='<PYTHON_VERSION>',
    framework_version='<TENSORFLOW_VERSION>',
    hyperparameters={
        'epochs': epochs,
        'learning_rate': learning_rate,
        'epsilon': epsilon,

        ...
    },
    input_mode=input_mode,
    metric_definitions=metrics_definitions,
```

```
        rules=rules,
        debugger_hook_config=hook_config,
        max_run=7200, # number of seconds
    )


    from airflow.contrib.operators.sagemaker_training_operator \
            import SageMakerTrainingOperator
    from sagemaker.workflow.airflow import training_config

    train_config = training_config(estimator=estimator,
                                   inputs=training_data_s3_uri)

    train_op = SageMakerTrainingOperator(
        task_id='train',
        config=train_config,
        wait_for_completion=True,
        dag=dag)
```

Now let's deploy the model:

```
    from airflow.contrib.operators.sagemaker_model_operator \
        import SageMakerModelOperator
    from sagemaker.workflow.airflow import model_config

    model_op = SageMakerModelOperator(
        task_id='model',
        config=model_config,
        wait_for_completion=True,
        dag=dag)

    from airflow.contrib.operators.sagemaker_endpoint_operator \
            import SageMakerEndpointOperator

    from sagemaker.workflow.airflow import endpoint_config

    deploy_op = SageMakerEndpointOperator(
        task_id='deploy',
        config=endpoint_config,
        wait_for_completion=True,
        dag=dag)
```

Let's define the pipeline:

```
    init.set_downstream(process_op)
    processing_op.set_downstream(train_op)
    train_op.set_downstream(model_op)
    model_op.set_downstream(deploy_op)
```

MLflow

MLflow is an open source project that offers experiment tracking and multiframe-work support including Apache Spark, but limited workflow support. While MLflow has some nice features, it requires us to build and maintain our own Amazon EC2 or EKS clusters. If we need a lightweight, simple way to track experiments and run simple workflows, MLflow may be a good choice.

TensorFlow Extended

TFX is an open source collection of Python libraries used within a pipeline orchestrator such as Kubeflow Pipelines, Apache Airflow, and MLflow. At a very high level, TFX is a collection of Python libraries that addresses every step of the machine learning pipeline. Most used within the TensorFlow community, TFX does have limited support for other frameworks, such as scikit-learn. If we are already using Tensor-Flow and looking to add some structure to our process, TFX may be a good choice for us. However, to scale, tune, and manage TFX beyond a single node, we should understand Apache Beam, which powers TFX's distributed data processing. Apache Beam has a bit of a learning curve but is pretty straightforward once you dive into it. Figure 10-13 shows the different libraries and components of TFX.

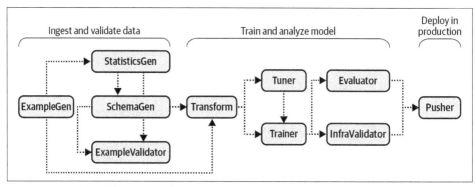

Figure 10-13. TFX libraries and components.

Human-in-the-Loop Workflows

While AI and machine learning services make our lives easier, humans are far from being obsolete. In fact, the concept of "human-in-the-loop" has emerged as an important cornerstone in many AI/ML workflows. Humans provide necessary quality assurances before pushing sensitive or regulated models into production. We can also leverage human intelligence by "crowdsourcing" data labeling tasks to humans.

We describe two services, Amazon A2I and SageMaker Ground Truth, that demonstrate how humans and AI can work successfully together. Amazon A2I enables

---

machine learning practitioners to integrate human review workflows into their applications. SageMaker Ground Truth leverages human workforces combined with an active learning approach to create accurate training datasets.

Improving Model Accuracy with Amazon A2I

Amazon A2I is a fully managed service to develop human-in-the-loop workflows, which include a user interface, role-based access control with IAM, and data storage with S3. Amazon A2I is integrated with services such as Amazon Rekognition for content moderation and Amazon Textract for form-data extraction. Figure 10-14 illustrates an Amazon A2I workflow to review model predictions from Amazon Comprehend. We can also use Amazon A2I with Amazon SageMaker and custom ML models.

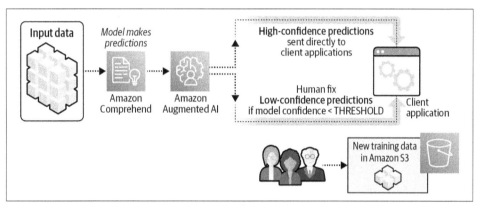

Figure 10-14. Amazon Augmented AI workflow to review model predictions.

In this example, Amazon Comprehend receives input data in a prediction request. We set a confidence threshold that defines when to involve the human reviewers. If the model's prediction meets the confidence threshold, Amazon A2I will send the prediction result directly to the client application. In case the model is unable to make a high-confidence prediction, Amazon A2I sends the task to human reviewers.

In our example of classifying product reviews, a low-confidence prediction could wrongly classify negative reviews as neutral or positive reviews. Our business may be negatively affected if we do not have an automated way to fix these low-confidence predictions and improve our model.

We may also want to randomly audit a sample of all predictions—both low and high confidence. This could be important for models that make critical decisions, for example in the healthcare/medical sector. In such situations, we probably want to have humans review and audit high-confidence predictions as well to make sure the model performs correctly.

Amazon A2I consolidates the human reviewer results and sends the final prediction response to the client application. Amazon A2I can also store the human review results in S3, which we could use as new training data.

Amazon A2I introduces a few new terms: Worker Task Template, Flow Definition, and Human Loop. The Worker Task Template defines the Human Task UI for the worker. This UI displays input data and instructions for workers. The Flow Definition defines the human review workflow. The definition contains the chosen workforce and provides information about how to accomplish the review task. The Human Loop represents the actual human review workflow. Once the human loop is triggered, Amazon A2I sends the human review tasks to the workers as specified in the flow definition.

Let's define some sample product reviews that we will send to Amazon Comprehend:

```
sample_reviews = [
                  'I enjoy this product',
                  'I am unhappy with this product',
                  'It is okay',
                  'sometimes it works'
                  ]
```

We also define a prediction confidence score threshold of 70%, which works well for our use case. If our model returns a prediction with a lower confidence score, Amazon A2I will trigger the human loop and our workforce team receives a task:

```
human_loops_started = []

CONFIDENCE_SCORE_THRESHOLD = 0.70

for sample_review in sample_reviews:
    # Call the Comprehend Custom model
    response = comprehend.classify_document(
            Text=sample_review,
            EndpointArn=comprehend_endpoint_arn)

    star_rating = response['Classes'][0]['Name']
    confidence_score = response['Classes'][0]['Score']

    print(f'Processing sample_review: \"{sample_review}\"')

    # Our condition for when we want to engage a human for review
    if (confidence_score < CONFIDENCE_SCORE_THRESHOLD):

        humanLoopName = str(uuid.uuid4())
        inputContent = {
            'initialValue': star_rating,
            'taskObject': sample_review
        }
        start_loop_response = a2i.start_human_loop(
            HumanLoopName=humanLoopName,
```

```
        FlowDefinitionArn=flowDefinitionArn,
        HumanLoopInput={
            'InputContent': json.dumps(inputContent)
        }
    )

    human_loops_started.append(humanLoopName)

    print(f'Confidence score of {confidence_score} for star rating of \
            {star_rating} is less than the threshold of \
            {CONFIDENCE_SCORE_THRESHOLD}')
    print(f'Confidence score of {confidence_score} for star rating of \
            {star_rating} is above threshold of \
            {CONFIDENCE_SCORE_THRESHOLD}')
    print('No human loop created. \n')
```

If we run this code, we will see the following responses:

```
Processing sample_review: "I enjoy this product"
Confidence score of 0.8727718591690063 for star rating of 3 is
  above threshold of 0.7
No human loop created.

Processing sample_review: "I am unhappy with this product"
Confidence score of 0.8727718591690063 for star rating of 3 is
  above threshold of 0.7
*** ==> Starting human loop with name: 72331439-0df9-4190-a42b-3e4048efb0a9

Processing sample_review: "It is okay"
Confidence score of 0.9679936170578003 for star rating of 4 is
        above threshold of 0.7
No human loop created.

Processing sample_review: "sometimes it works"
Confidence score of 0.6361567974090576 for star rating of 3 is
        less than the threshold of 0.7
*** ==> Starting human loop with name: e7994a4c-57bf-4578-aa27-dc5fb8c11d36
```

We see that two predictions didn't meet our confidence threshold and started human loops. When the assigned worker logs into the review system, the worker sees the submitted review tasks.

With Augmented AI, we can choose between a public or private workforce. Public workforces integrate with the Amazon Mechanical Turk service with hundreds of thousands of human labelers that have been pre-screened by Amazon. We can also use third-party, pre-screened workforce providers listed on the AWS Marketplace. Or we create private workforces with co-workers or employees.

The instructions are "Classify Reviews into Star Ratings Between 1 (Worst) and 5 (Best)." The worker sees the input data "sometimes it works" and might classify this as a 3-star rating. Note that we can assign a single task to more than one human reviewer to mitigate human bias. Amazon A2I consolidates multiple responses per task using weighted reviewer scores. Once all review tasks are completed, the UI clears the task from the worker's UI. We can use this newly labeled data in S3 to build a continuous pipeline for training and improving our Comprehend Custom model, as shown in Figure 10-15.

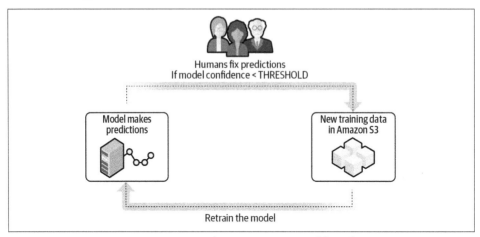

Figure 10-15. Continuous training pipeline to improve model predictions.

The more accurate our model becomes, the less reviews are sent to our workers. This concept is also called "active learning" and is implemented in SageMaker Ground Truth.

Active-Learning Feedback Loops with SageMaker Ground Truth

Active learning starts with a human labeling workflow and then transitions to self-labeling after enough samples have been seen. The active learning feedback loop is used to continuously retrain the model and improve the confidence of future label predictions. Active learning helps to scale the data labeling process by handling the high-confidence predictions and free up the workforce to focus on the low-confidence predictions that require specialized human intelligence.

Amazon SageMaker Ground Truth is an Augmented AI workflow implementation for automatic data labeling. With enough data, SageMaker Ground Truth combines human review workflows with active learning. As the human workforce labels more and more data, SageMaker Ground Truth proactively trains a model to join the workforce and perform automated labeling of new data as it arrives. If the model is not confident, the data is sent to the human workforce for review. Figure 10-16 illustrates the SageMaker Ground Truth workflow and transition from manual to automated labeling.

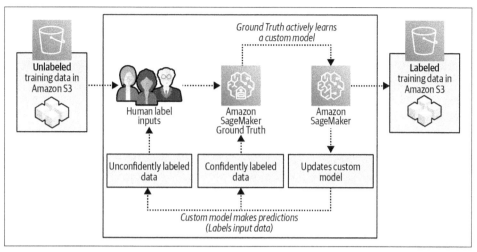

Figure 10-16. SageMaker Ground Truth uses active learning to augment human data labeling.

SageMaker Ground Truth offers pre-built labeling workflows and task templates to process images, text, and video. We can also define a custom workflow. In the following example, we will create an active learning pipeline for images. SageMaker Ground Truth will actively create a new object detection model beneath the covers as it sees more and more human labels. SageMaker Ground Truth uses this new model to automatically detect objects in the images with increasing accuracy. This allows humans to focus on labeling images that are more difficult to classify. Figure 10-17 shows a sample worker UI in SageMaker Ground Truth to detect and label objects in each image.

Figure 10-17. Sample worker UI in SageMaker Ground Truth.

Reduce Cost and Improve Performance

Most pipeline orchestration engines support some type of step caching to avoid reexecuting steps that have not changed. This is called pipeline "step caching." And because pipelines typically build upon other primitives such as SageMaker Training Jobs, we will highlight the Spot Instance cost savings for SageMaker Training Jobs used by our SageMaker Pipeline.

Cache Pipeline Steps

In some cases, we can reuse the results of previously successful pipeline steps and avoid running the step again. SageMaker Pipelines supports step caching by checking for previously successful step executions for the same input artifacts and parameters. Other orchestrators support pipeline step caching as well, including Kubeflow Pipelines.

To enable step caching in SageMaker Pipelines, we provide a cache configuration to each step upon creation, as shown in the following for the feature-engineering `Proces singStep`. If SageMaker Pipelines detects that the raw dataset and processing parameters have not changed, SageMaker Pipelines will skip the step execution, reuse the generated BERT embeddings, and continue with the pipeline:

```
from sagemaker.workflow.steps import CacheConfig

cache_config_prepare = CacheConfig(
    enable_caching=True,
    expire_after=<EXPIRE_TIME>
)

experiment_config_prepare = {
    'ExperimentName': experiment_name,
    'TrialName': trial_name,
    'TrialComponentDisplayName': 'prepare'
}

processing_step = ProcessingStep(
    name='Processing',
    code='preprocess-scikit-text-to-bert-feature-store.py',
    processor=processor,
    inputs=processing_inputs,
    outputs=processing_outputs,
    job_arguments=[...],
    experiment_config=experiment_config_prepare,
    cache_config=cache_config_prepare
)
```

Use Less-Expensive Spot Instances

SageMaker Pipelines build upon SageMaker primitives like Training Jobs, which support Spot Instances. We demonstrated how to enable Spot Instances for SageMaker Training Jobs in Chapter 7. Remember to also enable checkpointing when training with Spot Instances, as shown in the following when defining our estimator:

```
checkpoint_s3_uri = 's3://<BUCKET>/<CHECKPOINT_PREFIX>/'

estimator = TensorFlow(
    entry_point='tf_bert_reviews.py',
    source_dir='src',
    use_spot_instances=True,
    checkpoint_s3_uri=checkpoint_s3_uri,
    ...
)

training_step = TrainingStep(
    name='Train',
    estimator=estimator,
    ...
)
```

Summary

In this chapter, we described how effective machine learning pipelines help improve model quality and free up human resources to focus on higher-level tasks. We identified the key components to an effective machine learning pipeline, such as data-quality checks upon data ingestion and model validation after model training. We demonstrated how to orchestrate pipelines using SageMaker Pipelines and various other options, including AWS Step Functions, Kubeflow Pipelines, Apache Airflow, MLflow, and TFX.

We showed how to implement pipeline automation with SageMaker Pipelines. We discussed event-based triggers such as code commits and new data arriving to S3 to start a pipeline execution. And we learned how to set up time-based schedules and statistical triggers to automatically run a pipeline execution. We showed how to use human-in-the-loop workflows to automate data labeling, how to improve model accuracy using Amazon Augmented AI, and how to implement active-learning feedback loops with SageMaker Ground Truth.

With this knowledge on how to create repeatable and automated pipelines, we are now fully equipped to move our data science projects from experimentation into production. We increase productivity and ensure repeatability by automating all steps in the model development and model deployment workflow. We improve reliability by implementing GitOps practices to enforce consistency and quality. And we achieve auditability by keeping track of all pipeline steps and executions with SageMaker

Experiments and input/output artifacts with ML Lineage Tracking. We can also maintain high-quality models by automatically checking for changes to the statistical properties of our datasets, models, predictions, and explanations.

In Chapter 11, we extend our analytics and machine learning to streaming data. We will calculate real-time summary statistics, detect anomalies, and train models on continuous streams of product review data.

Streaming Analytics and Machine Learning

In the previous chapters, we assumed that we have all of our data available in a centralized static location, such as our S3-based data lake. Real-world data is continuously streaming from many different sources across the world simultaneously. We need to perform machine learning on streams of data for use cases such as fraud prevention and anomaly detection where the latency of batch processing is not acceptable. We may also want to run continuous analytics on real-time data streams to gain competitive advantage and shorten the time to business insights.

In this chapter, we move from our customer reviews training dataset into a real-world scenario. We will focus on analyzing a continuous stream of product review messages that we collect from all available online channels. Customer-product feedback appears everywhere, including social media channels, partner websites, and customer support systems. We need to capture this valuable customer sentiment about our products as quickly as possible to spot trends and react fast.

With streaming analytics and machine learning, we are able to analyze continuous data streams such as application logs, social media feeds, ecommerce transactions, customer support tickets, and product reviews. For example, we may want to detect quality issues by analyzing real-time product reviews.

In a first step, we will analyze the sentiment of the customer, so we can identify which customers might need high-priority attention. Next, we will run continuous streaming analytics over the incoming review messages to capture the average sentiment per product category. We will visualize the continuous average sentiment in a metrics dashboard for the line of business (LOB) owners. The LOB owners can now detect sentiment trends quickly and take action. We will also calculate an anomaly score of the incoming messages to detect anomalies in the data schema or data values. In case of a rising anomaly score, we will alert the application developers in charge to investigate the root cause. As a last metric, we will also calculate a continuous approximate count of the received messages. This number of online messages could be used by the digital marketing team to measure effectiveness of social media campaigns.

This chapter provides examples of both descriptive analytics (summary statistics) and predictive analytics using the BERT-based SageMaker models that we trained, tuned, and deployed in the previous chapters.

Online Learning Versus Offline Learning

In Chapter 9, we demonstrated how to perform near-real-time "online learning" by continuously training a reinforcement-learning model using real-time reward data from an example customer review application. Online, or incremental, machine learning is a small subset of machine learning and somewhat difficult to adapt to classical offline algorithms to effectively train online. With online learning, new data is incorporated into the model without requiring a complete retrain with the full dataset.

In general, linear algorithms such as linear regression, logistic regression, and K-Means Clustering are a bit easier to train with real-time data because of the relatively simple mathematics behind them. Scikit-learn supports incremental learning using the `partial_fit()` functions on certain linear algorithms. Apache Spark supports streaming versions of linear regression and K-Means Clustering.

Deep learning algorithms are also capable of online learning as well, since they continuously make small adjustments to the learned weights using mini-batches of new data. In fact, any time we train a deep learning model from an existing model checkpoint or pre-trained model (versus random initial weights), we are essentially performing online, incremental training—albeit relatively slowly as the data is usually presented to the algorithm from disk and not from a stream.

Streaming Applications

Streaming application data is not like traditional application data typically handled by REST APIs and relational databases. The 3 Vs that characterize big data also apply to streaming data: volume, velocity, and variety. The data, typically small and potentially with a different structure, comes in large quantities—and much more quickly than typical application data. The overhead of REST APIs and referential integrity of relational databases usually can't keep up with the performance requirements of high-volume and high-velocity streaming applications that may consume semistructured or unstructured data.

Distributed streaming systems such as Apache Kafka and Amazon Kinesis require multiple instances to communicate across a network to scale and share the load of processing high-volume and high-velocity streams. Since multiple instances are required to communicate across a network, the instances can sometimes process the data at different paces based on network stalls, hardware failures, and other unexpected conditions. As such, distributed streaming systems cannot guarantee that data will be consumed from the stream in the same order that it was placed onto the stream—often called "total order."

Streaming applications need to adjust for this lack of total order guarantee and maintain their own concept of order. While we don't cover total-order guarantee in great detail in this chapter, it is something to consider when building streaming applications. Some distributed streaming systems allow us to enable total order, but total order will negatively impact performance and may negate the benefits of building a streaming application.

Streaming technologies provide us with the tools to collect, process, and analyze data streams in real time. AWS offers a wide range of streaming-technology options, including Amazon MSK and the Kinesis services. With Kinesis Data Firehose, we can prepare and load the data continuously to a destination of our choice. With Kinesis Data Analytics, we can process and analyze the data as it arrives using SQL or Apache Flink applications. Apache Flink, written in Scala and Java, provides advanced streaming-analytics features, including checkpoints for reduced downtime and parallel executions for increased performance.

With Kinesis Data Streams, we can manage the ingest of data streams for custom applications. And with Kinesis Video Streams, we can capture and store video streams for analytics. AWS Glue Data Catalog helps us define and enforce the schema of structured-streaming data. We can use a self-describing file format like Apache Avro with AWS Glue Data Catalog, Kafka, and Kinesis to maintain structured data throughout our streaming applications.

Windowed Queries on Streaming Data

Descriptive streaming analytics is usually bound by windows to process—either by time or by number of input records. For example, we can specify a 30-second window or 1,000 input records.

If we implement a time-based window, our input records need to contain a timestamp column. Kinesis Data Analytics automatically adds a timestamp column called ROWTIME that we can use in our SQL queries to define time-based windows.

Kinesis Data Analytics supports three different types of windows: Stagger Windows, Tumbling Windows, and Sliding Windows. Later, we will use windowed queries to implement our streaming analytics and machine learning use cases with streaming product-review data.

Stagger Windows

Stagger windows are time-based windows that open as new data arrives and are the recommended way to aggregate data since they reduce late or out-of-order data. Hence, stagger windows are a great choice if we need to analyze groups of data that arrive at inconsistent times but should be aggregated together. We specify a partition key to identify which records belong together. The stagger window will open when the first event matching the partition key arrives. To close the window, we specify a window age, which is measured from the time the window opened. We define a stagger window with the Kinesis-specific SQL clause WINDOWED BY. The stagger window takes partition keys and window length as parameters:

```
...
FROM <stream-name>
WHERE <... optional statements...>
WINDOWED BY STAGGER(
    PARTITION BY <partition key(s)>
    RANGE INTERVAL '1' MINUTE
);
```

The partition key could be the time our product review message appeared, together with the product category:

```
PARTITION BY FLOOR(message_time TO MINUTE), product_category
```

The resulting stagger window is shown in Figure 11-1.

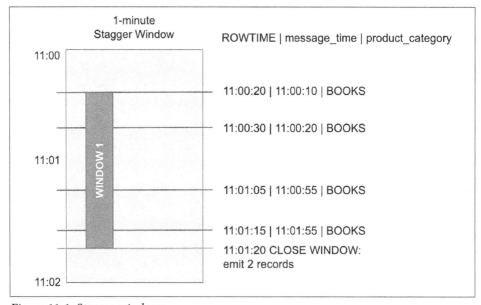

Figure 11-1. Stagger windows.

In this example, we see four data records arriving:

ROWTIME	message_time	product_category
11:00:20	11:00:10	BOOKS
11:00:30	11:00:20	BOOKS
11:01:05	11:00:55	BOOKS
11:01:15	11:01:05	BOOKS

Let's assume we are calculating a count over the data records per product category in our SQL query. The one-minute stagger window would aggregate the records like this:

ROWTIME	message_time	product_category	count
11:01:20	11:00:00	BOOKS	3
11:02:15	11:01:00	BOOKS	1

Our stagger window is grouping on a one-minute interval. The window opens when we receive the first message for each product category. In the case of BOOKS, this is happening at a ROWTIME of 11:00:20. The one-minute window expires at 11:01:20. When this happens, one record is emitted with the results that fall into this one-minute window (based on ROWTIME and message_time). The count in this example would be 3. The fourth data record has a message_time outside of the one-minute window and is aggregated separately. This happens because message_time is specified in the partition key. For example, the partition key for message_time in the first window is 11:00.

Tumbling Windows

Tumbling windows process the streaming data records in nonoverlapping windows and are best suited for distinct time-based windows that open and close at regular intervals. Here, each data record belongs to a specific window and is only processed once, as shown in Figure 11-2.

Aggregation queries using the GROUP BY SQL clause process rows in a tumbling window:

```
SELECT ...
FROM <stream-name>
GROUP BY <column>,
    STEP(<stream-name>.ROWTIME BY INTERVAL '60' SECOND);
```

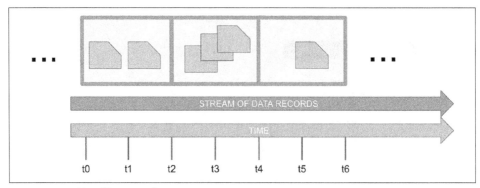

Figure 11-2. Tumbling windows.

In this example, the tumbling window is a time-based, one-minute window. We group the records by ROWTIME. The STEP function rounds down the ROWTIME to the nearest minute. Note that STEP can round values down to an arbitrary interval, whereas the FLOOR function can only round time values down to a whole-time unit, such as an hour, minute, or second.

Sliding Windows

Sliding windows aggregate data continuously using a fixed interval and fixed size. They continuously slide with time. We can create sliding windows with an explicit WINDOW clause instead of a GROUP BY clause and the interval can be time based or row based. Sliding windows can overlap, and a data record can be part of multiple windows. If a data record is part of multiple windows, the records get processed in each window, as shown in Figure 11-3.

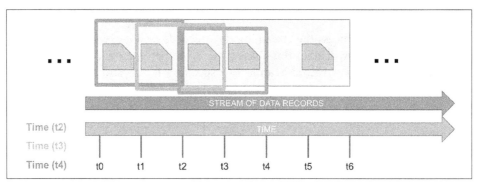

Figure 11-3. Sliding windows.

The following example creates a one-minute sliding window:

```
SELECT ...
FROM <stream-name>
WINDOW W1 AS (
   PARTITION BY <column>
   RANGE INTERVAL '1' MINUTE PRECEDING);
```

We can also define sliding windows based on number of rows:

```
SELECT ...
FROM <stream-name>
WINDOW
    last2rows AS (PARTITION BY <column> ROWS 2 PRECEDING),
    last10rows AS (PARTITION BY <column> ROWS 10 PRECEDING);
```

In this example, we create a 2-row sliding window and a 10-row sliding window. The 2-row sliding window will overlap the 10-row sliding window. Such a scenario is useful if we calculate average metrics over different-sized record batches.

Now that we have a better understanding of how to work with windowed queries, let's implement our online product reviews example using AWS.

Streaming Analytics and Machine Learning on AWS

We will use the Kinesis services to implement our online product reviews example. For simplicity, let's assume the streaming team already parsed the social media feed messages and attached a unique review ID and the relevant product category to each message.

We begin with the ingest of those messages. We set up a Kinesis Data Firehose delivery stream, which receives the messages and continuously delivers them to an S3 location, as shown in the Ingest and Store Messages column in Figure 11-4.

We also want to enrich the messages with the customer sentiment. We can leverage our fine-tuned BERT-based model from the previous chapters to classify the messages into star ratings, as shown in the Detect Customer Sentiment column of Figure 11-4. The star rating will act as a proxy metric for sentiment. We can map a predicted star rating of 4 to 5 to a positive sentiment, the star rating of 3 to a neutral sentiment, and a star rating of 1 to 2 to a negative sentiment.

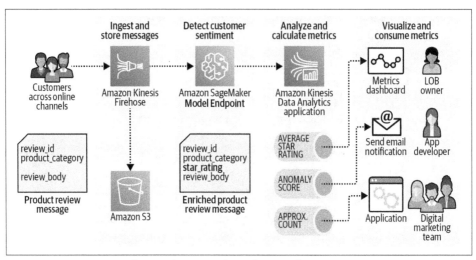

Figure 11-4. Streaming data architecture for online product review messages.

Next, we want to analyze our messages. We set up Kinesis Data Analytics to process our sentiment-enriched messages, as shown in the Analyze and Calculate Metrics column in Figure 11-4. Kinesis Data Analytics enables us to run SQL queries on streaming data. Kinesis Data Analytics SQL is based on the ANSI 2008 SQL standard with extensions to process streaming data.

We define a SQL query that continuously calculates the average star rating to reflect the change in sentiment and push the results to a real-time metrics dashboard, as shown in the Visualize and Consume Metrics column in Figure 11-4. We define another SQL query that continuously calculates an anomaly score based on the message data to catch any unexpected schema or data values. For example, we suddenly receive a star rating of 100, which doesn't exist. The application parsing the messages must have an error. In that case, we want to notify the team in charge to investigate the possible root cause and fix the issue. In a third SQL query, we continuously calculate an approximate count of messages that could be consumed by an application from the digital marketing team to evaluate and steer social media campaigns.

The SQL queries run continuously over our data stream of incoming product review messages. We can define mini-batches of streaming data records via time-based or row-based windows. We can limit our SQL query to just those mini-batches (windows) of streaming data records when calculating averages and approximate counts for each batch. This type of SQL query is called a *windowed query*.

Classify Real-Time Product Reviews with Amazon Kinesis, AWS Lambda, and Amazon SageMaker

We set up a Kinesis Data Firehose delivery stream to receive and transform the real-time messages from our customers, as shown in Figure 11-5.

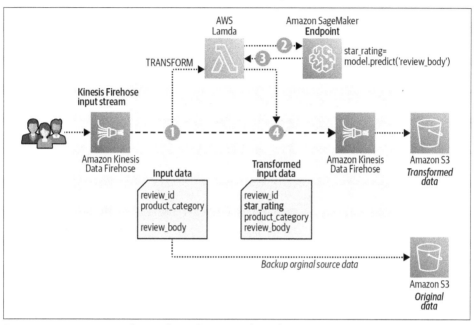

Figure 11-5. Receive and transform data records with Kinesis Data Firehose.

1. We receive the real-time input data and predict the star rating to derive the customer sentiment. The sentiment can be used to quickly identify customers who might need our high-priority attention.

2. Kinesis Firehose allows us to transform our data records with the help of a Lambda function. We build a Lambda function that receives the Firehose data records and sends the review message to a SageMaker Endpoint that hosts our fine-tuned BERT-based model.

3. The model predicts the `star_rating`, which our Lambda function adds to the original data record; the function then returns the new record back to our Firehose delivery stream.

4. The Firehose delivery stream then delivers the transformed data records to an S3 bucket we specify. Kinesis Firehose also allows us to keep a backup of the original data records. We can deliver those backup data records to another S3 bucket.

Implement Streaming Data Ingest Using Amazon Kinesis Data Firehose

Kinesis Data Firehose is a fully managed service for delivering real-time streaming data to destinations such as Amazon S3, Redshift, Elasticsearch, or any custom HTTP endpoint.

As a data source, we can select `DirectPut` or a Kinesis Data Stream. With `DirectPut` we can send data directly to the delivery stream or retrieve data from AWS IoT, CloudWatch Logs, or CloudWatch Events. We will choose `DirectPut` in our example.

Create Lambda Function to Invoke SageMaker Endpoint

Before we create our Kinesis Firehose delivery stream, we need to create the Lambda function to invoke our SageMaker Endpoint. Lambda functions help scale our Python code by providing a simple mechanism to dynamically increase or decrease the number of Python-based Lambda functions—each running its own Python interpreter—as the streaming load increases or decreases. This is similar in concept to scaling Python on a single instance by adding more processes and interpreters running on the instance. This auto-scaling feature of Lambda functions is similar to the auto-scaling feature of SageMaker Endpoints that we presented in Chapter 9.

We create a Lambda function that receives data records from the Kinesis Firehose delivery stream. In addition to Kinesis metadata such as the `recordID`, each data record consists of the `review_id`, the `product_category`, and the actual `review_body`. We parse the `review_body` and send it to the specified SageMaker Endpoint. We receive the prediction result, add it to our data record, and return the modified data record with the original `recordID` to Kinesis Data Firehose.

Following is an excerpt from the Python code for our Lambda function that invokes the SageMaker Endpoint as new data is pushed to the Kinesis Stream:

```
ENDPOINT_NAME = os.environ['ENDPOINT_NAME']
runtime = boto3.client('runtime.sagemaker')

def lambda_handler(event, context):
outputs = []

for record in event['records']:
            ...
            inputs = [
               {"features": [review_body]}
       ]

           response = runtime.invoke_endpoint(
              EndpointName=ENDPOINT_NAME,
              ContentType='application/jsonlines',
```

```
                Accept='application/jsonlines',
                Body=json.dumps(inputs).encode('utf-8')
        )
        ...

        output_record = {
                'recordId': record['recordId'],
                'result': 'Ok',
                'data': ...
        }
        outputs.append(output_record)

    return {'records': outputs}
```

We can create the Lambda function directly in the AWS Console or programmatically using the Python SDK as follows:

```
lam = boto3.Session().client(service_name='lambda',
                             region_name=region)

response = lam.create_function(
    FunctionName=<FUNCTION_NAME>,
    Runtime='<PYTHON_VERSION>',
    Role=<IAM_ROLE>
    Handler='<FUNCTION_NAME>.lambda_handler',
    Code={
        'ZipFile': code
    },
    Description='InvokeQuery SageMaker Endpoint.',
    Timeout=300,
    MemorySize=128,
    Publish=True
)
```

We can update the Lambda function with an environment variable referencing the SageMaker model endpoint to invoke:

```
response = lam.update_function_configuration(
        FunctionName=<FUNCTION_NAME>,
        Environment={
            'Variables': {
                'ENDPOINT_NAME': <ENDPOINT_NAME>
            }
        }
    )
```

We can now create our Kinesis Data Firehose Delivery Stream.

Create the Kinesis Data Firehose Delivery Stream

We configure the delivery stream type as `DirectPut` so that we can put our product reviews directly on the stream. Also, to store the streaming data records, we define the ExtendedS3DestinationConfiguration pointing to the S3 bucket. We add the Lambda function, which calls the SageMaker Endpoint and adds the predicted star rating to our data in ProcessingConfiguration. We specify another S3 bucket in S3BackupConfiguration to back up the original product reviews (before transformation).

Here is the code to programmatically create the Kinesis Data Firehose delivery stream with all the above-mentioned configurations:

```
firehose = boto3.Session().client(service_name='firehose', region_name=region)

response = firehose.create_delivery_stream(
    DeliveryStreamName=<FIREHOSE_NAME>,
    DeliveryStreamType='DirectPut',
    ExtendedS3DestinationConfiguration={
        'RoleARN': <KINESIS_ROLE_ARN>,
        'BucketARN': <S3_BUCKET_ARN>,
        'Prefix': 'kinesis-data-firehose/',
        ...
        'ProcessingConfiguration': {
            'Enabled': True,
            'Processors': [{
                'Type': 'Lambda',
                'Parameters': [
                    {
                        'ParameterName': 'LambdaArn',
                        'ParameterValue': '<LAMBDA_ARN>:$LATEST'
                    },
                    ...
                ]
            }]
        },
        'S3BackupMode': 'Enabled',
        'S3BackupConfiguration': {
            'RoleARN': <KINESIS_ROLE_ARN>,
            'BucketARN': <BACKUP_S3_BUCKET_ARN>,
            'Prefix': 'kinesis-data-firehose-source-record/',
            ...
        },
        ...
    }
)
```

We need to wait a few seconds for the delivery stream to become active. Then, we can put some live messages on our Kinesis Data Firehose delivery stream and see the results.

Put Messages on the Stream

To simulate our continuous stream of online product review messages, we can read in our sample customer reviews from the Amazon Customer Reviews Dataset and send messages containing the review_id, product_category, and review_body to Kinesis Data Firehose as follows:

```
import boto3
import csv
import pandas as pd

firehose = boto3.Session().client(service_name='firehose', region_name=region)

# Read in sample reviews
df =
 pd.read_csv('./data/amazon_reviews_us_Digital_Software_v1_00.tsv.gz',
             delimiter='\t',
             quoting=csv.QUOTE_NONE,
             compression='gzip')

# Generate 500 online messages
step = 1
for start_idx in range(0, 500, step):
    end_idx = start_idx + step

    # Create message (review_id, product_category, review_body)
    df_messages = df[['review_id',
                      'product_category',
                      'review_body']][start_idx:end_idx]

    reviews_tsv = df_messages.to_csv(sep='\t',
                                     header=None,
                                     index=False)

    # Put messages on Firehose
    response = firehose.put_record(
        Record={
            'Data': reviews_tsv.encode('utf-8')
        },
        DeliveryStreamName=<FIREHOSE_NAME>
    )
```

Once the messages arrive, Firehose calls InvokeSageMakerEndpointFromKinesis, the specified Lambda function, to transform the data. We can see the original message format, which contains the review_id, product_category, and review_body:

```
['R1066MVAFC477L', 'Digital_Software', "It's good"]
```

Our Lambda function that parses the review_body, "It's good", sends the review_body to the SageMaker Endpoint, receives the endpoint response, and decodes the star_rating prediction result of 5.

In the last step, the Lambda function adds the star rating to the original data record and returns it back to Kinesis Data Firehose:

```
R1066MVAFC477L        5    Digital_Software          It's good
```

We can also check the specified S3 bucket destination for Kinesis Data Firehose. Here, we should find the transformed data records:

And indeed, at *s3://<bucket>/kinesis-data-firehose/<year>/<month>/<day>/<hour>* we find a file with the following (shortened) output:

```
...
R2EI7QLPK4LF7U 5     Digital_Software     So far so good
R1W5OMFK1Q3I3O 3     Digital_Software     Needs a little more work.....
RPZWSYWRP92GI  1     Digital_Software     Please cancel.
R2WQWM04XHD9US 5     Digital_Software     Works as Expected!
...
```

These are our transformed data records. We also configured Firehose to back up our source data records. Similarly, we can check the S3 bucket we specified for the backup:

s3://<bucket>/kinesis-data-firehose-source-record/<year>/<month>/<day>/<hour>

And we find another file with the source records similar to this:

```
...
R2EI7QLPK4LF7U Digital_Software     So far so good
R1W5OMFK1Q3I3O Digital_Software     Needs a little more work.....
RPZWSYWRP92GI  Digital_Software     Please cancel.
R2WQWM04XHD9US Digital_Software     Works as Expected!
...
```

Note the missing star rating. The star rating is missing here, as this is the originally received product review message. This data represents the product review message before we invoked our BERT-based model (via the Lambda function) to predict and add the star rating to the streaming data record. We keep this original data as a backup.

This shows that the streaming data ingest and data transformation with Kinesis Data Firehose works. Now let's move on to the next step.

Summarize Real-Time Product Reviews with Streaming Analytics

The first business metric we want to continuously calculate is the average sentiment per product category. We could push the results to a real-time metrics dashboard. In our sample implementation, we will publish the average star rating (as a proxy metric for sentiment) to Amazon CloudWatch. The LOB owners can now detect sentiment trends quickly and take action.

Another business metric we continuously calculate is an anomaly score based on the message data to catch any unexpected schema or data values. In case of an application error, we want to notify the team in charge to investigate the possible root cause and fix it fast. For our implementation, we will use the Amazon Simple Notification Service (Amazon SNS) to send the calculated anomaly scores via email. Amazon SNS is a fully managed service to send SMS, email, and mobile push notifications.

As a last metric, we continuously calculate an approximate count of product review messages that can be consumed by the digital marketing team to evaluate and steer online campaigns. For our implementation, we will deliver the approximate count as a stream of continuous records to a Kinesis Data Stream. The digital marketing team could develop a custom application that reads the data records off the Kinesis Data Stream and processes the records as needed.

Figure 11-6 shows our evolved streaming data use case implementation.

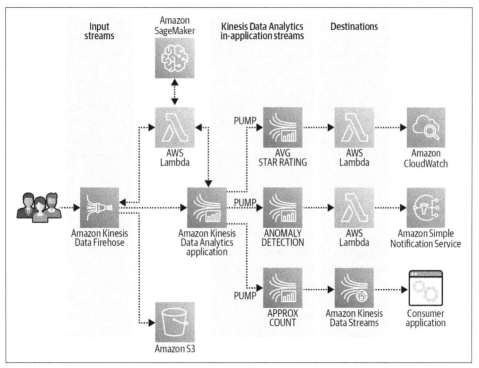

Figure 11-6. Analyze a continuous stream of product review messages with Kinesis Data Analytics.

Setting Up Amazon Kinesis Data Analytics

We will set up a Kinesis Data Analytics application to analyze our product review messages. Kinesis Data Analytics enables us to run SQL queries on streaming data.

We will use the Kinesis Data Firehose delivery stream as an input source for the Kinesis Data Analytics application. We will then develop a Kinesis Data Analytics application to execute SQL queries to calculate the average sentiment of the incoming messages, the anomaly score, and the approximate count.

Similar to Kinesis Data Firehose, we have the option to preprocess the incoming streaming data. We will reuse our existing Lambda function to invoke the SageMaker Endpoint and receive the star rating for our incoming messages. The star rating will act again as our proxy metric for sentiment.

> Why not reuse the transformed data records from Kinesis Firehose that already contain the star rating? Those transformed records get delivered straight to the S3 destination bucket. We only receive the source data records from the Firehose delivery stream in Kinesis Data Analytics.

Kinesis Data Analytics supports various destinations to send the analytics results to. We will set up two Lambda functions and an Kinesis Data Stream as destinations. We can leverage the Lambda functions to integrate with Amazon CloudWatch and Amazon SNS. Let's implement the needed components for this architecture, starting with the destinations.

Create a Kinesis Data Stream to Deliver Data to a Custom Application

Kinesis Data Streams are used to ingest large amounts of data in real time, store the data, and make the data available to consumer applications. The unit of data stored by Kinesis Data Streams is a data record. A data stream represents a group of data records. The data records in a data stream are distributed into shards. A shard has a sequence of data records in a stream. When we create a stream, we specify the number of shards for the stream. The total capacity of a stream is the sum of the capacities of its shards. We can increase or decrease the number of shards in a stream as needed.

In the context of streaming data, we often speak of producers and consumers. A producer is an application or service that generates data. A consumer is an application or service that receives the streaming data for further processing. Figure 11-7 shows the high-level architecture of a Kinesis Data Stream.

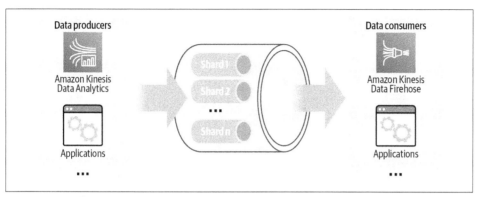

Figure 11-7. The Kinesis Data Stream architecture consists of data producers and con-sumers with data records distributed into shards.

Note that data is only stored temporarily in Kinesis Data Streams. The default data retention period for a Kinesis Data Stream is currently limited to 24 hours. However, we can increase the data retention period for long-term retention of up to one year. A longer retention period can help address compliance requirements without the need to move the data to longer-term storage like S3. The higher retention time helps in back-pressure scenarios as well, where the consumers cannot keep up with the producers during an unexpected increase in data pushed to the stream. In this case, Kinesis stores the streaming data until the consumers scale out to handle the spike—or the volume of data decreases and the consumers can catch up. A longer retention period also allows us to train models more quickly with online data directly from Kinesis—or combine the online Kinesis data with offline data in S3.

In our example, the Kinesis Data Stream will receive the results from our approximate count of messages, hence the producer is the Kinesis Data Analytics application. The consumer could be any custom application. In our example, we suggested an application from the digital marketing team. Figure 11-8 highlights the current step in our architecture that we are about to implement.

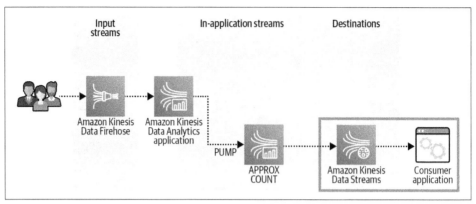

Figure 11-8. A Kinesis Data Stream is used as the Kinesis Data Analytics destination for the approximate count.

Here's the code to create the Kinesis Data Stream:

```
kinesis = boto3.Session().client(service_name='kinesis',
                                 region_name=region)

kinesis.create_stream(
        StreamName=<STREAM_NAME>,
        ShardCount=<SHARD_COUNT>
)
```

We need to wait a few minutes for the Kinesis Data Stream to become `active`.

We can programmatically check for the status of the stream and wait for the stream to become `active` with the following code:

```
import time

status = ''
while status != 'ACTIVE':
    r = kinesis.describe_stream(StreamName=<STREAM_NAME>)
    description = r.get('StreamDescription')
    status = description.get('StreamStatus')
    time.sleep(5)
```

Next, let's create an Lambda function that acts as the Kinesis Data Analytics destination for our anomaly score.

Create AWS Lambda Function to Send Notifications via Amazon SNS

In our Kinesis Data Analytics application, we will calculate an anomaly score for the data. In case the anomaly score rises, we want to notify the application developers to investigate and fix the issue. To send out notifications, we leverage Amazon SNS. We will send an email to the team in charge with the latest anomaly score calculated across our incoming messages.

As Amazon SNS is not directly supported as a Kinesis Data Analytics destination, we create another Lambda function as a proxy destination. Figure 11-9 highlights the step in our architecture that we are about to implement.

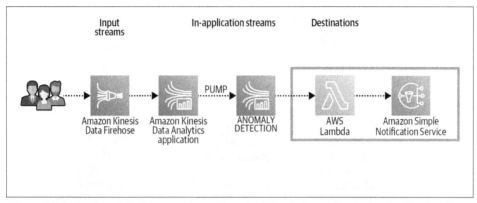

Figure 11-9. An Lambda function is used as the Kinesis Data Analytics destination for the anomaly score.

Here is the code to create our Amazon SNS topic:

```
import boto3

sns = boto3.Session().client(service_name='sns', region_name=region)

response = sns.create_topic(
    Name=<SNS_TOPIC_NAME>,
)

sns_topic_arn = response['TopicArn']
```

Following is an excerpt from our Lambda function code, *push_notification_to_sns.py*, which records the highest anomaly score from the batch of input records and publishes the score to an Amazon SNS topic:

```
import boto3
import base64
import os

SNS_TOPIC_ARN = os.environ['SNS_TOPIC_ARN']
sns = boto3.client('sns')

def lambda_handler(event, context):
    output = []
    highest_score = 0
    ...
```

```
r = event['records']

for record in event['records']:
    try:
        payload = base64.b64decode(record['data'])
        text = payload.decode("utf-8")
        score = float(text)
        if (score != 0) and (score > highest_score):
            highest_score = score
            output.append({'recordId': record['recordId'], \
                'result': 'Ok'})
    ...

if (highest_score != 0):
    sns.publish(TopicArn=SNS_TOPIC_ARN, \
        Message='New anomaly score: {}'\
            .format(str(highest_score)), \
        Subject='New Reviews Anomaly Score Detected')

return {'records': output}
```

Similar to the previous Lambda function, we can create this Lambda function programmatically and update the function with an environment variable set to our Amazon SNS Topic ARN.

We can subscribe to the Amazon SNS topic to receive the Amazon SNS notifications as follows:

```
response = sns.subscribe(
    TopicArn=sns_topic_arn,
    Protocol='email',
    Endpoint='<EMAIL_ADDRESS>',
)
```

We have one more Lambda function to implement.

Create AWS Lambda Function to Publish Metrics to Amazon CloudWatch

In our Kinesis Data Analytics application, we will also calculate the average sentiment over windows of streaming messages. We want to publish the average sentiment results as a custom metric to CloudWatch. Again, we will use the star rating as our proxy metric for sentiment. As CloudWatch is not directly supported as a Kinesis Data Analytics destination, we need another Lambda function as a proxy destination. Figure 11-10 highlights the step in our architecture that we are about to implement.

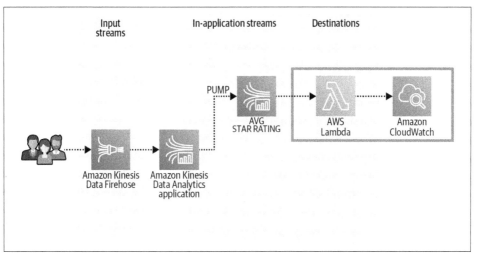

Figure 11-10. An Lambda function is used as the Kinesis Data Analytics destination for average star rating.

Following is an excerpt from our Lambda function code, *deliver_metrics_to_cloud-watch.py*, to publish the average star rating as a custom metric to CloudWatch:

```python
client = boto3.client('cloudwatch')

def lambda_handler(event, context):
    output = []
    ...

    for record in event['records']:
        payload = base64.b64decode(record['data'])
        datapoint = float(payload)

        client.put_metric_data(
                Namespace='kinesis/analytics/AVGStarRating',
                MetricData=[
                    {
                        'MetricName': 'AVGStarRating',
                        'Dimensions': [
                            {
                                'Name': 'Product Category',
                                'Value': 'All'
                            },
                        ],
                        'Value': datapoint,
                        'StorageResolution': 1
                    }
                ]
        )
```

```
        output.append({'recordId': record['recordId'], 'result': 'Ok'})
        ...

    return {'records': output}
```
After we create the Lambda function, we have all Kinesis Data Analytics application destinations in place and can now create the Kinesis Data Analytics application.

Transform Streaming Data in Kinesis Data Analytics

Similar to the data transformation feature in Kinesis Data Firehose, we can transform the incoming streaming data in Kinesis Data Analytics. We can use an Lambda function to transform, convert, enrich, or filter our streaming data. This step is executed before the Data Analytics application creates a schema for the data stream. In our example, we will reuse the Lambda function we created for the Kinesis Data Firehose data transformation. We will use the function to enrich our messages again with the star rating. Figure 11-11 visualizes the details of this step.

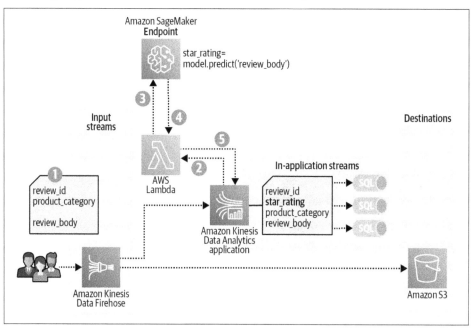

Figure 11-11. Preprocess streaming data in Kinesis Data Analytics.

The workflow looks as follows:

1. We receive the product review messages on the Kinesis Data Firehose delivery stream, which delivers the records to S3.

2. We set up the Kinesis Data Analytics application with the Firehose delivery stream as the input stream. The application receives the product review messages from the Firehose delivery stream and sends them to a Lambda function for pre-processing.

3. We are reusing the Lambda function `InvokeSageMakerEndpointFromKinesis`, which invokes the BERT-based model hosted on a SageMaker Endpoint to predict the star rating based on the review text in our product review message.

4. The Lambda function receives the predicted star rating from our model and attaches it to the product review message.

5. The Lambda function returns the product review message enriched with the star rating to the Kinesis Data Analytics application. The enriched product review messages are now used as the input for all subsequent SQL queries.

As we already have the Lambda function in place, we can continue to develop the SQL queries for our application.

Understand In-Application Streams and Pumps

An important concept in Kinesis Data Analytics applications is in-application streams and pumps. In our example, we will use the Firehose delivery stream as an input to our Data Analytics application. This input stream needs to be mapped to an in-application stream in the Data Analytics application. Once the mapping is done, the data continuously flows from the input stream into the in-application stream. We can think of the in-application stream as a table that we can then query using SQL statements. As we are not really dealing with a table, but with a continuous data flow, we call it a stream.

Note that Kinesis Data Analytics in-application streams only exist within the analytics application. They store the intermediate results of our SQL query. If we want to process the results outside of the application, we need to map the in-application stream to a supported Kinesis Data Analytics destination. Therefore, we set up three different destinations to capture the results of our in-application streams.

Here is an example for how to create an in-application stream (`MY_STREAM`) with three columns:

```
CREATE OR REPLACE STREAM "MY_STREAM" (
    "column1" BIGINT NOT NULL,
    "column2" INTEGER,
    "column3" VARCHAR(64));
```

To insert data into this stream, we need a pump. Think of a pump as a continuously running insert query that inserts data from one in-application stream into another in-application stream.

Here's an example that creates a pump (MY_PUMP) and inserts data into MY_STREAM by selecting data records from another INPUT_STREAM:

```
CREATE OR REPLACE PUMP "MY_PUMP" AS
INSERT INTO "MY_STREAM" ( "column1",
                          "column2",
                          "column3")
SELECT STREAM inputcolumn1,
              inputcolumn2,
              inputcolumn3
FROM "INPUT_STREAM";
```

Let's assume that the input stream (our Firehose delivery stream) in our Data Analytics application is called SOURCE_SQL_STREAM_001.

Amazon Kinesis Data Analytics Applications

Let's create three in-application streams to calculate the average star_rating, anomaly score, and approximate count of messages.

Calculate Average Star Rating

Our first in-application stream is called AVG_STAR_RATING_SQL_STREAM. We calculate the average star rating over a five-second tumbling window of received messages using the GROUP BY statement, which specifies INTERVAL '5'.

Here is the SQL code to implement this:

```
CREATE OR REPLACE STREAM "AVG_STAR_RATING_SQL_STREAM" (
    avg_star_rating DOUBLE);

CREATE OR REPLACE PUMP "AVG_STAR_RATING_SQL_STREAM_PUMP" AS
INSERT INTO "AVG_STAR_RATING_SQL_STREAM"
SELECT STREAM AVG(CAST("star_rating" AS DOUBLE)) AS avg_star_rating
FROM "SOURCE_SQL_STREAM_001"
GROUP BY
STEP("SOURCE_SQL_STREAM_001".ROWTIME BY INTERVAL '5' SECOND);
```

Detect Anomalies in Streaming Data

The second in-application stream is called ANOMALY_SCORE_SQL_STREAM. We leverage a built-in RANDOM_CUT_FOREST implementation to calculate an anomaly score across a sliding window of messages.

The random cut forest (RCF) implementation in Kinesis Data Analytics is based on the "Robust Random Cut Forest Based Anomaly Detection on Streams" research paper (*https://oreil.ly/0pDkv*), coauthored by AWS. The paper details using RCF for online learning with real-time data streams. However, AWS offers RCF for offline batch training using a built-in SageMaker algorithm. RCF is also used for anomaly detection in QuickSight.

The RANDOM_CUT_FOREST function in Kinesis Data Analytics builds a machine learning model to calculate an anomaly score for numeric values in each message. The score indicates how different the value is compared to the observed trend. The function also calculates an attribution score for each column, which reflects how anomalous the data in that particular column is. The sum of all attribution scores of all columns is the overall anomaly score.

As RANDOM_CUT_FOREST works on numeric values, we will calculate the anomaly score based on the star rating. The only required parameter for the RANDOM_CUT_FOREST function is a pointer to our input stream, which we define with the CURSOR function. Here is the SQL code to implement this:

```
CREATE OR REPLACE STREAM "ANOMALY_SCORE_SQL_STREAM" (
    anomaly_score DOUBLE);

CREATE OR REPLACE PUMP "ANOMALY_SCORE_STREAM_PUMP" AS
INSERT INTO "ANOMALY_SCORE_SQL_STREAM"
SELECT STREAM anomaly_score
FROM TABLE(RANDOM_CUT_FOREST(
    CURSOR(SELECT STREAM "star_rating"
    FROM "SOURCE_SQL_STREAM_001")
    )
);
```

Calculate Approximate Counts of Streaming Data

The third in-application stream is called APPROXIMATE_COUNT_SQL_STREAM. We calculate an approximate count over a five-second tumbling window of incoming messages. Kinesis Data Analytics has a built-in function to calculate an approximate count using COUNT_DISTINCT_ITEMS_TUMBLING, with the tumbling window size set to five seconds. The function uses the HyperLogLog algorithm, which stores a large number of approximate counts in a small data structure.

The following SQL code implements the approximate count of distinct items of the review_id column over a five-second tumbling window:

```
CREATE OR REPLACE STREAM "APPROXIMATE_COUNT_SQL_STREAM"(
number_of_distinct_items BIGINT);

CREATE OR REPLACE PUMP "APPROXIMATE_COUNT_STREAM_PUMP" AS
INSERT INTO "APPROXIMATE_COUNT_SQL_STREAM"
SELECT STREAM number_of_distinct_items
FROM TABLE(COUNT_DISTINCT_ITEMS_TUMBLING(
CURSOR(SELECT STREAM "review_id" FROM "SOURCE_SQL_STREAM_001"),'review_id', 5)
);
```

Create Kinesis Data Analytics Application

We are now fully equipped to create our Kinesis Data Analytics application, so let's first create a combined SQL statement that contains our three SQL queries to calculate the average star rating, detect anomalies, and calculate the approximate count of streaming data over a given window size. We pass this combined SQL query as the ApplicationCode when we create the application. Here is the code:

```
in_app_stream_name = 'SOURCE_SQL_STREAM_001' # Firehose input stream
window_seconds = 5

sql_code = '''
        CREATE OR REPLACE STREAM "AVG_STAR_RATING_SQL_STREAM" (
            avg_star_rating DOUBLE);
        CREATE OR REPLACE PUMP "AVG_STAR_RATING_SQL_STREAM_PUMP" AS
            INSERT INTO "AVG_STAR_RATING_SQL_STREAM"
                SELECT STREAM AVG(CAST("star_rating" AS DOUBLE))
    AS avg_star_rating
                FROM "{}"
                GROUP BY
                STEP("{}".ROWTIME BY INTERVAL '{}' SECOND);

        CREATE OR REPLACE STREAM "ANOMALY_SCORE_SQL_STREAM"
    (anomaly_score DOUBLE);
        CREATE OR REPLACE PUMP "ANOMALY_SCORE_STREAM_PUMP" AS
            INSERT INTO "ANOMALY_SCORE_SQL_STREAM"
            SELECT STREAM anomaly_score
            FROM TABLE(RANDOM_CUT_FOREST(
                CURSOR(SELECT STREAM "star_rating"
                    FROM "{}"
            )
          )
        );

        CREATE OR REPLACE STREAM "APPROXIMATE_COUNT_SQL_STREAM"
    (number_of_distinct_items BIGINT);
        CREATE OR REPLACE PUMP "APPROXIMATE_COUNT_STREAM_PUMP" AS
            INSERT INTO "APPROXIMATE_COUNT_SQL_STREAM"
            SELECT STREAM number_of_distinct_items
            FROM TABLE(COUNT_DISTINCT_ITEMS_TUMBLING(
                CURSOR(SELECT STREAM "review_id" FROM "{}"),
                'review_id',
                {}
              )
        );
    '''.format(in_app_stream_name,
                in_app_stream_name,
                window_seconds,
                in_app_stream_name,
                in_app_stream_name,
                window_seconds)
```

Next, let's create the Kinesis Data Analytics application. We set the application input to our Firehose delivery stream and configure the `InputProcessingConfiguration` to call our Lambda function invoking the BERT-based model. We then define the `InputSchema` to match our enriched product review messages with `review_id`, `star_rating`, `product_category`, and `review_body`.

For the application outputs, we reference the in-application stream names of our three SQL queries and define the destinations. We set the destinations `AVG_STAR_RATING_SQL_STREAM` and `ANOMALY_SCORE_SQL_STREAM` to the corresponding Lambda functions. We connect the `APPROXIMATE_COUNT_SQL_STREAM` to the Kinesis Data Stream destination. Here is the code that creates the Kinesis Data Application and references the `sql_code` defined earlier:

```
kinesis_analytics = \
        boto3.Session().client(service_name='kinesisanalytics',
                                region_name=region)

response = kinesis_analytics.create_application(
        ApplicationName=kinesis_data_analytics_app_name,
        Inputs=[
            {
                'NamePrefix': 'SOURCE_SQL_STREAM',
                'KinesisFirehoseInput': {
                    ...
                },
                'InputProcessingConfiguration': {
                    'InputLambdaProcessor': {
                    ...
                    }
                },
                'InputSchema': {
                    'RecordFormat': {
                        'RecordFormatType': 'CSV',
                        'MappingParameters': {
                            'CSVMappingParameters': {
                                'RecordRowDelimiter': '\n',
                                'RecordColumnDelimiter': '\t'
                            }
                        }
                    },
                    'RecordColumns': [
                        {
                            'Name': 'review_id',
                            ...
                        },
                        {
                            'Name': 'star_rating',
                            ...
                        },
                        {
```

```
                          'Name': 'product_category',
                          ...
                    },
                    {
                          'Name': 'review_body',
                          ...
                    }
                ]
            }
        },
    ],
    Outputs=[
        {
            'Name': 'AVG_STAR_RATING_SQL_STREAM',
            'LambdaOutput': {
                ...
            },
            'DestinationSchema': {
                'RecordFormatType': 'CSV'
            }
        },
        {
            'Name': 'ANOMALY_SCORE_SQL_STREAM',
            'LambdaOutput': {
                ...
            },
            'DestinationSchema': {
                'RecordFormatType': 'CSV'
            }
        },
        {
            'Name': 'APPROXIMATE_COUNT_SQL_STREAM',
            'KinesisStreamsOutput': {
                ...
            },
            'DestinationSchema': {
                'RecordFormatType': 'CSV'
            }
        }
    ],
    ApplicationCode=sql_code
)
```

Start the Kinesis Data Analytics Application

After creating a Kinesis Data Analytics application, we have to explicitly start the
application to receive and process the data. Here is the code to start our Kinesis Data
Analytics application:

```
input_id =
        response['ApplicationDetail']['InputDescriptions'][0]['InputId']
```

```
response = kinesis_analytics.start_application(
        ApplicationName=kinesis_data_analytics_app_name,
        InputConfigurations=[
            {
                'Id': input_id,
                'InputStartingPositionConfiguration': {
                    'InputStartingPosition': 'NOW'
                }
            }
        ]
)
```

Put Messages on the Stream

Once the application is running, we can test our streaming pipeline by putting messaging onto the stream. In order to simulate our continuous stream of online product review messages, we reuse our code from earlier. We read in our sample customer reviews from the Amazon Customer Reviews Dataset and send messages containing the review_id, product_category, and review_body to Kinesis Data Firehose. Our Kinesis Data Analytics application is configured to use the Firehose delivery stream as an input source.

Let's review the results from our Data Analytics application. If we open the Kinesis Data Analytics application in the AWS console, we can see the source and destination configurations, as shown in Figures 11-12 and 11-13.

	Source	In-application stream name	ID ⓘ	Record pre-processing ⓘ
🖉	Firehose delivery stream dsoaws-kinesis-data-firehose ⧉	SOURCE_SQL_STREAM_001	1.1	InvokeSageMakerEndpointFromKinesis ⧉

Figure 11-12. Kinesis Data Analytics application, source configuration.

The Firehose delivery stream gets mapped to the in-application stream SOURCE_SQL_STREAM_001. We also perform preprocessing of our input records with the Lambda function InvokeSageMakerEndpointFromKinesis.

	Destination	In-application stream name	ID ⓘ
🖉	Lambda function DeliverKinesisAnalyticsToCloudWatch ⧉	AVG_STAR_RATING_SQL_STREAM	1.1
🖉	Lambda function PushNotificationToSNS ⧉	ANOMALY_SCORE_SQL_STREAM	1.2
🖉	Kinesis stream dsoaws-kinesis-data-stream ⧉	APPROXIMATE_COUNT_SQL_STREAM	1.3

Figure 11-13. Kinesis Data Analytics application, destination configuration.

The destination configuration shows the correct mapping from our three in-application streams AVG_STAR_RATING_SQL_STREAM, ANOMALY_SCORE_SQL_STREAM, and APPROXIMATE_COUNT_SQL_STREAM to their corresponding destinations.

From that console, we can also open the real-time analytics dashboard to see our SQL query execution results as messages arrive. If we select the Source tab, we can see the incoming messages, as shown in Figure 11-14. The messages are already preprocessed by our Lambda function and contain the star rating.

ROWTIME	ANOMALY_SCORE
2020-11-12 16:22:31.173	1.056515594361638
2020-11-12 16:22:31.173	0.9871839401037168
2020-11-12 16:22:31.173	0.9791619936388584
2020-11-12 16:22:31.173	1.0562475887652574
2020-11-12 16:22:31.173	0.9789555993988099
2020-11-12 16:22:31.173	0.9031220381956967
2020-11-12 16:22:31.173	0.9789288160707215

Figure 11-14. Input stream of messages.

If we select the Real-time analytics tab, we can see the results of our three in-application streams, including average star ratings, number of distinct items, and anomaly scores, as shown in Figure 11-15.

ROWTIME TIMESTAMP	review_id VARCHAR(14)	star_rating INTEGER	product_category VARCHAR(24)	review_body VARCHAR(65535)
2020-11-12 16:07:26.899	R5RJEAB9MP170	5	Digital_Software	excelente
2020-11-12 16:07:26.939	R12IBIG2YN17HA	3	Digital_Software	after reading reviews on
2020-11-12 16:07:26.939	R3RHFEPMIFLC8X	4	Digital_Software	I feel safe having my phc
2020-11-12 16:07:26.939	R1JEQAB4GAWW4S	2	Digital_Software	Despite what this page a
2020-11-12 16:07:26.939	R3LZ1UZT7GV8KN	1	Digital_Software	Junk, errors out each tir
2020-11-12 16:07:26.939	R19GGQGDL3WY42	5	Digital_Software	not for me

Figure 11-15. In-application stream results for ANOMALY_SCORE_SQL_STREAM.

Finally, let's review our destinations. If we navigate to CloudWatch Metrics, we can find our custom metric AVGStarRating. We can add the metric to a graph and see the real-time sentiment trend of incoming messages. Our Amazon SNS topic also received the latest anomaly score and notified the application team via email.

Classify Product Reviews with Apache Kafka, AWS Lambda, and Amazon SageMaker

Amazon MSK is a fully managed service for an Apache Kafka distributed streaming cluster. We can create a Lambda function to invoke our SageMaker Endpoint using data from the Amazon MSK stream as prediction input and enrich our Kafka stream with the prediction output. This is similar to how our Kinesis stream triggered a Lambda function that invoked our SageMaker Endpoint with data from the Kinesis stream as prediction input and enriched our Kinesis stream with the prediction output. Figure 11-16 shows how to receive and transform data records with Amazon MSK, and we can describe the steps as follows:

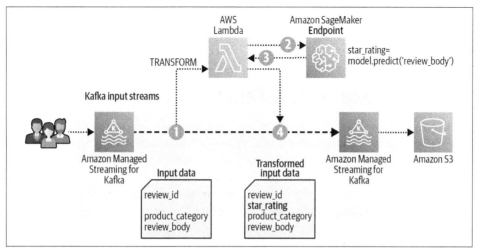

Figure 11-16. Receive and transform data records with Amazon MSK.

1. We receive the real-time input data and predict the star rating to derive the customer sentiment.

2. Amazon MSK allows us to transform our data records with the help of an Lambda function. We build a Lambda function that receives the Kafka data records and sends the review message to a SageMaker Endpoint that hosts our fine-tuned BERT-based model.

3. The model predicts the `star_rating`, which our Lambda function adds to the original data record; the function then returns the new record back to our Kafka stream.

4. The Kafka stream then delivers the transformed data records to an S3 bucket using an Amazon S3 sink connector for Kafka.

To set this up, we need to create an Amazon MSK cluster, a Kafka input topic (input stream) for the model inputs, and a Kafka output topic (output stream) for the model predictions. Next, we need to create a Lambda event source mapping using the Amazon MSK Python API `create_event_source_mapping()` to map our Kafka input stream to the input of the Lambda function that invokes our SageMaker Endpoint and writes the prediction to the Kafka output stream.

Here is the code to create the event source mapping between the Amazon MSK cluster and the Lambda function through the `reviews` topic:

```
response = client.create_event_source_mapping(
    EventSourceArn='<MSK_CLUSTER_ARN>',
    FunctionName='<LAMBDA_FUNCTION_NAME>',
    Enabled=True,
    Topics=[
        'reviews',
    ]
)
```

Reduce Cost and Improve Performance

We can further optimize the streaming data architecture for cost and performance. For example, Lambda functions are eligible for Compute Savings Plans, which offer a discount for one- or three-year term compute usage commitments. There are a couple of ways to reduce cost with Kinesis services. One best practice is to aggregate smaller data records into one PUT request. We can also consider Kinesis Firehose versus Data Streams to save money. We can improve the performance of Kinesis Data Streams by enabling enhanced fan-out (EFO).

Aggregate Messages

The cost of Kinesis Data Streams is based on the provisioned number of shards and our message PUT payloads in units of 25 KB. A best practice to reduce cost is to aggregate smaller messages into one PUT request. We can implement this technique with the Kinesis Producer Library (KPL). KPL aggregates and compresses multiple logical data records into one Kinesis data record, which we can then put efficiently into the stream.

Consider Kinesis Firehose Versus Kinesis Data Streams

Kinesis Data Firehose is best for use cases that require zero administration and can tolerate some data processing latency. Firehose provides near-real-time processing. It is fully managed by AWS and automatically scales to match the throughput requirements. We can also batch and compress the data to minimize the storage footprint at the destination. With Firehose, we only pay for the data that is processed.

Kinesis Data Streams is best for use cases that require custom processing for each incoming record. It provides real-time processing. We have to manage the through-put capacity of our Kinesis Data Stream ourselves. The cost of Kinesis Data Streams is based on the processed data *and* the number of shards provisioned to meet our throughput needs.

 If we choose to serve trained models using Lambda functions, we can connect a Kinesis Data Stream directly to the Lambda function. Lambda functions read the records directly from the Kinesis Data Stream and perform the prediction synchronously using the event data as the prediction input.

Enable Enhanced Fan-Out for Kinesis Data Streams

Without EFO, all consumers are contending for the read-throughput limit of each shard. This limits the number of consumers per stream and requires fanning out to additional streams in order to scale to a large number of consumers, as shown in Figure 11-17.

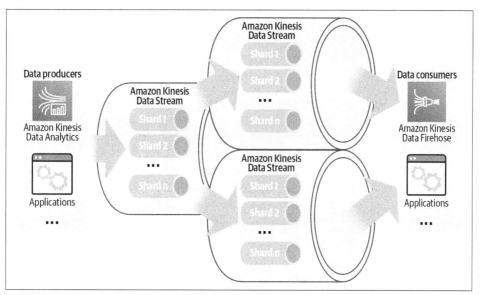

Figure 11-17. Scaling consumers without EFO using multiple streams.

With EFO, each shard–consumer combination can leverage its own dedicated, full read-throughput limit. Figure 11-18 shows the dedicated shard–consumer pipes with full read throughput.

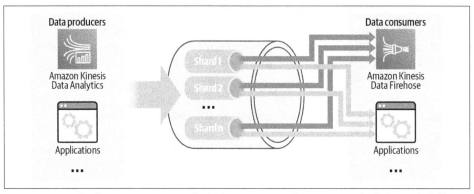

Figure 11-18. Scaling consumers with EFO using a single stream with dedicated, full-throughput shard–consumer connections.

In order to enable EFO, we use the functions `register_stream_consumer()` and `sub scribe_to_share()` from the Kinesis Data Streams Python API. When registering our consumers with EFO, Kinesis Data Streams will push data to the consumer using the highly parallel, nonblocking HTTP/2 protocol. This push mechanism results in more reactive, low-latency, and high-performance streaming applications that scale to a large number of consumers.

Summary

In this chapter, we showed how to perform streaming analytics and machine learning with streaming data. We set up an end-to-end streaming data pipeline using Kinesis streaming technologies to capture our product reviews, perform descriptive analytics, and apply predictive machine learning. We calculated summary statistics over the continuous flow of product reviews, performed anomaly detection on the streaming data, and enriched the data with predictions from our BERT-based SageMaker model. We visualized the results in a CloudWatch Metrics dashboard, sent email notifications to alert teams, and made results available to additional applications.

In Chapter 12, we will discuss how to secure data science and machine learning projects on AWS. After introducing the AWS shared responsibility model and discussing common security considerations, we will highlight security best practices for Amazon SageMaker in the context of access management, compute and network isolation, encryption, governance, and auditability.

Secure Data Science on AWS

It is important to maintain least-privilege security at all layers, from network to application, and throughout the entire data science workflow, from data ingestion to model deployment. In this chapter, we reinforce that security is the top priority at AWS and often called "job zero" or "priority zero." We discuss common security considerations and present best practices to build secure data science and machine learning projects on AWS. We will describe preventive controls that aim to stop events from occurring as well as detective controls to quickly detect potential events. We also identify responsive and corrective controls that help to remediate security violations.

The most common security considerations for building secure data science projects in the cloud touch the areas of access management, compute and network isolation, and encryption. Let's first discuss these more general security best practices and security-first principles. Then we will apply these practices and principles to secure our data science environment from notebooks to S3 buckets using both network-level security and application security. We also discuss governance and audibility best practices for compliance and regulatory purposes.

Shared Responsibility Model Between AWS and Customers

AWS implements the shared responsibility model, through which they provide a global secure infrastructure and foundational compute, storage, networking and database services, as well as a range of security services that we can use to secure anything we build and run on top of these services.

Security and compliance is a shared responsibility between AWS and the customer. AWS ensures the security "of" the cloud, while the customer is responsible for security "in" the cloud, as shown in Figure 12-1.

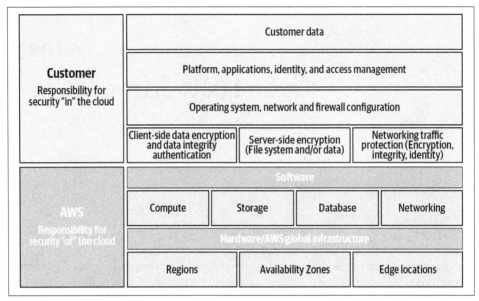

Customer **Responsibility for security "in" the cloud**	Customer data			
	Platform, applications, identity, and access management			
	Operating system, network and firewall configuration			
	Client-side data encryption and data integrity authentication	Server-side encryption (File system and/or data)		Networking traffic protection (Encryption, integrity, identity)

AWS **Responsibility for security "of" the cloud**	Software			
	Compute	Storage	Database	Networking
	Hardware/AWS global infrastructure			
	Regions	Availability Zones		Edge locations

Figure 12-1. Security is a shared responsibility between AWS and the customer. Source: Amazon (https://oreil.ly/DgY3n).

AWS protects the AWS cloud infrastructure that runs the AWS services. This includes all the components, from the host operating systems and virtualization layers down to the physical security of the facilities in which the AWS services run. The effectiveness of AWS security is regularly tested and verified by third-party auditors. We can access on-demand security and compliance reports and select online agreements via AWS Artifact (*https://oreil.ly/XFfgU*).

In return, AWS customers are responsible to ensure the security in the cloud. The scope of the customer responsibilities is determined by the specific AWS service. In addition, customers can choose from a variety of security services and features to build secure and compliant applications in the AWS cloud.

Applying AWS Identity and Access Management

IAM is a service that helps us to manage access to AWS resources. IAM controls who has access (authentication) to the environment and what permissions authenticated users have (authorization). We can use IAM to define users, groups of users, and roles. IAM implements the concept of principals, actions, resources, and conditions. This defines which principals can perform which actions on which resources and under which conditions.

We control access to specific resources by creating IAM policies and attaching them to IAM identities or AWS resources. Depending on different job roles or functions, we may want to grant different permissions to users. For example, some developers might just need to launch notebooks for ad hoc data exploration. Data scientists most likely require permissions to data stores, training jobs, and experiments. Data engineers and machine-learning engineers might need permissions to build repeatable data and model pipelines. DevOps teams require access to model deployments and performance monitors.

Amazon SageMaker leverages IAM for role-based access controls. We can also map any existing users/groups/roles from the AWS Directory Service, our enterprise user directory, or a web identity provider (called *federated users*).

IAM Users

We can create individual IAM users for people accessing our AWS account. Each user will have unique security credentials. We can also assign IAM users to IAM groups with defined access permissions (i.e., for specific job functions), and the IAM users inherit those permissions.

IAM Policies

Access permissions are defined using IAM policies. It's a standard security best practice to only grant least privilege by only granting the specific permissions required to perform a given task.

IAM User Roles

A more preferred way to delegate access permissions is via IAM roles. In contrast to an IAM user, which is uniquely associated with one person, a role can be assumed by anyone who needs it and provides us with only temporary security credentials for the duration of the role session. IAM service roles control which actions a service can perform on our behalf. IAM user roles are assumed by individual users.

The best practice is to create separate IAM user roles for individual job roles, such as the `DataScientistRole`, `MLEngineerRole`, `DataEngineeringRole`, `MLOpsEngineering Role`, etc. This allows for fine-grained and distinct policies for the different roles in the model-development life cycle.

IAM Service Roles

IAM service roles are assumed by AWS services. The best practice is to create separate service roles for distinct services and separate roles for distinct tasks per service. For Amazon SageMaker, we could separate service roles as follows:

`SageMakerNotebookExecutionRole`

The role assumed by a SageMaker notebook instance or SageMaker Studio Application, defining access permissions to SageMaker training or model hosting services

`SageMakerProcessingRole`

The role assumed by SageMaker Processing Jobs, defining access to S3 buckets for data input/output

`SageMakerTrainingRole`

The role assumed by SageMaker Training or Tuning Jobs, defining permissions during model training/tuning

`SageMakerModelRole`

The role assumed by the model hosting inference container on a SageMaker Endpoint, defining permissions during model inference

Figure 12-2 shows the data scientist IAM user role and the various SageMaker IAM service roles discussed.

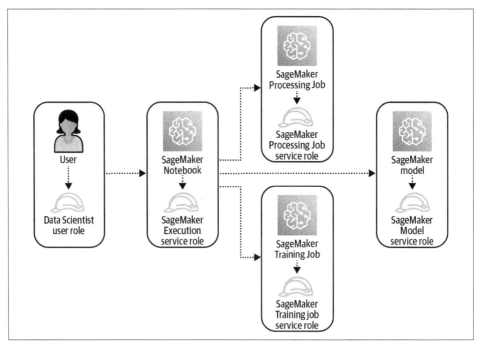

Figure 12-2. Sample IAM user and service roles for Amazon SageMaker.

When defining user and service permissions via IAM policies, we should always assign the least privilege needed to perform the task at hand.

Specifying Condition Keys for IAM Roles

We can use IAM condition keys to specify guardrails within our policies. When a principal calls a service API to create a resource, for example, the request information is compared to the conditions defined in the principal's IAM policy. If the condition statement passes, the API call succeeds; if the condition statement fails, the request will be denied. Condition statements generally look like this:

```
"Condition": {
   "{condition-operator}": {
      "{condition-key}": "{condition-value}"
   }
}
```

And here is a sample condition policy statement that denies uploads of any unencrypted objects to S3:

```
"Statement": [{
               "Sid": "DenyUnencryptedObjectUploads",
               "Effect": "Deny",
               "Principal": "*",
               "Action": "s3:PutObject",
               "Resource": "arn:aws:s3:::<bucket_name>/*",
               "Condition": {
                  "StringNotEquals": {
                     "S3:x-amz-server-side-encryption": "aws:kms"
                  }
               }
            }]
```

SageMaker supports global condition keys and also adds a few service-specific condition keys. The global condition context keys start with an `aws:` prefix. SageMaker supports the following global condition keys:

aws:RequestTag/${TagKey}
: Compares the tag key-value pair that was passed in the request with the tag pair specified in the policy

aws:ResourceTag/${TagKey}
: Compares the tag key-value pair that is specified in the policy with the key-value pair attached to the resource

aws:SourceIp
: Compares the requester's IP address with the IP address specified in the policy

aws:SourceVpc
: Checks whether the request comes from the Amazon Virtual Private Cloud (Amazon VPC) specified in the policy

`aws:SourceVpce`

Compares the Amazon VPC endpoint identifier of the request with the endpoint ID specified in the policy

`aws:TagKeys`

Compares the tag keys in the request with the keys specified in the policy

SageMaker adds service-specific condition keys that start with a `sagemaker:` prefix as follows:

`sagemaker:AcceleratorTypes`

Uses a specific Amazon Elastic Inference accelerator when creating or updating notebook instances and when creating endpoint configurations

`sagemaker:DirectInternetAccess`

Controls direct internet access from notebook instances

`sagemaker:FileSystemAccessMode`

Specifies the access mode of the directory associated with the input data channel (Amazon EFS or FSx)

`sagemaker:FileSystemDirectoryPath`

Specifies the filesystem directory path associated with the resource in the training and hyper-parameter tuning (HPT) request

`sagemaker:FileSystemId`

Specifies the filesystem ID associated with the resource in the training and HPT request

`sagemaker:FileSystemType`

Specifies the filesystem type associated with the resource in the training and HPT request

`sagemaker:InstanceTypes`

Specifies the list of all instance types for notebook instances, training jobs, HPT jobs, batch transform jobs, and endpoint configurations for hosting real-time inferencing

`sagemaker:InterContainerTrafficEncryption`

Controls inter-container traffic encryption for distributed training and HPT jobs

`sagemaker:MaxRuntimeInSeconds`

Controls costs by specifying the maximum length of time, in seconds, that the training, HPT, or compilation job can run

sagemaker:ModelArn
: Specifies the Amazon Resource Name (ARN) of the model associated for batch transform jobs and endpoint configurations for hosting real-time inferencing

Sagemaker:NetworkIsolation
: Enables network isolation when creating training, HPT, and inference jobs

sagemaker:OutputKmsKey
: Specifies the AWS KMS key to encrypt output data stored in Amazon S3

sagemaker:RequestTag/${TagKey}
: Compares the tag key-value pair that was passed in the request with the tag pair that is specified in the policy

sagemaker:ResourceTag/${TagKey}
: Compares the tag key-value pair that is specified in the policy with the key-value pair that is attached to the resource

sagemaker:RootAccess
: Controls root access on the notebook instances

sagemaker:VolumeKmsKey
: Specifies an AWS KMS key to encrypt storage volumes when creating notebook instances, training jobs, HPT jobs, batch transform jobs, and endpoint configurations for hosting real-time inferencing

sagemaker:VPCSecurityGroupIds
: Lists all Amazon VPC security group IDs associated with the elastic network interface (ENI) that Amazon SageMaker creates in the Amazon VPC subnet

sagemaker:VPCSubnets
: Lists all Amazon VPC subnets where Amazon SageMaker creates ENIs to communicate with other resources like Amazon S3

Enable Multifactor Authentication

SageMaker also supports multifactor authentication MFA. MFA adds extra security as it requires users to provide a second, unique authentication from an AWS-supported MFA mechanism. Supported MFA mechanisms include virtual MFA devices, U2F security keys, hardware MFA devices, or SMS text message–based MFAs.

As a best practice, we should enable MFA for users with administrator access. We should also add MFA as a second step of authorization—in addition to IAM policies —to prevent destructive operations such as the termination and deletion of resources. This is useful when compliance and governance policies require models to be stored for a period of time before deletion.

Least Privilege Access with IAM Roles and Policies

IAM policies control access to AWS resources. We attach IAM policies to IAM identities or AWS resources to define permissions of the identity or resource. By default, an IAM user or role starts without any permissions. An administrator has to grant permissions to that IAM user or role. When the user is part of a group, the user inherits the group's permissions.

We can define a pool of IAM policies as needed and then assign policies to our IAM identities as applicable. Figure 12-3 shows a sample many-to-many relationship of IAM policies to IAM users/groups/roles.

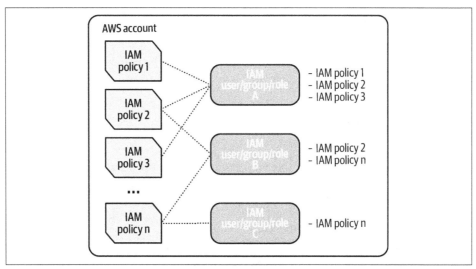

Figure 12-3. Relationship between IAM policies and IAM users/roles.

There are different types of policies, including identity-based and resource-based policies. Identity-based policies are JSON policy documents we attach to an IAM user/group/role. The policy defines the permissions for the user/group/role.

Resource-Based IAM Policies

Resource-based policies are JSON policy documents we attach to an AWS resource, such as S3 buckets. In the case of resource-based policies, the policy controls access to the resource, i.e., who is allowed to access the S3 bucket under what conditions.

Note that resource-based policies require a principal (who is allowed to perform actions on that resource and under what conditions). Principals can be AWS accounts, IAM users, IAM roles, federated users, or other AWS services.

Here is an example of a resource-based IAM policy. The following S3 bucket policy requires MFA to access the bucket. This is accomplished via the `aws:MultiFactor AuthAge` condition key:

```
{
    "Version": "2012-10-17",
    "Id": "123",
    "Statement": [
      {
        "Sid": "",
        "Effect": "Deny",
        "Principal": "*",
        "Action": "s3:*",
        "Resource": "arn:aws:s3:::<SAMPLE_BUCKET>/*",
        "Condition": { "Null": { "aws:MultiFactorAuthAge": true }}
      }
    ]
}
```

If Amazon S3 receives a bucket access request with MFA, `aws:MultiFactorAuthAge` carries a numeric value responding to the number of seconds since the temporary credential has been created. If the key is `null`, the credential wasn't created via an MFA device, and the access request will be denied.

Identity-Based IAM Policies

Here is an example of an identity-based IAM policy that could be attached to a Data Scientist IAM role. The policy grants the role access to a specific S3 bucket and Sage-Maker Studio environments:

```
{
    "Version": "2012-10-17",
    "Statement": [
        {
            "Effect": "Allow",
            "Action": [
                "s3:Abort*",
                "s3:DeleteObject",
                "s3:Get*",
                "s3:List*",
                "s3:PutAccelerateConfiguration",
                "s3:PutBucketCors",
                "s3:PutBucketLogging",
                "s3:PutBucketNotification",
                "s3:PutBucketTagging",
                "s3:PutObject",
                "s3:Replicate*",
                "s3:RestoreObject"
            ],
            "Resource": [
                "arn:aws:s3:::<BUCKET_NAME>/*"
```

```
            ]
        },
        {
            "Effect": "Allow",
            "Action": [
                "sagemaker:CreatePresignedDomainUrl",
                "sagemaker:DescribeDomain",
                "sagemaker:ListDomains",
                "sagemaker:DescribeUserProfile",
                "sagemaker:ListUserProfiles",
                "sagemaker:*App",
                "sagemaker:ListApps"
            ],
            "Resource": "*"
        },
    ]
}
```

Isolating Compute and Network Environments

We can isolate our development, staging, and production environments by creating separate accounts and separate VPCs within each account. This gives us the compute and network isolation needed to deploy our Amazon SageMaker, S3, CloudWatch, Redshift, and other AWS resources in a least-privilege and internet-free manner. Without compute and network isolation, we are at risk of leaking data outside of our network and into the wrong hands. Additionally, we are at risk of outside attackers viewing data on our compute nodes or inspecting packets on our network.

Virtual Private Cloud

We can specify allowed network communications to/from our VPCs via route tables. Route tables contain rules ("routes") that define where to send network traffic from our virtual private cloud's (VPC) subnets or gateways.

A VPC consists of one or more subnets. A VPC is a regional service and our VPC can span one or all of the Availability Zones (AZs) in the selected region by creating one or more subnets attached to an AZ. We can also add one or more subnets in each of the AZs. Subnets are defined as a range of IP addresses. For each subnet, we can further specify allowed communications to/from our Amazon EC2 instances, such as our SageMaker notebook instances, via Security Groups. VPCs can also be peered together to form secure connections within accounts and between accounts. Many popular SaaS products use VPC peering between the host and customer account.

Figure 12-4 shows the relationship between VPCs and related components, such as gateways, route tables, subnets, security groups, and instances.

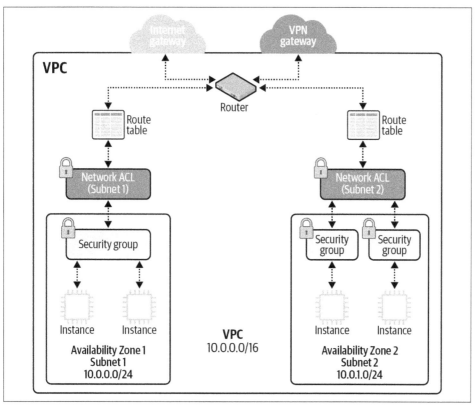

Figure 12-4. Relationship between a VPC and related components.

VPC Endpoints and PrivateLink

VPC Endpoints allow us to connect to services powered by the AWS PrivateLink eco-system, including most AWS services as well as third-party AWS Partner and Market-place offerings. The owner of the service is the "service provider." The consumer of the service is the "service consumer."

A VPC Endpoint is an ENI placed into a specific subnet accessible through a private IP address. We can control the network communications for that ENI via VPC secu-rity groups. To control access to the resources behind a VPC Endpoint, we specify VPC Endpoint policies.

We can create VPC Endpoints to make a private connection between our VPC and AWS resources, such as Amazon S3, SageMaker, Redshift, Athena, and CloudWatch. Without a VPC Endpoint, we are accessing these services over the public internet securely, not with a private tunnel, as shown in Figure 12-5. This is why we should use VPC Endpoints to access services that we use, as shown in Figure 12-6.

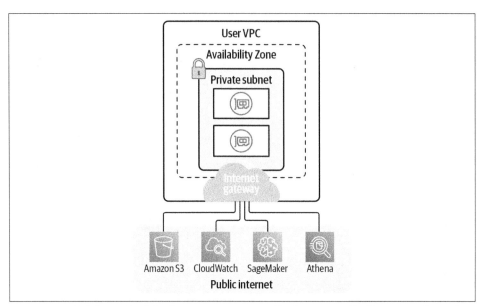

Figure 12-5. Without VPC Endpoints, our private VPC accesses AWS services through the public internet in a secure but public tunnel.

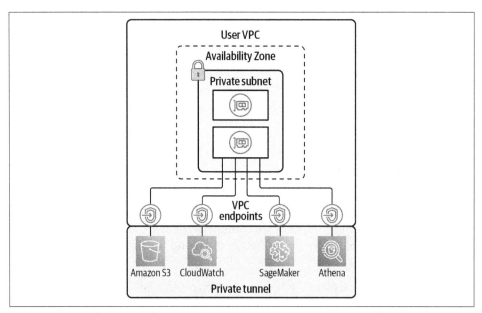

Figure 12-6. With VPC Endpoints, our private VPC communicates with AWS services through a secure and private tunnel.

Fortunately, most services, including Amazon S3, SageMaker, Redshift, Athena, and CloudWatch, support VPC Endpoints. But we should be cautious when integrating with third-party AWS Partner or Marketplace services that do not offer VPC End-points. The connections will be secure, but they will not be private unless using a VPC Endpoint.

Limiting Athena APIs with a VPC Endpoint Policy

We can create a VPC Endpoint Policy to only allow certain API calls for certain resources. For example, let's lock down an Athena VPC Endpoint to only a specific workgroup and set of Athena APIs with a resource-based policy as follows:

```
{
  "Statement": [{
    "Principal": "*",
    "Effect": "Allow",
    "Action": [
      "athena:StartQueryExecution",
      "athena:RunQuery",
      "athena:GetQueryExecution",
      "athena:GetQueryResults",
      "athena:CancelQueryExecution",
      "athena:ListWorkGroups",
      "athena:GetWorkGroup",
      "athena:TagResource"
    ],
    "Resource": [
      "arn:aws:athena:<REGION>:<ACCOUNT_ID>:workgroup/<WORKGROUP>"
    ]
  }]
}
```

Securing Amazon S3 Data Access

In today's world, keeping data secure and safe is a top priority. By default, all Amazon S3 resources are private so only the resource owner, an AWS account that created it, can access the resource. The resource owner can optionally grant access permissions to others by writing an access policy.

Amazon S3 integrates with AWS IAM for security and access management. We have learned that we can provide identity-based IAM policies, specifying what actions are allowed or denied on what AWS resource (i.e., the S3 bucket) by the IAM user/group/role the policy is attached to. We can also provide resource-based IAM policies, such as S3 bucket policies, which define the permissions by specific principals on the bucket. Without securing data access, we are at risk of sensitive data being exposed to the wrong audience.

Generally, we would use IAM identity-based policies if we need to define permissions for more than just S3, or if we have a number of S3 buckets, each with different permissions requirements. We might want to keep access control policies in the IAM environment.

We would use S3 bucket policies if we need a simple way to grant cross-account access to our S3 environment without using IAM roles, or if we reach the size limit for our IAM policy. We might want to keep access control policies in the S3 environment.

Note that we can apply both IAM identity-based policies defining permissions for a bucket as well as an S3 bucket policy for the same bucket. The resulting authorization would be the least privilege from the union of all defined permissions.

When we create S3 buckets for our data science and machine learning projects, we should consider creating separate buckets to match our data classification and data access control needs. In heavily regulated industries that must comply with standards and controls, such as the Payment Card Industry, we should align our S3 buckets with separate accounts that also comply with the same standards and controls. In this case, our sensitive and raw datasets would only be accessible from the compliant accounts, while the nonsensitive, transformed, and masked datasets would be accessible from the data science account, for example.

As a best practice, we should also consider creating separate buckets for different teams, feature stores, model artifacts, and automation pipelines. In addition, we should enable S3 bucket-versioning to keep multiple versions of an object or recover from unintended user actions. With versioned S3 buckets, we can also enable S3 Object Lock, which will enforce "write-once-read-many" to ensure that an object does not change—and is not deleted—after it is written. This is required to satisfy compliance regulations in financial and healthcare industries.

In other scenarios, we need to be able to delete specific user data on request. For example, we might need to comply with the "right to be forgotten" rule, which is an important pillar in many data protection regulations, such as General Data Protection Regulation.

Depending on which data store we use, there are various ways to implement this. For example, using Amazon Redshift Spectrum with the data stored in S3, we can copy the external table, which requires data deletion to a temporary Amazon Redshift table. We then delete the affected records and write the temporary table back to S3, overwriting the key name. In a final step, we delete the temporary Amazon Redshift table. If we need to scale and automate the data-deletion procedure, we could leverage Apache Spark to load the data from the data source into a temporary table, remove the data to be forgotten, and rewrite the data back to the original data store.

In cases where models have been trained and deployed using the data to be forgotten, we need to trace the lineage forward from the data to find all models trained with that data. After removing the data—and depending on the details of the data-protection regulation, we may need to retrain and redeploy the model to truly "forget" the user and delete their data.

Require a VPC Endpoint with an S3 Bucket Policy

Building on our discussion of IAM roles and VPC Endpoints, we can lock down access to specific S3 buckets by requiring a VPC Endpoint using an S3 Bucket Policy as follows:

```
{
    "Version": "2008-10-17",
    "Statement": [
        {
            "Effect": "Deny",
            "Principal": "*",
            "Action": [
                "s3:GetObject",
                "s3:PutObject",
                "s3:ListBucket"
            ],
            "Resource": [
                "arn:aws:s3:::<s3-bucket-name>/*",
                "arn:aws:s3:::<s3-bucket-name>"
            ],
            "Condition": {
                "StringNotEquals": {
                    "aws:sourceVpce": "<S3_VPC_ENDPOINT_ID>"
                }
            }
        }
    ]
}
```

Limit S3 APIs for an S3 Bucket with a VPC Endpoint Policy

We can also attach a policy to a VPC Endpoint for S3 and only allow a subset of S3 APIs on a specific S3 bucket as follows:

```
{
    "Version": "2012-10-17",
    "Statement": [
        {
            "Effect": "Allow",
            "Principal": "*",
            "Action": [
                "s3:GetObject",
                "s3:PutObject",
```

```
            "s3:ListBucket"
        ],
        "Resource": [
            "arn:aws:s3:::<S3_BUCKET_NAME>",
            "arn:aws:s3:::<S3_BUCKET_NAME>/*"
        ]
    }
  ]
}
```

Restrict S3 Bucket Access to a Specific VPC with an S3 Bucket Policy

Instead of completely locking down the S3 bucket, we could restrict access to a specified VPC as follows:

```
{
    "Version": "2008-10-17",
    "Statement": [{
        "Effect": "Deny",
        "Principal": "*",
        "Action": [
            "s3:ListBucket"
        ],
        "Resource": [
            "arn:aws:s3:::<BUCKET_NAME>"
        ],
        "Condition": {
            "StringNotEquals": {
                "aws:sourceVpc": <vpc_id>
            }
        }
    }]
}
```

With this S3 bucket policy attached to the S3 bucket, all access requests from outside
of the specified source VPC are denied.

We can verify that the access is denied as follows:

```
!aws s3 ls s3://<BUCKET_NAME>
```

We will receive an error message similar to this:

```
An error occurred (AccessDenied) when calling the ListObjectsV2 operation
```

Limit S3 APIs with an S3 Bucket Policy

We can limit the S3 API operations for a specific bucket by specifying the following
S3 Bucket Policy that denies the ListBucket API to the given bucket:

```
{
    'Version': '2012-10-17',
    'Statement': [{
```

```
        'Sid': '',
        'Effect': 'Deny',
        'Principal': '*',
        'Action': [
            's3:ListBucket'
        ],
        'Resource': [
            'arn:aws:s3:::<BUCKET_NAME>'
        ]
    }]
}
```

We can verify that the access is denied as follows:

```
!aws s3 ls s3://<BUCKET_NAME>
```

We will receive an error message similar to this:

```
An error occurred (AccessDenied) when calling the ListObjectsV2 operation
```

Restrict S3 Data Access Using IAM Role Policies

The following example shows how we can restrict access to our S3 buckets using an identity-based IAM policy:

```
{
    'Version': '2012-10-17',
    'Statement': [{
        'Sid': '',
        'Effect': 'Deny',
        'Action': [
            's3:ListBucket'
        ],
        'Resource': [
            'arn:aws:s3:::<BUCKET_NAME>'
        ]
    }]
}
```

We can verify that the access is denied as follows:

```
!aws s3 ls s3://<BUCKET_NAME>
```

We will receive an error message similar to this:

```
An error occurred (AccessDenied) when calling the ListObjectsV2 operation
```

Restrict S3 Bucket Access to a Specific VPC with an IAM Role Policy

We could restrict access to the S3 bucket to a specified VPC as follows:

```
{
    'Version': '2012-10-17',
    'Statement': [{
```

```
            'Sid': '',
            'Effect': 'Deny',
            'Action': [
                's3:ListBucket'
            ],
            'Resource': [
                'arn:aws:s3:::<BUCKET_NAME>'
            ],
            'Condition': {
                'StringNotEquals': {
                    'aws:sourceVpc': <VPC_ID>
                }
            }
    }]
}
```

With this IAM policy attached to a role, all `ListBucket` requests initiated with this role must come from within the VPC or they will be denied.

We can verify that the access is denied as follows:

```
!aws s3 ls s3://<BUCKET_NAME>
```

We will receive an error message similar to this:

```
An error occurred (AccessDenied) when calling the ListObjectsV2 operation
```

Restrict S3 Data Access Using S3 Access Points

Amazon S3 Access Points simplify access control for large, shared buckets such as data lakes. Traditionally, we accessed our S3 buckets through a unique bucket host name and defined access control with a combination of IAM policies and a single bucket policy. We can imagine that for shared datasets and a growing number of users, teams, and applications that needed access, this could quickly end up as a complex environment for us to maintain.

Amazon S3 Access Points simplify managing data access by providing a customized path into a bucket, each with a unique hostname and IAM access policy that enforces the specific permissions and network controls for any request made through the access point. This is particularly useful for managing access to shared datasets.

We can also require that all access points be restricted to a VPC, providing an extra level of security by basically firewalling our data to within our private networks.

Let's assume we have our sample S3 bucket called `data-science-on-aws` with prefixes (subfolders) called `feature-store` and `data-warehouse`. Our data science team needs read/write access to the feature store data, and our business intelligence team needs read access to the data-warehouse data stored in that bucket.

Figure 12-7 shows how that scenario would look without the use of S3 Access Points.

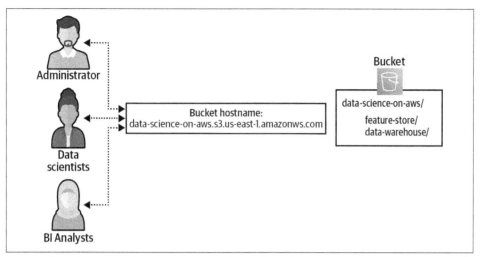

Figure 12-7. Accessing objects in Amazon S3 without S3 Access Points using a unique bucket host name.

A single S3 bucket policy would have maybe looked like this:

```
"Sid":"PrefixBasedAccessDataScience",
"Effect":"Allow",
"Principal":{"AWS":"arn:aws:iam::123456789012:group/ds},
"Action":["s3:GetObject","s3:PutObject"],
"Resource":"arn:aws:s3:::data-science-on-aws/feature-store/*"
...
"Sid":"TagBasedAccessBusinessIntelligence",
"Effect":"Allow",
"Principal":{"AWS":"arn:aws:iam::123456789012:group/bi},
"Action":["s3:GetObject"],
"Resource":"arn:aws:s3:::data-science-on-aws/data-warehouse/*"
...
```

Now let's see how we can simplify this with the use of S3 Access Points. The following sample command shows how to create Access Points called `ap1-ds` and `ap2-bi` via the AWS CLI command on our sample bucket called `data-science-on-aws`:

```
aws s3control create-access-point \
    --name ap1-ds \
    --account-id 123456789012 \
    --bucket data-science-on-aws

aws s3control create-access-point \
    --name ap2-bi \
    --account-id 123456789012 \
    --bucket data-science-on-aws
```

In an access point policy, we then grant the IAM group for our Data Scientist team ("ds") in account 123456789012 permissions to GET and PUT objects with the prefix feature-store/ through access point ap1-ds, and the IAM group for our Business Intelligence team ("bi") permissions to GET objects with the prefix data-warehouse/ through access point ap2-bi:

```
{
    "Version":"2012-10-17",
    "Statement": [
    {
        "Effect": "Allow",
        "Principal": {
            "AWS": "arn:aws:iam::123456789012:group/ds"
        },
        "Action": ["s3:GetObject", "s3:PutObject"],
        "Resource":
"arn:aws:s3:us-east-1:123456789012:accesspoint/ap1-ds/
object/feature-store/*"
    }]
}


{
    "Version":"2012-10-17",
    "Statement": [
    {
        "Effect": "Allow",
        "Principal": {
            "AWS": "arn:aws:iam::123456789012:group/bi"
        },
        "Action": ["s3:GetObject"],
        "Resource":
"arn:aws:s3:us-east-1:123456789012:accesspoint/ap2-bi/
object/data-warehouse/*"
    }]
}
```

Figure 12-8 shows how we can manage access to our S3 objects with S3 Access Points.

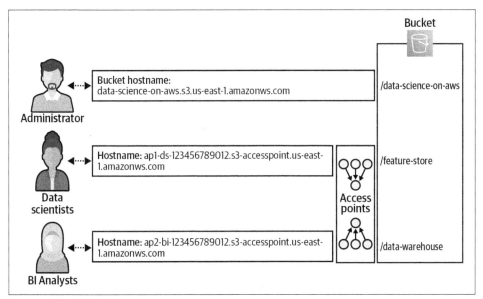

Figure 12-8. Accessing objects in Amazon S3 using S3 Access Points.

An AWS CLI request to an object in that bucket through the S3 Access Point would then look like this (if we are in the us-east-1 region and have the access permissions):

```
aws s3api get-object \
    --key sample_us.tsv \
    --bucket arn:aws:s3:us-east-1:123456789012:accesspoint/
ap1-ds feature-store/raw/sample_us.tsv
```

We can also access the objects in an Amazon S3 bucket with an access point using the AWS Management Console, AWS SDKs, or the S3 REST APIs. For an application or user to be able to access objects through an access point, both the access point and the underlying bucket must permit the request.

Encryption at Rest

Without encryption, data is readable by anybody who obtains access. All data should be encrypted as an extra layer of protection in case data ends up leaking into the malicious hands of an attacker—either internal or external to our organization.

SageMaker natively integrates with AWS Key Management Service (AWS KMS) to encrypt our data at rest using symmetric or asymmetric customer master keys (CMKs). CMKs, the primary AWS KMS resource, are a logical representation of a master key and include metadata such as the ID, description, creation date, and key state.

There are three types of CMKs: customer-managed, AWS-managed, and AWS-owned. They differ based on who manages the key, who can access the key metadata, how often the keys are automatically rotated, and how the keys are scoped across accounts. The summary is shown in Table 12-1.

Table 12-1. Different types of CMKs

Type of CMK	Can view CMK metadata	Can manage CMK	Used only for our AWS account	Automatic rotation
Customer-managed CMK	Yes	Yes	Yes	Optional every 365 days (1 year)
AWS-managed CMK	Yes	No	Yes	Required every 1095 days (3 years)
AWS-owned CMK	No	No	No	Varies

We should enable default encryption for all storage volumes, including Amazon S3, Amazon EC2 instance disks, network-attached Amazon Elastic Block Store (Amazon EBS), and distributed Amazon EFS. Additionally, it is recommended that we use deny policies to prevent uploads of unencrypted data to these storage volumes. We should encrypt all data artifacts, including notebooks, transformed features, trained models, batch predictions, and endpoint predictions. Also, we shouldn't forget to encrypt Docker images stored in Amazon ECR—as well as temporary "scratch" local storage and Amazon EBS volumes used during data processing and model training.

Create an AWS KMS Key

We start by creating a key with the AWS KMS to encrypt the storage volumes used in our SageMaker examples:

```
kms = boto3.Session().client(service_name='kms', region_name=region)

key_response = kms.create_key()

key_id = key_response['KeyMetadata']['KeyId']
```

Encrypt the Amazon EBS Volumes During Training

The following sample shows how to use an AWS KMS key with a SageMaker Training Job to encrypt the SageMaker instance's Amazon EBS volume:

```
estimator = TensorFlow(entry_point='tf_bert_reviews.py',
                       role=role,
                       instance_count=1,
                       instance_type='ml.p4d.24xlarge',
                       framework_version='<TENSORFLOW_VERSION>,
                       volume_kms_key=key_id)

estimator.fit(inputs)
```

Encrypt the Uploaded Model in S3 After Training

The following sample shows how to use encryption during a SageMaker Training Job using an AWS KMS key to encrypt the generated output assets, including our trained model in S3:

```
estimator = TensorFlow(
    entry_point='tf_bert_reviews.py',
    source_dir='src',
    role=role,
    instance_count=1,
    instance_type='ml.p4d.24xlarge',
    framework_version='<TENSORFLOW_VERSION>,
    output_kms_key=key_id<KMS_KEY_ID>)

estimator.fit(inputs)
```

Store Encryption Keys with AWS KMS

AWS KMS is a managed service that enables us to easily create and control the keys used for cryptographic operations. There are two ways to use AWS KMS with Amazon S3 to implement data-at-rest encryption. We can use server-side encryption to protect our data with a master key, or we can use an AWS KMS CMK with the Amazon S3 Encryption Client to protect our data on the client side.

If we select server-side encryption, we can choose between the following options:

SSE-S3
> Requires that Amazon S3 manage the data and master encryption keys

SSE-C
> Requires that we manage the encryption key

SSE-KMS
> Requires that AWS manage the data key but that we manage the CMK in AWS KMS

Enforce S3 Encryption for Uploaded S3 Objects

To require server-side encryption of all objects in a particular Amazon S3 bucket (enforcing data-at-rest encryption), we can use a bucket policy. For example, the following bucket policy denies upload object (s3:PutObject) permission to everyone if the request does not include the x-amz-server-side-encryption header requesting server-side encryption with SSE-KMS:

```
{
    "Version": "2012-10-17",
    "Id": "DenyIncorrectEncryptionalgorithmAES256",
    "Statement": [
```

```
        {
            "Sid": "DenyUnencryptedObjectUploads",
            "Effect": "Deny",
            "Principal": "*",
            "Action": "s3:PutObject",
            "Resource": "arn:aws:s3:::<bucket_name>/*",
            "Condition": {
                    "StringNotEquals": {
                            "S3:x-amz-server-side-encryption": "aws:kms"
                    }
            }
        }
    ]
}
```

In this case, S3 will encrypt every object before storing it and decrypt every object after retrieving it. This encrypt and decrypt process is done seamlessly behind the scenes. When we upload an object, we can specify the AWS KMS CMK using the header `x-amz-server-side-encryption-aws-kms-key-id`. If the header is not present in the request, Amazon S3 assumes the AWS-managed CMK.

Enforce Encryption at Rest for SageMaker Jobs

The following IAM policy will not allow a SageMaker Job to be created without Amazon EBS volume encryption:

```
{
  "Sid": "SageMakerJobVolumeEncryption",
  "Effect": "Deny",
  "Action": [
    "sagemaker:CreateTrainingJob"
  ],
  "Resource": "*",
  "Condition": {
    "Null": {
      "sagemaker:VolumeKmsKey": "true"
    }
  }
}
```

Enforce Encryption at Rest for SageMaker Notebooks

The following IAM policy will not allow a SageMaker Notebook instance to be created without Amazon EBS volume encryption:

```
{
  "Sid": "SageMakerNotebookVolumeEncryption",
  "Effect": "Deny",
  "Action": [
    "sagemaker:CreateNotebookInstance",
    "sagemaker:UpdateNotebookInstance"
```

```
    ],
    "Resource": "*",
    "Condition": {
      "Null": {
        "sagemaker:VolumeKmsKey": "true"
      }
    }
  }
}
```

Enforce Encryption at Rest for SageMaker Studio

The following IAM policy will not allow a SageMaker Studio domain to be created without Amazon EFS volume encryption:

```
{
  "Sid": "SageMakerStudioVolumeEncryption",
  "Effect": "Deny",
  "Action": [
    "sagemaker:CreateDomain"
  ],
  "Resource": "*",
  "Condition": {
    "Null": {
      "sagemaker:HomeEfsFileSystemKmsKey": "true"
    }
  }
}
```

Encryption in Transit

By default, all public AWS API calls are made over secure Transport Layer Security (TLS)–encrypted tunnels. This means that all network traffic is encrypted in transit, by default, between SageMaker and S3, for example. Without this encryption, data can be inspected by an attacker as it travels across the network in plain text. Remember that attacks can come from both inside and outside the organization.

For data in transit, SageMaker supports inter-container encryption for distributed training and HPT jobs. The information passed between training instances generally consists of model weights and other metadata versus training data itself, but enabling this setting can help meet regulatory requirements and add data protections.

Post-Quantum TLS Encryption in Transit with KMS

AWS KMS supports a quantum-resistant or "post-quantum" option for exchanging TLS encryption keys. While classic TLS cipher suite implementation is good enough to prevent brute force attacks on the key-exchange mechanism today, it will not be strong enough in the near future when large-scale quantum computers become accessible.

AWS KMS offers many key-exchange algorithm options for post-quantum TLS encryption, including Kyber (*https://oreil.ly/TPVel*), Bit Flipping Key Encapsulation (*https://bikesuite.org*), and Supersingular Isogeny Key Encapsulation (*https://sike.org*). Figure 12-9 shows the difference between Classical TLS 1.2 and Post-Quantum TLS 1.2.

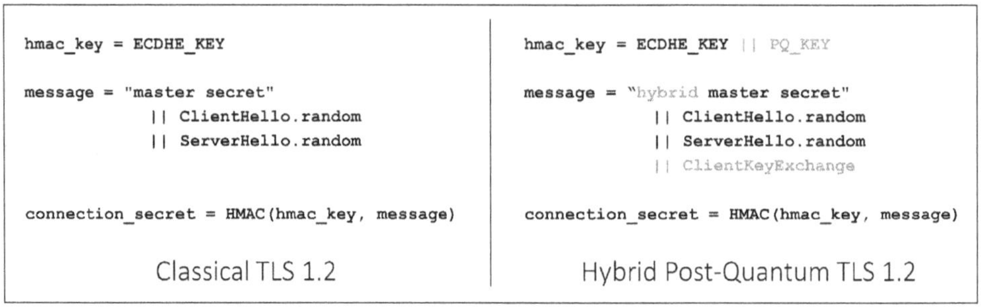

```
hmac_key = ECDHE_KEY                         hmac_key = ECDHE_KEY || PQ_KEY

message = "master secret"                    message = "hybrid master secret"
            || ClientHello.random                        || ClientHello.random
            || ServerHello.random                        || ServerHello.random
                                                         || ClientKeyExchange


connection_secret = HMAC(hmac_key, message)  connection_secret = HMAC(hmac_key, message)

            Classical TLS 1.2                       Hybrid Post-Quantum TLS 1.2
```

Figure 12-9. Classical and post-quantum TLS 1.2.

These post-quantum key exchange mechanisms will affect performance as they require extra computational overhead. Therefore, we should always test the performance of these algorithms thoroughly before deploying to production.

Encrypt Traffic Between Training-Cluster Containers

For distributed model training jobs, we can optionally encrypt internal network traffic between containers of our distributed-training clusters. While inter-container encryption can increase the training time, we should enable this setting to prevent sensitive data leakage.

Here is an example of how to encrypt inter-container communication with the encrypt_inter_container_traffic=True flag:

```
from sagemaker.tensorflow import TensorFlow

estimator = TensorFlow(entry_point='tf_bert_reviews.py',
                       source_dir='src',
                       role=role,
                       instance_count=2,
                       instance_type='ml.p4d.24xlarge',
                       framework_version='<TENSORFLOW_VERSION>',
                       encrypt_inter_container_traffic=True)
```

Enforce Inter-Container Encryption for SageMaker Jobs

The following policy will not allow SageMaker Training Jobs to run unless inter-container traffic encryption is enabled:

```
{
  "Sid": "SageMakerInterContainerTrafficEncryption",
  "Effect": "Deny",
  "Action": [
    "sagemaker:CreateTrainingJob"
  ],
  "Resource": "*",
  "Condition": {
    "Bool": {
      "sagemaker:InterContainerTrafficEncryption": "false"
    }
  }
}
```

Securing SageMaker Notebook Instances

By running our SageMaker notebook instances inside of our VPC, we create the network and compute isolation needed to prevent our sensitive notebooks from being accessed from outside the organization. Remember that notebooks, unlike typical software source files, often contain outputs such as visualizations and summary statistics that describe our datasets. These are just as sensitive as the data itself.

 If we want to implement centralized, governed, and self-service access to SageMaker notebook instances for our data science teams, we could use the AWS Service Catalog to define the SageMaker notebook instance as a product and preconfigure all required security policies.

When we create a SageMaker notebook instance, we can connect it to our private VPC by specifying subnet IDs and security groups as follows:

```
sm.create_notebook_instance(
    NotebookInstanceName='dsoaws',
    InstanceType='ml.t3.medium',
    SubnetId='<SUBNET_ID>',
    SecurityGroupIds=[
        '<SECURITY_GROUP_IDS>',
    ],
    RoleArn='arn:aws:iam::<ACCOUNT_ID>:role/service-role/<ROLE_NAME>',
    KmsKeyId='<KEY_ID>',
    DirectInternetAccess='Disabled',
    VolumeSizeInGB=10,
    RootAccess='Disabled'
)
```

Deny Root Access Inside SageMaker Notebooks

Note that the example also specifies the SageMaker Execution IAM role and the KMS key to encrypt the attached volumes, disables direct internet access from the notebooks, and disables root access for users. If we want to restrict users from creating notebook instances with root access enabled, we could attach the following IAM policy to the SageMaker Execution role:

```
{
  "Sid": "DenyRootAccess",
  "Effect": "Deny",
  "Action": [
    "sagemaker:CreateNotebookInstance",
    "sagemaker:UpdateNotebookInstance"
  ],
  "Resource":    "*",
  "Condition": {
    "StringEquals": {
      "sagemaker:RootAccess": [
        "Enabled"
      ]
    }
  }
}
```

Disable Internet Access for SageMaker Notebooks

Another best practice is to disable internet access from/to our VPCs that have access to our data. We can provide any external project dependencies via a separate, shared service VPC. This VPC could, for example, host a PyPI mirror with our approved Python packages.

The following example IAM policy will not allow SageMaker notebook instances to be created with direct internet access enabled:

```
{
  "Sid": "PreventDirectInternet",
  "Effect": "Deny",
  "Action": "sagemaker:CreateNotebookInstance",
  "Resource":    "*",
  "Condition": {
    "StringEquals": {
      "sagemaker:DirectInternetAccess": [
        "Enabled"
      ]
    }
  }
}
```

Securing SageMaker Studio

By locking down SageMaker Studio to our VPC, we are preventing outside attackers from accessing notebooks that contain sensitive data, such as visualizations and summary statistics that describe our datasets. SageMaker Studio also supports IAM and single-sign-on (SSO) authentication and authorization mechanisms. Using IAM and SSO, we can restrict Studio access to a limited number of individuals or groups using the least-privilege security principle. Without IAM and SSO authentication and authorization, malicious attackers could gain access to our notebooks and other Studio assets.

Require a VPC for SageMaker Studio

We can require SageMaker Studio access from our VPC by setting the parameter AppNetworkAccessType to VpcOnly. This deployment setting will create an ENI through which the resources in our VPC can communicate with the SageMaker Studio services using a VPC Endpoint. We can further control the communication by applying security groups to the ENI created by the VPC Endpoint.

The following example IAM policy will not allow a SageMaker Studio domain to be created outside of a private VPC:

```
{
  "Sid": "PreventDirectInternetforStudio",
  "Effect": "Allow",
  "Action": "sagemaker:CreateDomain",
  "Resource":     "*",
  "Condition": {
    "StringEquals": {
      "sagemaker:AppNetworkAccessType": [
        "VpcOnly"
      ]
    }
  }
}
```

With VpcOnly mode, all SageMaker Studio traffic is routed through the specified VPC and subnets. The default setting is PublicInternetOnly, which sends all non-Amazon EFS traffic through the AWS-managed service VPC, which has internet access enabled.

We define the IAM role for SageMaker Studio during domain creation. We can specify a private VPC for network communication via `AppNetworkAccessType=VpcOnly` and provide the relevant subnet IDs and the VPC ID. We can also pass a KMS key to encrypt the Amazon EFS volume set up by SageMaker Studio.

Here is an example of how to programmatically create the SageMaker Studio domain, a user profile, and the SageMaker Studio app with the mentioned settings:

```
sagemaker.create_domain(DomainName='default',
                        AuthMode='IAM',
                        DefaultUserSettings={
                            'ExecutionRole': <ROLE_ARN>,
                            'SecurityGroups': <SECURITY_GROUP_IDS>,
                        },
                        SubnetIds='<SUBNET_IDS>',
                        VpcId='<VPC_ID>',
                        AppNetworkAccessType='VpcOnly',
                        KmsKeyId='<EFS_KMS_KEY_ID>')

sagemaker.create_user_profile(DomainId=domain_id,
                              UserProfileName='default')

sagemaker.create_app(DomainId=domain_id,
                     UserProfileName='default',
                     AppType='JupyterServer',
                     AppName='default')
```

SageMaker Studio Authentication

SageMaker Studio supports two modes to authenticate users: SSO and IAM. In SSO mode, we map federated identity pools to users. In IAM mode, SageMaker Studio is fully integrated with AWS IAM and follows our IAM users, roles, and policy configurations. We authenticate with SageMaker Studio running in a SageMaker service account and platform VPC with private tunnels to our private account and VPC, as shown in Figure 12-10.

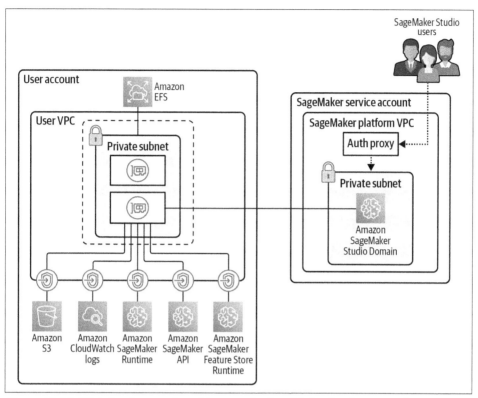

Figure 12-10. High-level network architecture for SageMaker Studio across the user VPC and SageMaker platform VPC.

Securing SageMaker Jobs and Models

We can also define permissions for SageMaker Jobs using service-level IAM roles to restrict permissions of IAM users/groups/roles, similar to the guardrails we discussed to restrict data access to our S3 buckets. We can restrict SageMaker Jobs to only have access to specific resources, such as S3 buckets or other data sources. Furthermore, we can require that SageMaker Jobs run in a private VPC to provide the compute and network isolation required to prevent external attackers from accessing data stored on the compute nodes or traveling across the network.

Require a VPC for SageMaker Jobs

In the context of SageMaker, we can specify IAM policies that require SageMaker to create resources without a VPC. Here is an example of such an IAM policy:

```
{
  "Sid": "SageMakerJobsVPC",
  "Effect": "Deny",
```

```
    "Action": [
      "sagemaker:CreateTrainingJob"
    ],
    "Resource": "*",
    "Condition": {
      "Null": {
        "sagemaker:VpcSubnets": "true",
        "sagemaker:VpcSecurityGroupIds": "true"
      }
    }
  }
}
```

Here is an example of how to connect SageMaker Training Jobs to our private VPC by providing `subnets` and `security_group_ids` to our SageMaker Training Job:

```
from sagemaker.tensorflow import TensorFlow

estimator = TensorFlow(
                entry_point='tf_bert_reviews.py',
                source_dir='src',
                role=role,
                instance_count=1,
                instance_type='ml.p4d.24xlarge',
                py_version='<PYTHON_VERSION>',
                framework_version='<TENSORFLOW_VERSION>',
                hyperparameters={...},
                subnets=[
                        "<SUBNET_ID>"
                ],
                security_group_ids=[
                        "<SECURITY_GROUP_ID>"
                ]
)
```

With this configuration, SageMaker will create the ENI to connect the training containers to our specified VPC.

We can enforce the specific VPC configuration via an IAM policy such as this:

```
{
    "Version": "2012-10-17",
    "Statement": [
        {
            "Sid": "SageMakerJobsVPC",
            "Effect": "Deny",
            "Action": [
                "sagemaker:CreateTrainingJob"
            ],
            "Resource": "*",
            "Condition": {
                "StringNotEquals": {
                    "sagemaker:VpcSecurityGroupIds":
                        "<SECURITY_GROUP_IDS>",
```

```
                "sagemaker:VpcSubnets": [
                    "<SUBNET_ID>",
                    "<SUBNET_ID>"
                ]
            }
        }
    }
  ]
}
```

Before we can run our training job within a VPC, we need to make sure that the VPC has access to S3 through an S3 VPC endpoint (or NAT device) set up within our VPC. This includes configuring subnet route tables, security groups, and network access control lists (ACLs). If we don't do this, we will see an error like this:

```
UnexpectedStatusException: Error for Training job: Failed. Reason: ClientError:
Data download failed:Please ensure that the subnet's route table has a route to
an S3 VPC endpoint or a NAT device, both the security groups and the subnet's
network ACL allow outbound traffic to S3.
```

With the example IAM policy, we are explicitly denying model creation as well as the creation of SageMaker Autopilot Jobs, Training Jobs, Processing Jobs, or Hyper-Parameter Tuning Jobs unless deployed with the specified VPC subnet IDs and security groups.

Let's run a Training Job without specifying the matching VPC parameters:

```
from sagemaker.tensorflow import TensorFlow

estimator = TensorFlow(
                entry_point='tf_bert_reviews.py',
                source_dir='src',
                role=role,
                instance_count=1,
                instance_type='ml.p4d.24xlarge',
                py_version='<PYTHON_VERSION>',
                framework_version='<TENSORFLOW_VERSION>',
                hyperparameters={...},
)

estimator.fit(inputs={...})
```

We will see a client error like this:

```
ClientError: An error occurred (AccessDeniedException) when calling the
CreateTrainingJob operation: User: arn:aws:sts::<ACCOUNT_ID>:assumed-role/<ROLE>/
SageMaker is not authorized to perform: sagemaker:CreateTrainingJob on resource:
arn:aws:sagemaker:<REGION>:<ACCOUNT_ID>:training-job/<JOB>
with an explicit deny
```

Figure 12-11 shows how the SageMaker Training Job started and stopped at 17:56 UTC.

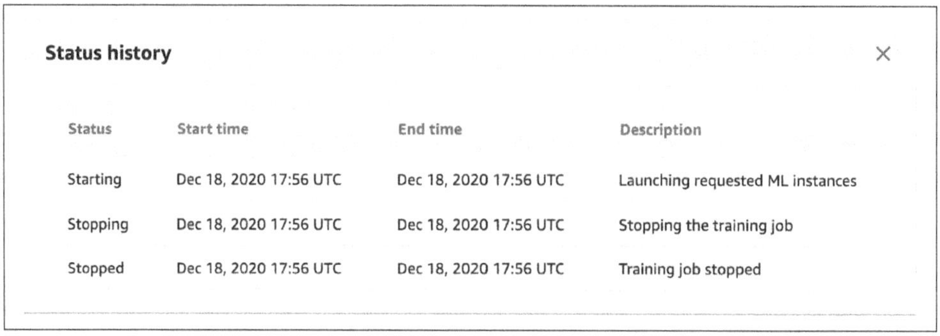

Status history				✕

Status	Start time	End time	Description
Starting	Dec 18, 2020 17:56 UTC	Dec 18, 2020 17:56 UTC	Launching requested ML instances
Stopping	Dec 18, 2020 17:56 UTC	Dec 18, 2020 17:56 UTC	Stopping the training job
Stopped	Dec 18, 2020 17:56 UTC	Dec 18, 2020 17:56 UTC	Training job stopped

Figure 12-11. SageMaker Training Job stopped because it doesn't comply with policies.

Require Network Isolation for SageMaker Jobs

If we need to completely isolate our model training jobs, we can enable network isolation for the containers performing model training. In this case, the container is restricted from all outbound network communication (including API calls to Amazon S3) and can only communicate with the local Amazon EBS volume. All required input and output data for the training job will have to be stored on the container's local Amazon EBS volumes, which should be encrypted.

Additionally, no AWS credentials are made available to the container runtime environment when network isolation is enabled. If we run a distributed training job, network communication is limited to the containers of the training cluster, which also can be encrypted.

Running SageMaker Jobs in network isolation mode is a strong protection against data-exfiltration risks. However, network isolation is not required to restrict traffic to specific AWS resources, such as S3 from within our VPC. For this, we use VPC subnet and security group configurations.

The following example policy will deny SageMaker Job creation if network isolation is disabled:

```
{
  "Sid": "SageMakerNetworkIsolation",
  "Effect": "Deny",
  "Action": [
    "sagemaker:CreateTrainingJob"
  ],
  "Resource": "*",
  "Condition": {
    "Bool": {
      "sagemaker:NetworkIsolation": "false"
    }
  }
}
```

If we try to access any resources outside of the container, we will see the following NoCredentialsError:

```
botocore.exceptions.NoCredentialsError: Unable to locate credentials
```

While the training containers cannot access S3 directly because of the network isolation, the SageMaker runtime can still copy the data between S3 and the underlying SageMaker instance where the training job containers are running. The container still has access to the training data through the */opt/ml/input/* directory mounted by Sage-Maker after copying the S3 data to the training instance. Similarly, the trained model will be placed in */opt/ml/output/*, which SageMaker will copy to S3, as shown in Figure 12-12.

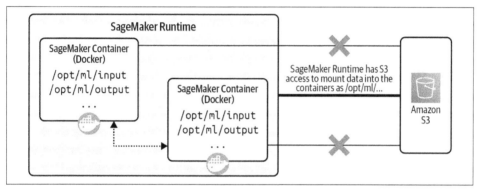

Figure 12-12. Network isolation does not prevent SageMaker from mounting data from S3 into the training containers.

We can further limit the SageMaker runtime's S3 access through additional IAM or S3 Bucket Policies. Additionally, network-isolation mode can be used in combination with a VPC, in which case the download/upload of data is routed via the VPC subnet. The model training containers would continue to be isolated, though, without access to resources in our VPC or the internet.

Securing AWS Lake Formation

AWS Lake Formation provides fine-grained access control to rows and columns of data for a given principal. With Lake Formation, we specify permissions on tables, rows, and columns versus S3 buckets, prefixes, and objects. With the Lake Formation "Data Permissions" UI, we can analyze all policies granted to users in a single view.

Lake Formation monitors and logs all data-access events in real time. We can subscribe to receive alerts when sensitive data is accessed. In addition to reviewing real-time dashboards and alerts, we can export data-access logs for offline auditing and reporting.

Securing Database Credentials with AWS Secrets Manager

We should never use hard-coded, clear-text credentials in our scripts, applications, or notebooks. By exposing usernames, passwords, and API keys, we create security vulnerabilities, which lead to malicious attacks and data breaches. Instead, we should store and retrieve our credentials from AWS Secrets Manager.

Secrets Manager encrypts secrets using AWS KMS and leverages AWS IAM policies to control access to the stored credentials. In addition to manually rotating credentials, we can also rotate credentials on a schedule using Secrets Manager. Many AWS databases are integrated with Secrets Manager, including Amazon RDS, Aurora, and Redshift. For these databases, we specify the unique ARN when executing our query. AWS then retrieves and validates the credentials in the background without exposing any usernames, passwords, or API keys.

Governance

We discussed several mechanisms to implement and enforce configurations that help us to comply with our organizational security policies. The examples showed controls specific to IAM users, roles, and policies within one AWS account. If we want to implement security and governance across AWS accounts and regions, we can leverage AWS Organizations, AWS Config, and multiaccount environments.

With AWS Organizations we can define service control policies (SCPs), which give us centralized control over the maximum available permissions for all accounts in our organization. If we need to set up new, secure, multiaccount AWS environments, we can use AWS Control Tower.

We can use AWS Config to evaluate AWS resource configurations across our accounts against best practices and our custom policies. AWS Config is an example of a detective control to alert us if configurations are out of compliance.

We can then apply the multiaccount setup to improve governance and security of our data science projects by, for example, separating the model deployment workflow across data science, staging, and production environments.

Secure Multiaccount AWS Environments with AWS Control Tower

AWS Control Tower enables us to set up and govern new, secure, multiaccount AWS environments in just a few clicks. Using AWS Control Tower, we can automate the setup of our AWS environment with best-practices blueprints for multiaccount structure, identity, access management, and account provisioning workflow. For example, we may want to disallow all public access to all S3 buckets, buckets that are not encrypted, or buckets that have versioning disabled.

Manage Accounts with AWS Organizations

AWS Organizations is an account management service that allows us to consolidate multiple AWS accounts into one organization. We can then centrally manage all accounts mapped to this organization.

If we need to group specific AWS accounts, we can create organizational units (OUs), add the relevant accounts, and attach different policies to each OU. Figure 12-13 shows how we can group individual accounts into OUs and attach policies.

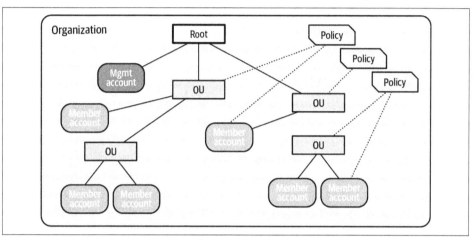

Figure 12-13. AWS Organization with OUs, member accounts, and policies.

Enforce Account-Level Permissions with SCPs

AWS Organizations allow us to specify SCPs to define permissions for member accounts in the organization. We can leverage SCPs to implement and enforce the discussed security controls across AWS accounts.

We can leverage SCPs to restrict access to AWS services, resources, and individual API actions for users and roles in each mapped AWS member account. Note that these restrictions will even take precedence over administrators of member accounts. In other words, SCPs give us a centralized control over the maximum available permissions for all accounts in the organization.

We can leverage SCPs as a guardrail or to define limits on the actions that the member account's administrator can grant to the individual account's IAM user and roles. We still have to create IAM policies and attach the policies to IAM users/roles in the member accounts. The resulting permissions are the intersection between what is allowed by the SCP and the member account's IAM policies.

Building upon condition keys for IAM, the following example defines an SCP to enforce encryption with a specific KMS key for all SageMaker Training Jobs created in the mapped AWS member accounts:

```
{
    "Version": "2012-10-17",
    "Statement": [
        {
            "Sid": "EncryptSageMakerTraining",
            "Effect": "Deny",
            "Action": "sagemaker:CreateTrainingJob",
            "Resource": [
                "*"
            ],
            "Condition": {
                "ArnNotEquals": {
                    "sagemaker:OutputKmsKey": [
                        arn:aws:kms:<REGION>:<ACCOUNT_ID>:key/<KMS_KEY_ID>"
                    ]
                }
            }
        }
    ]
}
```

Let's start a SageMaker Training Job in one of the attached member accounts without specifying the given KMS key:

```
estimator = TensorFlow(
            entry_point='tf_bert_reviews.py',
            role=role,
            train_instance_count=1,
            train_instance_type='ml.p4d.24xlarge',
            framework_version='<TENSORFLOW_VERSION>'
)
```

Here, we see the training job will fail with the expected `AccessDeniedException`:

```
ClientError: An error occurred (AccessDeniedException) when calling the
CreateTrainingJob operation: User: arn:aws:sts::<ACCOUNT_ID>:assumed-role/<ROLE>/
SageMaker is not authorized to perform: sagemaker:CreateTrainingJob on resource:
arn:aws:sagemaker:<REGION>:<ACCOUNT_ID>:training-job/<JOB>
with an explicit deny
```

To fix this, we will start the same Training Job with the specified KMS key, and the training job will start successfully:

```
estimator = TensorFlow(
            entry_point='tf_bert_reviews.py',
            role=role,
            train_instance_count=1,
            train_instance_type='ml.p4d.24xlarge',
            framework_version='<TENSORFLOW_VERSION>',
```

```
                subnets=<SUBNETS>,
                security_group_ids=<SECURITY_GROUP_IDS>,
                ouput_kms_key="<KMS_KEY_ID>"
    )

    estimator.fit(inputs)
```

Here, we see the SageMaker Training Job starts successfully using the KMS key provided:

```
arn:aws:iam:<ACCOUNT_ID>:role/service-role/<ROLE_NAME> \
    2020-10-30 16:04:01 Starting - Starting the training job.
training job.
```

Implement Multiaccount Model Deployments

We can leverage AWS Control Tower, AWS Organizations, and AWS Config to set up and manage multiple AWS accounts. To improve governance and security for model deployments, we should create separate AWS accounts for our data scientists, as well as for staging and for production environments. A simple AWS Organizations structure that defines the corresponding OUs and mapped AWS accounts could look like this:

```
ROOT
├── DATA_SCIENCE_MULTI_ACCOUNT_DEPLOYMENTS (OU)
│    ├── <AWS_ACCOUNT_DATA_SCIENCE>
│    ├── STAGING (OU)
│    │    └── <AWS_ACCOUNT_STAGING>
│    └── PRODUCTION (OU)
│         └── <AWS_ACCOUNT_PRODUCTION>
```

The data scientist should be able to freely build, train, and tune models in the data science account. Once a trained model qualifies for deployment, the data scientist approves the model, which deploys the model into the staging environment. The staging environment could be used by the DevOps team to run unit and integration tests before deploying the model into the production environment. In Chapter 10, we discussed how Amazon SageMaker Projects automate our model deployment pipelines across the data science, staging, and production environments. We can adapt the SageMaker Projects templates to any custom multiaccount setup.

Auditability

Besides implementing security controls, we also need to audit our environment by logging activities, collecting events, and tracking user activities and API calls. Auditability is a major requirement for implementing compliance frameworks and processes. There are several AWS services and features available to implement auditability. We can tag resources and leverage CloudWatch Logs and CloudTrail to receive logs and track API calls.

Tag Resources

We can add tags to any of our AWS resources. Resource tagging can be used as a mechanism for auditability. For example, we could enforce our SageMaker Studio applications to contain a specific team or project identifier via condition keys in our IAM policy as shown here:

```
{
    "Version": "2012-10-17",
    "Statement": [
        {
            "Sid": "EnforceAppTag",
            "Effect": "Allow",
            "Action": [
                "sagemaker:CreateApp"
            ],
            "Resource": "*",
            "Condition": {
                "ForAllValues:StringLike": {
                    "aws:RequestTag/Project": "development"
                }
            }
        }
    ]
}
```

If we attach this IAM policy to the principal belonging to the "development" project, the IAM user or role cannot create applications tagged with another project.

Log Activities and Collect Events

Amazon SageMaker automatically logs all API calls, events, data access, and interactions during our model development process. We can track and trace the interactions down to individual users and IP addresses.

We can leverage CloudWatch Logs to monitor, store, and access our SageMaker log files. Logs from SageMaker Studio notebooks, SageMaker Processing, or Model Training Jobs are also captured as CloudWatch events. We can keep track of metrics and create customized dashboards using CloudWatch Metrics. We can set up notifications or actions when a metric reaches a specified threshold. Note that SageMaker container logs and metrics are delivered to our CloudWatch environment, while the underlying infrastructure logs are retained by the SageMaker service platform.

Track User Activity and API Calls

We can track individual user activity and API calls with CloudTrail. CloudTrail will also show API calls that SageMaker instances make on our behalf, including the assumed IAM role. If we need to map the activities to each user, we need to create a separate IAM role for each user in each SageMaker service that assumes the role.

All captured API call logs are delivered to an Amazon S3 bucket that we specify. The API logs include the user and account identities for each API call, the source IP addresses, and the timestamps of the API calls.

Reduce Cost and Improve Performance

We can reduce KMS cost by reducing the number of KMS API calls required by our application. In addition, we can reduce SageMaker cost by using IAM policies to limit the instance types available to our users.

Limit Instance Types to Control Cost

We may want to allow only CPU instances types for our long-lived, real-time model endpoints in production—saving the GPUs for our relatively short-lived, compute-intensive, batch training jobs. The following policy limits the instance types to CPU-based instances when creating a SageMaker Model Endpoint:

```
{
    "Sid": "LimitSageMakerModelEndpointInstances",
    "Effect": "Deny",
    "Action": [
        "sagemaker:CreateEndpoint"
    ],
    "Resource": "*",
    "Condition": {
        "ForAnyValue:StringNotLike": {
          "sagemaker:InstanceTypes": [
            "ml.c5.large",
            "ml.m5.large"
          ]
        }
    }
}
```

We can also limit the instance types used for SageMaker notebook instances and SageMaker Studio domains. Since notebook instances and SageMaker Studio are long-lived resources, we may want to limit the instance types to CPU-based instances since the GPU-based heavy lifting of SageMaker Training Jobs should happen on a SageMaker cluster and not in our notebook. The following policies will limit the instance types of long-lived SageMaker notebook instances and SageMaker Studio applications to help control cost and encourage better utilization of the more expensive GPU instances:

```json
{
    "Sid": "LimitSageMakerNotebookInstanceTypes",
    "Effect": "Deny",
    "Action": [
    "sagemaker:CreateNotebookInstance"
    ],
    "Resource": "*",
    "Condition": {
        "ForAnyValue:StringNotLike": {
        "sagemaker:InstanceTypes": [
            "ml.c5.large",
            "ml.m5.large",
            "ml.t3.medium"
            ]
        }
    }
}
{
    "Sid": "LimitSageMakerStudioInstanceTypes",
    "Effect": "Deny",
    "Action": [
        "sagemaker:CreateApp"
    ],
    "Resource": "*",
    "Condition": {
        "ForAnyValue:StringNotLike": {
        "sagemaker:InstanceTypes": [
            "ml.c5.large",
            "ml.m5.large",
            "ml.t3.medium"
            ]
        }
    }
}
```

Quarantine or Delete Untagged Resources

To control cost, we should tag every resource to properly track and monitor our spending. We can enforce tags using the "required-tags" rule with the AWS Config service. This rule checks if a resource has the required tags. If the resource does not have the required tag, it can be quarantined or deleted to save cost.

Use S3 Bucket KMS Keys to Reduce Cost and Increase Performance

We can reduce cost for encryption by using S3 Bucket Keys, which decreases the number of API calls to the AWS KMS service when new objects are uploaded. We can add an S3 Bucket Key to our bucket with the following code:

```
response = client.put_bucket_encryption(
    Bucket=<BUCKET_NAME>,
    ServerSideEncryptionConfiguration={
        'Rules': [
            {
                'ApplyServerSideEncryptionByDefault': {
                    'SSEAlgorithm': 'aws:kms',
                    'KMSMasterKeyID': <KMS_KEY_ID>
                },
                'BucketKeyEnabled': True
            },
        ]
    }
)
```

Summary

In this chapter, we started by discussing how AWS cloud security is "job zero" and "priority zero." We introduced the relevant security concepts and AWS security services and features we can leverage—as well as the AWS shared-responsibility security model. We showed how to build secure data science and machine learning projects on AWS. We described how to implement preventive and detective controls that stop events from occurring—as well as responsive and corrective controls that helped to remediate security violations.

We described best practices in the area of compute and network isolation, authentication and authorization, encryption, and governance, as well as auditability and compliance. We learned how to protect our data by implementing access control with AWS IAM and restrict network access using VPCs. We highlighted some important concepts we should leverage to secure our data and showed specific examples of how to add different levels of security to our S3 data access and SageMaker Jobs. We showed how the use of S3 Access Points can help manage access to data in shared S3 buckets (aka our S3 data lake). We described data-at-rest encryption with AWS KMS and encryption-in-transit with traditional and post-quantum cryptography. Next, we discussed mechanisms to implement governance and auditability. Last, we finished the chapter by sharing tips on how to reduce cost and improve performance with the AWS security services.

Index

identifying and preventing privacy leaks, 43
increasing performance and reducing costs, 70-73
industrial predictive maintenance, 52
innovation across every industry, 29
Internet of Things (IoT), 53
product recommendations, 30-36
quantum computing, 65-70
self-optimizing cloud infrastructure, 55
text analysis and natural language processing, 45-50

V

validation datasets, 180
videos (see images and videos)
virtual private clouds (VPCs), 211, 452
visualizations
    bias reports, 159-166
    with CodeGuru Profiler, 72
    creating dashboards with QuickSight, 150
    open source libraries for, 14
    querying data warehouses, 142-150
    with QuickSight, 57
    visualizing data lakes with SageMaker Studio, 129-141

voice assistants, 44
VPC Endpoints, 453

W

warm start technique, 284-288
weights, 233
windowed queries
    sliding windows, 414
    stagger windows, 412
    time-based windows, 411
    tumbling windows, 413
word embeddings, 216
word of mouth, 101
word vectors, 216
Word2Vec algorithm, 217

X

XGBoost algorithm, 217

Z

zstd algorithm, 123

About the Authors

Chris Fregly is a principal developer advocate for AI and machine learning at AWS, based in San Francisco. He regularly speaks at AI and machine learning conferences around the world, including the O'Reilly AI Superstream Series. Previously, Chris was founder at PipelineAI, solutions engineer at Databricks, and software engineer at Netflix. Chris has been focused on building AI and machine learning pipelines with AWS for the past decade.

Antje Barth is a senior developer advocate for AI and machine learning at AWS, based in Düsseldorf, Germany. Antje is cofounder of the Düsseldorf chapter of Women in Big Data and frequently speaks at AI and machine learning conferences and meetups around the world. She also chairs and curates content for O'Reilly AI Superstream events. Previously, Antje was an engineer at Cisco and MapR focused on data center infrastructures, big data, and AI applications.

Colophon

The bird on the cover of *Data Science on AWS* is a northern pintail drake (*Anas acuta*). These large ducks cover the northern hemisphere in the breeding seasons (spring and summer), and migrate to the south for the winter.

Northern pintails are sexually dimorphic—only the males have the characteristic 4-inch-long central tail feathers. An average northern pintail weighs about 2 pounds and measures 21 to 25 inches long. They can live more than 20 years in the wild. In the spring, hens lay 7 to 9 cream-colored eggs and incubate them for about 3 weeks. The birds eat mostly plant matter, like seeds, roots, and grains, as well as some animal matter, including insects, mollusks, and crustaceans.

Northern pintail populations have seen some decline, but the IUCN Red List considers the species well-protected, classifying it of Least Concern. Many of the animals on O'Reilly's covers are endangered; all of them are important to the world.

The cover illustration is by Karen Montgomery, based on a black and white engraving from *British Birds*. The cover fonts are Gilroy Semibold and Guardian Sans. The text font is Adobe Minion Pro; the heading font is Adobe Myriad Condensed; and the code font is Dalton Maag's Ubuntu Mono.

CPSIA information can be obtained
at www.ICGtesting.com
Printed in the USA
JSHW020824220421
13785JS00001B/1